A Boy from Barnhart

A Boy from Barnhart
Times Remembered

Herbie R. Taylor

iUniverse, Inc.
Bloomington

A Boy from Barnhart
Times Remembered

Copyright © 2011 by Herbie R. Taylor.

All rights reserved. No part of this book may be used or reproduced by any means, graphic, electronic, or mechanical, including photocopying, recording, taping or by any information storage retrieval system without the written permission of the publisher except in the case of brief quotations embodied in critical articles and reviews.

iUniverse books may be ordered through booksellers or by contacting:

*iUniverse
1663 Liberty Drive
Bloomington, IN 47403
www.iuniverse.com
1-800-Authors (1-800-288-4677)*

Because of the dynamic nature of the Internet, any web addresses or links contained in this book may have changed since publication and may no longer be valid. The views expressed in this work are solely those of the author and do not necessarily reflect the views of the publisher, and the publisher hereby disclaims any responsibility for them.

*Any people depicted in stock imagery provided by Thinkstock are models, and such images are being used for illustrative purposes only.
Certain stock imagery © Thinkstock.*

*ISBN: 978-1-4620-3951-7 (sc)
ISBN: 978-1-4620-3953-1 (hc)
ISBN: 978-1-4620-3952-4 (ebk)*

Printed in the United States of America

iUniverse rev. date: 11/02/2011

CONTENTS

Preface ix
Acknowledgments xiii
Introduction xv

PART I
Beginnings
   1. The Clan of Taylor 3
   2. Shorty and Squirrel 14

PART II
Early Years
   3. What a Wonderful Way to Grow Up 31
   4. Learning and Other Things 52
   5. Make 'Em a Hand 67
   6. The Fighting Owls 79
   7. Bar S Ranch 91
   8. Married Man/College Student 110

PART III
Soldiering Years
   9. The Army 131
 10. An Ancient and Exotic Land 157
 11. My War 194
 12. Army Schooling 224
 13. The Land of the Rising Sun 235
 14. Command and General Staff College 274
 15. Mother MILPERCEN 284
 16. Land of the Morning Calm 300
 17. The Pentagon 330
 18. Fortress Polk 343
 19. A Unique Assignment 388

20. Army / Civilian Master's Degree 399
21. MILPERCEN Redux 408
22. Silent Warriors 426
23. Last Hurrah 459

PART IV
Later Years
24. Trying Times 493
25. Floating 512
26. A New Beginning 522

APPENDICES
I.   For My Descendants 527
II. Further Reading 537
III. Service Resume of Herbie R. Taylor 545
IV. Taylor, of Virginia: Documented Male Lines 551
V.   My Descendants 555
VI. Glossary 557

To my family . . . past, present, and future.

If you would not be forgotten as soon as you are gone, either write things worth reading or do things worth writing.

—Benjamin Franklin

Preface

Nikos Kazantzakis wrote, "Our first duty, in completing our service to humanity, is to feel within our lives our ancestors. Our second duty is to throw light on their onrush, and to continue their work. Our third duty is to pass on to our children the great mandate to surpass us." These elegant, profound words have meaning for me and perhaps for you, my descendants, as this book is written for you. How well I met the mandate of Mr. Kazantzakis may be revealed herein.

Who then is the man who wrote this book, these words, and why did he write them? Simply stated, I wrote this book as my legacy to you. It is the legacy I wish my ancestors had left me. It would bring me great pleasure to hold in my hands a book written by one of my family, especially my great-grandparents, chronicling their lives, their hardships, joys, sorrows, failures, successes, and achievements.

Who, then, am I? If you keep reading, you may find that out, as well as a little history about the Taylor clan and the world I lived in for half of the twentieth and part of the twenty-first century.

I began to think seriously about compiling some of the stories of my life to leave to my grandsons, Micah Jeb and Jared Ross, when I reached the cusp of my pending dotage at age sixty-two. I also had an acute awareness that my memory of past events was slowly fading, as was the energy needed to complete such an endeavor. I felt a need, a responsibility that Micah and Jared have some knowledge about their maternal grandmother, whom they did not know, her family, and my family.

I did not intend to write a book, but somewhere along the way, the project took on a life of its own. I began to put pen to paper in May 2004 and worked on it in fits and spurts, only interrupted for lengthy periods because of illness, travel, and lethargy. I had no clue the project would take this long or require this much effort. Had my toil not become a labor of love, I would have quit long ago.

Reputation is what man thinks about you. Character is what God knows about you.
—Unknown

This book is my understanding of what happened in my life, my recollection of my life. I have tried not to be cynical, calculating, or self-aggrandizing. How well I have done this is problematic, because ego, pride, and self-centeredness are three of my base character defects. The quest for immortality is an inherent trait of the human experience, and I, too, desire to be remembered regardless of how insignificant my actual life may have been.

A change of opinions is almost unknown in an elderly military man.
—C. K. Chesterton

I realize this book contains biases, insights, and opinions developed over more than sixty-nine years on this planet. If they offend, I apologize. My intention is not to demean, embarrass, or convince as to their rightness but rather to call it as I see it or as I lived it. To do otherwise would be dishonest and deny insight into how this old fellow viewed the world. In a few places, I have omitted or changed names and identities to protect the innocent (or to shield myself from the not-so-innocent). If you find your name herein, you may be assured of two things: one, I remember you for the impact you had on my life, be it a small or large way, and two, you are a part of my life, my story. And for that, I am grateful.

Memory can be a tricky companion at times, especially as one ages, and I would not be taken aback if a few factual errors and faulty remembrances were reflected in these pages. I can promise that all within—conversations, events, and dates—are as truthful as I remember them; however, I know that three versions of the truth always exist, namely mine, yours, and what really happened. This axiom was proved when I sent some of my stories to my mother and sister for comments. Each had a different view of the incident. Most differences concerned nuances, but some were significant in the details. It was as if we had all been witnesses to the same vehicle accident but had seen it from different angles.

Vanity, too, plays lurid tricks with memory. Will Rogers wrote, "When you put down the good things you ought to have done and leave out the bad ones you did do, well, that's memoirs." Someone also said, "Autobiographies are neither fact nor fiction but the truth as the author remembers it."

This is what I remember as I remember it.

So this is my story, but it does not remotely intend to include everything. It is part genealogy, history, travelogue, and memoir, reflecting my interests and personality.

I have included an appendix that suggests readings that might amplify or assist you if you have further interest in the times in which I lived. All are part of my personal library.

I enjoyed writing this tome and reminiscing as I worked. I hope you will enjoy reading it. Years from now, when I start pushing up daisies, I do not want you to say, "I wish he had told us his stories or at least written them down."

Here they are.

These are the tales this boy from Barnhart would tell you if we could spend a lot of time together like we would on a long car trip or ocean voyage.

Acknowledgments

In acknowledging all those whose help and inspiration helped me to write this book, I first think of my sister, Tippe, who initially encouraged and then gently pushed me along to first start and then finish this book. I recall her e-mail of May 24, 2005, when she wrote, "You have so many good stories to tell about *your* life, and you are a great storyteller. Just enjoy this adventure—don't obsess so over it. Look at this as a love gift to your family." Tippe, I could not have done it without you.

I owe a deep debt of gratitude to my father and mother for their help, guidance, love, and encouragement. They have both gone to a far better place than I can imagine. I honor their memory.

Then there are the friends, teachers, soldiers, and mentors who touched my life in countless ways to my benefit. Many are mentioned herein, but far more could not be included without extending these pages endlessly. They know who they are and what they did for me. I thank them all.

I particularly want to recognize two childhood friends from Barnhart days, Janet Parry Hackleroad and Donna Brunson Daugherty, for not only their input into this effort but their friendship these many years. They, too, are family.

The folks at iUniverse held my hand while guiding me through the Byzantine world of self-publishing. Through their exceptional efforts and understanding, I had a positive publishing experience.

To my son, Ross, with whom I am pleased, and his wife, Kristi: thank you both for giving me the gift of my grandsons, Micah and Jared.

Micah and Jared, you continue to make me proud.

Staci "Tinkerbell" Autrey, my girl, the daughter I would have never had if you had not come into my life, my life is so much richer now that you are part of it.

Last but not least, my wife and best friend, Janice, who rarely complained when I disappeared into my office to work on and obsess over this effort. You were my best critic, proofreader, and advisor. You came into my life during a difficult time, and for that, I will be eternally grateful. Your love is my most precious possession.

Thank you all for the memories.

Introduction

The remnants of this small, dusty, desolate village are located off US Highway 67 and State Highway 163 in southwestern Irion County, Texas. It is but a speck on the map, a place of no particular importance that time has relegated to obscurity. It is at best a minor footnote in history.

If you were traveling Highway 67 today, you would not give it a second thought. However, for those of us who lived, played, worked, and went to school there, it remains a part of us. Barnhart defined us; it was where we were from and who we were. We were from Barnhart, Texas!

Established in 1910 during the construction of the Kansas City, Mexico, and Orient Railway, Barnhart was named for William F. Barnhart, an agent for the railroad. A school was acquired in 1912; Mrs. Maude Wood Branch, a relative, was the only teacher. The Barnhart Independent School District became a reality on February 27, 1917, and operated until 1967. By 1920, the town also had a post office; a bank, the Barnhart State Bank; a newspaper, the *Barnhart Range*, three groceries; four cafés; two hotels; and a variety of other businesses.

In the 1920s and 1930s, Barnhart became a large-volume inland shipping point for livestock because of its location between major rail lines, and many considered it the largest within the United States. During this time, most area ranchers fenced their land, preventing their neighbors from driving sheep and cattle to the railroad shipping point at Barnhart. The Ozona-Barnhart Trap Company, organized in Ozona in 1924, offered a solution to the problem.

By buying or leasing land for trails, traps (small pastures), pens, and water wells, the company established a corridor through which ranchers could drive their livestock to the railroad without crossing fences or destroying grass supplies. The main trail extended about thirty-four miles from south of Ozona to Barnhart with branch lines throughout the area. Sale of stock to area ranchers financed the enterprise along with a charge per head of livestock paid for services used. The Ozona-Barnhart Trap Company saved the ranching industry when it was the only important business in the area. The need for the trail dwindled with the rise of truck transportation, but drives continued until the 1950s.

In 1942, the year of my birth, Barnhart had over 250 residents, six businesses, a post office, and a school. At the time of this writing (2011), the population is around a hundred souls, and the town has only a post office, a gas station/convenience store, a couple of oil patch-related shade tree businesses, but no school.

The railhead, once occupied by a myriad of wooden corrals, chutes, and alleys long ago dismantled or simply fallen down and deteriorated, offer mute testimony to a way of life now extinct. All too soon, those of us who were there will pass from this land, and there will be no one to pay tribute to those who went before.

Standing there at midday in the West Texas sun, three days past the beginning of autumn, the pickup's digital thermometer reading 104 degrees, my mind returns to the time of my youth. I stand lost in thought, and I am transported to another time and place. I once again hear the bawling of the cows, the whoops of the cowboys, and the shrill whistle of the steam locomotive.

I am a boy from Barnhart!

PART I

Beginnings

1

The Clan of Taylor

If you don't know your family's history, then you don't know anything. You are a leaf that doesn't know it is part of a tree.
—Michael Crichton

The name Taylor was as common in the seventeenth century as it is now. This makes tracing one's ancestry difficult. Fortunately, my branch of the Taylor family has a lineage that has been well researched and documented by a distant cousin, Nathaniel Lane Taylor. Dr. Taylor, a native of New England and holder of a PhD in medieval European history from Harvard University (1995), has graciously allowed me to use material from his unpublished work titled *An American Taylor Family: Descendants of Richard Taylor (d. 1679) of North Farnham Parish in the Northern Neck of Virginia*. This work is on the Internet at http://www.nltaylor.net/Taylorgen. Dr. Taylor's research is based on an exhaustive search of the paper trail, and today, it is being substantiated by DNA testing, of which I am a participant.

My twig of the Taylor tree may be characterized as hardworking "tillers of the soil." They were referred to by some as the "salt of the earth." They were neither presidents, captains of industry, educators, noted authors nor orators, physicians, or politicians. Primarily stewards of the land, some served their country under arms. I am a tenth-generation descendant of one Richard Taylor. A synopsis of the life of this man and his male descendants follows:

It is of no consequence of what parents a man is born, so he be a man of merit.
—Horace

Richard Taylor was a planter in the Northern Neck of Virginia. Likely born by 1642, he may have immigrated to Virginia from England in the 1650s, but he was certainly here by 1663, when he witnessed a deed for Colonel Moore Fauntleroy. Because of his association with Colonel Fauntleroy and because he named a son Simon and a daughter Constance, it is probable his father was the Simon Taylor who is listed as a headright of Colonel Fauntleroy in a Northern Neck land patent dated May 22, 1650. Dr. Taylor's research has led him to consider that Richard is the son of Simon Taylor and Constance Berrington, who were married at Stanford-on-Soar, Nottinghamshire, England, on June 14, 1641. A record of baptism for Richard has not yet been found to verify this premise.

Richard died in North Farnham Parish, Virginia, between March 22, 1678, and May 7, 1679 (the drafting and proving of his will). Richard could sign his name, which suggests a certain level of practical education and perhaps social standing. Records show Richard purchased two hundred acres of land on May 1, 1671, placing him in the planter class. He married Sarah in 1663. Her surname, parentage, date, and place of birth are unknown. She survived Richard or at least was alive when he wrote his will. Richard and Sarah had three children, a girl and two boys.

Simon Taylor, son of Richard and Sarah, born between 1667 and 1670 in North Farnham, Richmond County, Virginia, died there on January 10, 1729. Simon, an heir to a portion of his father's agricultural estate, married Elizabeth Lewis, the eldest daughter of Edward and Mary Lewis, in or before 1691. She was born March 8, 1674, in North Farnham Parish and died October 7, 1727. They had eight or nine children. Additional land came into the hands of Simon through his wife, Elizabeth. Simon owned at least one slave, a woman named Jeney.

John Taylor, born about 1704 in North Farnham, the fourth child of Simon and Elizabeth, died there on February 28, 1741. He married Hanna Harrison by 1728. No record of Hanna's birth or death has been located. John died without a will, and it appears he was not particularly prosperous based on a court-ordered inventory of property after his death. Court records indicate John, as his father, probably had an alcohol problem. John and Hanna had five children.

Harrison Taylor, born August 11, 1735 in Richmond County, Virginia, died November 22, 1811, in Ohio County, Kentucky. The third child of John and Hannah, he married Jane Curlet on November 27, 1759, in Winchester, Frederick County, Virginia. Jane, the daughter of Nicholas and Rachel Jane Curlet, was born September 5, 1742, in Virginia. She died August 5, 1812, in Ohio County, Kentucky. They had twelve children. Harrison and Jane are buried in the Milton Taylor Cemetery in Hartford, Kentucky.

In 1777 and again in 1787, Harrison bought land from Captain Jeremiah Smith on Back Creek near Gore in what is now on the fringe of the Virginia horse country. This land lay along the great road leading from Winchester, Virginia, to Romney, West Virginia. On the initial tract, he built a large mill known locally as "the Big Mill," and he became known as "Honest Old Taylor at the Mill." This mill did the grinding for many miles of the surrounding country. On this property, Harrison spent some thirty years, built a house that still stands today, and built and operated the mill, which remained until 1973.

According to Wilmer L. Kern's *Frederick County, Virginia: Settlement and Some First Families of Back Creek Valley, 1730–1830*, the mill was built in 1794 (the second of Harrison's mills) and demolished in 1973. The structure was prominent in Willa Cather's novel *Sapphira and the Slave Girl*. Cather, a Pulitzer Prize-winning novelist, was born on a farm in the Back Creek Valley.

A photograph of the mill taken in 1972 by William J. Shull was printed in the *Ohio County Time-News* of Kentucky, on June 13, 1974, along with a photo of Harrison's home. The North Farnham Church, Richmond County, Virginia (Church of England, 1737; heavily restored 1924), located in the parish seat where most of the third generation of Taylors were baptized and married, still stands. Photos of the home, church, and mill are contained in Dr. Taylor's work.

Harrison, an American patriot during the Revolutionary War, rendered invaluable service to the Continental Army by furnishing supplies and other assistance. My sister, Norvel Nantippe Taylor Cox, is a Daughter of the American Revolution #674108 based on Harrison's lineage.

Harrison and Jane's personalities have been the object of considerable eulogy. Harrison D. Taylor (grandson of Harrison) in his history of the Taylor family, republished in *Ohio County in the Olden Days,* writes at length of Harrison, the patriarch of the family. J. B. Lutz wrote extensively of Jane's character and career as a midwife and ad-hoc surgeon.

In 1799, Harrison, Jane, and most of the children left Virginia and moved to Kentucky.

Septimus Taylor, born February 22, 1773, in Frederick County, Virginia, died in 1814 in Ohio County, Kentucky, and is buried in the Reid-Taylor Cemetery. The seventh child of Harrison and Jane, he married Mary McMahon on August 10, 1797, in Frederick County, Virginia. Mary long outlived Septimus, dying around 1846 in Ohio County, Kentucky. Septimus and Mary had seven children.

Richard McMahon Taylor, born June 17, 1798, in Winchester, Virginia, died October 5, 1880, in Ohio County, Kentucky. He was the elder child of Septimus and Mary. Richard married Delilah Frances Wise, the daughter of Tobias and Mary Grisby Wise, on March 19, 1819, in Ohio County, Kentucky. Delilah was born May 6, 1801, in Ohio County, Kentucky, and died there on July 18, 1847. Richard and Delilah had eleven children.

After Delilah's death, Richard married Sarah Rock on October 26, 1848, in Kentucky, in a joint marriage ceremony with his third daughter, Laura. Sarah was born in 1814 in Pennsylvania. They had four children.

Richard served in Captain George Trotter's Troop of Cavalry, First Regiment, Kentucky Volunteer Light Dragoons in the War of 1812. In later life, he was known as "Major Dick." We know from the 1860 census that he owned at least one slave, a male of age thirty-five.

Richard and Delilah are buried in the Old Taylortown Cemetery in Ohio County, Kentucky. Sarah went to live with a son after Richard's death, and no record of her death or burial has been located.

My father, a great-grandson of Richard, my mother, and my sister, Tippe, traveled through Kentucky in the early 1980s on their way to Virginia to visit me and see the sights of Washington, D.C. They stopped at our ancestors' old home place and the cemeteries where so many are buried. They spent a very enlightening evening with the Berryman family in Beaver Falls, Kentucky. The Berrymans are relatives with a vast knowledge of the Taylor family. The Berrymans explained that Richard owned a large tract of land in Kentucky, and as each child and grandchild married—and there were scores of them—they received a parcel of land. The parcels kept getting smaller and smaller, and the land was wearing out, tobacco being particularly hard on the soil. This, most likely, explains why my great-grandfather, Woodford Mitchell Taylor, moved to Texas.

Woodford "Woop" Mitchell Taylor was born on May 19, 1841, in Hartford, Ohio County, Kentucky, the tenth child of Richard McMahon and Delilah Wise. He died on January 31, 1926 in Bethel, San Saba County, Texas. He married Sarah Peter Rust, the daughter of Daniel and Elizabeth Simmons Rust, on June 24, 1863, in Skylesville, Muhlenberg County, Kentucky. Sarah was born February 6, 1844, in Logan County, Kentucky and died February 18, 1922, at Locker, San Saba County, Texas. They had ten offspring. My grandfather Emmett was their youngest child.

Woop stood five-foot-seven, and he had a ruddy complexion, brown eyes, and dark hair.

Woodford Mitchell and Sara Peter Rust Taylor.
Likely a wedding photograph, 1863. Woodford wears the insignia of a lieutenant in the US Army.

Sarah and Woodford's marriage bond, dated June 23, 1863, is quoted:

I, W. M. Taylor, who applies for a marriage license do certify that a marriage is intended to be solemnized between myself and Sarah P. Rust at Mrs. Cowans' in this county on the 24th day of June 1863. That I am 22 years of age and was born in Ohio County, Kentucky, that my father R. M. Taylor was born in Virginia, that my mother Deliah Taylor was born in Ohio County, Kentucky. That she the said Sarah P. Rust is about 18 years of age and was born in Logan County, Kentucky, that her father Daniel Rust was born in Virginia, that her mother Elizabeth Rust, now deceased, was born in this state, that neither I, the said W. M. Taylor, nor she the said Sarah P. Rust have ever been married.

Texas history permeates the education of Texas children from an early age, and it began to fascinate me as soon as I was able to digest small comic books used by teachers as early as the third grade. Stories of the French and Spanish explorations, the Texas revolution, the Alamo, the Republic, statehood, the Civil War, and Reconstruction molded my character and development. Much to my chagrin, the grandiose image of Texas I had developed was tarnished somewhat by two incidents in my childhood.

On a trip to San Antonio with my friend Ikey Tom Ault and his parents, staying at the Crockett Hotel, I saw the Alamo for the first time. A ten-year-old from West Texas expected an immense, walled fortress, not a small, weather-beaten, old chapel surrounded by large buildings. I now realize the Alamo fortress was large, and the chapel was only a small part of the complex.

This disappointment was only exceeded by my shock at seeing my great-grandfather's Civil War uniform for the first and only time. I could not believe my eyes when I looked into the trunk where it was being stored. The uniform was not Confederate gray but Yankee blue! Kentucky, a border state, remained neutral during the War between the States. Some hundred thousand Kentuckians served in the Northern Army and forty thousand in the Southern Army.

Great-grandfather Woop joined Company B, 26th Kentucky Infantry Regiment at Bowling Green, Kentucky, on September 28, 1861, as a private. He served in Company B throughout the war, steadily rising in rank, and he was discharged on April 12, 1864, as a captain. Woop was the last of six captains who commanded Company B. It was obvious from reviewing his service record and noting his rise in rank from private to captain that as his fellow soldiers, who were higher in rank, were killed, wounded, or transferred, he took their place.

He fought in several battles, the battle of Shiloh having the notoriety of the bloodiest. He fought as a lieutenant at Shiloh, and the regimental commander, Lieutenant Colonel Cicero Maxwell, mentioned in dispatches the gallant conduct of Lieutenant Taylor and others.

During the period 1974 to 1977, while I was serving as chief of the Army's Retirement Branch, I had access to all individual military service records archived at the National Records Center in St. Louis, Missouri. I was unable to locate Woop's records, which left me in a quandary. A woman at the National Records Center told me of an archivist at the National Archives in Washington, D.C., one well known for his ability to locate lost or missing records. I contacted the man who informed me that if Woop's records existed, he could find them. He said that it might take some time and not to call him, that he would call me.

I forgot about my quest until he surprised me by calling some nine months later to let me know that he had found the records and that he was forwarding a copy to me. I was elated to receive the records and eagerly perused them. The documents included Woop's entire pay record, record of promotions, dates of service, and several other documents. The Army kept excellent records even in those days. All were handwritten in beautiful script. One document of particular importance was his application for pension based on his Civil War service and approved by the War Department (now the Department of Defense). Woop was receiving a pension of $50.00 per month at his death. Woop's records had been moved from the National Records Center to the Bureau of Pensions (now the Social Security Administration) when his pension was approved, and that is where they were found.

In 1984, while I was a student at the Army War College in Carlisle Barracks, Pennsylvania, I had some time on my hands and visited the Institute of Military History located on this historic military installation to look for additional information about my great-grandfather. I located a book titled *The Union Regiments of Kentucky* published in 1897 that explained how the 26th Infantry Regiment was organized, how they fought, the units involved, the men and officers who served, and dispatches from the battlefield. This book contained an entry mentioning Lieutenant Taylor for gallant conduct at the battle of Shiloh.

Woop also served for a short time as a Texas ranger under the command of Captain L. H. McNelly as part of the Washington County volunteer militia.

An item from the *San Saba News*, dated June 4, 1914, follows:

> Mr. & Mrs. Woop Taylor who live on the old homestead place in the Bethel Community spent the last week in town as guest of Mr. & Mrs. R. G. Holden. These two good people were among the first to settle on Richland Creek. They came from old Kentucky, stopping one year in Ellis County and landed on Richland Creek about Christmas, 1875. Mr. Taylor was

an officer in the Union Army and participated in some of the great struggles of that fateful period. He yet has the sword he wore in the battle of Shiloh. He had not been to town since the new courthouse was built or the railroad came. He attended his first moving picture show.

Woop lived with his youngest son, Emmett, after Sarah died. As a youngster, my father spent many hours with Woop and remembers him clearly. Daddy said Woop could do anything with his hands. (So could my dad.) He remembers pedaling a manual lathe for his grandfather as the man carved wood to make furniture. Woop talked to him of many things but never about the war.

Mother remembers Woop and Sarah as a wonderful Christian couple. An influenza epidemic resulted in her family being quarantined, and they were unable to leave their home when she was a child. Woop and Sarah would visit daily and put a basket of food on the porch, and Sarah would inquire how they were doing. Mother said as they walked away, Woop would ask Sarah what the Shaws had to say. Mother told me Woop was extremely deaf, probably from riding to the "sound of the guns" too many times.

The following taken from his obituary in the *San Saba News* is quoted in part:

> Grandpa Taylor probably did not have an enemy in the world, and he left a host of friends and relatives to mourn him, many whom attended the last rites. Three of his old time friends, Willis Smith and Pete and "Tuck" Davenport, who moved to the county at the same time with him, were present at the burial ceremonies, and placed the first earth upon the casket, enclosing his remains.

Woop and Sarah are buried in the Old Algerita Cemetery near the former community of Bethel in San Saba County. The cemetery, which is located on ranch land, is fenced, mowed, and has several large, majestic live oak trees around the site. It is a beautiful pastoral setting and a wonderful final resting place. There are twelve Texas rangers including Woop buried in the cemetery. My son, Ross, and I visited their graves on April 10, 2005, and had a pleasant time reflecting on the lives of those who came before.

Woop's marker reads, "Resting until the Resurrection Morn," and Sarah's reads, "Empty is the home bereft of its Mother." The words are barely distinguishable as time and weather have blurred them, but Woop and Sarah's memory remain vivid. Theirs were two lives well lived.

Emmett Overton Taylor, my grandfather, was born July 2, 1882, in San Saba County and died March 15, 1963, in a San Saba nursing home. He married my daddy's mother, Mamie Beatrice Wood, the daughter of Warren and Polly Harkey Wood, on January 31, 1904, in San Saba County. Mamie was born May 3, 1887, in San Saba and died March 5, 1915, at the family home in the Bethel community during childbirth. Emmett and Mamie had six children, and my daddy was the fourth.

Emmett Overton Taylor

Grandfather Emmett is buried in the Richland Springs Cemetery, and Grandmother Mamie is buried in the Old Algerita Cemetery.

Mamie Beatrice Wood Taylor

Emmett soon married Willie Rhee Graham, the daughter of Hugh and Zilpha Wood Graham, on December 8, 1915. Willie was my grandmother's cousin. Emmett and Willie had one child, Woodie Lavon. Willie died in February 1982 at Rockdale, Texas, and was buried at Richland Springs beside Emmett.

I knew Emmett, a farmer in the Bethel community, after he retired and moved to San Saba. He was a handsome man of medium height and weight, reserved in demeanor, and dignified. He was apparently a successful farmer in the Bethel community, owning one of the few two-story farmhouses in San Saba County. I did not know him well, and I only visited with him for short periods when I was young.

Why did I not know Grandfather Taylor? He was neither mean and argumentative nor arrogant. He was simply distant. Always uncomfortable around my grandfather, I felt he was studying me, evaluating me, and silently asking, "Does Shorty's boy have what it takes?" He was not an easy man to get to know, and I never did!

2

Shorty and Squirrel

Mother arrived on November 30, 1919, at her parent's home near Locker in San Saba County. The daughter of Walter Green (Pappy) and Martha (Momma Shaw) Samatha Blasingame Shaw, her birth certificate lists her name as El Nora Shaw; however, Mother has always used Elanor as her first name. Alyene is not on her birth certificate. A relative named Vivian Alyene Reavis Taylor gave mother that name. Mother spelled it Allene, but her sister, Gladys, changed the spelling to Alyene when she was Mother's third-grade teacher at Locker.

Regardless, we knew her as Elanor Alyene. Her friends call her Alyene, and Daddy affectionately called her "Squirrel," a name given to her by her brother, J. R. Shaw, who thought she looked like a little squirrel when she was a baby.

She grew up on a 160-acre dry-land farm immediately adjacent to a dirt road that remains unpaved. Pappy Shaw grew cotton primarily. Other cash crops were watermelons and peanuts. He always had a garden of potatoes, corn, onions, tomatoes, green beans, black-eyed peas, carrots, radishes, and many other wonderful things, including grapes and peaches. In addition, there were chickens for eggs, fried chicken, the stew pot, hogs for bacon and ham, and an occasional squirrel or rabbit for the table. Rarely was beef available because of a lack of refrigeration. Consequently, though poor, they never went without food even during the Great Depression.

One of my earliest childhood memories is the sweet, syrupy smell of yellow-fleshed peaches cooking on Momma Shaw's stove as my mother and aunts went about canning fruits and vegetables. There was a concrete storm cellar located near the house where the canned goods were stored. The cellar, which was dark, musty, and cool, maintained a constant temperature. Anytime the weather looked threatening, we would go to the cellar. We thought it great fun to play in the cellar while we were waiting for the storm to pass.

While my mother and the aunts were cooking and visiting, my cousins, Travis and Jarvis Shaw, Clyde Cockrum, sister Tippe, and I would wandered over Pappy's farm, looking for bugs, arrowheads, rattlesnakes, and anything that would allow us to get into mischief. We were supposed to stay on Pappy's land, but we would often slip through the fence and head for Corn Knob mountain. Corn Knob, the highest point in the area, seemed particularly tall at the time. Covered with mesquite, cedar, a few oak trees, cactus, and slippery rocks, it became a chore to climb, skinning knees and elbows, but what a marvelous, breathtaking, panoramic view at the top. I remember that we could see all the way to the Colorado River . . . or maybe not. Maybe all we could see were the trees outlining its banks or maybe a draw, a tributary. Anyway, we could see a long way.

The five of us once had a dirt clod fight with Travis and me against the three younger ones. They were bruised, bleeding, and battered, but they kept coming and would not quit. Some of the clods started to hit Travis and me, and we decided the game was no longer fun. We could get hurt. It was certainly no fun when we got to Pappy's house and the aunts found out what had happened.

A delight from this time was Momma Shaw's "depression soup" filled with all manner of fresh, recently gathered, mouth-watering vegetables. Momma Shaw called it "depression soup" because it contained no meat. Mother made it, too, but it was not as good as Momma Shaw's, even though the ingredients were the same. My taste buds were probably more defined as a child.

Not so delightful was the periodic barefoot trek to the one-seat outhouse shaded by mulberry trees. This was where the chickens hung out and searched for the juicy, dark-colored fruit that had fallen from the trees. I dreaded the journey that invariably occurred early in the morning or late in the evening, and having to negotiate the chicken's poop and their incessant pecking at my heels didn't make matters easier.

Mother walked to school at Locker, which was perhaps a mile away, until the ninth grade, and then she rode the bus to Richland Springs for high school. She was the only one of her sisters who did not "board out" in either Richland Springs or San Saba for high school. Mother graduated Richland Springs High School in 1938, and again, she was the only one of her sisters who did not graduate college, for which she expressed bitterness during her later years. Mother said that Pappy had no money to send her by that time.

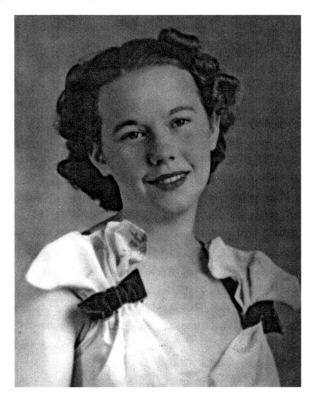

Mother, high school graduation, 1938.
This was Daddy's favorite photo of Mother.

The reason her sisters "boarded out" was that there was no school bus to take them to high school at that time. Pappy may have given financial help to her sisters, but it was meager at best. The girls worked to pay for their education, teaching school from September to May and taking college courses in the summer. That was how it was done in those days.

I do not understand Mother's resentment. She had the same opportunity as her sisters, but she failed to take advantage of the opportunity, either because she was hurt, depressed, or simply did not (or could not) understand the opportunity before her. She has always been of a pessimistic nature, with Daddy the eternal optimist. They were a good combination, a balanced blend for sister Tippe and me. She was a good mother and wife. Daddy, Tippe, and I loved her, but Daddy was the only one who understood her. Only he could cut through her dark side.

I am so like my mother, and Tippe so like my daddy.

Mother was the youngest of five children. In chronological order, they include the following: Thelma Gladys, Bessie May, Billie Iva, J. R., and my mother. Bessie died in 1932 of cancer, J.R. in 1983 of a heart attack, Gladys in 2004 of old age, and Billie in 2004 of Alzheimer's.

Mother first met Daddy at the all-county high school meet in San Saba. In those days, there was a farm with a family on every 160 acres. Therefore, the children had to either walk or ride a horse or mule to school, so there were many small schools located throughout the county. Each year, the schools would assemble to determine the San Saba county champion in such activities as picture memory (recognition of famous artists by their paintings), spelling bees, declamation, math, and other academic endeavors. There were also athletic events, such as track and field, baseball, and basketball. For each student entered in an activity, schools received points toward the overall county championship. Mother entered in tennis (although she had never held a racket in her hand) and the picture memory contest. She did not enter the math contest, because she had the same problem with math that I do today.

At that time, Mother was fifteen, and Daddy was twenty-five.

When I asked what he was doing there, she exclaimed, "He was checking out the high school girls!"

A mutual friend introduced them, and Daddy asked her for a date. I found it difficult to believe that Momma Shaw and Pappy would allow her to date a twenty-five-year-old man when she was only fifteen. She explained that girls dated and married much younger in the 1930s.

Later, Daddy lived on the O'Neal ranch, near Mother's home, which he and Uncle Herbert Taylor had leased and where they were running cattle. Daddy and Pappy hunted nightly. Some animal hides, such as bobcat or fox, would bring as much as a dollar, and as times were hard, this was a good way to make extra money. They had a couple of hunting dogs and roamed up and around Walbarger Creek, trying to make a kill.

Daddy became a fixture at the Shaw place. He ate there, played dominoes with Pappy, and courted Mother—or so he thought.

Mother did not know they were courting, and once when she and Daddy were visiting a neighbor, she left with another boy. This upset Daddy, and he told her he had thought she was his girl.

Mother responded, "Oh, I didn't know."

I suspect she was playing hard to get.

He was a roper, a rider, a fighter, and a damn good windmill man.
—Unknown

The fourth child of six born to Emmett Overton and Mamie Beatrice Wood Taylor, Norvel Ross "Shorty" Taylor was born at home near the Bethel community, San Saba County, on April 9, 1910.

He received the nickname "Shorty" as an infant from his Uncle Emery Ross Wood when Uncle Emery said, "He is a real 'Shorty,' isn't he?"

Daddy was not that short, standing five-foot-nine and weighing around 165 pounds. Wiry, strong, smart, energetic, determined, strong-willed, and gentle are words that describe him. He could be short-tempered when aroused, had a very high pain threshold, and could always be heard singing or whistling when working. I always knew where he was when we were in a pasture rounding up cattle or sheep, because I could hear him. He especially like to sing "Just Molly and Me and the Baby Makes Three," "Alexander's Rag Time Band," "Across the Alley from the Alamo," and "Roly Poly."

One of the highest accolades is the comment, "If he says so, you can bank on it."
—James L. Hayes

Daddy's word was his bond, and a handshake his contract. He was honest and fair in all his dealings. The world could use more men like Shorty Taylor.

My daddy, N. R. "Shorty" Taylor, around 1947, when we lived at Suggs Switch.

Daddy was no stranger to work, because any boy who lived on a farm during that time could be expected to work as a man.

Daddy went to school in Bethel through the eighth grade.

He once told me, "Son, I probably have a better education than you, even though you graduated college." He went on to say that he wanted to learn and the teacher's wanted to teach. Because time was short, they taught the basics of reading, writing, spelling, and arithmetic, and they taught him well. They sure did! Daddy could add, subtract, multiply, and divide faster in his head than I can on a calculator.

Daddy did have the opportunity to continue his schooling, but for some unknown reason, he did not. His uncle, Noel Wood, who taught school at Mercedes in the Rio Grande Valley asked Daddy and a cousin named Clyde Wood to come live with his family and go to school. They did, but they then changed their minds, left without telling Uncle Noel, and hitchhiked home to Bethel, which took them about a week.

After the eighth grade, Daddy went to work for his other uncle, Herbert Taylor, who owned several farms in San Saba County and was president of the Richland Springs Bank. He also worked for Emery Wood, another uncle, who owned a couple of farms around Bethel. He continued to work for and with his uncles, owning a few cows with Uncle Herbert and Mother's brother, J. R. Shaw, until he married Mother.

During this time, he heard about the oil boom in West Texas and decided he should check it out. He rode with another fellow to McCamey and got a job with a company from Pennsylvania, building oil storage tanks. On his way, he passed by Suggs Switch and Barnhart. At both locations, cowboys were delivering cattle to the railhead. Daddy thought that was the sort of life he would like to live. Little did he know, however, some fourteen years later, he would be one of the cowboys.

Daddy initially worked in the oil field by delivering water to the workers until the supervisor became impressed with him and kept giving him better jobs and more pay. Eventually, he got homesick and told the supervisor he was going home. The supervisor asked him to stay and go to Pennsylvania with him, because he was smart and hardworking and because he could have a future with the company. Instead, he headed back to San Saba County, his family, and eventually, my mother.

Daddy's siblings included his brother Willard Overton, his sister Verma Ray, his brother Carmen Overton "Billy," and his younger sister, Roxie Octavia Beatrice Taylor. A brother Bernard died in 1905 before Daddy was born, and his brother Willard died in 1990. Verma Ray Telecamp died in 2000. In 2002, Daddy and I took a trip to see all the places he had lived. We visited Roxie Grumbles and his brother Billy, and we had an enjoyable visit. Aunt Roxie died in 2005, and Uncle Billy passed away in 2010. He and his brother Billy could pass for twins, and I look more like them each year. The acorn does indeed fall close to the tree!

Three significant events happened during Daddy's early childhood.

First, his mother died when he was five while she was giving birth to Roxie. He remembers a black hearse pulled by horses taking her away from the farm, but he does not remember her funeral. His mother is buried in the Old Algerita Cemetery, not far from Bethel, with many of our relatives.

Second, his father married Willie Rhee Graham, the cousin of Daddy's mother, shortly after his mother's death. I suppose that was the way they did things in those days, especially when you had a farm to run, mouths to feed, and an infant in the house. Daddy loved his stepmother and always treated her as if she were his natural mother.

The last event took place when Daddy was eleven or twelve. Ed Knight, a neighbor, had cleaned out a dirt stock tank for Daddy's father. Ed's daughter and Daddy's sister, Verma, decided to go swimming. The girl could not swim, and the tank was deep. Unfortunately, the girl began to sink. Verma got a tree limb for the girl to grab; however, as Verma pulled her toward the bank, the limb broke, and the girl drowned. Daddy's father sent him by horseback to tell her parents. Shortly after his ninety-fifth birthday, I asked Daddy about the reaction of her parents, and he told me they had been upset but had not blamed Verma or his parents. The times were difficult, and accidents, injury, and death were part of the era.

One day when in his twenties, he and Uncle J. R. Shaw were taking a truck load of cattle to the O'Neal ranch, north of Locker on the Colorado River. They were traveling from Algerita on Cottonbelt Lane, and they had to cross a bridge over Richland Creek. The bridge collapsed, and the load of cattle dumped into the creek, killing some and injuring others. Daddy and Uncle J. R. were lucky they were not hurt.

Daddy and truck, Richland Creek, San Saba County, Texas.

Another time, Daddy and Uncle J. R. were driving cattle along the railroad that ran through San Saba. Some of the cattle drifted off the railroad right-of-way and wandered through people's yards. One old lady, who was madder than a wet hen, came up to Daddy and asked him who owned the cattle, because they were going to have to pay for the cattle tearing down her clothesline and ruining her clothes.

Daddy told her, "The fellow back there at the end of the herd owns them, so you need to talk to him." The fellow at the end was Uncle J. R. Daddy owned the cattle.

When he was middle-aged, Daddy told me about some of the things he had done that he was not particularly proud to admit. In his old age, when I would ask him to tell me the stories again, he would just smile and say, "I don't remember," or he would say, "That was a long time ago, Herb." I will try to relate a couple of the stories to the best of my recollection.

Emery Ross Wood, Daddy's uncle, gambled and enjoyed partaking of John Barleycorn. Cards, dice, and horses were his specialty. He also ran bootleg whiskey from the Kerrville area to San Saba County. The local law enforcement folks figured this out and knew the make of the car he drove, thus making his avocation a dangerous one. Daddy had his own car, so Uncle Emery asked Daddy to make the runs, which he did several times without incident. I suspect Daddy drank some of that whiskey, as he was known to toss one back in his youth.

Insanity is doing the same thing over and over again expecting different results.
—Anonymous

At a dance in Lometa one Saturday night, he kept cutting in on a truck driver and his date. The girl told Daddy that the trucker could be mean. If Daddy kept cutting in on them, the trucker would take him outside and whip him. Daddy did, and the trucker did. Daddy told me it was not much of a fight, because the trucker was much larger. Being the ornery sort and not one to give up, Daddy would go to Lometa each Saturday to wait for the trucker to return from a trip, and they would go at it again. This happened several Saturdays in a row with the same result.

Finally, the trucker told him, "You are wearing me out whipping you. If you want her this bad, you can have her."

I do not think the girl had anything to do with it. One of them had to give in, and it was not going to be Daddy.

Daddy spotlighted deer with his brother-in-law, Ray Graves, when Ray was teaching school at the small town of Castell near Mason. Spotlighting was illegal then just as it is now. Uncle Ray had a rifle with a powerful flashlight attached that was "zeroed in" so that the bullet would impact exactly in the center of the light beam. They would hunt along the county roads, make the kill, dress the deer, and have venison whenever they wanted. Ray wanted to take some of the meat to school board members to earn brownie points. Daddy told Ray that would get him fired, maybe jailed. The ironic thing is that years later, when Ray owned a place near Locker on the Colorado River, he would go ballistic if he thought someone hunted on his land. He would never give permission to hunt on his land, much less spotlight.

A justice of the peace in Kerrville married Mother and Daddy on September 30, 1939. Because it was early in the day, they went to see the *Wizard of Oz* at the local moving-picture show, but they only stayed for half the show. Mother was twenty, and Daddy was thirty.

Shortly thereafter, they began their married life by moving to Maryneal, where Daddy took a ranch job and became a genuine cowboy. G. P. Jones, who was single and somewhat eccentric, owned the ranch. Daddy told of Mr. Jones having him catch rattlesnakes, which were plentiful, and keeping them in a fifty-five-gallon drum. Once a year, Mr. Jones would invite the administration and students from Hardin-Simmons University in Abilene for a barbeque. All got a big kick out of looking at the rattlesnakes. This was especially true of the girls who rode the six white horses for which Hardin-Simmons is known.

While Daddy was shaving early one morning, a lightning strike hit near their house and traveled down the wind charger's electrical line to the single bulb hanging in the bathroom, striking Daddy. Though he was knocked unconscious, Mother somehow got him to their pickup and drove him to the doctor in Roscoe. The doctor told Daddy he was lucky to be alive.

I once asked Daddy whether he suffered any lingering side effects. In his West Texas drawl, he said, "You know, Herb, not really." Then embarrassingly, he said as an afterthought, "It did turn my 'ding dong' black as coal for a few days."

Mother cooked and cleaned house for Mr. Jones. His history was that he liked either the man or the woman who worked for him, but not both. In this case, he liked Mother. They worked for Mr. Jones for two years until Daddy got another ranch job. They were both glad to leave.

Jim Henderson hired Daddy to work as a ranch hand at Suggs Switch in 1941. Mr. Henderson was running sheep and cattle on some thirty sections, and Daddy would be responsible for managing it all. The house where Mother and Dad were to live had been used by single cowboys and needed repair and expanding in the worse way before they could move. Mr. Henderson agreed to take care of it.

Later, Mr. Henderson leased part of the ranch to his brother, Loftin "Honey" Henderson, and the remainder to Clifton B. "Cotton" Brooks. Cotton hired Daddy to run his lease.

Daddy on horseback at Suggs Switch.

Cotton and Daddy hit it off from the beginning. Cotton told Daddy that in his experience, a hired hand would be more conscientious taking care of the owner's livestock if he had a personal interest in them. Therefore, Daddy borrowed money from the First National Bank in Mertzon to buy five calves to run with Cotton's cattle. Daddy was no longer just a hired hand but now a cattleman. Later, Cotton agreed for Daddy to lease the Fry Place, which consisted of four sections, to run his own stock while he continued to work for Cotton.

The Brooks were more than good to the Taylors. Cotton and his wife, Lillian, had three boys: Larry, four years older than me; Bill, a year or two younger; and Joe David, the youngest. There were no girls. Consequently, when sister Tippe arrived, the Brooks treated her as their own and spoiled her lavishly. I received clothes that Larry had outgrown, which were always welcomed. I particularly remember a white sport coat and a pair of blue suede shoes. Cotton's family lived in San Angelo during the winter, but they spent the summer at their ranch near Mertzon. Bill and I helped our fathers work during the summer, and we got to swim, play cars, and participate in other games at the Mertzon ranch.

Also living at the Mertzon ranch were Rance, Lois, and Donna Brunson. Donna, some four years older than me, became a surrogate big sister. Once, she took me to the drive-in picture show in Mertzon. I must have been about twelve. I thought it a big deal. She was so sophisticated, driving and all.

Each summer, the Brooks, Brunsons, Peeks, and Taylors would camp on Dove Creek near the site of the Dove Creek Battlefield. Here in January 1865, twenty-six Texas rangers and militiamen were killed in a losing, five-hour battle with Kickapoo Indians who were on their way to Mexico. Eight miles southeast of Mertzon on private land along Dove Creek, a Texas historical marker erected in 1963 reads, "Around this mountain a battle was fought on Jan. 8, 1865, between 2000 Indians and Texas rangers and State Troops. Four officers and 22 of their men lie in unmarked graves nearby."

The grownups would play dominoes and cards while we kids swam, fished, and romped up the steep, rocky sides of the bluffs along the creek. Donna and I would walk and talk. We were both going through the maturation period from adolescence to adult.

Cotton had another ranch between Big Lake and Ozona, so there were times Daddy did not see him for several weeks. Their relationship was such that Cotton gave Daddy signature authority on his bank account at the First National Bank of Mertzon. This allowed Daddy to pay his own salary each month and to purchase necessary supplies for the ranch without having to contact Cotton. Cotton told Daddy, "If you need to borrow money for the kids or an emergency, write a check and pay me back when you are able."

Years later, when Daddy and Cotton no longer had a business association, Cotton told Daddy he had never changed the signature authority and did not intend to do so. I cannot fathom that happening today. People were more trusting then, because they could be.

Cotton always gave Daddy a bonus at Christmas even when stock prices were low and feed bills high. He would make a special trip to the ranch and place an envelope containing the bonus check on a branch of the Christmas tree. He also placed wonderful, wrapped presents from Hemphill Wells in San Angelo under the tree for all of us. Daddy would not open the envelope until Christmas day, so it was always a nice surprise. I am sure he used the money to pay for the gifts he bought Mother, Tippe, and me.

Cotton Brooks was one of my early role models.

PART II

Early Years

3

What a Wonderful Way to Grow Up

Bless those who curse you, pray for those who mistreat you.
—Luke 6:28 NIV

I drew my first breath at 0325 on June 28, 1942, a Sunday, at the Shannon Hospital in San Angelo with Dr. R. L. Powers, the attending physician. Daddy was thirty-two, and Mother twenty-two.

Daddy had been sending his sister, Verma, the bookkeeper at the hospital, money each month to place in an account so all hospital bills were paid prior to my birth. The total cost was less than a hundred dollars, even though the hospital stay was five days. I detest being in debt to anyone, a trait I obviously got from my father.

Dr. Powers gave Mother a book on how to raise a child, and on the inside cover, he wrote, "Keep him dry, fed, and leave him alone." A picture of me, the earliest I have found, shows me with a "cheesy" smile and plump cheeks. I appear to be a happy and well-fed child.

Baby Herbie, 1942.

My name came from Daddy's uncles, Herbert Wood Taylor and Emery Ross Wood. In my opinion, Herbert would have been a better choice than Herbie. Even today, I receive official documents addressed to Herbert. Apparently, people assume Herbie is a nickname. At least I was not named after my father. Thankfully, my sister, Tippe, got the name Norvel. Daddy had probably decided I would never make a cowboy by the time Tippe was born. By giving her his name, he might be able make one of her.

I vaguely remember the birth of my sister, Norvel Nantippe "Tippe," in San Angelo on February 28, 1947, and her being brought home to Suggs Switch.

Tippe was a tomboy, a nuisance, wanting to do everything I did. She is all lady today, but she was as rough as a cob as a youngster. She has been a significant part of my life during both good and bad times, and for that, I am both blessed and grateful.

A typical Tippe stunt took place when our cousins Travis and Jarvis had come to visit. Tippe and Jarvis were riding a horse bareback, with Tippe in front and Jarvis in back, when she reined the horse hard under Mother's clothesline. She ducked, and Jarvis never saw the line until it was too late, knocking him to the ground.

We were eating in a Mexican restaurant in San Angelo, and when the waiter brought us our menus, Daddy ordered for all of us. The waiter brought our drinks, tostadas, and hot sauce. Tippe asked who ordered the soup, and both Jarvis and Travis piped up that they had.

Tippe told them, "You'd better eat it while it is hot." I suppose they had not eaten much Mexican food, because each took a large spoonful of the hot sauce, swallowed, turned beet red, and began to gulp their water. Such was her nature.

She convinced Jarvis that there were bears at Suggs Switch. Today, Jarvis will ask jokingly if there are any bears around.

Tippe had no trepidation as a child, and I am not sure she has any now.

She would pester Daddy to let her barrel race.

Daddy would refuse, finally admitting, "You have no fear. I am afraid you might end up like Tom Owens's daughter."

Tom Owens was a neighbor, and his daughter, Margaret, was a professional cowgirl. She was killed in a vehicle accident late one night as she was returning from a rodeo. I am told the police had to shoot her two large dogs, which were faithfully guarding her body.

Suggs Switch is located six miles east of Barnhart on a dirt road. The road had originally led from San Angelo to Big Lake and places farther west before Highway 67. The name originated from its location on the Kansas City, Mexico, and Orient Railway, and it was a livestock shipping point for the Suggs Ranch and other ranches in the area. A spur or switch off the main railway allowed trains to pass and boxcars to be positioned at the shipping pens for the loading of livestock.

Living on a ranch in West Texas was a wonderful way to grow up! Horses, dogs, pigs, sheep, goats, cattle, dove, bobwhite, blue quail, prairie dogs, rattlesnakes, skunks, coons, coyotes, horned toads, an occasional bobcat or deer, and other assorted animals were all part of the varied but arid landscape. Rabbits, both cottontail and particularly jackrabbits, were present in large numbers, and it was great fun to hunt them. There was all the space imaginable to ride, play, shoot, drive, and dream.

My formative years were at Suggs Switch. I had good role models in my parents and an excellent environment to grow. Hard work rounding up livestock, branding, marking, shearing, building fences, burning pears, fixing water gaps, milking cows, riding, roping, feeding livestock, unloading truck loads of hay and hundred-pound sacks of feed, going to work at daylight, and working until dark all build character as well as a healthy body. City kids then as well as now miss a wonderful way to grow up.

The water was always sweeter, the food tastier, and the sleep deeper after making a hand during a hard day's work. I will always be grateful for the opportunity I had to experience this way of life. It served me well as I made my way in the world. Even so, I understood early on that we did not own our land and never would; therefore, I would need to find another way to earn a living.

Our house consisted of a kitchen, bathroom, living room, two bedrooms, and a screened front porch. The wood-frame house was not painted. It had no electricity, but did have running water. We had a battery radio; butane heaters, kitchen stove and icebox; and kerosene lamps for lighting.

During the summer, we slept on the screened porch covered in thick, prolific Virginia Creeper vines with blue and white flowers, because it was cooler.

Mother in front of Virginia Creeper vines at Suggs Switch.

The yard was fenced with wire and had one mesquite tree in the front and one outside the fence at the back and side of the yard, where our car and pickup were parked.

Mother washed clothes outside the house on a gas-powered Maytag washing machine, filling it with a garden hose and wringing the clothes out by hand. She put the clothes in a metal tub and later took them to a clothesline near the yard for drying, using a little red Radio Flyer wagon. My cousin, Travis Shaw, and I took the wagon to the Barnhart Draw and rode it down the sides until it was destroyed. Mother is still mad at us for that.

We had a crank telephone that hung on the wall, and it had a party line. The line connected to a central office in Mertzon. Donna Brunson worked at the central office after school and during the summer, so it was always nice to hear a familiar voice. The line served only the ranchers who had participated in laying the line, which resulted in each being connected to the other. If you wanted to call someone, you had to crank the phone a certain number of times to correspond to a set number of rings. Ours was three longs and a short crank. The rings were hard to distinguish. Therefore, anytime the phone rang, everyone on the party line would listen to find out if the call was for them, and if not, some would continue to listen. You dared not discuss anything that you did not want others to know.

The house was about forty yards from the railroad track. When the train went by, it was noisy, but we became accustomed to the noise and hardly noticed. The wire fence out front was part of a holding pen for livestock. Near the house, there was a barn that was about five feet from the rail spur, and attached to it was a saddle, tool, and equipment shed. A bit farther away were the large wooden corrals, dipping vat, water troughs, weighing scales, and wooden chute for loading the livestock into the railcars.

A wooden windmill and a large rock water tank sat on a hill about 150 yards from the house. The windmill supplied water to us as well as the animals. Daddy built an elevated storage tank on the side of the rock tank for our drinking water. The water came through the pipe to the house by gravity. The sides of the rock tank were two feet wide, and it had a concrete top. The tank was ninety feet across and six feet deep. From the top of the windmill, you could see Barnhart and anyone coming for several miles. I spent many a happy hour there by myself or with family and friends. The windmill became a castle, fort, or whatever my imagination dreamed, and the tank made a terrific swimming pool.

I often wished that a little girl by the name of Penny would come, and she did once with Janet Parry. I was embarrassed by our house with no paint and surroundings. Penny did not seem to mind, shy as she was, and my feelings for her grew stronger, much stronger.

Many incidents occurred during our time at Suggs Switch, some funny, some sad, most just about life. They are in no particular sequence, but hopefully, they provide a flavor of what life was like at Suggs Switch in the late 1940s and early 50s.

Daddy was on his way home one afternoon when his horse caught a foot in a prairie dog hole and fell on Daddy, breaking his leg. He was about a quarter mile from the house and called for Mother, but she could not hear him. He dragged himself on his elbows until she heard him when he was near the house. He told her what had happened and to get the pickup and come get him. There were several gates—some wire, some wooden—between the house and Daddy. Mother did not bother to open any of them. She just drove through them. Daddy was watching her and thinking, "Here, I'm going to be laid up with a broken leg. She has torn the gates down. Cattle and sheep will be scattered all over the county, and there is not a thing I can do about it."

Daddy bought me a pair of handmade boots and a Stetson hat from M. L. Leddy's in San Angelo. I presume he thought he would make a rancher out of me if I had the proper accessories. I rarely wore them, except to church, preferring a straw hat or no hat and off-the-shelf boots for school and work. This greatly disappointed Daddy. Mother probably had only two dresses in her closet, and both were well worn and washed. I am sure the money could have been better spent on her.

Herbie Ross, age three.

We had several pets, including the horses, dogie lambs, and milk pen calves that remain bright in my memory, the first being Bruno the Bear. Bruno was a figment of my imagination, but he was real to me just the same. He lived on a fence post near the house. I would visit him to tell what was happening in my life, usually when I had my feelings hurt by my parents. Bruno existed when I was four or five years old, probably because I rarely had other children to talk or play with. Bruno became my friend, confidant, and playmate. He must have been quite shy, because I do not remember him talking much. I clearly remember how Bruno looked and the fence post on which he sat.

Mother and Daddy would talk and laugh about a white pig following me on my tricycle. The pig would be laying in the shade during the heat of the day, and I would take off on the tricycle. He would grunt and snort, not wanting to get up, but he could not stand my leaving him, so here he would come. He followed me everywhere. I do not remember what happened to him, and neither do my parents. We probably ate him. Surely not!

Our dog, Blackie, of medium-size with white paws, belly, and a white tip on his tail, was worth keeping. Once, we were unable to find Blackie, so Daddy decided he had probably gone to Barnhart to find a girlfriend. Sure enough, Daddy found him in Barnhart at Bart Westfall's Texaco warehouse. Bart held Blackie while Daddy castrated him. Poor Blackie bled all over the bed of the pickup on the way back to Suggs Switch. He was one sick dog, but he never ran off to Barnhart again.

Later, Daddy told me, "Son, I should not have done that to Blackie."

I agreed, especially in light of what transpired later.

Mother was working in the yard and had Tippe with her. Tippe was just a toddler, and Mother heard Tippe saying, "Big bug, Mommy. Big bug." Mother turned around and saw a rattlesnake crawling toward Tippe. Thankfully, Blackie positioned himself between Tippe and the snake, giving Mother the time to get her daughter out of danger. The rattler did not bite Blackie, but he was bitten later by a rattlesnake and almost died. He lay in the vines and shade beside the house for two weeks before he was able to get up and about.

Rattlesnakes were a part of the scene in West Texas, but I never became accustomed to them. It is a miracle that more people were not bitten. The only folks I know who were bitten are my cousin Clyde Cockrum and Buck Owens. I saw more than one horse and several cattle that had been bitten. The damn things were everywhere, and they still are. Rattlesnakes and cockroaches will always be with us, regardless of how we mistreat this fragile planet of ours.

The family was at Barnhart one evening, and as one of us stepped on the porch to go into the house, we heard a rattlesnake rattling. The rattling seemed to come from underneath the porch steps or the vines around the front porch. Daddy went inside and got a flashlight, looked around, and decided the snake was under the house. He got a .22-caliber rifle and entered the crawl space under the house, Mother begging him to come back but to no avail.

The house could not have been more than two feet off the ground, and it rested on rock pillars that were spaced every few feet. They were some very tight quarters and no place to be on a dark night, crawling around on your belly looking for a snake. The advantage had to be with the snake.

Daddy told us to be quiet so he could hear the snake rattle and locate him.

After several tense minutes, we heard the crack of a shot, and Daddy hollered, "Got him."

That was my daddy. If he made his mind up to do something, he was going to do it, come hell or high water.

Blackie came to an untimely end as dogs that chase cars often do.

An oil well was being drilled east of the house, and a roughneck going home was driving faster than the conditions of the dirt road would allow. Blackie heard him coming and ran out to the road. The driver swerved, hit Blackie, lost control in the soft bar-ditch dirt, and turned over, spilling tools everywhere.

Daddy walked calmly to the wreck as the man was crawling out a truck window.

"You hurt?"

"No," the man said.

Daddy quietly explained to the man that he had killed the children's dog, that he had been driving too fast, that the children often played near the road, and that he could have hit us. Daddy then picked up a pipe wrench lying on the ground and proceeded to break any glass not already broken on the truck. When he had finished, the front windshield, back window, side windows, front headlights, and back taillights had all been shattered.

He then softly but firmly said, "You tell your buddies that if they speed within a half mile of this house, they will have to answer to me."

Daddy helped the roughneck turn the pickup back on its wheels and load his tools. The roughneck said absolutely nothing, got in his truck, and left.

From then on, we could hear those fellows a mile from the house, but when they got close, you could hear them slow. They would creep by the house and then gun their engine, and away they would go.

That old dog was my first experience with the death of someone I cared for, but he would not be the last.

During the summer of '55, some of my pals and I planned to go camping on the ranch, and had asked Charles Roe to go with us. For some reason, his dad, Everett Roe, would not let him.

We were camped where the Barnhart Draw and another draw come together when Daddy came to tell us that Charles had been killed. He was playing with a younger boy, Don Childs, and they were throwing rocks. Childs accidentally had hit Charles behind the ear, killing him. He was twelve years old. Charles's funeral was my first funeral and the first time I saw a dead body.

All present shuffled past the coffin. I really did not want to see. His face looked like wax. He was there—or his body was there—but Charles was gone. I did not like it then, and I do not like it now.

I have seen too many lifeless, wax faces. I simply no longer view an open casket.

Everett later told Daddy that if he had let Charles go with us, he would still be alive.

For those who believe, no explanation is possible.
—St. Ignatius Loyold

I have often thought about life being preordained, but I have decided that cannot be so. If God gave his only son to die for our sins and he gave us the freewill to either accept or not accept his son as our lord and savior, then that choice cannot be preordained. To me, this is one of life's great mysteries.

Everett's oldest son, Franklin, was killed several years later in a car accident. Everett said at his funeral, "I will never have to go through this again. He is the last one."

Good judgment comes from experience and a lot of that comes from bad judgment.
—Will Rogers

On the lighter side, I was an observer or participant in several life lessons at Suggs Switch.

Loftin (Honey) Henderson, a neighbor and old-time cowboy, wore his pants in his boots, rolled his own Bull Durham cigarettes with one hand, drove GMC pickups and a Cadillac, and called everyone "Honey," whether they be man, woman, or beast.

One day, we were going to one of our pastures, which joined Honey's lease, and as we rounded a curve, there was Honey standing legs spread beside his Caddy. He was rolling a cigarette and relieving himself. Honey was hard of hearing, so Daddy drove up very quietly behind the Caddy and honked. Honey was startled and quickly jerked around, and Bull Durham and pee streaked across our windshield. Honey was terribly embarrassed, as Mother and Tippe were in the pickup.

After he regained his composure, he told Daddy, "Honey, if you ever do that again, I will kill you," and I think he meant it. *You do not do some things to another man!*

Herbert Peek, his wife, and daughter, Lorena, worked for Honey. I called both Herbert and his wife Peek. The Peeks had a worn-out paint horse they wanted to sell. I saved my money and finally had enough to buy the horse. Daddy told me, "Son, offer Peek twenty-five dollars for that horse, and only offer him more if he insists that he won't sell the horse at that price."

I had thirty dollars, and I was nervous, as this was my first experience dealing. I went to Peek and told him, "Peek, I will give you twenty-five dollars for that horse, but if you won't take that, I will give you thirty." Well, I bought the horse for thirty. *Never tip your hand while doing a deal!*

Tippe had a baby kitten that she was dunking in a water trough when Peek walked up and asked what she was doing. She told Peek,

"I'm baptizing it." Now that kitten had an aversion to being baptized and was fighting for all it was worth.

Peek told Tippe, "You stop drowning that cat, or I'm going to baptize you." *You should not try to baptize a man or critter unless they have a sincere desire to be baptized!*

When rounding up a pasture of livestock, one rider stays in sight of the outside fence while starting any livestock found moving toward the rider to his right. Each rider stays in sight of the rider to his left and does the same, eventually moving all livestock to the middle of the pasture. The fence rider is usually the youngest or greenest. He cannot get lost because he has the fence to guide him, but it is the hardest job because he has to ride at a hard lope the entire time. I was often the fence rider. *The fence rider and a fellow wanting to get ahead in life are similar. Both have to ride a little harder and faster than the other fellow!*

It occurs to me that the hierarchy for a herd of cattle is the same as for men. *You have those out front—the leaders who get the fresh grass, get to drink first, do not have dust blowing in their face, and can see the world in front of them. You have the middle of the herd where most dwell, and then you have the drags, those at the tail end, which get no fresh grass, drink last, eat dust, and can only see the backside of others!*

One morning, Daddy, a couple of other men, and I rounded up a pasture of wild cows and calves that had been in the brush for some time. As we were penning the cattle, I decided that I wanted to ride one of the calves and began to pester Daddy to do so.

He said, "No, we have too much work to do," but I continued to badger him.

One of the cowboys said, "Hell, Shorty, let the kid ride one and get it out of his system."

Daddy nodded and said, "Do it." The cowboys flanked a calf. I got on him. He took two jumps, and I landed hard on my face.

Daddy hollered, "Get him another."

I protested but ended up having to ride three more of those calves, each throwing me hard. I had all the calf-riding I wanted to do for a while. *Sometimes the smart thing is keep your mouth shut and leave well enough alone!*

Suggs Switch had coyotes, and they were killing sheep. Daddy decided to have a coyote hunt. A fellow volunteered to fly his Piper Cub, and fifteen to twenty pickups showed up with an average of three rifles to a pickup. We were at the lower end of the ranch, and the pickups were lined up side-by-side, gunning their engines, looking like a tank battalion fixing to cross the LOD (Line of Departure) into Iraq. The Piper Cub was flying overhead, and once the pilot spotted a coyote, he was to drop a roll of toilet paper to mark the coyote's location.

After several minutes, the toilet paper came fluttering out, and the hunt was on. Pickups went in every direction. It looked like a chase scene out one of the *Bandit* movies with Burt Reynolds. They ran over wire fences and gates, bouncing around, throwing up dirt, hitting mesquite trees, and having a grand ol' time. There were few coyotes killed.

When it was over, Daddy said, "Herb, those coyotes could have killed a lot of sheep for what it is going to cost to fix these fences." *Often the cure is worse than the disease.*

We hunted dove during dove season at every opportunity. Often, Clyde Parry, his son, James Lee, a couple of other family friends, and I would hunt together. The best hunting we usually found was along the county road from Suggs Switch to the Fry place. The bar ditches were normally full of sunflowers, and doves loved the seeds, so they provided good hunting. We would clean our kill, and Clyde would take them to Barnhart to store in his freezer.

Hunting in a pasture named Mineral Well for the windmill, which pumped drinkable but "gyppy" water, we had killed many doves, and we cleaned them as we walked and hunted. The birds' craws were full of sunflower seeds, and Daddy began to eat the seeds, telling us they were good. Soon, several of us were eating them. Shortly thereafter, Daddy, James Lee, one or two others, and I were all producing bodily fluids from both port and aft. Recently, James Lee informed me he had never been that sick again. I have, but I do not remember when.

The end of dove season signaled the time for the bird fry at Suggs Switch.

Friends and neighbors came for a night of festivities. There would be tubs of iced-down sodas for the kids and beer for the adults. The men would fill a large iron pot with lard, build a wood fire around the vessel, and dump the birds into the pot when the lard began to boil. They fried the birds until they were crispy, and we would come and have our plates filled. There would be potato salad, pinto beans, and all the fixings as well as homemade ice cream and watermelon. It was fun to play with the other kids, and the adults had a fine time as well.

Life was good for this boy from Barnhart.

Ikey Tom Ault was one of my first playmates. He lived on a neighboring ranch across Highway 67 near Barnhart. We would ride horses together and play on the railroad boxcars at Suggs Switch, usually on Sunday after church. Ikey Tom had the peculiar habit of repeating himself. He would say, "Let's play cowboys and Indians Let's do. Let's do," or he would say, "Let's ride horses. Let's do. Let's do."

His father, Sam Ault, was born in 1912 at Big Hollow, west of Mertzon, the grandson of Thomas Jefferson Ault, one of the early settlers of Irion County. In 1929, Sam married Marie Jones, and they left for California so Sam could be in the movies.

He met director Jack Sullivan with Warner Brothers Studio while he was looking at an apartment in Hollywood, and Sullivan hired him on the spot. Sam was in various movies, including the Buck Jones serials. In addition, he also acted in *Dive Bombers*, *The Westerners*, *One with the Gun*, *The Santa Fe Trail* with Errol Flynn, and *The Outlaw* with Howard Hughes and Jane Russell. He then met his longtime friend, Ben Johnson (who won an Oscar for best supporting actor as Sam the Lion in the movie *Last Picture Show* in 1971). Johnson was on his first trip to Hollywood, bringing paint horses from Oklahoma. When Ikey Tom was born in 1941, Sam was Gary Cooper's double in *Sergeant York*. He also doubled for Ronald Reagan on several occasions. Sam trained horses while in Hollywood, including Roy Rogers's horse, Trigger. The Aults had several pictures of Sam with Trigger.

After he returned to Texas, he bought livestock for the movie studios and transported cattle and horses to California. In his lifetime, he had partnerships with several auction barns in West Texas, the first being the Producers Auction in San Angelo, which he, his father, and his brother started. He spent many years dealing in livestock and real estate in Texas, New Mexico, Arizona, and California. Sam died in 2007. Sam Ault was a good man, and all man.

Bruce Edwards, a school friend, would often visit. His father, Morris Edwards, owned the only grocery store in Barnhart. I had told him about riding calves, so he decided that was what he wanted to do.

We were probably eleven or twelve. Daddy and I caught the milk pen calf, but Bruce thought he should ride the calf with a saddle, so we put a saddle on the calf.

Bruce turned to Daddy and quite seriously said, "Mr. Taylor, how should I get off him?"

Daddy equally serious replied, "Don't worry about it, Bruce."

The calf took two jumps and bucked under an elevated horse trough catching Bruce about chest high. Bruce hung up in the stirrups, and the calf dragged him off, skinning Bruce from head to toe. The calf continued to try to throw the saddle and bucked into a water faucet, which he broke and sent water skyward some twenty feet. What a mess. Bruce never asked to ride a calf again, and I am sure if he had, Daddy would have told him no.

One Sunday, Bruce and I decided to go swimming at the big tank on the hill. Mother and Daddy took a nap Sunday afternoon and did not want to be disturbed. Daddy told us not to holler for help unless we truly needed it and asked if we understood. He probably did this knowing that hollering for help when not needed was right up Bruce's alley. Bruce and I were having a good time swimming and decided that I would hold my breath, duck under the water, and try to hear Bruce call my name. I should have known better. I held my breath as long as I could, came up for air, and told Bruce that I could not hear a thing and suggested Bruce try to hear me.

The next thing I knew, Daddy was at the side of the tank, out of breath, hollering, "Where is Bruce? Where is Bruce?"

Bruce had been shouting, "Help, Herbie. Help, Herbie!"

There were three five-foot wire fences between the house and the tank, and Daddy had jumped all three. He was too tired and scared to be mad.

Later, after he had rested, he loaded Bruce up and drove him to Barnhart.

I learned a life lesson from Daddy and Mr. Edwards that has stuck with me all these years. Perhaps it was the most important lesson of all. The family was buying a few staples in Mr. Edwards's grocery. Mr. Edwards's accounting system was to write each purchase on an invoice and file the charge in a box for each family. At the end of the month, he would send an itemized bill for payment. Daddy gave me a $1.25 a month credit at Mr. Edwards's store, which would buy a lot of Cokes, chewing gum, and popsicles, but it was my responsibility to show Mr. Edwards what I was taking from his store. This day, I had taken a pack of gum, put it in my pocket, and did not show the gum to Mr. Edwards. On the way home to Suggs Switch, I was stuffing the gum in my mouth, and Daddy asked, "Did you pay for that gum?"

"No, sir," I said.

"Did you show the gum to Mr. Edwards?"

"No, sir."

"Then you stole it."

"No, sir, I don't steal."

"Son, if you took it and did not pay for it, then you stole it. Is that right?" he asked.

"Yes, sir."

"Then you are a thief." He stopped the car and began to turn around and said, "Thieves must be punished. We are going back to Mr. Edwards's, and you are going to tell him you stole from him and ask what you can do to make it right." Daddy went on to say that it did not matter if it was a five-cent pack of gum or fifty thousand dollars in a robbery, stealing was stealing.

I reluctantly told Mr. Edwards what I had done and asked what I could do to make it right. He told me he saw me put the gum in my pocket and now knew I could not be trusted. This both hurt and embarrassed me. He then told me to be at the store at 0630 for a week, and he would have a job for me to pay off my debt.

Mr. Edwards bought fresh eggs from a local woman who had a few chickens, cleaned them up, jacked up the price, and sold them to his customers. My penance was to clean them up. *I vowed then to never again get myself in a position where I had to clean up my or someone else's chicken shit.*

My cousin, Travis, would come to visit each summer, and we would get into more trouble than I have words to relate. Once, Daddy had worked all day building a wire fence. He had just finished stretching the wire, and he was getting ready to nail the wire to the fence posts. I talked Travis into taking wire cutters and cutting the wire. The wire went limp, and Daddy's work was all for naught. Fortunately, he was too tired to whip us.

Daddy chained a truck tire to the back of the pickup, and we rode the tire. We would swing across the road from bar-ditch to bar-ditch, kicking up dirt, weeds, and rocks. We were filthy and headed for the tank when we got home. Mother was furious that Daddy had let us ride the tire, knowing we could have been hurt. We could have, but instead, we had some great fun.

> *It takes a mighty tough hombre to ranch in West Texas.*
> —Shorty Taylor

The 1950s were a terrible time for West Texas and particularly West Texas ranchers. This was the time it never rained. The land west of the ninety-eighth meridian has always been plagued by sparse rainfall, generally less than twenty inches a year. When it does rain, it often comes all at once, resulting in flash floods.

Daddy often remarked, "This land will promise less and give more than any land I know if it only gets a little rain."

He also believed that if you took care of the land, the land would take care of you. However, to do so, it had to rain at least a little.

From 1950 until 1957, it simply did not rain.

West Texas ranchers are a hardy bunch, but they have short memories. Drought has always been a given, but normally, it did not last for six years. I visited Suggs Switch and the surrounding environs in 2001 and again in 2004. Mesquite trees and prickly pears had taken over, and they both sucked out what little moisture there was in the soil. Mesquite is a particularly insidious intruder. Slowly, over many decades, this tough, resilient plant with its thin, lime-green leaves and large seedpods has been making its way northward out of Mexico and South Texas. Cattle, which ate and then disgorged the undigested seeds, aided its migration. For centuries, Indians had been moving cattle from Mexico to camps along the base of the Llano Estacada and the Texas Caprock.

In 2001, desolate, dry, dusty, and depressing was the only way I can describe the whole area. It made me glad to live in Central Texas, where we had creeks, trees, and grass. However, that old country does get into your blood. It must for anyone to continue to live there. It was a wonderful place to grow up, but I left as soon as I could. Nevertheless, I would not have traded my childhood with anyone.

The day after a rain is the first day of the next drought.
—West Texas adage

When I visited in 2004, it had rained more than normal, and the land looked as good as I had ever seen. The mesquite and prickly pear were still there, and drought always will be. I suspect that the only way a rancher can make it today is if he owns his own land or has a cheap university lease, his momma and daddy left him some money in the bank when they passed, and he has some nice Dallas or Houston lawyers to lease his land for hunting. An oil well or three is also helpful. Cattle prices have been good for several years, but ranching in West Texas is a crapshoot at best.

View of corrals and railroad tracks at Suggs Switch
(2004)

I was only vaguely aware of the fear and desperation my parents felt during those years. Outwardly, there was no change, but inwardly, their lives were in turmoil. Their small investment in sheep and cattle had a real chance of drying up and blowing away on the wind of high feed bills and an unbelievably low livestock market. Further complicating the situation, the possibility existed that Cotton Brooks would be unable to continue his lease, which would leave Daddy without a job. Daddy was in his forties; therefore, starting over would forever force him to be a ranch hand.

Daddy began burning cactus (prickly pear) for his cattle early on, as they were eating it anyway. Cotton initially would not let him burn pear for his cattle, believing it was no way to ranch, but relented as the drought wore on. Pear burning was a seven-day-a-week job, which displeased Mother, because Daddy could not attend church. It was hot, dirty, and bone-tiring. Daddy kept on whistling though.

Daddy decided to sell his livestock while he could get something for them.

This upset Cotton.

"I thought you wanted to be a rancher!"

"I do, but I don't want to go broke doing it."

Cotton later told Daddy, "You were the only rancher in West Texas who had any sense."

I remember most the dust storms. You could see them coming miles away—a deep, dark brown, almost-black, billowing, frightening cloud of dirt rising thousands of feet in the air. A fine, silky dust would cover everything—floors, tables, and cabinets in the house—once it had blown over. People driving would often have to stop, as headlights would not pierce the darkness. It would appear most of New Mexico and the Texas panhandle had blown across Suggs Switch.

Late one afternoon in the summer of '55, Daddy and I were working near the middle of the ranch and saw a dust storm on the horizon. The storm was a bad one. We immediately started at a lope for home, but the storm caught us. We unsaddled, took the bridles off the horses, and let them go, placing our heads under the saddles to wait out the storm. The huge, boiling cloud of dirt quickly obliterated the sun, plunging us into darkness. It was suffocating hot, difficult to breathe, and the dirt and fine sand stung as it hit exposed extremities. It was scary. I thought I would choke on New Mexico dirt. It was the worst storm I remember experiencing, and there were several.

Adding to the misery of the drought were bitterweed and the screwworm fly. The screwworm fly caused untold loss to Texas ranchers, particularly in West and South Texas. Wounding was a prerequisite for a screwworm fly's strike. Accordingly, the navel of a newborn calf or fawn, castration wounds, or even brands provided an ideal location for the flies to deposit their larvae. Sheep could be struck in the absence of a wound. The corner of a sheep's eye was a common site for a screwworm strike. A screwworm strike has a very unpleasant smell, especially when the weather is hot. Additionally, the larvae feeding deep inside a wound is not a pleasant sight.

Daddy would spend many an hour roping sheep with screwworms, then tie them to a mesquite tree, go back that night to load them in the pickup, and take them home for doctoring. Sometimes he could not find one or two in the dark, and he would have to go look for them the next morning.

As he rode near the county road that divided Suggs Switch and the Fry Place and looked for "wormies," Aubrey DeLong, a neighboring rancher, drove up.

Aubrey, who noticed all the "pigging strings" on Daddy's saddle, asked, "Shorty, why do you need all those 'pigging strings?'"

Daddy told him, "I'm roping and tying 'wormy' ewes to take in to doctor."

Aubrey pointed to a rifle he had in a gun mount in his pickup and said, "This is what I use!"

I am not sure how many sheep Daddy saved, if any, but he kept bringing them in.

Some fifty years ago, the folks at the USDA came up with a program to release sterile male screwworm flies to break the life cycle and eventually eliminate the population. Texas ranchers considered this on the magnitude of Jonas Salk developing the polio vaccine. This scientific breakthrough also allowed a decimated deer population to flourish. Now liberal lawyers and egocentric doctors, graduates of the University of Texas, can lease and hunt deer on Suggs Switch, thanks to the brilliance of government scientists. Talk about irony, not to mention a windfall for the rancher.

The early '50s were also the time of the polio epidemic. This terrible disease could strike anyone, but it seemed to favor the young, often ending in paralysis or death. The virus hit West Texas particularly hard. There were several deaths from polio in and around San Angelo, and many were paralyzed. Any time Daddy, Tippe, or I felt puny, Mother was sure we had the malady. I do not remember anyone in the Barnhart area suffering from the virus, but perhaps my memory fails me. Thankfully, the previously mentioned Jonas Salk developed his vaccine, and later, an oral vaccine was developed by Albert Sabin, and the disease was defeated.

Mother Nature brought much misery to West Texas during the 1950s.

Bitterweed covered the Suggs Switch country. Cows would not eat it; however, sheep would, and if they ate enough, it would kill them. Daddy's solution was to fence an area with minimal bitterweed, pen the sheep, and feed them hay, which was not cheap. That, in addition to cow cake for the cattle, butane for the pear burner, as well as normal ranch expenses, caused a problem with cash flow and a bottom line that rapidly drifted into the red.

Another problem was the cocklebur. These plants were all over the sides and bottoms of the draws that ran through the ranch. They attached themselves to the sheep's wool and became a sheepshearer's nightmare, reducing the value of the wool. Needle grass was also a problem.

Daddy let me have the wool of any sheep that died to sell for spending money. I would shear them by hand, which was not fun if the sheep had begun to decompose. I would bag the wool separately from Daddy's at shearing time and send it with his to the wool and mohair warehouse in Mertzon to sell. Daddy always told the wool buyers which bag was mine and where the wool had come from, because it was of a lesser quality. The buyers would usually give me the same price they gave Daddy for his wool.

> *Be thankful we are not getting all the government we are paying for.*
> —Will Rogers

Eventually, the federal government came to the aid of the rancher in the form of federal drought relief, and invariably, some of the recipients of the federal largesse abused the program.

My father was one of them.

Some feed store owners and dealers allowed ranchers to use the feed vouchers for equipment and operating supplies rather than livestock feed. Some big ranchers abused the program in a big way, and some small ranchers like my father abused the program in small ways. Some ranchers did not abuse the program at all. They simply refused to acccept a government handout.

The bureaucrats in Austin and Washington caught on to the scheme being perpetrated against the American taxpayer and said it was time to render unto Caesar what was due Caesar. My father knew what he was doing was wrong and reimbursed Uncle Sam. Others did not. Some had political connections and got their elected officials involved, resulting in the scandal "going away."

Do we not ever learn?

In 1957, it finally rained, and near normalcy returned to the arid land of West Texas and Suggs Switch.

4

Learning and Other Things

A one-room building that was erected in the fall of 1912 enabled school to begin for the first time in Barnhart. Mrs. Maude Wood (Granny) Branch, a relative, was the only teacher instructing all grades. The building also served as a church for service, community dances, and other groups that needed a place to meet.

The construction of a two-story rock and stucco school building authorized in 1917 was started at a cost of fifteen thousand dollars, which was borrowed from the First State Bank of Barnhart. The building, which was completed in 1918, consisted of six classrooms, a superintendent's office, and an auditorium and stage.

Construction of a new high school and gymnasium began in 1935 at a cost of forty-seven thousand dollars. The staff totaled eight teachers for the entire school system. The old building became the elementary school, and people continued to use it until 1959 when it was destroyed by fire caused by faulty wiring.

The Barnhart School consisted of twelve grades. Two grades were taught together in one room through the sixth grade. The grade school had two floors with two classrooms, an auditorium, stage, and restrooms on the bottom floor. There were two classrooms and a cafeteria on the second floor with an inside and outside stairwell serving the floors. The high school had a gym with girl and boy dressing rooms and restrooms, a science/biology room, four or five classrooms, a very small library, a math room, and an office for the superintendent.

Both buildings had electricity but no air-conditioning, and they were heated by coal. Rooms in the grade school had a coal stove. The high school had a central furnace. As one of my responsibilities during the first and second grade, I had to keep the stove in our classroom stoked and filled with coal. It was a nasty job. There simply was no way to keep the coal dust off my hands and clothes.

There was a playground with swings, a merry-go-round, a teeter-totter, an area for dodge ball and baseball, and a makeshift dirt track.

I started school in 1948, and I attended the first through sixth grade in the grade school building and the six through eighth grade in the high school building.

Barnhart schools.

Three buildings were moved onto the grounds in 1952 and converted into a teacherage and a home economics building. Four apartments were in one building, and an apartment and home economics room was in the others. The families that I remember living in the teacherage were

Mr. and Mrs. Ray Moore with sons Charles and Gary; Mr. and Mrs. H. B. Porter with sons Robert and Lewis and daughter Marcella; and Mr. and Mrs. Cole with son Ronnie. Mr. Moore was superintendent, and Mr. Porter was the principal. Mr. Cole was the superintendent before Mr. Moore. All three of their wives were teachers.

My classmates in the first grade were James Thomas Kessler, Charles Roe, Janet Parry, Nancy Cox, Linda Taylor (no relation), a very special, pretty, and shy little girl by the name of Penelope (Penny) Ann Farr, and several others I cannot recall. Older schoolmates and friends were Marcella Porter, Bruce Edwards, Mary Sue Griffin, Preston Porter, Carolynn Ethridge, Tommy Clint Owens, and James (Bubba) Parry. Louis L. (Bud) Farr IV, Steve Elkins, Mike Elkins, and Bill Farr had not started to school, but they were playmates.

Miss Floy H. Williams was my first-grade teacher. I had Mrs. W. DeFord for second grade, Mrs. Elizabeth Cole for third and fourth grade, and Mrs. Azalee Ashcraft for fifth and sixth grade. I had several teachers in the seventh and eighth grades, including Mrs. M. M. Newman, Ken Williamson, Buck Owens, Mr. H. B. Porter, and Mr. Ray Moore. Coach Williamson and Buck Owens were outstanding basketball coaches and prepared me well for high school.

Coach Williamson became the basketball coach at Reagan County and later San Angelo Central. Buck, a rancher southwest of Barnhart, picked up a few dollars teaching during the drought. Buck could have been a success as a high school coach, but he went back to ranching full-time once the drought ended. He did keep his hand in basketball as a referee, and refereed a couple of my high school games.

I saw Buck in 2004 at the Rocker b Ranch reunion, and we had a nice visit. His youngest son, Mickey Tom, is a successful high school football coach, and his oldest son, Rusty, is ranching with his dad.

Mrs. Cole and Mrs. Ashcraft were excellent teachers, especially Mrs. Ashcraft. They taught me my three R's—reading, writing, arithmetic—and they were certainly challenged. It cannot be said I was a good student. Learning was difficult at best. Nevertheless, I can read and write, although after you read this book, that may be questionable, and I can also do basic math but not algebra or geometry. I am truly grateful for their patience, understanding, friendship, and professionalism.

Mrs. Ashcraft sent the following note on June 6, 1954, from Big Lake:

Dearest Herbie,

I enjoyed having you in my classes for the last two years. Since we aren't "teacher" and "pupil," I hope we can be good friends, always. Please let me help you in any way I can.

Lovingly,
Azalee Ashcraft

After I transferred to high school in Big Lake, I attended school with both her eldest son, Bruce, and youngest, Bill. Bruce was a year ahead of me, and Bill was a freshman when I was a senior. Consequently, I continued to see Mrs. Ashcraft throughout my high school years. Several years ago, I saw Bill at an informal reunion of Reagan County High School graduates in Salado. Bill told me his mother asked about me and wondered if I was "still having trouble diagramming sentences."

She lived with Bill at the time in Gatesville only fifty miles from Salado. I regret I did not make the effort to go see her. It was the least I could have done for all she had done for me. Mrs. Ashcraft died in 2005.

A thank you is always appropriate and never too late.
"Thank you, Mrs. Ashcraft."

The following words, which were written by my mother, were pasted in a scrapbook she made documenting my school years from first grade through college. She had written them on a loose-leaf sheet of paper, and they apparently represented a synopsis of my life from fifth through the eighth grade. The sentences are exactly as she wrote them:

Nothing has been the same since his 5 year. He started playing basketball went to all the games as a sub. Finally got to play in a game shot at the wrong goal.
6 year first parties official calf untier for roping club-Teeth kicked out. Didn't loose his baby teeth when other kids did started the 7

year 8 teeth missing Certainly wouldn't have been voted the most handsome boy.
8 year-Captain of basketball team
Nothing outstanding
Very average in grades
Meaner more stubborn than most
Janet and Linda gave him a dancing lesson the other night. That might lead to something someday

It is hard to fool your mother!

Almost everything revolved around the school. The school served as a community center and YMCA all rolled into one. The entire town as well as ranch families living near Barnhart would come to whatever social activity happened to take place at the school. Dances, plays, cakewalks, declamation contests, recitals, reunions, sports banquets, king and queen contests, elections, basketball, and volleyball were some of the activities held at the school.

The largest event held annually was the Barnhart Christmas Dance. People from all over West Texas would come to the dance held in the school gym. It was widely known and a highlight of the Christmas season. The Christmas spirit and spirits of another kind would be in abundance. Even so, it was a family affair, and children of all ages and their parents would come to dance the cotton-eyed Joe, two-step, waltzes, jitterbug, foxtrot, and sometimes even the Charleston to a live band.

The dancing was nonstop, but many took the opportunity to go to their cars to take a break, imbibe, and sometimes do a little courting. A couple of times, there was a fight in the parking lot but never on the dance floor.

The Owens family would always perform during intermission. June Owens Scott would sing "White Christmas" with Mother Edith on piano and Brother Tommy Clint on guitar. I attended my first dance when I was in grade school and my last as a senior in high school.

Another good memory is the annual Christmas Eve kids' party held in the auditorium of the grade-school building. There would be a tree. Parents would bring gifts. There would be stockings filled with apples, oranges, and nuts for everyone, and Dutch Ethridge would dress up and play Santa Claus. Some parents did not have the money to buy a gift, but Bode and Edith Owens would bring extra gifts so that no child went home without one.

Santa Claus was still very real to me, and on the way back to Suggs Switch from the Christmas party, Daddy would shout, "Look, there goes Santa Claus and his reindeer."

I would look out the car window and see them floating across the moonlit sky, and I still can. Santa Claus would come to Suggs Switch that night after we went to sleep.

Basketball became my passion when I was in the sixth grade, probably because it was the only sport for boys that the school sponsored other than track. Daddy built me a wooden basketball backboard with a metal goal and attached it to our barn at Suggs Switch. It was hung eleven feet high even though a regulation goal was ten feet. I suspect Daddy thought the higher the goal, the more energy I would expend, thus training me to shoot from longer range more accurately. I do not think his idea improved my shooting, but I did spend many hours practicing and dreaming of making the winning shot in an important game.

My first coach, Ken Williamson, had an old green Nash that he would load with players and take to such exotic places as Water Valley, Christoval, Grandfalls, Imperial, Mertzon, and Rankin to play games. I was not very good, primarily because I had to play with and against older players; however, I kept trying, and by the eighth grade, I was good, and so were some of my teammates.

Our eighth-grade team did very well, and an end-of-season tournament for both boys and girls was held at Barnhart. There were eight or nine teams entered, with Wall and Mertzon being two of the best. The starting five for Barnhart were Milton Tomlinson, James Thomas Kessler, Gary Moore, J. R. Sparks, and me. Buck Owens was our coach. The team follows in the picture:

Left to right: Herbie, Gary Moore, Milton Tomlinson, Coach Buck Owens, James Thomas Kessler, Jesse Carney, J. R. Sparks, unknown.

We whipped Mertzon and played Wall in the championship game.

Wall had several excellent players that were later good in high school and college. James Glass, Ken Dierschke, and Frankie Kuapil are ones I recall. We beat them, a feat I was only able to do once at Reagan County, and won the championship. It was a big thrill for this boy from Barnhart.

> *Disappointment is often the salt of life.*
> —Theodore Parker

There was a large crowd at the game, including Penny Farr, and I was sure that I would receive the MVP award, as did Daddy. When the awards were announced, I was selected for the all-tournament team, but Milton Tomlinson was chosen as MVP. I was crushed. I received a small gold basketball for my efforts, and Milton received a trophy. Daddy and Buck, according to Daddy, had words after the award ceremony, and Buck told Daddy that I barely made the all-tournament team and that not only did Milton play better than me, but James Thomas did also.

In the cold light of day, the incident is meaningless, but at the time, it was devastating. I went home and threw the gold basketball in the tank at Suggs Switch. I regret that now and wish I had it back. Interestingly, Buck refereed the game my senior year when Reagan County upset Wall at the Ozona tournament.

I correspond with Jan Owens, Buck's wife, by e-mail. Recently, I sent her an e-mail telling of the time Barnhart was playing Water Valley and during a timeout, Buck said to me, "Son, you have one thumb in your mouth and the other up your ass, and you keep switching them."

I knew exactly what Buck meant. Jan e-mailed me back and told me Buck got a good chuckle out of my remarks.

Buck and the entire Owens family are West Texas legends. You can go two hundred miles from Barnhart and mention the Owens name, and someone will know them and have a story to tell about them—some funny but all favorable. The Owens epitomize the West Texas ranching family.

An Owens tale or two told me by others include the following:

Edith would come to Morris Edwards's grocery store and announce, "If Bode does not fix the bathroom floor, he will fall through." This went on for some time. One day, Edith came in and softly, unemotionally said, "Bode fell through."

Bode was going to show a sheep buyer around, hoping to get a good price for his lambs.

Edith wanted to go.

Pregnant with Tommy Clint, Bode tried to talk her out of going. "You have to take a whiz every hour, and there is no place to do that."

Edith had a plan.

"When we come to a gate and I need to take a whiz, I will nudge you, and while the buyer is opening the gate, I will slip out and do what I need to do behind the pickup."

Bode agreed.

About the second gate, Edith slipped out.

Bode drove through the gate, and there was an exposed Edith and the sheep buyer looking at each other.

Boy Scouts was also one of my childhood interests. Clyde Parry, who owned one of two filling stations in Barnhart, was the scoutmaster.

In those days, we called them filling stations. The attendants would fill your vehicle, sweep the inside, clean your windows, and even wash your car if you had the oil changed. Today, we call them service stations; however, there are no attendants, and we fill our own vehicle.

Clyde was a good man, a Christian man, active in the community, and he enjoyed kids. He and his wife, Lorene, had three children: James Lee, Janet, and Norma. James Lee, nicknamed "Bubba," was two years older. Janet and I were the same age. Janet, James Lee, and I were good friends and remain so today. The Parrys had the first television in Barnhart and perhaps the area. I remember seeing Elvis on the *Ed Sullivan Show* at their house around 1956. The picture was snowy, blurry, and it rolled constantly; however, I was mesmerized.

Our troop took trips each year and went to the area scout encampment at Camp Louis Farr near Mertzon each summer. I especially remember two trips, one camping for several days on the Pecos River and another on the Devil's River. We caught a large turtle and cooked it for our night meal when we were on the Pecos, and we caught a sixty-five-pound catfish on a trotline during the Devil's River trip.

One of the fun activities when scouting was to play "steal the flag." Sides would be chosen, and one side would guard the troop flag while the other side tried to steal it. The flag had to be in a visible location, and there were rules to be followed, now lost to memory; however, it was great fun. We would play that game for hours. I always wanted to be the leader, but Bubba Parry and Tommy Clint Owens would invariably be chosen as team leaders, because they were the oldest and most natural leaders.

Once, while I was working on a merit badge for cooking, the troop hiked from Barnhart to Suggs Switch. Each scout was required to cook his own breakfast, lunch, and dinner over an open fire. We cooked breakfast in Barnhart, lunch at a windmill beside the road to Suggs Switch where water was available, and dinner at the windmill on the hill at my house. I was glad when that trip ended so I could get something decent to eat.

Bicycling became one of my favorite scouting activities and a primary means of transportation. We had a bicycle fair each year during which we decorated our bicycles and performed tricks. I was not the best by any means, but I could ride a long distance with no hands, do wheelies, and make jumps using a board ramp. We raised money for our scouting trips at the fair and did quite well.

One weekend, Steve Elkins, James Thomas Kessler, Bud Farr, the great-grandson of the gentleman for whom Camp Louis Farr was named, and I rode our bikes from Barnhart to the Bar S Ranch. This was before State Highway 163 was built, so we had a twenty-one-mile, hilly, dusty, and tiring dirt road to travel. We camped on Tepee Draw near the Bar S Ranch headquarters. Bud's father, Louis L. Farr III, the ranch manager, and his mother, Lou Dickey Baucus Farr, came to check on us. They brought with them Bill and Phil Farr, Bud's brothers, and his sister, Penny. They sneaked up on us and gave us quite a scare, but even so, I was sure pleased to see Penny.

Another bicycle incident that I will never forget took place during this time. Most of the kids had bicycles that they rode to school. We rode them during the noon hour and after school. I do not remember where I kept my bicycle, probably at James Thomas's house, but I always had it in Barnhart until I started driving. Nancy Cox, who was my age, walked home for lunch and was halfway down the hill from the school. James Thomas had a big, heavy bicycle that was larger than he was, and he was barreling down the hill, out of control, rocks flying, heading straight for Nancy. Nancy heard him coming and turned to meet him, standing with her legs spread and hollering, "James Thomas, don't you run over me!" His front tire hit Nancy directly in the crotch. She went one way, James Thomas another, and the bicycle still another. Thankfully, only Nancy's feelings were hurt. James Thomas was too tough to hurt, but the bicycle was not in very good shape. I realize this was not funny to Nancy, but it was a sight one twelve-year-old still laughs about fifty-seven years later.

James Thomas Kessler was ornery, mean as a one-eyed snake, and my best friend. We learned to smoke together, snitching Chesterfields, Lucky Strikes, and Pall Malls from his uncle Cato's café and smoking them in the abandoned lumberyard. We would swipe his granddad's wooden leg while he was taking his afternoon nap and hide it. We would put our hands in an ant bed and watch the red ants sting until one of us could no longer stand the pain. We would lie on the railroad track with a train coming and its whistle shrilling and wait until the last second to jump away.

The first day of the first grade, Miss Williams asked each of us to introduce ourselves.

Each child had their head down, embarrassingly mumbling their name until she came to James Thomas. In a very loud voice, he announced, "My name is James Thomas Quit That!"

I suppose he really thought that was his name, because his mother, Billie, addressed him that way most of the time.

Scouting at Camp Louis Farr was a lot of fun. We were able to interact with kids from other towns and troops and work on merit badges, such as knot-tying, first aid, plant identification, and other useful activities. The camp was located on Spring Creek, so we got to swim, fish, and canoe. One of the largest oak trees in Texas was on the Tankersely Ranch near the camp, as was the main spring for Spring Creek, which we would hike to see. The last time I went to camp was the summer before the seventh grade. By then, I had reached the rank of first-class scout. When I realized girls were more than soft boys, my priorities changed.

My first girlfriend was the little girl previously mentioned—Penelope Ann Farr. I first knew her as Penny, and later, I lovingly referring to her as Pen. Her daddy called her "Cutch" for some unknown reason, and Alma and Theodore Washington, the black couple who cooked and cleaned for her parents, referred to her as "Sistah." We met in the first grade and gravitated toward each other immediately. She was extremely shy and cried every morning, begging her mother not to make her go to school. She told her mother that the other kids were mean to her. I do remember her slipping off the merry-go-round and holding on for dear life and begging James Thomas Kessler to stop pushing her around and around. This skinned her knees, but I do not remember her being mistreated by the other kids.

One year, the school had a contest to choose a king and queen. They were chosen with a penny per vote, the money going to the senior class for their annual senior trip. Penny and I represented the third grade. We won because her dad and Fred Elkins waited until the last minute before the voting ended to put a significant amount of money in the ballot box in our names. A photo of that event follows. Penny is holding on to my sleeve, and her dad told me more than once, "Even then, she did not want you to get away."

Penny and Herbie, third grade, Barnhart, 1951.

Penny and I continued to be friends through the sixth grade, at which time her mother and father decided to send her to school in Big Lake. I saw very little of her the next two years but thought about her often.

My first real date was in the seventh grade with Mary Sue Trotter, and so was my first kiss. We had several dates. I also remember an informal date or two with Mary Sue Griffin. I also took Marcella Porter to a sports banquet in the seventh grade.

Peggy Trotter was my date at the sports banquet in the eighth grade. Peggy was a junior in high school and Mary Sue's older sister. Peggy and I double-dated with James Parry and Lucrecia Porter, and we went "parking" after the banquet. Peggy was a gorgeous girl, and she was "fully growed," as we say in West Texas. In addition, boy could she kiss! That was a memorable night indeed.

That night was also the time that Penny had to eat in the school kitchen during the banquet. Pat Muir had asked Penny for a date to the banquet. She did not want to go, but her parents believed it would be impolite for her not to go. Mrs. Muir drove them to the banquet, but when they got there, Penny was told that she could not eat with the rest of the children because she did not go to school at Barnhart. That was a terrible way to treat a child. It was, however, payback for her parents sending her to school in Big Lake. The school population at Barnhart was dwindling, and even then, we should have known that the school would eventually have to close.

I would rather believe there is a God and find out there is not one than believe there is no God and find out there is one.
—Unknown

Religion played a large role in my childhood and early adolescence. One of my earliest memories is assisting my mother dusting and polishing the pews and altar in the small, wood-framed Baptist church in Barnhart on Saturday afternoons. It seemed like she, Tippe, Daddy and I were in church every time the doors opened. Sunday school, church, and Sunday evening services along with Wednesday night services we attended weekly. Vacation Bible school was a joint effort between the Methodists and Baptists, and was conducted during the summer at the Methodist church, better known as the Cowboy Church, because the church was larger. Today, the Baptist church no longer exists, but the Cowboy Church still serves the religious needs of the area.

I memorized all the books of the Bible, both New and Old Testament, and could recite from memory many of the scriptures.

Around the second grade, I signed a total abstinence pledge in which I pledged to God and myself that I would never use beverage alcohol and that I wouldn't give, sell, or serve it to others.

There were several spiritual advisors during this time who worked diligently to bring me to the Lord and save my soul. Teddy Russell, Mrs. Jim Shaw, Neville Davis, Faye Southerland, Pastor Marshall Southerland, and of course, my parents were prominent in this undertaking. They prayed for me and with me, and I had many long talks with them as they sincerely strived to point me in the way of the Lord.

All were fundamentalists who interpreted the Bible literally. They believed that a person reached the age of accountability around twelve and that if they had not accepted Jesus as their Lord and Savior, they were doomed to burn in hell for eternity. Sermons were about the devil, hellfire, and brimstone, and invitation hymns would extend for several verses as the preacher exhorted the unsaved to come forward to the altar and accept Christ as their Lord and Savior. I felt that every eye, every verse sung, and every word the preacher spoke was directed toward me.

Those old invitational hymns—"Just as I Am," "Just a Closer Walk with Thee," "O Why Not Tonight?" and "The Old Rugged Cross"—echo through my mind and remain a part of my Christian heritage. However, it was "Softly and Tenderly Jesus Is Calling" that always tugged at my heart and often had me tightly gripping the back of the pew in front of me: *Softly and tenderly, Jesus is calling, calling for you and for me. Come home, come home, you who are weary come home: Earnestly and tenderly, Jesus is calling. Calling, O sinner, come home!*

Eventually, I did have a spiritual awakening, a "God consciousness." It was vivid, and it was real. I saw Jesus or God with his beard and long, flowing white robe beckoning me to the altar. I was baptized shortly thereafter at the First Baptist Church in Mertzon. I was twelve, and I was clean, pure, and not soiled by the vicissitudes of life.

Puberty was on the way, and soon, heaven was not of God but getting in some girl's pants. My first drink of alcohol and first drunk soon followed. Slowly but surely, I became a "backsliding Baptist," losing my way and taking the wrong path, breaking most of the Ten Commandments not once but many times until years later I woke up and realized I was spiritually bankrupt.

In retrospect, the religion of my parents was one of a fearful and intimidating God, but I do not doubt the sincerity of their beliefs. Today, I am a member of the First Methodist Church of Salado. I find the theology of the Methodist branch of Protestantism to be kinder, gentler, and more loving than the Baptist or Old Testament brand of religion.

I started driving on the ranch as soon as my feet could touch the foot-feed. When I was eleven or twelve, Daddy decided I could drive to school. The roads were all dirt, even those in Barnhart, except where I had to cross Highway 67. Daddy checked with Vic Atwood, the local state trooper, to make sure it would be all right. Mr. Atwood said if he caught me crossing the highway, he would give me a ticket. However, he would not make a special effort to catch me. He did not, and I continued to drive Tippe and myself to school.

5

Make 'Em a Hand

The summer of 1956 found us moving to the Wood place. The drought had finally convinced Cotton that he needed to give up his lease at Suggs Switch, but divine providence in the form of Teddy Russell intervened for the Taylor family.

Teddy Russell is one of the finest men I have known. He had been a pilot during WWII, flying the Burma Hump. He had tried his hand in the restaurant business then as a banker with his father's bank in Hamlin, Texas, and he was now running the Murphey Estate Ranch located between Highway 67 and Highway 163.

The Wood place was part of the Murphey Estate, and was located two miles off Highway 67, with the Reagan and Irion County line running through the center of the ranch house. It was fifteen miles from Big Lake and six miles from Barnhart. Mrs. Tom Murphey owned the Murphey Ranch. She had two daughters and a stepdaughter, each of whom had inherited one third of the ranch from their father.

Teddy had married the oldest of Mrs. Murphey's daughters. Teddy was no rancher; however, he was a dreamer, and his faith was strong. Teddy had leukemia and needed the help of an experienced hand. Teddy offered Daddy the lease of the Wood place, some seven sections, if he would come to work for him. Daddy continued to lease the Fry place, so he now had more land to run sheep and cattle than he had had before, and he also had a paying job.

Teddy (on the left) and Daddy (on the right) are having a serious discussion apparently about barbed wire.
Murphey Estate Ranch around 1959.

    The Fry place consisted of four sections of good ranch country located between Suggs Switch and the Noelke Ranch. Barnhart Draw traversed the entire length, and it was intersected by two other draws. It had an unpainted, wood-frame house where we camped one summer and a wonderful, tree-lined, dirt stock tank with the largest frogs I have ever seen. The land had not been overgrazed, so with the seven sections at the Wood place, Daddy now had around seven thousand acres to run cattle and sheep—enough land to make a living as a rancher in West Texas but barely. The movie star Matthew McConaughey now owns the ranch, and he and Sandra Bullock, the actress, have been seen in Barnhart.

    The move pleased me, because with part of the home in Reagan County, it meant that I could go to school in Big Lake, play football, and see Penny Farr every day. In addition, we had electricity, television, a dial phone, and all the comforts that city folks were accustomed to enjoying. Moreover, I had my own house. The ranch house had only two bedrooms and one bathroom, so Daddy had a small building built beside the main house for me. It was a bedroom with space for a couple of chairs and desk, a bathroom, and a closet. It was private, and it was mine. And Tippe now had her own bedroom.

By this time, I had a driver's license and needed a car to drive back and forth to school. Reagan County Independent School District would send a bus to the county line to pick up and take kids to and from school, but because I would be playing sports and finishing after the bus run, that would not work for me.

The Big Lake booster club wanted me to play sports, so they agreed to pay for my gasoline if I drove myself to school. A Big Lake gas station delivered a fifty-five-gallon drum of gas anytime I said I needed it. I had to pump the gas by hand and did not like that, so I would fill up at the station in Big Lake. My friends from town often used the gas out of the drum. Gas was cheap at twenty-seven cents a gallon, and for four years, the booster club kept my friends and me in gas.

I bought my first car from Ray Boothe, who owned a ranch outside Sweetwater. Ray had married Tommie Murphey, Teddy's sister-in-law, who had inherited the Wood place. Ray had been an instructor training Women Air Force Service Pilots (WASP) during World War II at Avenger Field near Sweetwater. The car, a 1951 two-door black Chevrolet with a manual transmission, was the first and last General Motors vehicle I owned. I paid $250.00 for the car. It had a hundred miles per hour on the speedometer; however, eighty was the top speed, and the radio did not work most of the time. It's rounded shape made it look like a humpbacked turtle going down the road. It did last me through my first year of college until wrecked.

More and more, I liked ranch work less and less.

Daddy gave me an allowance for chores that I did around the house, and I worked for him on the weekends.

Dignify and glorify common labor. It is at the bottom of life that we must begin, not at the top.
—Booker T. Washington

I decided I would find a summer job at the end of my freshman year rather than work full-time on the ranch, so I went to work digging post holes. Highway 67 had been widened, which resulted in the right-of-way fence having to be replaced. If I remember correctly, I made ten cents a hole. It was me, a boss Mexican, and nine or ten "wetbacks," so named because they had illegally crossed the Rio Grande from Mexico into Texas. I could dig five holes with my high-tech equipment while the Mexicans were digging one.

A San Angelo bar, a seventeen-pound, steel-forged, six-foot pole with a tapered end, and a two-pound coffee can were my tools. Obviously, I made no money, and I sure as hell realized I did not want to dig any more postholes.

I still have the San Angelo bar, a visual reminder of my youth, hard work, and little pay.

It was during this time that Daddy told me, "Son, if you take another man's pay, you have to make 'em a hand."

It was advice I took to heart and never forgot. It served me well then and later. I can honestly say I earned every paycheck and then some over the years. Later in the army when I had men and some women working for me, I expected the same from them. I never asked them to do what I would not do. Most gave me more than I asked, and outstanding evaluation reports, promotions, and awards rewarded their efforts. Some did not, and I gave them an early career start in civilian life.

During the summer of my sophomore year, I got a job with a construction company, building a wing on the Reagan County Memorial Hospital and roofing the Reagan County Library at less than minimum wage. Perhaps it was the other way around—I am not sure—but I do know I worked on the two buildings, and that I was paid less than legally required. Even so, I was glad to have the job.

One of my fellow workers was a black man, and he kept pestering me to go out on the town with him. He told me, "You be a black boy just one Saturday night, and you never want to be a white boy again." I was tempted, but I decided against it. Big Lake and the schools were segregated in 1958, and I was afraid of pushing my luck.

Shortly before two-a-day football practice began, I helped level cement on the roof of the library. My knees were in the cement, and none of us had protective gear. That night, my knees began to burn, and by morning, I was in real pain. I had burn holes in my knees that left scars still visible today. A doctor was able to stop the burning, but the damage had been done. I was unable to practice football for three weeks. It was disappointing not to be able to practice twice a day during August when the temperature averaged 105 degrees in the shade.

Finally, I got a job with the Texas Highway Department located in Barnhart during the summer prior to my senior year. Pay was $1.05 an hour. I had been trying to get the job for two years, and Everett Roe, who was the area supervisor, hired me. James Parry and I were the only high school kids. The summer before college, Everett raised my pay to $1.15 an hour, and that particular summer, I got time and a half for overtime and got plenty of overtime. We resurfaced a portion of Highway 137 between Big Lake and Stiles to Stanton. To get in a full day's work, we left Barnhart at 0630, stopped in Big Lake to get ice for our water cans, and arrived at the job site around 0800. We worked until 1700 and then headed home, arriving around 1800. The whole time I was on the clock, even when I was riding in the truck.

One afternoon, I was flagging and stopping traffic and telling people to drive slowly to get around our work crew. It was hot. I was sleepy, and I looked up and saw a car coming in the distance at a high rate of speed. I waved my flag wildly to get the driver's attention but to no avail. He ran me off the road, hit the hot asphalt we were laying, throwing it thirty feet in the air, and continued speeding through the asphalt until he saw the work crew. He veered into the bar ditch, almost turning over in the process, and continued on his way.

Here came Everett in his yellow state car, hollering, "Why didn't you stop him?"

"I tried, but he wouldn't stop," I shouted.

Everett hollered, "Get in."

Away we went in chase, which seemed to last forever. Eventually, we saw their car at a store, which I remember as either a bar or café. It was easy to spot because it was covered in asphalt. Everett told me to stay in the car and went inside.

He came out after a while and told me, "The sheriff is coming to get them, and you will have to make a statement." I knew who those two old boys were at the time, but their names have been lost to memory.

Another time, I was flagging cars between Mertzon and Barnhart, and I had to stop cars for a few minutes. Traffic was again light when a Cadillac pulled up, and I went to the car to let the driver know it would only be a few minutes. It was a woman. She was naked from the waist up. It was hot, and I could feel the cold from her air-conditioning and the heat from my loins as she rolled the window down and asked how long it would be. I suppose I stared, but it did not seem to bother her. I stammered, "Only a few minutes," and went back to standing in the middle of the road. That was a very unpleasant few minutes. I was embarrassed; however, she was an attractive thirty-something, and I had a real desire to stare. I know who she was, but I am not telling.

When he was working livestock, Daddy would often hire kids of local ranchers to help. This particular weekend, we were rounding up a pasture of sheep, and he hired Steve Elkins, Mike Elkins, Bill Farr, and another cowboy. He told me that he had to go to San Angelo, that I was in charge, and that he would be back by the time we got the sheep penned. I decided that because I was the boss, I would ride Daddy's favorite horse, Old Rex. No one was allowed to ride Old Rex except Daddy. He was the best horse I have known. He was small but strong, could turn on a dime, and knew what an animal was going to do before the rider and perhaps the animal did. If you were riding Old Rex, you had damn well better be alert.

We had gathered the sheep and were moving them into a trap when one ewe drifted off. I decide I would go back and rope her later.

It was then that Daddy drove up. He saw the ewe and me on his horse and said somewhat unpleasantly, "Get off that horse. I'm gonna catch that ewe."

He mounted Old Rex and loped off to rope the ewe. He was standing up in the saddle, had a loop built, and was poised to rope her when the ewe ducked back. Old Rex cut after her, and Daddy kept on going. He landed belly-first in the dirt, kicking up so much dust you could barely see him.

I knew he was hurt, but after the dust cleared, he looked over his shoulder to see if anyone had seen what had transpired. We all had and were doing our best not to laugh. He got up, brushed himself off, caught Old Rex, and walked him back to where I was standing.

He handed me the reins and said, "Go catch that old ewe. I'll meet you at the pens."

He is now ninety-six, and I still kid him about that incident.

Our horses were kept in traps at the Wood place and the Murphey Ranch headquarters. We would pen the horses with the pickup when we needed to work that part of the ranch. One morning, the horses would not pen at headquarters, and Daddy had his dander up. He was right on their tails. Dirt was flying from the horses hooves, so we could not see, and we were running over mesquite trees. All of a sudden, I saw the horses break off hard to the right, and then I saw the milk cow ambling along and chewing her cud. Daddy slammed on the brakes. The pickup bounced and slid sideways, and we rolled up the poor old cow. Daddy said, "Damn, Herb! I think I killed the milk cow."

Me astride Old Rex at the Wood Place.

The Wood place also had rattlesnakes.

We were on our way to Barnhart when we saw a huge rattler and killed him. Daddy decided he would have some fun with a fellow by the name of Red. Red worked for the Texas Highway Department during the week and for Clyde Parry at the Texaco filling station on the weekend. Red was the nervous type and often the butt of a joke.

We wrapped the snake around the spare tire in the trunk of the car, and when we got to Clyde's, Daddy told Red, "Herbie and I had a flat on the way in this morning that needs fixing. How about fixing it while we are at the café drinking coffee?"

Red said he would, and Daddy gave him the keys to the car.

Red opened the trunk, reached down to get the tire, saw the snake, hollered, "Oh, my God. Oh, my God." He raised up, hit his head on the trunk lid, cursed, went down again, hollered, "Oh, my God," and again hit his head on the trunk. This went on two or three times before Red realized the joke.

He walked over and very shakily said, "Mr. Taylor, if you ever do that again, I'll kill you." Seems my father had several people tell him that.

One cold morning, we stopped by headquarters to talk with Teddy. When we got in and started the pickup, it made a strange sound. Daddy thought he'd better have Griff, who owned Griffin's Garage in Barnhart, take a look. We drove to Griff's. He opened the hood, backed out, began to gag, heave, and then vomit. A cat had crawled up to warm itself on the engine block while we were visiting with Teddy, and when the engine started, it had jumped into the radiator fan. Griff was leery of working on any of Daddy's vehicles after that.

A young fellow of eighteen or nineteen named Roger Hendricks was traveling from Illinois to California on horseback. He was riding a gelding and leading a mare loaded with supplies. The mare was about to drop her foal when he saw the lights of our house. He came to the door, told his story, and asked if he could stay until the colt was old enough to travel. We could always use another hand, so we were glad to have him. The foal, "Little Devil," arrived, and Roger and his menagerie stayed with us from May 14, 1959 until June 8, 1959.

Roger had promised his mother that he would go to church every Sunday while he was on his journey. Each Sunday, he would ask the clergy to sign the church program, and he would mail it to his mom. We were members of the First Baptist Church in Big Lake, so Roger would attend Sunday service with us. One Sunday morning, I asked him if he had been to a Catholic church, and he said he had. I had never been, but I thought it would be interesting, so we decided to go. After the service, Roger presented the program to the priest and asked him to sign it. The priest thought he was a felon on probation and had to attend church as a condition of his probation. Roger explained what he was doing, and the priest asked us to eat lunch with him so he could learn more about Roger's adventure. We dined on a very simple meal of beef stew and bread in the priest's private quarters, and I found the priest to be an interesting and charming fellow.

Later when I was an Army officer and had chaplains assigned to my unit, I was impressed by Catholic chaplains and less so by Protestant chaplains. The Catholic chaplains were motivated, dedicated, and in the field with the soldiers, which was where they were needed. Protestant chaplains often tried to beg out of field duty. They had to get ready for Vacation Bible School or perform a marriage, wedding, or something.

Roger sent us a picture of him and the three horses in the surf of the Pacific Ocean along with a nice letter after he reached California. Later, he wrote a book chronicling his adventures, and the Taylor family comprised a chapter of the book.

We worked many "wetbacks" at Suggs Switch, the Murphey ranch, and Fry Place during the '50s. Those who worked these people were not breaking the law, unless they transported them on a highway, at which time interstate laws came into effect. If we had to cross a highway, we would let the Mexicans out, have them walk across the highway, and pick them up on the other side.

These unfortunate souls were poor workers at best. They had no knowledge of machinery, and they were used strictly for manual labor. Often, we would have one or two working for us from different Mexican states, and they could not understand each other because the dialects were different. They could understand our border Spanish or "Tex-Mex," and we would translate for them.

The Border Patrol knew we worked "wetbacks" and would call the house to ask if we had any. If we did, they would ask how long we needed them. Daddy would tell them on what day and where they could be picked up. Both Daddy and the Border Patrol had an itch, and both got their itch scratched. Daddy got his work done, and the Border Patrol could accomplish their mission without breaking a sweat.

Remuneration for these fellows was two dollars a day, all the food they could eat, and a roof over their heads. Most spent no money except to buy rolling paper and tobacco for cigarettes. If they wanted candy or anything special, Daddy would buy it for them. We often gave them used clothes and shoes. They were not mistreated. I do not remember one ever stealing from us.

If we had several working for us, one would be designated cook and sent in early to prepare the night meal. After a hard day's work, Daddy and I would often eat with them as we enjoyed their tortillas and the way they cooked beans and meat. We would then go to the house and find Mother cooking a large supper for which we were no longer hungry. This displeased her, but we got to eat it warmed up the next night.

A young illegal in his late teens named Pedro walked up to the house one day, wanting work. Daddy quickly realized the kid was a cut above the rest and trainable.

The government Bracero Program allowed ranchers to work these people legally with an approved application. There were certain conditions: Pay had to be $90 a month, and there had to be running water in their living area, among other conditions. Daddy applied to employ one, and he was asked to be in the bullring in Nuevo Laredo, Mexico, across from Laredo, Texas, on a certain day to select the one he wanted. That was a roll of the dice, so he had Pedro walk back (after he had driven him close to the border) to Mexico and get in the bullring on the appointed day. Pedro was there, and Daddy chose him.

Pedro stayed with us for three years, my high school years, and became a member of the family. He went to my football and basketball games and participated in most family activities.

Once a horse threw him and broke his leg, which sent him to the Reagan County hospital for several weeks. We would visit him each day, and he would cry like a baby. We cared for him, and he cared for us. He finally went back to Mexico with a large sum of money, as Daddy had saved all his wages. He and Daddy corresponded for several years, but eventually, Pedro was heard from no more.

The mindset of these folks, Pedro being no exception, borders on the thick. Pedro told Daddy he needed to return to Mexico for corn-planting season his first year with us. Daddy asked how much it would cost to hire locals in his village to plant the corn. Pedro admitted it was much less than what he was earning, but Daddy told me Pedro never grasped the concept.

Did we exploit the Mexican? The rationale for hiring them was that they and their families were starving, and it was impossible to find locals who were willing to work on a ranch for the pay being offered. The same rationale is used by corporate America today.

The pain of the mind is worse than the pain of the body.
—Publilus Syrus

I share many personality traits with my mother and only a few with my dad, while it is just the opposite with my sister. One of their traits is the ability to tolerate pain.

The family was eating breakfast one morning when Tippe left to saddle her horse. She returned shortly to inform us that she thought her horse, Bouquet, was sick. Daddy told her he would take a look at him, and the three of us headed toward the barn.

Bouquet was standing easy but had froth around his mouth. Daddy thought he had a foreign object stuck in his throat and began to examine him. This agitated the horse, and by now, Tippe was sobbing, "My poor Bouquet. My poor Bouquet."

We loaded Bouquet in a trailer and drove to a veterinarian in San Angelo. The vet took one look at the horse and told us that he was sure the horse had rabies and that he would have to euthanize him and send his head to Austin for testing. He then asked if anyone had touched the horse around his mouth. Daddy told him Tippe had been loving on the horse and holding its head and that he had stuck his hand and arm in its mouth. The vet recommended they see a doctor immediately and take rabies shots.

We drove to a doctor who told Daddy and Tippe that they needed to have the shots. Daddy asked how many, and he was told sixteen, one each day for fifteen days and the final shot a week later. The doctor explained the shots were given around the navel, were extremely painful, and became more painful after each shot. Daddy told him he had a ranch to run, that he could not come the sixty miles to San Angelo for daily shots, and that he was not going to do it. The doctor informed

Daddy that he had no choice, because without the shots, he and his daughter would most likely die, and that it was not an easy death.

Daddy asked the doctor to give him the serum and said that he would give the shots to himself, as he often gave himself and the family penicillin shots for various ailments. The doctor shook his head and very quietly said, "You will be back."

Daddy did give the shots, fifteen of them. Tippe would come home from school, lie on a bed, and lift her skirt, and Daddy would administer the shot. Daddy would then lie on a bed for an hour to rest, prepare his mind, and then give the shot to himself. He would only allow Mother in the room for his shot. The needle was long. I hurt thinking about what they went through.

The day of the sixteenth shot, Daddy told Tippe, "I can't do it. I would rather die."

Tippe agreed.

Bouquet did have rabies.

Daddy and Tippe did not die.

6

The Fighting Owls

I was fortunate to attend Reagan County High School in Big Lake, Texas, the home of the Fighting Owls. My freshman class would be the initial class to go through all four years in the new high school. The facility was the most modern, best equipped, and the envy of every town in West Texas. We were the first school in the area to have glass backboards in our gymnasium. The teachers were outstanding, and if a student had the desire to attend college, he or she could be confident that they would be well prepared.

How was small-town Big Lake able to have such a fabulous school? A short history of Big Lake and Reagan County tells the tale.

Oil, that is, black gold, Texas tea!
—theme from The Beverly Hillbillies

Reagan County is in West Texas at the northwest edge of the Edwards Plateau on Highway 67, Farm Road 137, and the railroad. The county's northwestern corner lies on the Llano Estacado. Big Lake, the county seat, is twenty-one miles west of Barnhart and some seventy miles southwest of San Angelo.

The town is named for a large (thousand-acre) natural depression on Big Lake Draw, which was once fed by springs. I think the lake has only been full four times in my life. In the early days of the cattle drives, the lake was the only fresh water between the Middle Concho River and Comanche Springs at Fort Stockton some ninety miles west.

One of the oldest cattle trails in Texas, the Loving-Goodnight Trail, crossed the area during the pioneer days.

In 1912, the Kansas City, Mexico, and Orient Railroad built tracks from Mertzon to Barnhart to Girvin by way of Big Lake. A town was laid out, and a stock pen was built to hold cattle for rail shipment. Between 1916 and 1920, many railcar loads of steers were unloaded at Big Lake each year to winter in the Ozona country before they were sent north to fatten for market.

In May 1923, the focus of the area economy changed from agriculture to petroleum when Santa Rita Number 1 "blew in" six miles west of Big Lake. The ten-cent-an-acre land, if a buyer could be found, where the well was located had been given to the University of Texas by the Texas legislature in 1876. Early on the morning of May 28, the Santa Rita, named for the saint of the impossible, roared to life, spraying oil over the top of the derrick and covering a 250-yard area around the site. This was the beginning of the "oil boom" in the oil-rich lands of West Texas and the Permian Basin.

In 1940, the Santa Rita rig moved from its original site to the University of Texas campus in Austin, where it remains today. The rig symbolizes the establishment of the Permanent University Fund (PUF), through which thousands of Texas children have been educated at the University of Texas and Texas A&M University. Oil also provided the Reagan County Independent School District with a significant tax base. Today, oil and gas continue to be the main source of Reagan County and Big Lake's economic development, with agriculture as a secondary industry.

Today, Big Lake, especially the downtown area, has the look of a third-world village as do most small West Texas towns. The school, which was remodeled with money from the recent oil boom, remains the pride of West Texas.

I played football because that is what you do in Texas, especially at the smaller schools. If you want to commit a robbery in small-town Texas, do it on Friday night, because everyone will be at the game. I can only remember one or two boys who did not play football but instead played in the band. I thought that strange. Today, kids play football and also play in the band and even perform at halftime. I like that.

The game of football can be a rush of adrenaline for those who are not afraid to hit or be hit. In truth, football is anti-intuitive. You were not born to strap on shoulder pads and smack someone in the nose and bring snot or blood to their face. It is not for everyone. Football is something you must learn either through instruction or through watching others. I had some good ones to watch in David Jacobs, Tommy Reese, Howard Johnson, James Matlock, Jimmy Nossent, and others.

Before a game, my stomach filled with butterflies, often to the point of nausea, but after the first hit, the adrenaline kicked in. I cannot remember being afraid of hitting or being hit by an opposing player, regardless of size or reputation. I simply played the best I was capable of playing, which was not very good. Football builds character, certainly more than basketball, baseball, or track and field. Golf builds character though. In fact, you had better have a little character before you start to play the game.

The game kids play today is soccer. I think that it's a "sissy" game and that kids are coerced into playing by their mothers who are afraid their little darlings might be injured and their self-esteem hurt if they play football. Football will certainly do that to you, but gutting through adversity is good even if you bleed a little.

Because I had never played football, I did not know how to assemble my uniform. Teed Boyd and Wayne Hermann had to show me how to put on my knee and thigh pads and adjust my shoulder pads. The entire time I played high school football, I never had a helmet that fit my small head. I believe I would have been a capable receiver if I had had a helmet that had fit and did not rotate as I ran down the field. Probably not, though, because I had small hands and could not catch the ball, either.

The first football game I saw, I also played in. I do not remember if we had even practiced when we went to Ozona for a scrimmage. The coach told me to play left defensive end. I had no clue where I was to line up or what I was supposed to do, so I asked the coach. He looked at me rather peculiarly and told me, "Just knock the crap out of the guy with the ball."

I understood that, but where was I supposed to go? I thought better of asking the coach again, so I ran out on the field, and one of my teammates put me in the correct place.

The very first play, the Ozona halfback took the handoff, started around our right end, broke through our secondary, and started tiptoeing down the sideline headed for a touchdown. I had the angle on him and cut across the field. I caught up with him, but like a dog chasing a car, I was not sure what I was going to do with him. I had not been taught how to tackle, so I jumped on the kid's back, which is an unorthodox but successful way to bring an opponent down. I brought him down all right. We hit the ground. My helmet rotated around my head, and I bounced around inside that uniform.

I thought, *So this is football. I believe I like basketball better.* Still, I was proud of myself. I had knocked the crap out of him like the coach had said to do.

The coach called me over when I got to the sideline and told me, "Good job, son, but you need a little work on your tackling technique."

Big Lake had some excellent athletes. Most were two grades ahead of me or one or two grades behind me. The Reagan County Owls fell on hard times during my junior and senior year. Some of the better athletes ahead of me were Howard Johnson, David Jacobs, Jim Tom Mills, Butch Stout, Roy Holmes, Riley Featherston, Bill Loftin, Tommy Reese, Jimmy Nossent, and James Matlock. My junior year, Wayne Hermann, Teed Boyd, Karman Weatherby, Jimmy Evans, and John Edgar were the best of the lot. Karman was an all-around good athlete and excelled in football, basketball, and track.

My senior year, Howard Love at six-foot-one, 190 pounds, and 9.9 speed could have been good, perhaps outstanding, as a football player, if he had had the heart for it. George Tucker was an above-average high school football player, and I was slightly above average as a basketball player. James "Tunkie" Mann and his brother, Kenny, were good football and basketball athletes, and Bobby Hubbard and Finn Watkins could play basketball. Gary Miller, Tommy Franklin, and Bud Farr were outstanding football players. Marion Daly and Charles McKinney represented the school well, placing third in the state golf tournament.

Do not judge or you to will be judged. For in the same way you judge others, you will be judged, and with the measure you use, it will be measured to you.
—Matthew 7:1–2

A new football coach was hired prior to my senior year. One of the great truths in life is that you can learn from certain people how not to do things, which is often as valuable as learning how to actually do things.

I learned a great deal from this man. I learned how not to motivate people, how not to treat people, how not to represent myself, how not to lead, and how not to succeed. He was a preacher in the First Baptist Church and could preach a pretty good "hellfire and brimstone" sermon on Sunday morning and treat you like dirt at football practice Monday afternoon. He lasted one year!

I did not know where he went, and I didn't hear of him again until recently. My hope had been that wherever he had gone, he had found employment suitable to his nature rather than working with young people. His obituary read that he had coached at several schools in the Texas panhandle and north central Texas, but apparently, he was never a head coach. He was twenty-eight when he was at Big Lake. Perhaps over time, he realized there was a difference between bullying, coaching, teaching, and leading.

One aspect of my high school athletic career I vividly remember is the horrendously long bus and car trips. It is a far piece between towns in West Texas. We traveled 301 miles to Fabens, 180 miles to Marfa, 154 miles to Alpine, and 135 miles to Junction, all one-way trips to play district games. We also took a three-day trip to El Paso, traveling 327 miles to play basketball, and a 152-mile trip to Del Rio to play in a basketball tournament.

We rode in school station wagons for basketball games and buses for football games. Either way, we were worn out when we got to our destinations.

The trips to El Paso and Del Rio were a lot of fun. In El Paso, we stayed in a hotel, played much larger schools, usually beating them, and we got to go across the border to Mexico on Saturday night. In Del Rio, we stayed in the guesthouse of one of the wealthier families, played some good basketball teams, and got to go across the border every night.

The long trips did often have a reward. The cheerleader and pep squad bus would return to Big Lake before the team bus, so Penny and Carolyn Becknell would wait in a car for their boyfriends to arrive. Carolyn's dad, Stacy Becknell, was the Big Lake city police officer, and he would drive around the parking lot to ensure all the kids' cars were safe. Penny and Carolyn would see him coming and duck down on the car seat because they were supposed to go straight home. Karman and I would arrive, and we would get in a little "smooching" before we took the girls home. I do not think Stacy was fooled, because he would always shine his spotlight on the car where the girls were hiding.

Carolyn is now Mrs. Karman Weatherby. They have four children and a slew of grandkids. Dr. and Mrs. Weatherby live in San Angelo.

Herbie and Penny, Senior Prom, 1960.

My junior year, we were playing Del Rio in Del Rio, and they had a black player. He was the first black player I had played against, as most small West Texas towns remained segregated. This young fellow was a good athlete. He was tall and quick, and he could jump out of the gym. Our center, John Edgar, quickly got into foul trouble trying to guard him, as did our reserve center, Joe Lee Kosel. Coach Alton Green told me to guard him, and I had my hands full, literally. I held him, banged him, pushed him, but did not stop him. As I was trotting down the court, the referee sidled up to me and whispered, "Son, you can hold him some of the time but don't hold him all the time."

Big Lake is 150 miles from Ciudad Acuna, Mexico, across from Del Rio. The drive is three hours from Big Lake. From Ozona to Juno and Juno to Comstock, the road is winding and hilly, with many low water crossings, which makes it dangerous.

I suspect most but not all boys from Big Lake before and since have made that journey. They were not going to Mexico to sightsee. They made that trip for sex, booze, or both. More than one Reagan County Owl learned to fly in Ciudad Acuna's "Boys Town," where the women were cheap, and so was the whiskey!

Some Owls experienced the hospitality of Miss Hattie's, a high-end brothel located just outside the city limits of Austin on the old San Antonio highway (Congress Avenue) in 1959 while they were attending the state basketball tournament held at Gregory Gym on the University of Texas campus. The brothel burned in late 1959, and because of media interest, it was not rebuilt. However, the "Chicken Ranch" at LaGrange, which was caricatured in the movie *The Best Little Whorehouse in Texas* starring Burt Reynolds and Dolly Parton, provided a satisfactory, alternate destination for some Owls again attending the state basketball tournament in 1960.

Reagan County's athletic teams and individual athletes often did not meet their full potential. I think the main reason was that too many of us smoked, drank, and caroused—conditions not conducive to performing at your best. Our coaches, while not condoning this behavior, ignored our extracurricular activities. Coaches Lewis Hayden, Alton Green, Dick Wynne, and Keith Aycock were all good coaches and teachers but short on discipline.

The highlight of the year athletically was the annual Reagan County High School Boys Basketball Tournament, which was held over the Christmas holidays. My senior year, twenty-four teams entered, with the teams playing over a three-day period. The tournament attracted teams from all over West Texas. The Colorado City Wolves, Alpine Bucks, San Angelo Lakeview Chiefs, Iraan Braves, Monahan Lobos, McCamey Badgers, Sonora Broncos, Uvalde Coyotes, Brady Bulldogs, Abilene Christian Wildcats, and Crane Golden Cranes were some of the teams participating. My senior year was the twenty-ninth year the tournament had been held, and fifty years later, it is still held.

My formal athletic career, such as it was, ended upon graduation from high school, as it does for most kids. Second team all-district in basketball, honorable mention all-district in football, and captain of both the basketball and football teams, I was selected to receive the Ralph O'Bryan Award, which was given annually to the outstanding senior athlete.

I was the only senior on the basketball team.

Billy Williams, Charles McKinney, George Tucker, and I were the only seniors on the football team.

There were excellent administrators and teachers at Reagan County: Ben Featherston (superintendent), Erma Lee Cole (English), Jackye Havenhill (librarian), Harold Watkins (science), Billy Tom Curry (math), J. M. Wheat (industrial arts), and Jeanne Wynne (journalism), just to name a few. All were not only fine teachers but also good citizens from whom I learned much. My favorites were Robert Magruder (high school principal) and Ellis M. Mills (English).

Mr. Magruder was tough but fair, and he ran a tight ship. He would have made an excellent army officer. Students, including myself, did not dare get on his bad side. Mr. Magruder liked me for some reason, and I liked him. My senior year, I was class president, and Mr. Magruder allowed me to go to a local grocery store to buy candy for the seniors to sell for our senior trip. I did this during class time. Some kids thought I must have been "sucking" up to him, because it was unheard of for him to allow a student to miss class.

Mr. Mills was ever-so-precise in speech, dress, and manner. He can best be described as professorial. He had one goal, and that was to prepare students to pass college English. He believed that most college students had a difficult time with their first year of English, and universities used those courses to weed out the weaker students. Accordingly, he taught us how to write and drilled us on English literature at the college level. I was prepared when I arrived at Tarleton State. I did not make A's, but I did receive solid B's. I am truly grateful to Mr. Mills for his dedication and devotion to teaching.

Penny's favorites were Mr. Mills and her Spanish teacher, Mrs. Montfort. Mrs. Montfort, an elegant lady, wrote in Penny's 1960 yearbook: "*Buena suerte a una alumna simpatica y buena ya una oradora muy buena! Sinceneamente, Tomasita Montefuerte.*"

Another favorite of Penny and her brother, Bud, was Billy Tom Curry, a math teacher. Bud told me Curry got him through freshman algebra at A&M, and Penny mentioned several times Mr. Curry had been a good teacher.

My freshman year was not my best year at Reagan County High School. I was the new kid. I was learning to play football, and I was having a difficult time adjusting to a larger school. I thought that Miss Penelope Ann Farr would help with the transition, but she ignored me, which only made me more miserable.

Penny's best friend was a cute girl by the name of Verlis Branch. Verlis's mother was deceased. She and her dad, Riley, lived on their ranch, which joined the Wood place on the east and the Bar-S on the north. During the school year, Verlis stayed in Big Lake at her Granny Branch's home. Granny Branch was a Wood before her marriage, and Verlis and I were third cousins; however, I did not know that at the time. Verlis and I also shared the same birth month and year, June 1942. Verlis and I had several dates going to the drive-in movie and other activities during my freshman year. I truly enjoyed being with her. She was a sweet girl and quite popular, and she helped me adjust to my new surroundings. Nevertheless, I still had a crush on Penny.

If you cannot make someone love you, all you can do is stalk them and hope they panic and give in.
—Unknown

The summer before my sophomore year, I got the nerve to call Penny and ask her for a date to go to the drive-in movie. I could tell by her voice that she did not want to go, but instead of saying no, she said she had to ask her parents and would call me back. I found out later that her mother talked her into going. I do not remember the details of the date or other dates that summer, but sometime around Christmas that year, Penny and I were double-dating with Wayne Hermann and his date. We were parked, and they were "smooching." They began to kid us by saying, "Herbie, kiss her," and I did. And it was all and more than I could ever imagine. We were "going steady" soon after.

I think that "going steady" morphed to "going together," and today, it is "going out." I believe "going steady" is the better description, as it has a degree of permanence and commitment.

Our dating caused friction between Penny and Verlis, some that was not resolved until after high school. George Tucker came into Verlis's life, and they "went steady" their junior and senior years; however, Penny and Verlis were very much in competition for awards, leadership positions, and popularity for the remainder of high school. Verlis was salutatorian of our graduating class, Penny finishing third. Me? Well, I was in the middle of the pack.

Patsy Davis was the class valedictorian.

Graduates of the class of 1960 included the following: Verlis Branch, Grover Dean Chamberlain, Marion Daily, Patsy Davis, Tommy Gordon, Kay Easter, Marie Childress, Gigette Goertz, Howard Love, Gene Foster, Penny Farr, Margret Pettit, Patsy DuPree, Patti Johnson, Patsy Ellison, Barbara Moore, Sharon Foster, Charles McKinney, George Tucker, Billy Johnson, Linda Way, Billy Williams, Larry Smith, Eugene Zaiontz, Fidel Fuentes, Beth Odom, Billy Parsons, Ronnie Ray, and me.

The death of a classmate was again experienced when Benny Rogers was killed my senior year in a car accident while he was returning from a band activity in Del Rio.

Penny and I receive numerous honors in high school:

Penny: Student Council 1 2 3 4, Recording Secretary 4; Basketball 3 4, Captain 3; Class Favorite 2; Basketball Sweetheart 3 4; Annual Staff 1 2 3 4; and Assistant Editor *Owl's Hoot* 4; Pep Squad 1 2 3 4, President 3, Vice President 4;

Choral 2; Class Treasury 3; Secretary 4; FHA 4; Candidate for Miss RCHS 3; One-Act Play 2 3; Declamation 1 2 3 4; Quill and Scroll 4; Football Sweetheart 4; and the Lead Role Senior Play.

Penny's annual photo her senior year.

Herbie: Football 1 2 3 4, Captain 4; Basketball 1 2 3 4, Captain 4; Track 1 2 3; Class Favorite 3; Class President 4; Mr. RCHS Candidate 3; Best All-Around Boy 4; Sport's Editor *Owl's Hoot* 4; Quill and Scroll 4; and the Ralph O'Brien award as outstanding senior athlete.

My senior year annual photo.

I had a plan that mapped out what I wanted to do with my life by my senior year. I wanted to marry Penny, attend Tarleton State, participate in ROTC, graduate, and be commissioned as a US Army second lieutenant. And of course, I wanted to live happily ever after.

I had the blessing of my parents and Penny's parents on all aspects of my plan except one. My father had suggested many times that I become a military officer. His rationale was the Vietnam War was in its infancy and would get worse. It was better to go to war as an officer than an enlisted soldier. The military had a good retirement system, and I could see the world. Penny's father had been a captain in George Patton's Third Army during WWII after he had graduated from Culver Military Academy, and he also encouraged me to go to college and then into the military. Therefore, I decided to tread this path.

The one aspect of my plan that both sets of parents did not agree with, and rightfully so, was getting married. This roadblock in my path did not get successfully resolved until the summer.

7

Bar S Ranch

Much of my life has been intertwined with the Farr family. It is only fitting and proper that I include a chapter on their lives as well. The place to begin, I believe, is with the Bar S Ranch, today known as the Rocker b.

The ranch sprawls over 173,000 contiguous acres in Irion and Reagan counties, and it has over twelve miles of the Middle Concho River meandering through its vastness. The river is dry today, a victim of irrigated farms farther north around the German community of Saint Lawrence, drought, overgrazing, mesquite trees, oil drilling, and a steadily shrinking aquifer. It runs only when it rains on its watershed of Centralia Draw, Kiowa Creek, Teepee Draw, and South as well as North Mustang Draw. The river then is a rolling, thundering torrent of water uprooting trees and destroying all in its path. The river flowed as late as 1962.

The Bar S is well known in Texas. It is the story of a big land, big men, and history. Today, the ranch fills the coffers of the Scottish Rite Hospital for Crippled Children in Dallas at approximately ten million dollars a year, primarily from oil revenue. In its beginning, it lined the pockets of Phileteus H. Sawyer, a man already wealthy from Oshkosh, Wisconsin. A prominent politician and businessman, Sawyer bought a section of land on the Middle Concho River at Centralia Draw in 1871. The land along the river was being homesteaded, but by buying or burning out those who refused to sell, Sawyer and his partner, Louis L. Farr, Sr., were able to control large areas of land away from the river having no water.

Before the Bar S, there was the land steeped with history, sweat, and blood. It was the land of the Comanche, the trail driver herding cattle to New Mexico and Colorado, the outlaw, the wagon train of settlers heading farther West, and the stagecoaches of the Butterfield Overland Mail Company. And it was the US Army manned by the black "Buffalo Soldiers" of the Tenth Cavalry stationed at Fort Concho across the river from the bars and brothels of Saint Angela, now San Angelo, that patrolled the area.

All crossed the Middle Concho and traversed the land of the Bar S. Black Jack Ketchum, Colonel Benjamin H. Grierson, Colonel Ranald S. Mackenzie, Charles Goodnight, and Oliver Loving, Head of Concho Station, and Camp Charlotte are just some of the names from the past.

In the Spring 1994 *Concho Valley Archaeology Society News*, Don R. Franks quoted a participant in the 1993 archaeological project at Head of Concho Station, a stage stop on the Butterfield Trail. This individual speaks to the remoteness of the site even today:

> [The] Butterfield Overland Mail Route stop . . . on the Rocker b Ranch [is] on a portion of the ranch known as the 'Head of the River Pasture'. There remained on the site only rocks . . . a set of walls remained, though not to high and somewhat in disarray. A refreshing, though lonely place, with a view of the world I had not had before—trying to recall what I thought it might have been like to be situated at such a remote, isolated, dry, barren spot. All sorts of pictures came to mind.

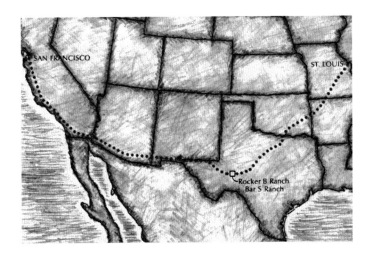

Butterfield Overland Mail Route.
(*Courtesy Texas Parks and Wildlife Magazine*)

This is the way I remember (and want to remember) the site. The land has always been there—rough, untamed, and almost alien. It is a land where only the strong survive. It has always been and always will be.

Louis Lee Farr, Sr., became the first of three generations of Farrs to be associated with the Bar S Ranch, all serving consecutively as ranch manager. Farr, a surveyor, rancher, banker, businessperson, and politician, was born in Greenville, Texas, on August 19, 1865, and died June 10, 1930, in a Temple hospital in Texas. He is buried in Fairmount Cemetery in San Angelo. He came to San Angelo in 1884 as a surveyor and worked for a time as a typesetter for the *San Angelo Standard*.

In 1899, Mr. Farr became San Angelo's first city engineer. He was twice elected Tom Green County tax assessor, and in 1906, he was elected mayor of San Angelo. In 1907, he was vice president of the Park Land and Cattle Company, the company that developed the Mertzon area. In 1909, he helped organize the Wool Grower's Central Exchange Storage Company and served as director and vice president. He was secretary-treasury of Eldorado Town Site Company and a partner in Broome, Farr, and Lee Real Estate and Insurance. In 1919, he became vice president of the Central National Bank and board chairman in 1927.

In 1911, in partnership with Ira Yates, he bought a ranch in Crockett County. About 1913, Mr. Yates bought a dry-goods store in Rankin, and by 1915, he was doing five thousand dollars' worth of business a month, a sum unheard of in those days. Mr. Yates sold the store in 1915, and he bought an unfenced, desolate ranch, one with no water and no visible value, over the objection of Mr. Farr and other friends. On October 28, 1928, oil was struck, and Yates was an instant millionaire. The Yates field near the Pecos River, a major Permian Basin strike, continues to produce today. The town of Iraan was named after Ira and his wife, Ann.

Ira Yates chose Louis Farr as his business manager and attorney after his ship came in. The two had been friends since 1885.

Phileteus Sawyer, after he had made his initial purchase in 1871, dispatched his son, Edgar P. Sawyer, to Texas in 1884 to increase his holdings, and increase them he did. Edgar met Louis Farr, and together, they begin to assemble the property that became the Sawyer Cattle Company's Bar S Ranch. Farr became the general manager and part owner of the Bar S in 1918, and he served as director and secretary of the Sawyer Cattle Company until his death.

In 1930, his son, Louis L. Farr, Jr., became general manager of the ranch. Louis, Jr., educated at Rice Institute in Houston (now Rice University), played end on the Owls football team and once pitched an exhibition game against the New York Yankees. I remember him instructing me on how to ward off blockers as a defensive end one Saturday afternoon at the ranch headquarters. He knew his football.

Louis, Jr., a large, handsome man, arrogant and self-assured like his father, had other ranching interest during his tenure with the Bar S, and he was well known in Texas ranching circles. He married Nola "Mudgie" Rattan, who was a truly remarkable woman of old stock. Both Louis, Jr., and Mudgie were teetotalers. Mudgie especially would harp on the pitfalls of, in her words, that "damnable, damnable liquor." This deep bias toward drink originated from her father being an alcoholic during her youth in Anna, Collin County, Texas. Both Louis, Jr., and Mudgie were opinionated and difficult to get to know.

The story is told of Mudgie playing poker for payday stakes with the single cowboys on the ranch, relieving them of their wages and saving them from painted women and that "damnable, damnable liquor."

Mudgie had a wonderful command of the English language and wrote beautiful but disordered letters with numerous strikeovers on her manual typewriter.

She had a nickname for all. She referred to me as "him" in her letters to Penny. A typical example was "you tell 'him' he had better treat you well or he will suffer my wrath, and that he does not want to do," and I did not. She ignored me when I was in her presence, and I am quite sure she felt Penny married below her station. Mudgie was short and stocky, but she had a pretty face when young. She stood in sharp contrast physically to her husband.

Physically different but temperamentally alike, these two people had four children: Louis Lee Farr III, Martha Jane "Turk" Farr, James Rattan "Jim" Farr, and Ellen Elizabeth "Bitsy" Farr. The children were tutored at the ranch until high school, at which time they were sent to private schools. The boys went to Culver Military Academy in Indiana, and the girls went to Hockaday Academy in Dallas. Twice a year, the girls were taken to Neiman Marcus and outfitted with new wardrobes. They were raised as royalty, and they were as near to royalty as existed in West Texas. Their upbringing, most certainly, contributed to difficulties they experienced in later life.

In 1954, William A. Blakley bought the Bar S and an eighty-thousand-acre ranch, the San Cristobal, at Lamy, New Mexico, near Santa Fe. The New Mexico ranch had been named for the Tewa Indian pueblos located on the ranch. Louis, Jr., was part owner of the New Mexico ranch.

Blakley, a Dallas magnate who in his youth had been a cowboy from Oklahoma working on a ranch near the Bar S, was self-educated. He was an attorney and accountant during the days when only a competency test was required, and he was a millionaire. His wealth came from banking, insurance, and real estate. At one time, he was a major stockholder and director in the now defunct Braniff airline. He and his wife had no children. His political opponents derisively called him either "Cowboy Bill" or "Dollar Bill Blakely."

Blakley is best known for serving two appointments in the US Senate and a lost senate election. The governor of Texas initially appointed him to the senate in January 1957 to fill the vacancy created by the resignation of Price Daniel. He was an unsuccessful candidate for the senate in 1958, losing the Democratic nomination to Ralph Yarbrough. Again, Blakley was appointed to the senate in January 1961 to fill a vacancy after the resignation of Lyndon Johnson. Subsequently, he lost in a general election to a Republican, John Tower, a nondescript college professor from Midwestern State University in Wichita Falls.

Tower was the first Republican since Reconstruction elected to the senate from Texas. He paved the way for many more Republicans to win state offices, including another fellow who was nondescript in all but his name, George W. Bush.

I met Bill Blakley once at the Rocker b ranch headquarters and shared a meal with him at the Farr family table. He looked the part of a Texas senator. Stetson hat, bow tie, white shirt, craggy, sunburned but handsome face, and genteel manner all added to his persona. I also remember the old Lincoln car he was driving as well as his poor table manners.

Mr. Blakley, when he bought the two ranches, made two quick changes. First, he fired Louis Farr, Jr., and appointed his son, Louis Farr III, as ranch manager of both properties. I understand he did this because Louis, Jr., held out for more money for his share of the San Cristobal than did the others. Second, he changed the name of the Bar S to the Rocker b. The ranch brand is a script "b" rather than a capital "B" so it would be less likely to scab from a hot branding iron and attract a screwworm strike.

Louis Lee Farr III met his future wife, Lou Dickey Baucus, when they were children. Her father, William Nichols Baucus, a cattle buyer on the Kansas City Livestock Exchange, routinely bought cattle from the Bar S. Mr. Baucus, his wife, Francis Louise Dobyns Baucus, and their three children would often visit the ranch during the summer staying in the ranch guesthouse.

Later, when he was attending Culver Military Academy, Louis Lee would ride the train to the Baucus home in Richmond, Missouri, during holidays. Mr. Baucus owned a beautiful, manicured farm with a large, two-story antebellum plantation home, and Lou Dickey was quite fetching. The surroundings were apparently attractive to Louis Lee, and a romance blossomed.

Their courtship resulted in marriage on September 14, 1940, in Kansas City, Missouri. The newlyweds honeymooned in Topeka, Kansas, at the Nighthawk Hotel, and traveled to San Antonio to spend the remainder of their honeymoon at the Saint Anthony Hotel. Shortly after their arrival, Louis III received a call from his father, one telling him that he was needed to supervise sheep shearing at a ranch Louis, Jr., owned in South Texas. That call ended the honeymoon, and off to "Africa" they went. Mudgie had named the South Texas ranch "Africa" because of the thick brush on the ranch.

Louis, Jr., owned another ranch in South Texas that Mudgie named "Hell." A business associate phoned Louis, Jr., at the Bar S, and Mudgie answered the phone. She told the caller, "Louis is in 'Hell,' and they don't have a phone down there." Mudgie had to do some explaining to that fellow to overcome his confusion.

Louis Lee III, the epitome of the tall, dark, and handsome man, had a superior intellect and was equally comfortable on the back of a horse or behind a desk. He was well read and had a beautiful baritone voice. He would have been a magnificent general officer in the mold of Patton and Schwarzkopf or a success as a lawyer. He was one of the best if not *the* best man I have known in a crisis. He had an innate sense of what needed to be done, and he did it.

He was not without faults. He was arrogant, profane, egotistic, opinionated, and quick-tempered. He had no clue in managing his own finances, and he was generous to a fault. Sentimental, he became teary-eyed easily and could be quite gentle or harsh with those he loved. In short, he was a man.

Louis Lee Farr III
Culver Military Academy

Lou Dickey was a beautiful, genteel lady with impeccable manners. She was of solid Midwestern stock with a finishing school background, and she went without the hard edge of many West Texas women. Above all, she was adaptable. The showplace farm in Missouri was a long journey to the rough-and-tumble world of a West Texas ranch. She never changed Louis Lee, but she did "gentle him somewhat."

A Boy from Barnhart

Lou Dickey Baucus Farr

Mr. and Mrs. Louis L. Farr III, Louis Lee and Lou Dickey, settled in at the Bar S and worked for Louis, Jr. They lived in the main house at the ranch headquarters, as Louis, Jr., and Mudgie were now living in San Angelo. Their time at the ranch was short, interrupted by the events of December 7, 1941.

Louis Lee and Lou Dickey were driving to San Angelo, pulling a horse trailer, when they heard the news of the Japanese attack on Pearl Harbor over the car radio. The United States of America was at war! Louis Lee was to play polo with the Mertz brothers—Mertzon was named after their father—and other friends. They played the polo match, and all retired to Steve's Ranch House Restaurant for dinner; however, their minds were only on the winds of war blowing hot over West Texas.

The next morning, Louis Lee returned to San Angelo and Goodfellow Army Air Base to take a physical and accept his reserve commission in the army. He failed the physical because of poor hearing.

The following day, he and Lou Dickey drove to Brooke Army Hospital in San Antonio, and he again got in a line to take a physical. This time, he memorized what he was supposed to hear by talking with those who had already passed the test. He passed, completed his paperwork, and returned to the Bar S to wait for orders.

Orders came in March 1942 to report to Camp Roberts, California, for officer orientation. Second Lieutenant Farr and Lou Dickey drove to California, securing a room at the Paso Robles Inn in Paso Robles, California. After a couple of months in California, Lieutenant Farr was ordered to Fort Sill, Oklahoma, for training in the field artillery. Lou Dickey, now pregnant, returned to her parents' farm in Missouri.

Penelope "Penny" Ann Farr was born August 13, 1942, in Saint Luke's Hospital, Kansas City, Missouri. Dr. Hamilton, the same physician who had delivered her mother, delivered her. Her father, who was notified at Fort Sill of her birth, was granted leave to visit his new daughter and wife.

When Penny was three months old, her father received orders to report to Fort Knox, Kentucky. The family drove from Richmond, Missouri, where they secured a room at a motel in Elizabethtown, Kentucky, near Fort Knox. They were awakened during the night by the manager and told they would have to leave the next morning, as infants were not allowed.

Getting up, Lieutenant Farr found an ad in the local newspaper for two rooms in the little railroad town of Cecelia, which was also near Fort Knox. He drove to the home of the people who had the rooms for rent, Dr. and Mrs. Cecil. The Cecils were willing to rent the rooms, but they first wanted to meet the wife and baby. The family met the Cecils and passed inspection.

They shared a bathroom with the Cecils, but they had no sink or running water in their two rooms. A coal-burning fireplace provided heat. They opened their Christmas gifts in bed because it was so cold. Penny slept in a baby buggy, as they had no crib for her. They were young and in love, and the family was together, so all was right in their world.

The town of Cecelia had been named for Dr. Cecil's family. He was a retired dentist, and several times, moonshiners came down from the hills to have him pull their teeth. I'll bet I know what they used to pay him with.

Later, Lieutenant Farr was transferred to Camp Bowie near Brownwood, Texas, and assigned to the 4th Infantry Division. Today, the 4th Infantry Division is stationed at Fort Hood just down the road from Brownwood. The 4th ID is refitting and training after a third tour in Iraq for relocation to Fort Carson, Colorado.

Louis, Jr., had rented a nice place for Lieutenant Farr and family at the Harlow Courts in Brownwood, so they felt "uptown" after their meager quarters in Kentucky. During the tour at Camp Bowie, they met Rusty Heitkamp. Rusty had been the Corps commander at Texas A&M College as a student and was later awarded the Silver Star for bravery in Germany. He mustered out of the Army as a brevet lieutenant colonel.

Inviting Rusty to the Bar S one weekend, he met Lieutenant Farr's sister, Bitsy. Rusty and Bitsy later married. Such are the fortunes of war.

A temporary duty (TDY) trip to Fort Knox interrupted the stay at Camp Bowie. The family again rented the Cecils' two rooms. It was spring by then. Penny was able to play outside, and she had a playpen to sleep in. Louis Lee (Bud) Farr IV was conceived there.

Lieutenant Farr returned to Camp Bowie and the 4th Infantry Division, where he participated with the division in the Tennessee maneuvers. Lou Dickey and Penny returned to her parent's home.

Reassigned to Panama, the Army, in its infinite wisdom, thought that because he was from Texas, he could speak fluent Spanish. He could not, so after a few months, he was shipped to California and assigned to the 768th field artillery battalion.

Louis Lee (Bud) Farr IV arrived while Lieutenant Farr was at Fort MacArthur and commanding a shore battery that was guarding the California coast from possible Japanese attack. Dr. Hamilton also delivered Bud. Lieutenant Farr, given leave after Bud's birth, visited the family in Kansas City. Lou Dickey was thrilled to produce a boy, because Mudgie, in very specific words, let her know at Penny's birth that, "Farr women never have girls first, especially blue-eyed ones."

The 768th moved to Needles, California, for desert maneuvers in preparation for oversea deployment. Lou Dickey left her babies with her mother and drove to Needles with a soldier's wife she had met at the travelers aid station in Kansas City's Union Station. This young woman could not drive, spoke hardly a word the entire trip, but did have a ration card.

There was no place to stay in Needles, but they finally found a place for Lou Dickey on the back of a porch with another wife. A blanket hung between beds provided privacy. The husbands were rarely able to come in from the field.

The 768th ordered to the port of embarkation in New York landed in Swanage, England, for combat duty with George Patton's Third Army following the Battle of the Bulge. The unit crossed the English Channel into France and later Germany, where it remained until war's end. Lieutenant Farr, now Captain Farr, was awarded the Bronze Star medal for distinguished service while in Germany.

Captain Farr returned to the United States in November 1945 and met Lou Dickey in St. Louis, where they celebrated. They returned to the Baucus farm, picked up Penny and Bud, and headed for Texas and the Bar S.

A special breed of men will sacrifice everything for the security and freedom of so many unthankful others.
—Unknown

The difficulties Louis Lee and Lou Dickey experienced during WWII reinforced my belief that serving in the uniform of our country is not easy and requires sacrifice, sometimes the ultimate sacrifice. The Bill Clintons, Dick Cheneys, Barack Obamas, and their ilk who took the easier, softer way appall me. These men who are so willing to send others in harm's way but who themselves lack the courage and conviction to serve their country in the same manner are, in my mind, unworthy of their elected office.

We owe the Louis Farrs and Rusty Heitkamps and the millions of others who fought and died in WWII and the many wars since a debt of gratitude that can never be repaid.

A veteran, whether active duty, honorably discharged, or retired, is someone who at one point in his or her life wrote a blank check made payable to "the United States of America" for an amount up to and including their life. There are way too many people in this country who no longer accept, much less understand this fact.

By the time Penny and I had started going "steady" and I had become a frequent visitor to the Rocker b, Louis Lee had made his mark on ranch operations. Mr. Blakely and Louis Lee purchased at a dispersion sell registered Anxiety 4th Herefords from the Windsor Farms, Boonville, Missouri. They bought six bulls for about six thousand dollars each and a hundred cows at a thousand dollars each. This was a major acquisition to improve the already large commercial herd.

On Christmas Eve of 1965, Louis Lee and I spent the night pulling calves for cows that were having their first calf. For the uninitiated, "pulling calves" means just that. The cows were small, the bulls big, and the calves large; therefore, the heifers needed some help. Louis Lee had given the ranch hands time to be with their families, and his boys were out with their girlfriends.

It was a memorable night, watching all that new life come into the world. Around 0600 on Christmas morning, we headed to headquarters to open presents.

My heroes have always been cowboys, and they still are it seems, sadly in search of and one-step in back of themselves, and their slow moving dreams.
—Willie Nelson

In the late 1950s through the 1960s, ranch employees remained relatively stable. Cowboys and their families lived at line camps, each responsible for around eighty sections. B. A. Basham, wife Elvie, and sons Dwayne and Ronnie Pat and later Eddie and Nancy Hale were at "Elbow." Howard and Sue Ann Swearingen were at "West Line." Tom and Marm Wilson were at "Voodoo." Glenn McFarland, wife Norma, and their children, Kenneth and Marsha were at "Vat." Dobbs Hermann, his wife, and his son, Wayne, lived a couple of miles from headquarters. Dobbs was responsible for the registered herd. Jim Ed Basham and his wife, Dorothy, lived at headquarters. Jim Ed was the ranch foreman. Harper McFarland, the brother of Glenn, was foreman of the New Mexico ranch and reported directly to Louis Lee.

Theodore and Alma Washington lived at headquarters. Theodore was the chuck wagon and bunkhouse cook. Alma cooked and cleaned for the Farrs and served as surrogate mother for the Farr children when their parents were gone to the New Mexico ranch or to other places on ranch business. Theodore would also help cook at the "Big House" and was a better cook than Alma.

Louis Lee and Dickey lived in the "Big House" at headquarters, and their family now consisted of Penny, Bud, William (Bill) Baucus Farr, and Phil Sawyer Farr. There was usually at least one single cowboy living at the line camps and ten to twelve at headquarters, depending on the time of year and work to be done. The ranch was fenced, and pastures ran between fifteen and twenty sections with numerous corrals and pens. The outside fence measured some hundred miles, and inside fencing consisted of some 280 miles of woven wire. There were sixty-three windmills. The ranch ran ten to twelve thousand sheep, 2,500 mother cows in addition to the registered herd of some 250 animals, and numerous goats.

There were some one hundred saddle horses, twenty-five to thirty broodmares, and four registered stud horses. The ranch contained several hundred feral hogs along the Middle Concho River, which were hunted, and the piglets were roped and raised for meat at headquarters and the line camps. Antelope and deer proliferated after the screwworm epidemic was contained and numbered several thousand. Turkey, bobcat, dove, quail, javelina, and an assortment of other critters also made the Rocker b home.

The Bar S and later the Rocker b operated just as you see it in the movies—chuck wagon, bedrolls on the ground, horses tied to a string line, and work much the same as in the 1880s. This continued until around 1962 when pickups and trailers replaced the old way.

Louis Lee Farr III

Edna Ferber visited the Bar S and later the King Ranch, researching material for her book, *Giant*, published in 1952. The book was made into a movie starring Rock Hudson, Elizabeth Taylor, and James Dean (1956). Much of what she saw and was told during her stay at the Bar S appeared in the book and also in the movie.

Some say she based her characters of the larger-than-life Texas rancher and Virginia-born horsewoman on Louis Lee and Lou Dickey. Others say the characters were based on Robert Kleberg and his wife, Helen of the King Ranch, the daughter of a Kansas congressional representative. Only Ferber knew, and she never told; however, I suspect it was an amalgamation of the two men and women. I do know this: Rock Hudson and Elizabeth Taylor did an outstanding portrayal of

Louis Lee and Lou Dickey from appearances, mannerisms, and clothes. Mercedes McCambridge's role as the rancher's sister was Mudgie Farr personified.

Louis Lee did not like Ferber, probably because she was a pushy, opinionated, Jewish woman. They had several spirited discussions, and she pointedly told him he was wasting his talents on a West Texas ranch.

The Texas rancher and oilman did not favorably receive her book or the movie. I personally think the movie is a classic.

Miss Ferber and Lou Dickey corresponded for several years afterward, but the letters and photos taken during her visit were destroyed in a fire in 1958.

Many notables visited and hunted on the ranch over the years, but perhaps none better known than Astronaut Jim Lovell, who commanded the ill-fated Apollo 13 flight to the moon. Actor Tom Hanks in the movie *Apollo 13* portrayed Lovell.

Astronaut James Lovell and Lou Dickey Farr in the Farr home.

Daddy and I were spraying cattle for ticks at the Murphey Ranch headquarters and saw black smoke rising in the distance. The smoke appeared to be coming from the Bar S some ten miles away. The large sprayer tank was full, and we headed for the Bar S headquarters. The "Big House" built in the 1880s was ablaze. The house constructed of native rock quarried on the ranch was the victim of antiquated electrical wiring and was not to be saved. The Farrs lost everything. Only Penny saved anything—the formal she was to wear to the prom at school year's end.

A new main house made from brick and designed by Lou Dickey, one consisting of five bedrooms, four baths, a large kitchen, and a 20x48 great room was completed in 1959. This home proved very comfortable for the Farr family.

Today, the home serves as the ranch "guesthouse." A new manager's home has been constructed, and the old guesthouse/office complex was replaced by a brick building with manager's office, conference room, and reception area, much as you will find in any executive suite.

During the construction of the new home, the Farrs lived in the old guesthouse and took their meals in a makeshift kitchen in the ranch commissary.

The commissary consisted of a large room for storing staple goods, a walk-in freezer for meat and frozen vegetables, and a cold room for storing fruit and vegetables. Once a month, the ranch would order food from the M System food chain in San Angelo and dispatch a ranch truck to bring the food to the ranch headquarters. M System offered S&H Green stamps, and the stamps were saved until year's end when they were redeemed for items to be used in the ranch families' homes.

The wives of the cowboys would come to headquarters, and Theodore Washington would disburse two weeks' worth of groceries to the families. A family on the Rocker b could live quite well. Their home, water, electricity, and food were provided by the ranch, and also included health insurance and a retirement plan. Though not large, their salary was only encumbered by taxes and personal needs.

I could write a chapter on the exploits and escapades of the Farr boys, but I think one anecdote will suffice.

William Baucus "Bill" was the middle child and the most gregarious of the three. Bill loved trucks and still does. Bernie Henson was a trucker and hauled cattle for the ranch. Bernie loved Bill, and Bill loved Bernie's truck. Bernie would stop by headquarters, and if Bill was around, he would take Bill with him.

Bernie told Louis Lee that Bill's language was getting rough and that maybe Bill, being just a five-year-old, was spending too much time at the bunkhouse with the cowboys.

Louis Lee had a talk with Bill about his language, but the next time Bernie came by the ranch, Bill refused to ride with him. Bernie felt badly about this so he brought Bill some candy.

Bernie handed the candy to Bill. Bill looked at Bernie and said, "I don't want any of your Goddamn candy, you tattletale son of a bitch."

It was a round trip of a hundred miles when Penny and I went on a date to see a movie at the drive-in theater in Big Lake, and much of the drive was on dirt roads. Straight-line distance or as the crow flies was about fifteen miles from my house to hers, but the roads did not run in straight lines.

Alma would stay in the Farrs' home when Pen's parents were away so that she could protect the "chillins." Alma was afraid of the dark and would not have been much help in a crisis, but Phil or "the baby," as she called him, was also scared of the dark, so she was there for him.

Penny and I would come home late from a date, and every door would be locked. Alma and the boys were sound sleepers, so it would take much shouting to awaken Alma and get her to the door. She would say, "Sistah, is that you?" open the door, and stick a big pistol in our face. We knew what would happen and hoped the pistol was not cocked.

Alma called Louis Lee "Mr. Bob," Lou Dickey "Miss Dickey," Penny "Sistah," Bill, "Richard," Phil "the Baby," and Bud "Bud."

When I first started dating Penny, Alma called me that "cauliflower-eared boy." For example, she said, "Sistah, is that cauliflower-eared boy coming for suppah tonight?" Later, as I became a fixture at the Rocker b, she called me "brother-in-law." Both nicknames were embarrassing.

Alma and Theodore were superstitious. Often, the boys and Pen would ride with them to Barnhart to get the mail. If anyone forgot something and had to return to headquarters, all would have to get out of the vehicle, draw a circle on the ground, spit in it, and walk around the circle three times. If anyone got sick, they believed a hex had been put on the person. Theodore had a chant or potion for just about every hex.

After Penny learned to drive, Alma would ride with her. Penny always drove quite fast, even on dirt roads. She was her daddy's girl in many respects, and that was one of them.

Alma would tell her, "Sistah, I just loves to hears that gravels hitting this cars." That meant slow down.

Alma and Theodore were good people. I remember them fondly.

Penny and I were in love and desperately wanted to marry after high school graduation. Our parents had another idea, and the idea was this: "The two of you have never dated anyone but each other. You need to separate for a time, go to different colleges, meet and date others, and then after a year if you want to get married, we will discuss it."

The wisdom of Solomon, and we were not in a position to refuse.

Therefore, I was off to Tarleton State and Penny to Christian College, a girl's school in Columbia, Missouri.

8

Married Man/College Student

Tarleton State University is located in Stephenville, Texas. Stephenville had a population of around six thousand in 1960 (approximately sixteen thousand today). It is located in north-central Texas some seventy miles from the Dallas-Fort Worth metroplex. The town promotes its image as the "Dairy Capital" and the "Cowboy Capital" of Texas based on the large number of dairy farms and professional rodeo cowboys who live in the area. The town is quite charming, with some diversified light industry, and it is rapidly becoming known as a nice place to retire. Then as now, the university remains its focal point.

The university received its name from an eccentric New Hampshire Yankee who bought ten thousand acres of prime Texas ranch land near Stephenville and amassed a large fortune. This man, John Tarleton, bequeath $85,000 to establish the college, provided it bear his name, in order to help rural children receive the education he had been denied. The institution was founded in 1899, although some historians believe it opened in 1896, as John Tarleton College.

In 1917, the college became part of the Texas A&M system, and the name was changed to John Tarleton Agricultural College and operated as a two-year institution. In 1963, the college graduated its first class as a four-year institution under the name Tarleton State College. The college was granted university status in 1973, and currently, it has an enrollment of over 9,600 students.

The largest non-land-grant agriculture university in the United States, Tarleton educates more agricultural education teachers than any other institution in the nation.

We sleep safely in our beds because rough men stand ready in the night to visit violence on those who would cause us harm.
—George Orwell

Tarleton has had an ROTC program since 1917, a program from which I am a proud graduate. More than 250 Tarleton faculty, staff, and students lost their lives in World War II, and others have been lost since, the most recent being Master Sergeant Kelly Hornbeck, class of 1987, killed on his second tour in Iraq.

Lieutenant Colonel Earl Rudder, Colonel James Bender, Lieutenant Colonel Edwin Dyess, Lieutenant Colonel Robert Gray, Colonel Will Tate, Major General Bill Garrison, and Major General Chris Adams are but a few names from Tarleton's storied military past. The names of the deceased, prisoners of war, general officers, and recipients of the Silver Star to Distinguished Service Cross may be viewed on the Tarleton State University Military Memorial, which is located in Heritage Park on the university campus.

Through the years, there have been attempts by misguided or uninformed citizens and politicians to change the name of Tarleton. Names put forth include Texas A&M-Stephenville, Texas A&M-Tarleton Station, and others equally horrendous. I now believe enough right-thinking Tarleton Texans and a few local politicians have convinced the Texas legislature, which is not known for right thinking or even thinking, that Mr. Tarleton's will is a legal and binding document. We may be affiliated with Texas A&M; however, we are not A&M. We are the Tarleton State University Texans, and damn proud of it.

I began my first year at Tarleton in September 1960 and graduated on May 31, 1964, with a bachelor of science in general business. During those four years, my life changed dramatically.

I lived in Bender Hall, a long, two-story, brick building on the west side of the campus, adjacent to Stephenville's main thoroughfare, Washington Street. Bender Hall, built in 1953, was named for Colonel

James Bender, who had been the professor of military science at Tarleton at the beginning of WWII. Bender participated in the D-Day invasion and was killed in action in France one month later.

My two-man room on the first floor consisted of a bunk bed, two desks, two chairs, and a lavatory. Communal showers were located on each floor in the middle of the building. The room was austere. On the north end of the building, there was a lounge with couches, overstuffed chairs, a game area, and a flickering TV.

Tarleton in 1960 could best be described as a quasi-military school. Almost everything centered on the ROTC Corps of cadets. While ROTC was not mandatory, the majority of the male students participated in the program. ROTC provided the student government leaders and the membership of the various clubs and activities on campus. Most of the athletes were ROTC members. Even the female students were involved. Each lettered company had its sweetheart called the "Little Colonel." She wore a special uniform just as the cadets did and participated in our military activities. The selection as "Little Colonel" was quite an honor at Tarleton. Only the prettiest and most popular girls were selected.

The Cadet Corps was composed of a corps commander, battalion staff, four letter companies—A, B, C, and D—and a band company. The professor of military science was a regular army lieutenant colonel assisted by a major, two captains, and several noncommissioned officers (NCOs). The composition of the regular army cadre remains much the same today. I was assigned to Delta (D) Company as a private and remained in that company all four years. My sophomore year, I was a sergeant, junior year a lieutenant, and I commanded the company as a captain the final semester of my senior year.

Major Joseph Burkett, one of the cadre during my freshman and sophomore years, was killed in an ambush in Vietnam in 1963. He was awarded the Silver Star. His death was a wake-up call for those of us who planned to enter the army as second lieutenants. My interest in military subjects intensified. Map, sand table, weekly drill, and weekend field exercises took on new meaning.

Hazing was an integral part of the freshman experience, and even those few freshmen who were not in the ROTC were not denied character-building sessions with upperclassman. The hazing, while it was annoying at times and downright indecent or cruel at other times, was but a rite of passage. No one was seriously injured or hurt, although some folks' self-esteem may have been temporarily bruised. Hazing was one reason I spent as little time as possible in my dorm room. The library offered a temporary haven, and it was one of the few places I could find to study without interruption.

I was lucky, because my roommate, Gene Wehmeyer, a sophomore, provided a buffer from upperclassmen. Gene was from Ingram near Kerrville, and we became fast friends. I visited his home a couple of times, as he did mine. He had a pretty sister, and I dated her once while we were visiting his family. Gene had an older friend who had an apartment in Stephenville, where we were able to hang out. The friend was a jeweler, and we used his tools to polish our uniform brass and belt buckles. Our brass always sparkled at inspections.

The second or third day at Tarleton, I met with my academic advisor, a heavyset, gruff man who looked like a constipated bulldog. He had been a football coach, and now he had earned a PhD and worked as an instructor in the physical education department. Motioned into his presence, he indicated I take a seat in front of his desk.

He looked me in the eye, turned his attention to some papers on his desk, looked up, and stated, "Son, I have reviewed your test scores, and I want to give you some advice. Save yourself some time, your parents their money, go get a job, and get on with your life."

I do not know if this man gave the same advice to all freshmen, but I do know this: If his intention was to motivate me—and I do not think it was—he did. It took me several days to process what he had told me and to regain a smidgen of my self-esteem and then make myself a promise, "I will show him that I can make it," and I did, but not without difficulty!

I never again experienced a professor with his attitude. My Tarleton professors wanted us to succeed and were willing to help in any way they could. They were competent, caring, and above all, good citizens. Dick Smith, Virginia Yearwood, Mary Sue Staig, O. A. Grant, Oscar Frazier, Elmer Henningsen, Lamar Johanson, Donnie Campbell, Johnny Dunn, and Clinton Smith, all PhDs, were outstanding teachers, and each made their mark on Tarleton in other ways as well.

Penny and I wrote often and talked on the phone once a month. We were anxious for Christmas vacation to arrive. She had gone to her grandparents for Thanksgiving, so we had not seen each other since college had started. The Christmas holidays finally arrived, and we were together constantly. Then the time came to say good-bye and return to school. We sat in front of her parents' home until early in the morning, not wanting to say good-bye. We wanted to go in and talk with them about marriage; however, we decided we had made a commitment, and we would stick to it.

Penny and her parents were to drive to Dallas the next day and see the Cotton Bowl game on New Year's Day, and then Penny would fly out of Love Field to Columbia, Missouri, the day afterward. My parents drove me back to Tarleton on New Year's Day, and my plan was to study for final exams.

Her parents told me that they would be coming through Stephenville on January 2nd and would take me to lunch. I was lying on my bunk, and there was a knock on the door. It was Pen's father, and he wanted to know if I was ready to get a bite to eat. We walked out into an empty parking lot, and there was Penny in the backseat of their car.

Her father said, "I am tired of hearing Penny crying and not wanting to go back to Missouri. You two are getting married. Go call your father and tell him to meet us in San Angelo. Penny is eighteen and doesn't need someone to sign for her, but you do."

It was a very quiet ride to San Angelo, but periodically, Penny and I would look at each other and grin.

Daddy met us in San Angelo. Penny and I got a marriage license and a blood test, and I borrowed Daddy's car and drove back to Tarleton. Daddy rode to Barnhart with the Farrs.

This was a difficult week, as I had to study for finals, look for a place to live, and try to resolve in my mind what marriage actually meant. I do not remember talking with Penny that week, but we must have at least once.

The pickings were slim in locating places to live in our price range. Finally, I found an apartment off Washington Street behind the Ford dealership, four blocks from the Stephenville Courthouse. The apartment building, which was owned by a dentist and his wife, Dr. and Mrs. Lester G. Martin, contained three furnished apartments, two on the second floor and another apartment and a garage on the ground floor. An apartment on the second floor was vacant. It was tiny—a living room, one-person kitchen, dining room, bathroom, and bedroom. It was cooled by a swamp cooler and heated by gas stoves. A small deck off the kitchen provided a magnificent view of the Ford dealership service bays.

Mrs. Martin knew of Penny's family. I told her that Penny had been a student at Christian College in Columbia, Missouri. She did not want to rent me the apartment. She told me Penny would not like it and that I could find other apartments that were nicer. I convinced her I needed that apartment, and she finally agreed to rent it to me. The cost was forty-five dollars a month with all bills paid.

Gene and I returned to the Wood place on the night of January 5, 1961. The morning of January 6th, Penny and I met with the Reverend Jack London, a Farr family friend, who had driven to the Rocker b from Hobbs, New Mexico, to marry us. We then drove to San Angelo and bought wedding rings. The cost of Pen's small diamond ring was $125.00.

Penny and I were married at high noon on January 7, 1961, in the Farr home on the Rocker b. Verlis Branch was her maid of honor. Gene Wehmeyer was my best man. Travis Shaw was the ring bearer, and Tippe was the bridesmaid.

Penny and Herbie, wedding, Rocker b Ranch, January 7, 1961.

We left the Rocker b in a "gulley washer," and it rained all the way to Brownwood, where I had made reservations at a motel to spend our wedding night. I had to stop several times because the windshield wipers on our 1951 Chevy could not keep up with the deluge of water.

When we arrived at our destination with me in a high state of anticipation, Penny informed me that she had forgotten some personal items and asked if I would please go purchase them while she cleaned the bathroom. The remainder of our married life, we carried a cleaning kit for Penny to clean the bathroom of any motel, guesthouse, or hotel where we might stay.

I dutifully departed in the rainstorm and proceeded to locate the items in a grocery store. This took some time because I did not want to ask a store employee where the items were located. Because I had no experience buying female-type items, I had to search aisle by aisle to find them.

When I returned to the motel room, I found the bathroom cleaned and Penny asleep. She was worn out from a week of wedding showers, luncheons, and the general excitement of it all. The Farrs had placed a bottle of champagne in the car, and I proceeded to celebrate our marriage by drinking the champagne. The Farrs called around 2100 to offer congratulations, but the ringing phone did not wake Penny. The next morning, we departed for our new home at 143 Devine Street, Stephenville, Texas.

I had a slight hangover.

Dr. and Mrs. Martin, Doc and Zana, liked Penny a lot, and I believe they liked me. Their daughter was also named Penny. They took us under their wing and made sure that I had enough work around their home and dentist office to pay the monthly rent and then some. They put me in charge of the apartments, and I would do the cleaning and painting after people moved out. They also bought new carpet for their home, and we used the old carpet in our apartment.

The Martins were extremely generous. They had us to dinner several times and entertained both our families at the Stephenville Country Club on the evening of my college graduation. We continued to correspond with them for many years after college. Both Doc and Zana are now deceased.

Penny enrolled at Tarleton, and we were both students for a semester. It soon became evident that money was a problem. My parents had purchased a life insurance policy, paid up at age eighteen, which they gave to me. I redeemed the policy for $750.00 and paid up a policy of a thousand dollars, which I still have. The $750 was placed in a savings account and used for my tuition which at the time was $3.00 a semester hour.

We were adamant that we wanted to pay our own way and depend on our parents as little as possible. The only way to do this was for Penny to quit school and go to work, which she did after one semester.

I worked in the college store between classes. George Cook, the manager of the college store, hired Penny as his secretary and allowed me to continue to work in the store. He also allowed me to use without cost the used books sold by the store. The only books I had to buy were those new books professors required. This arrangement continued the remainder of our time at Tarleton.

George Cook was a saint. I recently called him in Arkansas, where he is now retired from the University of Arkansas bookstore, and told him how much I appreciated all he had done for Penny and me.

Money continued to be a problem. We would cash dollar checks. Spam became a staple, and a ten-dollar grocery bill was a budget-breaker.

Around the end of my sophomore year, I went to Mr. Cook and told him I needed more money and asked if he would hire me as his assistant manager and allow me to take some college courses. He told me he thought that would be a mistake, a big mistake, but he would discuss the proposal with Dr. Stuart Chilton, the college registrar. Mr. Cook and Dr. Chilton decided that they would hire me and allow me to take six hours a semester on college time. Penny, Mr. Cook, and Dr. Chilton all thought I was making a mistake.

I worked three weeks as the assistant manager and realized my error. I went with hat in hand and told them I would never graduate from college taking six hours a semester, and I asked if we could go back to the previous arrangement. Thankfully, they agreed, and no one said we told you so.

I see Dr. Chilton when I visit Tarleton for different functions, and we both have a good chuckle about my short tenure as assistant manager of the college store. Dr. Chilton, now retired, periodically writes a column for the *Stephenville Empire-Tribune*.

An incident took place during my senior year that changed the lives of my parents for the better, although I did not realize it at the time.

Our parents had come to Tarleton for Parents' Day toward the end of the school year. I was commanding Company D, and it was to be recognized as the Honor Company during a military review conducted by the ROTC the next day.

Dad's face was bruised, scratched, and generally a mess. Daddy explained that he had been working cattle and a bull had hit him in the face. Something did not ring true, and I got Pen's dad alone and asked him to level with me.

No man can think clearly, when his fists are clinched.
—George Jean Nathan

I will now relate what I have been told then and later. Since I was not there and because there are usually three sides to every story—each side has a version, and then there is what actually happened—I cannot vouch for the facts in their entirety.

Daddy was having coffee at the only café in Barnhart, as was another rancher. This rancher and Daddy had bought a railroad car of cow feed, each to pay for half. A second rancher told Daddy he wished he had known they were buying the feed, as he would have gone in with them. Daddy told this rancher he could have half of his part and to pay the first rancher.

The first rancher was unaware of this arrangement, and unknown to Daddy, the second rancher had not paid for his share. The first rancher accused Daddy of cheating him on the deal, and they decided Barnhart was not big enough for the two of them and that one would have to leave. They stepped outside the café for fisticuffs, Daddy thrashing him fairly well.

Later that afternoon, Daddy received a call from the rancher's son demanding Daddy meet him in Barnhart, as he was going to whip him for trouncing his daddy. Daddy told the son he had no quarrel with him and that he would come but he would not fight. He instead would just take a beating.

The son was in his thirties, and Dad in his fifties. And it would not have been a fair fight, even if Daddy had tried to fight. Daddy arrived at Clyde Parry's service station, and a crowd had already formed to watch. The son threw all the punches, and I guess finally got tired of hitting Daddy. Seems to me someone should have stepped in and stopped a young man from beating an older man, but that did not happen.

I went ballistic when I heard this, and I was soon on my way not to fight the son but to kill him. Penny's father was the voice of reason convincing me I had too much to lose and I should take the high road and let it go.

Daddy only had a handshake deal with Teddy on the Wood place lease. Teddy had died. Teddy's widow decided soon after the fight she wanted the lease and did not need Daddy to work for her any longer. She and the rancher that Daddy had whipped were now dating and were going to marry. Daddy had to sell out and leave the ranching business.

He had a friend in Big Lake named Lewis Evans, who owned a chain of grocery stores throughout West Texas. Daddy asked Lewis to hire him and help him to learn the grocery business. Lewis told Daddy, "Shorty, I can't picture you in an apron, but if that is what you want, I will do it."

Daddy worked in Lewis's store in Crane for two years, learned the business, and bought his own "Mom and Pop" store in Big Spring. The Airport Grocery, located adjacent to Webb Air Force Base, was a gold mine. Daddy retired at age sixty-two and lived comfortably thereafter.

Daddy sent the son a letter a few years ago with payment for the other rancher's part of the cattle feed. The son sent the money back with a nice letter.

I saw the son at the Rocker b reunion, and we had a short, cordial visit.

Do not wait for six strong men to take you to church.
—Unknown

Penny and I decided we needed to attend church regularly. She had been raised as a Presbyterian, but I convinced her we should try the Baptist church, although she preferred the Methodist as a compromise.

The first Sunday service we attended was the last day of a revival, and the guest preacher was wound up preaching hellfire and brimstone and slipping in inappropriate commentary about the Catholic president, John Kennedy, and the Pope. We sang several verses of the invitational hymn without the preacher getting any response to his strident plea for all sinners to come forward and be saved from everlasting damnation.

> *I like your Christ. I do not like your Christians. Your Christians are so unlike your Christ.*
> —Mohandas Gandhi

The preacher then said that he knew there were many lost souls in the sanctuary—those saved knew who they were—and asked each Christian to take a nonbeliever by the arm and lead them to the altar and salvation. We both had a problem with that and the comments about Kennedy, even though we had not voted for him. It was the last time we were in a Baptist church for many years. We started attending the Methodist church with our friends John and Merline Riggs. There, we found the Methodist service based more on a loving God than a fearful God.

November 22, 1963, remains etched in my memory. I was behind one of the cash registers in the college store, and Penny was helping sort mail when Dr. O. A. Grant walked in and announced President Kennedy had been shot, and his next words were, "They sure as hell will think we are all a bunch of right-wing crazies now."

I did not understand his comment but realized later that he very concisely summed up the prevailing attitude about Texas, particularly Dallas, by the rest of the nation.

Tarleton came to a standstill as students, faculty, and administrators crowded before the few black-and-white televisions scattered across campus. All were shocked, and some wept as we tried to make sense of what had happened and why it had happened.

It was not a good time for our nation, Texas, and especially Dallas.

My grades overall at Tarleton were satisfactory, but there were three classes that gave me great difficulty: zoology, algebra, and accounting.

Dr. Lamar Johanson had not been a Tarleton professor for very long when I twice withdrew from his zoology class with a WF (withdraw failing). Those two black marks are the only failures on my transcript. Years later, I mentioned to Lamar that he had twice failed me. Lamar responded, "You should have studied harder."

Lamar and his lovely wife, Marilyn, are good friends and have retired on their ranch between San Saba and Goldthwaite. Marilyn knows as much about me as anyone, because she taught in the public school system with my aunts, Geneva and Gladys. Lamar is the former dean of the College of Arts and Sciences at Tarleton and was the executive director of Tarleton State University-Central Texas in Killeen prior to his retirement. A sports enthusiast, Lamar served for many years as the NCAA compliance officer for Tarleton. He and Marilyn attend every Tarleton sporting event, whether they are in Texas, New Mexico, Oklahoma, or California.

Ross tells of the time the Tarleton basketball team was to play an away game his freshmen year. Ross went to one of his professors and told him he would miss a lab and test and asked when he could make them up. The professor went into a tirade, telling Ross that he needed to decide if he was a student or an athlete and that if he missed either the test or lab, he would flunk the course. Ross went to Coach Perry, who always called him "Bigun," and asked what he should do.

"Don't worry about it, Bigun. Dr. Johanson will take care of it," and he did.

When he returned from the trip, the professor was most friendly to Ross, telling him he could make up the lab and test at his convenience. During warm-ups before the next home game, Ross noticed the professor at the game. The professor along with his young son attended all home games thereafter. When Ross returned from a road trip, the professor would query him if Tarleton had won and how many points he had scored, and he would engage Ross in conversation to explain the intricacies of the game.

When you are dissatisfied and want to return to your youth think of Algebra.
—Will Rogers

Algebra and its formulas completely baffle me. $X + Y = Z$ makes absolutely no sense, and it has no practical value in my everyday world. Therefore, why are college students required to take algebra? Algebra teachers tell me that it trains the mind to think in the abstract. They, of course, are only protecting their jobs. I have lived sixty-nine years, and I do not know anyone who uses algebra in his or her life or work. I know why students are required to take algebra. Colleges need a way to flunk freshmen.

Again, Tarleton, George Cook, and my algebra teacher, Coach Oscar Frazier, took a different approach. Mr. Cook let Penny take the course with me. Coach Frazier and Penny tutored me immediately following class, and Penny tutored me again at night. I passed with a low, low D.

Business majors were required to take four semesters of accounting. The first semester I made a B, the second semester a C, and the third semester a D. Accounting is progressive, with each course building the foundation for the next, but I was obviously not progressing. I waited until the final semester of my senior year to take the last course. I had to pass to graduate. I went into the final exam needing to make a high B to receive a D. I left the final exam knowing that I had not done so.

My whole life was passing before my eyes. What would I tell Penny, my parents, her parents? I would not graduate. I would have to take the course over during the summer and probably not pass. I would lose my Army commission.

Grades were posted outside the classroom after an exam, so I went to check my results. There was no grade beside my name, but I did have a note to see the professor. When I entered his office and took a seat, the conversation went something like this:

"Mr. Taylor, are you married?"

"Yes, sir," I said.

"Do you have a child?"

"Yes, sir."

"Does your wife work in the college store?"

"Yes, sir."

"Do you work in the college store?" he asked.

"Yes, sir."

"Do you need to pass this course to graduate?"

"Yes, sir," I said.

"Are you going into the Army?"
"Yes, sir."
"Will you have to go to Vietnam?"
"I probably will, sir."

He then mumbled something about me having enough trouble without him giving me more and dismissed me. I received a much-undeserved grade of a D for that course.

It is obvious that a significant event happened in our life while we were at Tarleton. We became parents, two children raising a child. The honeymoon, which we did not have, was not over, and eleven months later, we were parents.

Given maternity leave from her job, another example of Tarleton taking care of its own, Penny had returned to her parents on the Rocker b a week before to await the birth.

The call came around three in the morning from Pen's mother. Penny was in labor, and I should get on the road to San Angelo, as the baby could come at any time. The morning was dreary and foggy with limited visibility, and I was driving much too fast for road conditions. Somewhere between Santa Anna and Ballinger, I almost rear-ended an eighteen-wheeler. This scared me, and I slowed down. I realized I could have been killed or seriously injured. I would not have known if my child had been born or the sex, because sonograms did not exist at the time. I arrived at the hospital long before the baby arrived. There had been several deliveries that morning, and the doctor had slowed Pen's labor, so she had to wait her turn. She was in much pain, but finally, her turn came.

Herbie Ross Taylor, Jr., was born at 1247 on December 6, 1961, in the Clinic Hospital, San Angelo. Dr. Roy E. Moon was the attending physician. Herbie, Jr, weighed seven pounds and one ounce, and he was twenty-one inches long.

Life is not measured by the breaths you take but by the moments that take your breath away.
—Unknown

The first time I saw him, the nurse brought him out of the delivery room, holding him by his ankles. He was wet, somewhat bloody, and he had a pointed head, large mouth, all arms and legs, and boy was he mad. He looked like a plucked chicken throwing a temper tantrum. I knew there had to be something wrong, but I was told that all babies looked like that at birth.

This boy from Barnhart had a boy.

I was pleased.

Later that afternoon, the nurse told me that she would be bringing the baby to his mother and that I would be the only one allowed in the room. Pen's mother overheard the nurse and said that she was going in as well, and she did. I guess the nurse decided to leave well enough alone. The first thing Pen did was unwrap the blanket and count his fingers and then his toes. Then she smiled and said, "He is beautiful," and he was. And so was she.

I spent the night at Mudgie's house, and after I visited the hospital, I drove back to Tarleton for classes.

Sometime that afternoon, the nurse asked Pen to complete the forms to name the baby. Both her mother and my mother were there, and some discussion took place about the appropriateness of using Herbie as a first name. Penny and I had agreed that if he were a boy, he would be named after me.

We had not discussed a girl's name, simply because it was not a possibility.

Pen's mother believed that Herbie was a nickname and that he should be named Herbert. My mother insisted I was Herbie, not Herbert, and if he were to be a junior, he had to be named Herbie. Pen's mother, being the lady she was, demurred, and Herbie it was; however, he has always been called Ross, except by Mudgie, who called him "Feller."

Ross's first trip from the Rocker b allowed him to play baby Jesus in the Christmas pageant at the First Presbyterian Church in Big Lake. He was ten days old. I am told he did not cry and he was the perfect baby Jesus. I wish I could have seen the pageant, but I was in Stephenville.

Penny and Baby Ross at the Rocker b.

Ross brought a new dimension to our lives. The first priority of working parents is finding affordable day care with someone you trust. We found the best, and her name was "Big Momma." I do not remember her last name, if I ever knew it. I always wrote the check to "Big Momma."

Big Momma kept no more than one infant and eight to ten kids from toddler to around six years of age. Usually, she had five or six children in her house. She fed three meals a day, if needed. Our routine was to feed Ross breakfast. He would eat the noon meal at Big Momma's and the evening meal at home. I would retrieve Ross after classes or work, depending on my schedule. There were times when he was there all day.

Big Momma loved kids, and Ross was quite comfortable with her just as were we. I would fix things that Big Momma needed fixing around her house and yard, and when I came for Ross, she would usually give me some of whatever she had cooked to take home for supper.

One afternoon, I came to get Ross and walked into her house to find her holding an infant and crying. I took one look at the baby, knew that it was dead, and told her so. She was in shock, but she had called the fire department.

I left her with the infant, took all the kids to a back room, and began to call parents to come get their children. The infant had died from sudden infant death syndrome. It was sad, because the parents were older and this was their first child.

Big Momma was devastated and resolute that she would no longer keep children.

Louis Lee and Lou Dickey, now Grandmother and Granddad Farr, met us in Ballinger and took Ross to the Rocker b. Penny and I waited two weeks, went to Big Momma, and told her that it was not her fault that the child died and that we wanted her to continue to keep Ross. She agreed only until we found another caregiver. After a few days, other parents did the same, and soon, she was keeping most of the original group. This was best for Big Momma, Ross, and us.

Our best friends during college were John and Merline Riggs. The Riggs were from Galena Park near Houston. John was a football player, and Merline worked for one of the local banks. John and I were in ROTC and both majoring in business. The four of us had much in common, as there were few married couples attending Tarleton.

John and Merline had not yet had a child, and they enjoyed keeping Ross and did so often. One or the other would show up on our doorstep and ask if they could keep him for a while, and we were more than glad to oblige.

One Saturday, John called and wanted us to go to the picture show with them that night. The movie was *Ice Palace*, which was based on Edna Ferber's book of the same title. We begged off, as we were not about to try to take Ross with us. He was an infant and would surely get restless and cry. John kept calling and saying that Ross would be okay.

Finally, I told him, "John, we will go if you agree to take Ross to the lobby if he starts crying."

John agreed.

John saw very little of the movie.

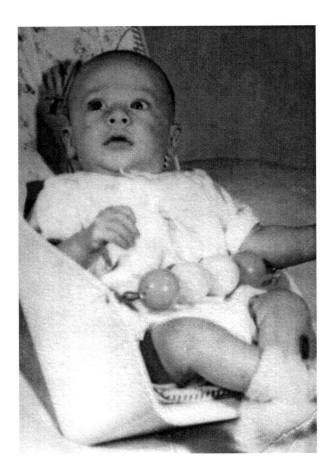

Mr. Ross Taylor

John was an outstanding football player, first-team small college all-American at linebacker, and his senior year, he played in at least one all-star football game. Commissioned as second lieutenants, we went into the Army together. John did not intend to make the Army a career, as the Army required too much moving, so he did his time, got out, and went to work in the communications industry. I followed John's career. He moved more often than I did. Today, he is retired on a golf course near Houston.

The Herbie Taylor Family

During my time at Tarleton, a fellow by the name of Marshal Proctor set the all-time scoring record in basketball. Little did I know that twenty years later, Ross would break Marshal's record, graduate Tarleton, and be inducted into Tarleton's Athletic Hall of Fame alongside John and Marshal.

The world had turned over many times by then.

PART III

Soldiering Years

9

The Army

The evening of May 31, 1964, I walked across the auditorium stage and was handed a diploma as a graduate of Tarleton State College. Immediately following, I was administered the oath of office as a commissioned officer in the US Army by Lieutenant Colonel John Miller, Tarleton's professor of military science. Mother and Penny pinned on my gold "butter bars" as a second lieutenant. I was in the Army now! It was a significant moment in my life. I was very proud, and I am sure Penny and Mother were as well.

My oath of office read:

> I, Herbie Ross Taylor, having been appointed an officer in the Army of the United States, in the grade of Second Lieutenant, do solemnly swear that I will support and defend the Constitution of the United States against all enemies, foreign or domestic, that I will bear true faith and allegiance to the same; that I take this obligation freely, without any mental reservation or purpose of evasion; and that I will well and faithfully discharge the duties of the office I am about to enter. So help me God.

A simple oath with no loopholes, "no" when it suits my purpose and "yes" if I agree. There it is—take the oath or walk away. I took it. All professions have oaths. The oath is one of the distinctive marks of a profession. The preceding is for an officer. Enlisted soldiers take a similar oath, except they swear their oath to the officers appointed over them rather than the US Constitution, an important distinction. My profession was now the profession of arms.

Penny, Herbie, and Alyene, Tarleton Graduation, May 31, 1964.

I received orders to report to active duty at Fort Benjamin Harrison, Indianapolis, Indiana, for attendance at the adjutant general officer basic course (AGOBC). The accompanying letter suggested I not bring family members with me, as the post had no quarters for second lieutenants. Off-post rental property was in short supply and expensive, and the course would be quite rigorous and require my full attention.

My journey outside the familiar confines of Texas had begun. A trip to Ruidoso and Carlsbad Cavern, New Mexico, and several trips to Old Mexico were the only times I had been outside Texas. I was looking forward to seeing the Mississippi River.

Penny, Ross, and I made the trip in our almost-new 1964 Ford Fairlane. As I continued to hang around the Ford dealership, looking at new cars and wishing, retrieving Ross from their service bays and offices for three years, I became friends with the owner. One day during my last semester at Tarleton, he said, "Taylor, I have a couple of new Fairlanes on the lot. Pick the one you like. I will cover the insurance, and you can start paying me when you graduate and start earning an army salary." I was overwhelmed then and now that this man would do such a thing. I think he was sweet on both Penny and Ross.

When we arrived in Indianapolis, we found an unfurnished, short-term rental at 2159 North Arlington, quite a distance from Fort Harrison. We got cots, bedding, cooking utensils, and other items from the Harrison lending closet, and we set up housekeeping. The apartment was not air-conditioned, and it is hot in Indianapolis in the summertime. We were camping out; however, the course was only nine weeks, and we were together. There were many children Ross's age in the apartment complex, and the kids would play together in the common area. Ross quickly earned a reputation from the other mothers. All the kids had a tricycle, except Ross. He would go to a kid, pull them off their tricycle, and take it. No amount of whippings or talking to Ross improved the situation. We decided to buy him a tricycle, even though we could not afford one. This did not solve the problem. Ross was often so busy playing that he forgot to go to the bathroom. Other kids would come up to Penny and tell her, "Ross smells." He was now almost three.

I reported to my class advisor on July 23, 1964, and began the AGOBC. There were fifty or so second lieutenants in the class, mostly from the east coast. I was the only student from Texas.

The military is one of the few institutions in this country that focuses on developing leaders and improving leadership. The military's hierarchical structure is designed to identify the best and brightest at each level and push them upward. Officers are expected to mentor those below them. I was part of a very clear structure, which was comforting. I knew my place. I was embarking on the first of several military schools I would attend over my career, each more innovative, introspective, and demanding.

I soon realized I was the only student proficient in all military subjects, such as map reading, land navigation, drill and ceremonies, and physical training, and I was the only one who scored expert with the M-14 rifle and the Colt, US Army M1911 45 ACP pistol. My officer development officer (ODO), Major Dorsey Greene, an Armor officer, wanted to see me. I thought I had been doing quite well academically with an average in the mid-to high eighties, but Greene did not think so. He told me I was the top man in the class based on leadership and pure military performance but that academically, I was in the middle of the pack. He told me that if I would get my grades up, I could be the honor graduate. I told him I was doing my best. Guess those Ivy League types spent all their time studying. They sure as hell could not shoot. Maybe it was what they were smoking.

One morning, we had a lecture presented by a warrant officer from the Criminal Investigation Detachment (CID). He asked us to look to our right and then our left. He stated that at least 50 percent of us had experimented with marijuana; therefore, either the man on the left or the man on the right or both had smoked marijuana. I had no idea what he was talking about. There hadn't been any marijuana in Barnhart. I had done more than my share of cigarettes and whiskey, but I had never used marijuana. I would not be exposed to marijuana until Vietnam.

Completing the basic course, this boy from Barnhart was off to the real Army, "the Mean, Green, Fighting Machine" at Fort Hood, Texas.

Located adjacent to Killeen, Texas, Fort Hood is the Army's largest installation and its only two-division post. The post is named for Confederate General John Bell Hood, who commanded the Texas Brigade at the Battle of Gettysburg. It is sixty miles north of the capital city, Austin, 160 miles from Dallas, and 150 miles from San Antonio. Fort Hood encompasses 339 square miles and supports a population of 218,000. This population consists of 4,733 officers, 39,262 enlisted soldiers, 74,000 family members, 90,000 retirees, and 8,900 Department of Army Civilians (DACs), and Nonappropriated Fund (NAF) employees.

I reported in to Fort Hood on September 25, 1964, and I was assigned to the 1st Armored Division (Old Ironsides). The 2nd Armored Division (Hell on Wheels) was the other division at Fortress Hood. Today, only the names have changed. The 1st Cavalry Division, the 3rd Armored Cavalry Regiment and the First Army Division West now call Hood home. Fort Hood was also the home then as now of the III Armored Corps (Phantom Corps) of WWII fame.

Fort Hood has changed significantly from 1964 to the present, and the change has not been in just brick and mortar, although that change has been prominent. The change at Fort Hood mirrors the change in the Army, and that change has been pronounced.

In 1964, the Army was an Army of conscripts, many, probably most, who did not want to be in the Army. Today, we have a volunteer Army—the majority of whom want to be in the Army. Disciplinary and training problems have been greatly reduced. The fact that the soldier of today and the soldier of 1964 still come from the middle to lower end of the socioeconomic ladder remains, but it is reality. This reality does not speak well for the nation and does not serve the nation well. It is part of the "me" mentality. Let the other poor bastard serve their country, or as Vice-President Cheney so eloquently stated when asked why he had not served in Vietnam, "I had better things to do."

There are the names of over fifty-eight thousand Americans on the panels of the Vietnam Memorial in Washington, D.C., and most of them had better things to do. Because I have served in both the draftee and the volunteer Army, I can tell you that our Army is a better Army today. That is not to say that the soldier of the Vietnam era was not as good as today's soldier. Several million great soldiers served during the Vietnam years. Smart soldiers and highly educated. I had several soldiers who served under me and had master's degrees. The majority did their duty and went home. A few did not, and that small percentage took up an inordinate amount of a leader's time.

Another significant difference is that today's Army is a married Army. In 1964, almost all of the conscripts were single, as were many of the junior officers. Today, there are 5,304 enlisted quarters for families on Fort Hood. In 1964, enlisted family quarters were almost nonexistent. These quarters are located in various areas within Fort Hood and are centered around a community neighborhood consisting of a chapel, childcare, and post exchange facility. Single enlisted soldiers live in ninety-eight separate enlisted barracks. These are not the WWII wooden barracks most people remember. They are brick and configured much as you would expect to find in a university residence hall. Over 80 percent of the enlisted force now lives on Fort Hood.

The housing situation for married officers is almost as dismal today as it was in 1964. Some new quarters have been built for the generals, of course, and others are being built; however, the demand still greatly exceeds the supply. The Wherry Housing at 210 Wascow Avenue, which was built in the early 1950s, the place where Penny and I lived when

I was a first lieutenant in 1965, is now used to house junior enlisted soldiers and their families. Most officers live off-post in the surrounding communities. Officers receive a housing allowance based on the grade of the officer when they are not residing in government quarters, and the higher the grade, the larger the allowance. Realtors and civilians owning rental property know exactly what this allowance is and always charge over the allowance to allow you to rent their property, and they want a long-term lease. If you want to keep your family with you, then you pay and cut costs elsewhere.

When I first came into the Army, there was an old saying that went, "If the Army wanted you to have a wife, the Army would have issued you one." That was true. But even then, the times were a-changing, and attempts were being made to improve conditions for the family.

Officers' wives were expected to volunteer their time to work in the thrift shop and the Red Cross office, belong to the Officers' Wives' Club, host monthly teas, and teach classes to young enlisted wives on how to balance a checkbook, shop, or cook, and they had to participate in all the charitable organizations and fund-raisers on post. They were expected not to work. If a wife worked or failed to participate as appropriate, a comment to this effect was placed in her husband's officer evaluation report (OER). A complimentary report about the wife was also included when it was fitting. Penny was always mentioned as an asset to me and the Army in my reports. The Army considered you a team, and the wife also served. I saw wives make or break their husbands' careers.

I bought into this thinking for a long time, as did Penny. That was just the way it was. This thinking, rightfully so, has changed. Today, many officers' wives work, mainly to make ends meet. Military pay for officers continues to lag behind the civilian sector for similar education and responsibility. Those wives that work generally volunteer and help where they can. There is no mention of the wife in the OER of today, either good or bad. In fact, it is prohibited.

The saying that you hear today is, "The soldier enlists, and the family reenlists." How true. If Momma is not happy, then nobody is happy.

Consequently, the Army and the US Congress have made great strides in improving the living conditions of the Army family, but much work remains to be done, especially in the areas of health and childcare, housing, and pay. The Army is experiencing difficult times in reenlisting the family primarily because of the short turnaround time to a war zone or other deployments. Simply stated, the Army is too small to perform the missions that our president and the civilian leadership have given it. Wives and children live in constant fear that something will happen to Daddy. He is home for a short period, and as soon as all adjust to being a family again, he is gone once more. I can tell you from experience that the easy part is the soldiering, because you are too busy to dwell on your misery. The hard part is the waiting family who remain in a state of limbo.

The status of the units at Fort Hood is another big change from the 1960s. When I arrived at Fort Hood, the 1st and 2nd Armored Divisions could not move across US Highway 190, which parallels Fort Hood much less to Europe to fight the Soviets which was their contingency mission. The Vietnam Conflict was rapidly escalating, and there was not much use for large, heavy armored forces in the rice paddies and jungles of the Republic of Vietnam (RVN). Therefore, the two divisions were used as a source for replacements to staff the force in the RVN. Most M60A1 main battle tanks were placed into administrative storage, as there were insufficient crews to operate and maintain them.

> *To be prepared for war is one of the most effectual means of preserving the peace.*
> —George Washington

Once again, our Army was fighting the politician's war in a far and distant land, and once again, the Army was unprepared. Vietnam was the war of the "ninety-day wonder lieutenant," the "shake-and-bake NCO," the one-year combat tour, the six-month command tour, and of all things, Project 100,000.

Lyndon Johnson and Robert McNamara cooked up Project 100,000 under the guise of providing minority and disadvantaged youth, ones who were unable to pass the Army's mental aptitude test, the opportunity to join the Army, learn a skill transferable to civilian life, and improve their lot in life. I kid you not! The other part of the deal was that they would go to Vietnam, fill the empty foxholes, serve as riflemen, and have the opportunity to die for their country. What a deal. The great society at its best.

> *God and the Soldier, we adore,*
> *In time of danger, not before,*
> *The danger passed and all things righted,*
> *God is forgotten and the Soldier slighted*
> —Rudyard Kipling

I first heard "No more Task Force Smiths" when I was an ROTC cadet, and it has continued to be the Army's mantra. Task Force Smith was an undermanned, poorly equipped and provisioned, untrained, 406-man infantry unit sent to Korea in July 1951 to conduct a delaying action while the Army organized to come to the aid of the South Koreans. General Douglas MacArthur haughtily called this small, ill-equipped unit an "arrogant display of strength" as they flew out of Japan. This great battle captain thought that the mere presence of US troops would stop the North Koreans in their tracks when they met the "invincible" US Army. The soldiers of Task Force Smith fought bravely, but they were soundly routed.

The end of World War II, the Korean War, the Vietnam War, the Cold War, and the first Gulf War all saw the predictable and inevitable downsizing of the Army. Our Army is not manned or prepared to fight the next war. Americans love the soldier when he is bleeding and dying on a foreign battlefield, but how quickly they forget!

Our small, over tasked, and inadequately equipped Army of today is a direct result of the so-called "Peace Dividend" that was supposed to accrue from America's victory over the Soviet Union at the end of the Cold War. The nation had no more "big bad bear" to fight, so the politicians said, "Let's reduce the size of the Army, stop procurement of any new weapon systems, reduce base support, and training and maintenance funds. And while we are at it, have them transform themselves into a smaller, lighter, leaner force that makes maximum use of new technology." This plays well at election time, but not so well with the sergeant first-class, first sergeant, captain, and lieutenant colonel who are expected to fight the next war.

The Army's problems, this time, started with the first President Bush. All of the plans to emasculate the Army were drawn up during his administration, and they were in the process of implementation when the first Gulf War required that they put the plans on hold. The war ended, and the plans were implemented. The second President Bush and his successor struggle under the constraints of an Army much too small for the missions it is expected to accomplish.

My first office at Fort Hood was a WWII building. This building now houses the 1st Cavalry Division Museum, and the building looks a hell of a lot better today than it did in 1964. I later moved to the old hospital area when a new modern hospital was built. That hospital is now near fifty years of age and showing it, and is soon to be replaced, thanks to stimulus funding.

The leadership of the 1st Armored Division (Old Ironsides) was superb. Major General Jablonski, a former football player at West Point, was the division commander. Colonel Albert Wing and later Colonel George Taylor (no relation) served as the division chief of staff. My immediate supervisors were Captain Dandolo M. Janutolo, Captain Richard E. Hohl, Major E. C. Lytle, and Lieutenant Colonel John Weston, the adjutant general.

I rarely saw Weston except for briefings and ceremonies.

Major Lytle had served in most grades in the Army, ranging from private to master sergeant and warrant officer, and he received a direct commission to captain. He was promoted to lieutenant colonel while I was at Fort Hood and eventually retired as a full colonel. He was tiny, around five-foot-six and 135 pounds. He had a tanned, leathery face with a permanent scowl and gravelly voice, and I never saw him happy. He also had a little man's ego. Lytle was one of the finest teachers and leaders that I had the privilege to serve.

Once Captain Janutolo and I had done something that upset him, and he called us into his office for a "come to Jesus" meeting. He motioned us to a chair after we had reported to him. His chairs almost sat on the floor. Even so, he had his legs crossed and was sitting on them behind his desk to make himself appear even taller. He looked us in the eye and said, "Janutolo, you have two bars, and Taylor, you have one. And neither one of you will have any if you fuck up like this again. Now get out."

We did and quickly.

Both Dick Hohl and Dan Janutolo were fine, experienced officers. In fact, they were very experienced. Promotions had come almost to a standstill after the Korean War. Both officers had been in the Army between twelve and fourteen years. In comparison, I was promoted to captain after only thirty-one months in the Army, thanks to the Vietnam War. I lost track of Dick Hohl over the years, but I know Dan retired as a lieutenant colonel. In one of my Army magazines, I read that Dan had died. They were both good officers, and they taught me a lot.

I spent the first nine months in the field. My unit would participate in training exercises for a couple of weeks and return to main post, clean up our gear, and then be off for three or four days, and then we would do it all over again. I liked that, and so did Penny. I would leave for the field, and she and Ross would leave for the Rocker b and then return the day before I came out of the field.

Penny and Ross at the Rocker b.

This got her out of the dump at 724 Carrie Avenue in Killeen, where we were living at the time and paying too much money, but it was a place we had been very lucky to find. My basic pay as a second lieutenant was $222.30 a month. Even so, we were living better than we had been in college. I remember visiting with newly married second lieutenants and their wives over twenty-five-cent drinks at the Officer's Club on Friday nights and listening to them complain about how little they made and how much they could be making on the outside if it were not for the Vietnam War. Their current life did not measure up to their carefree college days when they were spending Daddy's money.

The Friday night officer calls at the Officer's Club was an Army tradition. Officers were expected to meet by unit at the club and develop comradeship and "*esprit de corps.*" Often the officers and their ladies were invited to meet at the club, have drinks during the social hour, and later eat dinner at the club. This was an opportunity for the junior officers to hobnob with their bosses and their ladies and one for the bosses and their ladies to get to know their junior officers and their ladies. If the ladies were present, the affair was more subdued, but you could be assured that your boss's lady was making mental notes about you and your lady. Today, the Army has deemphasized alcohol, and the tradition is less prevalent. The "dining in," a formal affair, is now used to achieve the same purpose.

The last line of my OER when I was leaving Hood read, "Lieutenant and Mrs. Taylor are active socially and make the perfect military family team." Penny did well. She did not always go to the Rocker b while I was in the field, especially if she was expected to attend a social function.

I would usually return from the field at least once to pick up supplies, and I would drop by the house. We had a standing greeting that we used throughout our time in the Army. She would say, "Are you home for clean underwear, sex, or booze?"

I would answer, "All three."

After the nine months or so in the field, Lytle assigned me to be the assistant chief of personnel management, working for Dan Janutolo. My job was to fill all levies received from Department of the Army (DA). Weekly, a cable would be received from DA, directing that the 1st AD ship a specified number of soldiers to Vietnam or elsewhere, but rarely elsewhere. The cable contained the numbers of soldiers by grade and military occupational specialty (MOS).

I recommended that we first ship those who had been at Hood the longest. The command group approved this.

Soldiers I initially identified for shipment had been at Hood for eight or more years (homesteaders) and were largely in the grade of sergeant first-class or master sergeant. Upon receipt of orders, some showed up on my office doorstep with their wives, kids, lawyers, bankers, or prominent businesspersons. Their petition was that they could not be reassigned because they were assets to the community and/or owners of businesses, had a loan they could not repay in Vietnam, were out of shape, had to take prescription drugs. And the reasons went on and on.

My reply was, "Sergeant, you have your orders. Comply."

They and theirs often appealed to the command group of the 1st Armored Division, III Corps, or their congressman, which resulted in me writing responses justifying my reasons for sending them to Vietnam. Not once was I overturned. Some tried to retire, but that, too, was disapproved. I do not remember one of these "homesteaders" beating the system, but several Killeen businesses went belly-up.

Another policy I established was that we would take volunteers. And many volunteered, but often with caveats. "Don't tell my first sergeant, sergeant major, commander, or wife that I am volunteering," they would say.

And to those, I would respond, "I am only taking volunteers, but I won't tell your wife."

Most said, "I understand. Put me down as a volunteer."

And I did.

Receiving a levy from DA for a particular grade and MOS held by a volunteer, one of my soldiers would call his brigade sergeant major, and tell him that one of his soldiers had volunteered. The sergeant major would also be told that it was not his brigade's time to provide a soldier or that if it was, he could provide the name of another soldier rather than the volunteer. It was the brigade's choice, but they had two days to decide.

One morning, I looked up from my desk and a brigade commander (full colonel) and his sergeant major were standing there. I rose to an abbreviated position of attention, and the brigade commander proceeded to accuse me of selling assignments. The more he shouted, the madder he got, and it was not pretty. He was going to the Criminal Investigation Detachment (CID) to have me investigated. He was going to the commanding general, and he was going to have me thrown out of the Army, if not in prison.

The colonel said all this in front of perhaps eight of my soldiers, as I did not have a private office.

He wheeled and departed along with his sergeant major.

Major Lytle had heard the ruckus, and after the colonel's departure, he told me to come with him. We got in Lytle's jeep, he driving, and proceeded to the chief of staff's office, where I explained what had happened.

The next day, I was again at my desk when I looked up to see the same brigade commander, his sergeant major, Major Lytle, Dick Hohl, Dan Janutolo, and the soldiers of the Personnel Management Branch assembled. The brigade commander then apologized to my soldiers and me. I do not know if he was contrite, as my eyes were fixed on his sergeant major. The sergeant major soon volunteered for Vietnam. The brigade commander did not object.

An aside to all this is that when assigned as assistant chief of personnel management, my NCOIC, a master sergeant (E-8), was one of the first I sent to Vietnam. I realized that he had a paying position as a NAF employee overseeing various activities at Fortress Hood to include the bowling alley and that he had not "hit a lick" for the Army in years. His departure got the attention of those I worked for and who worked for me, establishing the credibility I would need later.

The soldier I made my NCOIC was a staff sergeant (E-6). He showed up at my office one day after he had been transferred to Hood from another post. He told me he was broke, out of gas, family in his car, no place to stay, and he asked if I could help. He did not beg, but intuitively, I knew he was telling the truth. When I walked out the front of the building, I saw his worn-out car, his wife, and four kids. I told him to bring his family inside out of the heat while I made phone calls. When I called Army Emergency Relief (AER), I got him a small interest-free loan. The finance office was willing to give him an advance on his next paycheck. Transient billeting agreed to put him and his family up for a few days, and I gave him my personal check for seventy-five dollars.

When I told Penny that night, she was not happy. We did not have seventy-five dollars to loan to anyone. She thought I would never be repaid. She asked how I could have done what I had and given money to a perfect stranger when she, Ross, and I had our own needs. However, it was one of the best investments I have ever made. The sergeant did repay me, and with interest, by being completely loyal and one of the best NCOs I had assigned over the years. He was promoted to sergeant first-class (E-7) before I left Hood.

Another success story is a fellow I will call Ray. When Lytle initially assigned me to permanent field duty, I inherited a few NCOs from the lieutenant I was replacing. All were good NCOs, but I had the feeling something was missing. They were young. None had combat experience, and I thought we all needed the expertise of a grizzled, old warrior, someone who had been there and done that.

As I wandered around Lytle's outer office one day, I spied what had to be the Army's oldest private. His name was Ray.

I struck up a conversation with Ray and found he had been a buck sergeant in a rifle company during the Korean War. He had reached the grade of master sergeant but had gone AWOL for almost a year over a love affair gone wrong, and classified as a deserter. A hillbilly from Appalachia, he hid out in the mountains until he was turned in by one of his kinfolk for a fifty-dollar reward. Ray was staying in the Hood detention facility and awaiting transfer to the military prison at Fort Leavenworth when the 1st Armored Division began desert maneuvers in California.

A battalion commander by the name of George Smith Patton, the son of General Patton of WWII fame, asked, because he was short troops, to take selected prisoners in the detention facility with him to California. This was approved, and Ray was one of the prisoners selected. Ray performed admirably in the desert, and Patton was able to get Ray's sentence commuted, except the part that busted him to private. Patton was transferred, and Ray ended up working for Lytle.

I told Dick Hohl that I wanted Ray. He said he would discuss it with Lytle. Lytle agreed, and Hohl told me, "Good choice."

During the remainder of my time as the field lieutenant, I had Ray by my side. A natural leader, all my soldiers looked up to him, as did I. Nightfall, when things usually got quiet, I would get Ray aside and ask him for advice and constructive criticism. Ray would say, "Lieutenant, you are the boss, and whatever you order, the men will do. They are good soldiers. But if you really want to know, I would have done this or that this way."

When I departed Hood, Ray was a buck sergeant and he was still keeping lieutenants straight in the field. I am told Ray retired as a sergeant first class.

One of the fun things I did as a second lieutenant was acting as the defense counsel for soldiers being court-martialed. You talk about having the deck stacked against you. The prosecutors on a court-martial were a judge advocate general officer, a lawyer, and normally at least a captain, and the defense counsel was a wet-behind-the-ears second lieutenant who knew next to nothing about the law. You learned quickly, though. Further, the Army would not bring a case to court-martial unless they had an airtight case. If there was a chance the soldier could get off, the matter was handled by nonjudicial punishment.

Very few of my cases actually went to trial. I would tell my soldier-client that he was likely going to do hard time in federal prison at Fort Leavenworth and the best bet would be to plead guilty and go for a plea bargain to get a reduced sentence. Most soldiers agreed, and I would go to the president of the court-martial board, a full colonel, and ask for a lighter sentence. Usually, the board president would agree.

I had one soldier who wanted a trial. He had been caught peeping into the bathroom of one of the VIP quarters in front of the III Corps headquarters. There were several VIP quarters located on a U-shaped street. The colonel's lady had seen the soldier peeping through the bathroom window and had shouted to the colonel, who called the MPs. The MPs arrived, and the soldier was still at the window. He saw the MPs and ran into the street and then into a second MP car that had arrived on the scene. This young degenerate was guilty, and the colonel and his lady were pissed

Appointed defense counsel, and as was my way, I went to his chain of command to find out what I could about the soldier. Sometimes I would discover information about a soldier that could have caused him to commit an act that he would not have normally done. For instance, his mother had recently died. His sister had been raped. He had been orphaned and raised in a foster home. I could use this information in extenuation or mitigation when I was working a plea bargain.

I visited with his first sergeant, and he told me, "Lieutenant, I got 149 of these hard dick sons of bitches, and 148 of them will lie, steal, or cheat to get between a woman's legs. And all this dumb bastard wants to do is look at it."

That pretty well summed it up for me, so it was plea bargain time.

The soldier had a different idea. He wanted a trial, and he wanted senior enlisted soldiers on his board. Obviously, he had been listening to a loudmouthed soldier who thought he knew it all, commonly called the "barracks lawyer." An enlisted soldier should never ask for senior enlisted members on his court-martial board. Senior enlisted soldiers take a dim view of soldiers getting into trouble and besmirching the enlisted reputation. Officers are generally more lenient toward an enlisted soldier.

In addition, he did not want me for a lawyer. He wanted a civilian lawyer. I explained to him that was his right but that he would have to pay for the lawyer and that he was still going to go to jail. I tried to tell him that he would be better off seeking a plea bargain.

He found a civilian lawyer in Killeen to take his case, and the lawyer wanted to see me. The lawyer asked me what I thought, and I told him the soldier was guilty and going to jail. He acknowledged that it was pretty much an open-and-shut case. He then told me he would put up a good defense, and he wanted me to interview a number of people and get this record and that document. I responded that my job was to introduce him to the court and nothing more. It was his job to do the legwork—that was why he was being paid. This sleazebag thought he could bluff me, a poor, dumb second lieutenant, into doing his work.

Mr. Lawyer put up a lousy defense. The soldier got the maximum sentence, and he still had to pay the lawyer. Today, a military lawyer represents the accused, so the playing field has been leveled.

There was one time at Fort Hood that I thought I might need a lawyer. The NCOs were having a farewell party for another NCO and invited me to come say a few words. I was told the time and that it was located at the corral on West Fort Hood. In 1965, West Fort Hood was a secretive place. When told the party was at the corral, a set of wooden pens to a boy from Barnhart, I had some difficulty in understanding where the party was actually located.

West Fort Hood was home to a US Air Force base at the time. Later, in cooperation with the Defense Atomic Support Agency, the

Army took control of West Fort Hood and renamed the airfield Gray Army Airfield in honor of Robert "Bullet" M. Gray. "Bullet" Bob Gray was a Killeen native and a former student at John Tarleton Agricultural College. Gray, a B-25 pilot, flew the third ship off the aircraft carrier *USS Hornet* on the famous Doolittle Raid on Tokyo in April 1942. He was killed six months later. He was flying another combat mission when his plane crashed near Assam, India. Unknown to the citizens of the surrounding area, West Fort Hood was one of the largest storage areas for nuclear weapons in the United States. Nuclear weapons were stored there from 1947 until 1969.

I did not want to go to the function by myself, so I dropped by the Officer's Club and talked a couple of my lieutenant friends into going with me. Both of these men had been imbibing and were already somewhat lubricated. Off we went after a couple of whiskeys, clearing security at the main gate of West Fort Hood and turning right onto the first road I came to as I had been told. (I was supposed to turn left.) It was a dirt road, and the night was quite dark; however, because I was going to a corral, that seemed reasonable. All of a sudden, I was blinded by an incredibly bright light, and I was brought to a quick stop.

I could see nothing, but I heard this authoritative voice from out of the light say, "Right-front passenger, disembark vehicle with hands over head and proceed to right front headlight. Rear-seat passenger, disembark vehicle with hands over head and proceed to rear of vehicle. Driver, disembark vehicle with hands over head and proceed to left front headlight."

I did as instructed and saw the outline of a man about twenty feet in front of me, and I saw very clearly the pistol he was holding. The barrel was the size of a 105mm howitzer. The lieutenant on my right exclaimed, "Oh, swell, it's a Mattel."

And I said, "Shut up, you drunk bastard."

We were spread-eagled, frisked, and interrogated, and our military ID cards were reviewed. When it was determined we were not spies, we were escorted off West Fort Hood and released. The incident was written up in the military police blotter, and Major Lytle read the blotter first thing every morning. I will not repeat what he had to say to me.

I later found out the Corral was an NCO club. Today, it is called the Longhorn Club.

In its infinite wisdom, the bigger Army decided that since the 1st AD was combat ineffective, the division could be used to conduct basic combat training (BCT) for new recruits. I was selected to head up this effort. I had been promoted to first lieutenant by this time. Colonel George Taylor (no relation), the chief of staff of the 1st Armored Division, and Penny did the honors.

Colonel Taylor, Lieutenant Taylor, and Penny Taylor.
Promotion to First Lieutenant.

What a difference between first and second lieutenant. Gone were the grudging salutes and "yes, sir," and "no, sir," from the enlisted soldiers. Changing the color of that gold bar to a silver bar made a world of difference. The soldiers, NCOs and even the senior officers treated you differently, almost as if you were one of them, not quite but almost.

Given a small staff to begin the process of receiving and processing basic trainees, I grew my own staff. I would pull one or two of the smarter soldiers graduating from basic training and assign them to me. The drill was that I would receive quotas by MOS for each graduating class by cable from DA for further assignment to another installation. There, the trainee would receive advanced individual training (AIT) and ultimate assignment as individual replacements for units in Vietnam. I sent soldiers to Fort Knox for training in armor, Fort Benning for training in infantry, Fort Sill for artillery, and so on.

How did I decide who went where? It was quite an advanced process. I usually received the quotas a couple of days before a class graduated, so the decision and assignment procedure had to be done quickly so that orders could be processed and placed into the soldiers hands upon graduation. I would go to my quarters (we now lived on post), and I would take a sheet of paper and write, "Infantry-96, Field Artillery-5, Signal-3 or Military Intelligence-2," until I had a sheet of paper for each quota. The number on the paper signified how many BCT graduates I had to select for training in that particular field. I would then review the trainees Armed Services Vocational Aptitude Battery (ASVAB) test results and how well they had done in BCT and then make a decision. If I decided infantry, I pitched his record in the infantry pile. If signal, in the signal pile, and so on.

I generally had too many in one pile and not enough in another. I would repeat the process until I had the right numbers in each pile and a degree of confidence that I had placed round pegs in round holes and square pegs in square holes. I was aware that my decision might be a death sentence for some of the soldiers, especially the ones I assigned for training in the combat arms. The next morning, I would take the files to the clerks to issue orders. That was the way it was done! I assigned over eleven thousand soldiers in this manner.

A few trainees that came to Hood had rare and unusual skills. One trainee had been a camera operator on movie sets in Hollywood and had received Academy Award acclaim for his work. I reported these soldiers to HQ DA, and DA provided me with assignment instructions. They usually got a job working in their civilian skill without further training.

I kept some soldiers at Fort Hood for on-the-job (OJT) training. These were soldiers needed to fill critical vacancies. I assigned several soldiers with law enforcement experience to military police units, some with accounting and finance degrees to the finance office, and if they could type, they were a candidate for my staff. This was not in my charter, but I quickly realized DA did not have a good handle on how many troops were being trained and where, so I cooked the books a little here and there, which made me quite popular with certain elements on post.

The recruits the 1st AD received to train were from army training centers, such as Fort Benning, Georgia; Fort Knox, Kentucky; Fort Sill,

Oklahoma; Fort Polk, Louisiana; and Fort Dix, New Jersey. They were excess to the training capacity at those installations and were shipped by bus or airplane to the 1st AD for BCT.

My brother-in law, Bill Farr, had been drafted and sent to Fort Polk, Louisiana, for basic training. I called my counterpart at Polk and asked him to hold Bill until Polk reached capacity and then send him to Hood to be trained, and he did. I assigned Bill to a training company commanded by a friend of mine from Muleshoe, Texas, named Captain Gaylord Tate. I do not think that Bill was aware of how he got to Fort Hood, although he did know I was assigned to Hood. I waited three weeks and called Gaylord and asked him how Bill was doing and when could I see him. Gaylord told me that Bill was one of his finest and that if I would drive up to the back door of his office around 1800, I could have him for a couple of hours.

Private Farr was scared that he had done something wrong, because it was highly unusual for a trainee to be summoned to the company commander's office. He was quite surprised, shocked actually, to see me pop through Gaylord's back door. I took Bill to our quarters, and Penny cooked a fine meal for her brother. This continued once a week or so until Bill graduated.

Some years later, Gaylord, then a major, was killed when his helicopter crashed on the north side of Fort Hood. Bill and I reminisce about him each time we see each other. Gaylord's wife, Ginny, grew up in Middle America, and she was visiting relatives when she was notified of Gaylord's death. Her plane had a layover in Indianapolis, where we were stationed at the time. Penny and I met Ginny at the airport and consoled her as best as we could. I have been in that airport many times since, 2005 being the most recent, and I always remember that sad day when we tried to comfort Ginny and understand why Gaylord had been taken much too early. Perhaps it is true that only the good die young.

Soon, I asked Bill what he wanted to be, and he declared a military policeman. I called the MP operations officer, another captain friend of mine, and told him the deal. He agreed to take him on if Bill had a clean record. I knew that Bill had an alcohol incident while at Texas Tech and that he might be a hard sell as a military policeman. I let my friend know that Fort Hood would most likely not receive any more trainees with lily-white records and law enforcement backgrounds. My friend got the picture. Later, he told me that Bill was the best young trooper in his outfit. Bill later served in an MP unit in Germany, where he did well.

I would meet every bus and planeload of trainees arriving at Fort Hood with cadre from the receiving training unit. I would account for the soldiers based on a roster from the sending installation and take possession of their records completed at a military entrance and processing station (MEPS) prior to their entry into the army. Each group of soldiers, usually around a hundred to 125, had a designated group leader. This trainee hand-carried the roster and records. If the trainees came by plane, the contract read that the pilot would bring them to Temple Airport. The airport had little navigational aids, no radar, and no operational tower, but it did have a long runway. The pilot was on VFR, and if he could not land because of weather, he was to go to the nearest airport where he could land. He was to call the Fort Hood Operations Center, which would relay his location to me, and I would go get the trainees.

A plane was due in late one evening, and I headed to Temple Airport to meet it. The weather was cloudy and stormy, with a ceiling around 900 feet. I was quite sure the plane would divert when it popped out of the clouds. It was a Constellation, a beautiful airplane, and everything was looking good until the plane rolled right and the right wing almost touched the runway. I guess it caught a crosswind. Somehow, the pilot got the plane level and was gone. I was in constant communication with the Hood Operations Center, but the pilot had not called in. I was also calling Love Field in Dallas, the Waco, Austin, and San Antonio airports with no luck. Around midnight, I called Major Lytle to tell him the situation, and his response went something like this, "Damn it, lieutenant. Why are you calling me in the middle of the night? You know what the mission is. Find those people and bring them to Hood. Out!"

Finally, I received a call from Hood Operations. They had received a call from the Austin airport that there were soldiers running loose all over the place and would someone please come get them. The pilot had never called. He had dumped the trainees on the tarmac at Austin and departed. I had a staff car and was able to travel faster, a lot faster, so I got the senior training NCO and headed for Austin. The trainees were indeed all over the inside and outside of the airport. I located the group leader and his roster, and I now knew how many by name we were looking for. We had all accounted for, and we had them formed up in a parking lot of the airport when the buses arrived.

In late 1965, I got the itch to move to an overseas assignment and see the world. To scratch that itch, I called the Adjutant General Officer Assignment Branch in Washington, D.C., and spoke with a little old lady who was responsible for lieutenant assignments. I told her I wanted to go overseas, and she asked, "Where?"

I said, "Anywhere."

She told me that she had no overseas vacancies for a lieutenant except Vietnam but that she could fill those requirements, and because I was so nice, she would check with the captain assignment officer and see if he had an overseas requirement for me. I wish I could remember this lady's name, because she was an institution. All lieutenants of my era would remember her.

When she called me back, she told me that there was a captain position in Turkey that I could fill. I had no idea where Turkey was located, but for a boy from Barnhart, it sounded exciting. I asked her about the job, and she said something like "cosmic registry," which meant nothing to me. I did not care what the job was, so I told her to "issue the tissue." I also asked that when she called Lytle to tell him that she was putting me on assignment orders, to please not tell him I had called her as that would make him very unhappy. She understood.

A couple of days later, Lytle called and asked, "How do you like Turkey?"

I said, "I don't eat it much. Usually just at Thanksgiving and Christmas."

"Damn it, lieutenant, not that turkey, the country Turkey. You'd better start liking it, because that's where you're going."

About two weeks later, the little lady called back in a tizzy and said, "You have got to go regular army, as your active duty commitment is about to expire. You must apply for a Top Secret clearance. You need a passport," and the list went on.

Now none of this can be accomplished overnight, and with the exception of the passport, all occurred after arrival in Turkey.

One of the folks who interviewed for my Top Secret clearance was Cotton Brooks. Cotton phoned Daddy and exclaimed, "What the hell is Herbie involved in? I have FBI people out here wanting to know all about him."

Commissioned in the reserves rather than the regular army, I had a two-year active duty commitment. I had wanted to be commissioned regular army out of college, but that had not happened.

The summer before my senior year, I attended ROTC summer camp at Fort Sill, Oklahoma. Summer camp is basic combat training for potential officers. The course was eight weeks, and if you finished in the top 20 percent of your hundred-man training company, had the required college grade point average, and the recommendation of your professor of military science, the Army could approve you for a regular army commission as a distinguished military graduate. If you planned to make the army a career, the regular army was the way to go.

Throughout summer camp, it appeared that I was in the top 20 percentile, and I was quite satisfied with my performance. A couple of days before graduation, the company tactical officer, a regular army captain, called each cadet in individually for a critique of their performance during the eight weeks and to tell them their final standing in the company.

He had some bad news for me. The tactical officer had me in the top 20, but the tactical NCO had me at the bottom of the class. The tactical NCO had rated another cadet with a last name of Taylor, well known by the cadets as a "screw-up," in the top 20. The tactical officer said he had discussed the situation with the tactical NCO and had asked if he had us mixed up, but the tactical NCO denied that had happened. The tactical officer told me he had also discussed the situation with the company commander, a regular army major, who had declined to discuss the matter with the tactical NCO. Thus, both Taylors had their scores averaged, and both finished in the middle of the pack.

We cadets had long-suspected that the tactical NCO had a drinking problem. He was often late for 0530 morning formations and disappeared during night tactical problems, and in general, he had a difficult time keeping up with us young bucks. I suspect the company commander was aware of the problem and did not want to deal with it during summer camp. The two officers and the NCO were all from different universities, and the company commander probably decided that it was the parent university's problem.

This taught me a valuable lesson: It is an officer's responsibility to deal immediately with a disciplinary problem. Disciplinary problems do not improve with age.

A side note is that many years later when I was chief of the Adjutant General Officer Assignment Branch, I had the responsibility to recommend officers with a poor performance record over an extended period to a "show cause" board. This other Taylor was one of several officers I recommended to appear before the board. I could say that what goes around comes around, but although the board decision was that he be separated from active duty, he had enough time to retire.

People make choices. Choices make people.
—Unknown

Penny and I discussed the Army as a career and decided that if we were going overseas for three years, I should either apply for a regular army commission or get out. The process dictated that you apply and then appear before a board of officers, and the board recommendation would be forwarded to DA for decision. I applied. The board recommended me, and DA approved my selection as a regular army officer in September 1966 after I had arrived in Turkey.

The officers of the Adjutant General Division had a fine farewell party for us. Lytle had been promoted to lieutenant colonel, and he was now the 1st Armored Division adjutant general. He gave a nice talk and made flattering remarks about Penny and me.

Lytle was a teetotaler. I had never seen him drink. He came up to me and told me he wanted to talk. He said that he did not drink but that this was a special occasion. We found a quiet corner of the club, and while I sipped my whiskey, he gave me some very valuable career tips and advice. I was quite moved that a senior officer would speak to a lieutenant in the manner that he did.

Lytle never touched his drink.

The next day, he presented me with the Army Commendation Medal in the 1st Armored Division headquarters conference room. I now had something to wear on my uniform.

We had been assigned to government quarters on Fort Hood in June 1965 at 210 Waskow Avenue. Penny loved having a nice home close to all facilities. The house, which was built in the early 1950s, was small with a kitchen, laundry room, dining room, living room, two bedrooms, a bath, and a carport. The day I signed for the quarters, this boy from Barnhart thought that he was in hog heaven. The house was so much better than anything we had lived in during our married life. Today (2011), the house still stands, and a corporal (E-4) and his family now make it their home. The Army and taxpayer have recouped their investment in this property countless times over. There are many reminiscences of our time at 210 Waskow Avenue. I periodically drive by the house when I am on Fort Hood and remember those times.

I recall the time I came home from work and found Penny and Ross hiding in our bedroom underneath the bed. It seems Ross had had a disagreement with some neighborhood boys and had "cleaned their clocks" in a scuffle. One of the boys had an older sister, an overweight, potty-mouthed teenager, and she had threatened to beat the shit out of both Penny and Ross if they came out of the house. She taunted them by beating on the front door. It took me little time to straighten out the situation with the girl's father, a warrant officer, and to get peace restored to the neighborhood.

Clearing government quarters is never easy, and the first time around was even more difficult. The inspectors literally check every nook and cranny, and it is a white-glove inspection. It is a pain when you are leaving, but it's very nice when you're arriving, because you know you are moving into quarters that are spotless. The source of my difficulty was paint on the brick. We had a small area of brick on the front of our quarters. The post engineers had once been painting a house across the street when they had gone to lunch. Ross had borrowed their paint and proceeded to paint a part of our brick. I thought it funny at the time, as he was a little tyke, but not when I had to remove the paint.

I took a couple of weeks leave, and we then drove to New York. We were to fly out of Kennedy Airport, so we found a hotel near the airport. The next morning, I was to take our car to the military terminal at Bayonne, New Jersey, for shipment to Turkey, and we were to fly out that evening. We were worn out from the trip to New York, so we decided to go to the hotel restaurant for dinner rather than looking for a restaurant nearby.

Wow, the prices were clearly too much for a family on a lieutenant's pay. We were too tired and too embarrassed to leave, so I started looking for a hamburger on the menu and found none. I did find Salisbury steak, which was the cheapest item. I said to Penny, "Can you believe these Yankees? Steak is the cheapest thing on the menu?" Talk about country coming to the city. Well, that was me.

The next morning, I put on my tan uniform and went to get the car. The door attendant stopped me and inquired as to where I was going. I told him. He wanted to know how I was planning to get back to the hotel and if I was familiar with the area. My plan was to ride the bus. I was not familiar with the area, but I did have a map to get to Bayonne. He informed me there was a transit strike in progress and the only way to get around was by taxi.

He said, "Lieutenant, with your accent, you are going to see a lot more of New York than you would ever want to see."

He wrote out specific instructions for me to tell the cabdriver and how much it should cost. He told me he had been a soldier, the Army had been good to him, he wished he had stayed in, and he wanted to make sure I was not taken advantage of by a local. What a guy. The trip back to the hotel was a piece of cake, thanks to him.

The three of us flew to Turkey via Frankfurt, Germany, landing in Istanbul.

10

An Ancient and Exotic Land

Turkey, a land of contrast—exotic, backward, ancient, modern—it is where Europe meets Asia. The division between the two runs from the Black Sea to the north down along the Bosporus Strait through the Sea of Marmara and the Dardanelles Strait to the Aegean Sea and the larger Mediterranean Sea to the south. The Republic of Turkey is located mainly in the Middle East, with a small portion in Europe. It is bordered by Bulgaria and Greece on the west in European Turkey.

In 1966, it was bordered on the east by the Soviet Union, but today, it is bordered by the former satellite states of Georgia, Armenia, and Azerbaijan. Turkey is in a rough neighborhood, Iran also on its eastern border and Iraq as well as Syria on the southern border. The Tigris and Euphrates Rivers have their source in Turkey, and the book of Genesis describes Turkey's highest mountain, Mount Ararat, as the resting place of Noah's Ark. Turkey joined NATO in 1952 and has been a key partner of the West and the United States since that time, although the relationship has been severely strained during various periods.

Turkey dates from antiquity with a wide variety of civilizations and kingdoms occupying its territory. The Persians, Greeks, Romans, Hittites, Byzantines, and Ottomans each ruled at one time. The ancient cities of Troy, Smyrna, Constantinople, and Ephesus are all well known, as are the names of Homer, Anthony, Cleopatra, Herodotus, Alexander the Great, Suleiman the "Magnificent," Saint John, Saint Paul and Mary of biblical times, and Mustafa Kemal Ataturk from modern times.

The Republic of Turkey was established on October 26, 1923, and Mustafa Kemal Ataturk (meaning father of Turks) was her first president.

Ataturk initiated a series of reforms with the aim of westernizing Turkey. These included a secular government and education, exile of the sultan, introduction of the Latin alphabet and Gordian calendar, equal rights for women, introduction of Western attire, the adoption of surnames, among others. My observation is that Ataturk's modernization program succeeded primarily in the three major cities of Istanbul, Ankara, and Izmir but less so in the provinces. I traveled throughout Turkey and found the people in small villages, especially in eastern Turkey, living much as you would have found in the United States in the 1870s, carrying rifles and sidearms.

Nominally, 99.8 percent of the population is Muslim, with the majority belonging to the Sunni branch of Islam. Unlike other Muslim countries, there is a strong tradition of separation of church and state. This means the subordination of religion to the state rather than what we Americans would consider separation of church and state. This is probably because in modern times, generals, starting with Ataturk, rather than the *imams* and Muslim clerics, have usually led the country.

Into this strange and forbidding land came a boy from Barnhart, his wife, Penny, and his four-year-old son, Ross. We arrived late in the evening of May 12, 1966, proceeded through customs to a military welcome desk staffed by the US Air Force, and took a taxi to a hotel that had been leased by the military to spend the night.

The hotel dining room served American meals (hamburgers, hot dogs, and French fries), but none like I had ever seen. The guestroom had one bed for all three of us. The mattress was about a half of an inch thick. The toilet paper was crepe paper (really), and the worst part was that the hotel was located near a hide tanning factory and the whole area smelled. To make matters worse, an enlisted couple in the next room argued the entire night, and the walls were paper-thin. They were also on their way to Izmir, and the wife did not want to go. Ross was too tired to complain, and I think Penny was shell-shocked.

The next morning, we took a cab to the Istanbul airport and boarded a Turkish Air flight for the short trip to Izmir. We taxied out to the runway, picked up speed as we went, and then made a screeching turn on the runway, and away we went. There was no setting the brakes and bringing the engines up to power for these fellows. The flight to

Izmir was uneventful, and we arrived at what was to be home for the next twenty-eight months.

Our sponsor, Captain Don Gumm, met us and loaded us in an Army staff car for the drive to Izmir, which was around forty-five minutes from the airport. I quickly realized that driving in Turkey was to be a unique experience. The roads were narrow and cobblestone, filled with pedestrians, thick with animals ranging from cats to camels, peddlers with pushcarts, and horse-drawn taxis. There were also trucks, but cars were rare.

All were fighting for possession of the road, and none seemed to care about their personal safety, much less the safety of anyone else. Both a green light and a red light meant the same thing—keep pushing forward. The horn on the sedan, which was required to be operational when inspected by Turkish police, was not to be tooted, because it violated an anti-horn law. It was honked constantly. No one—and I mean no one—paid any attention to it.

Izmir, a truly magical place located on the Aegean Sea and surrounded by mountains, brings back memories of a time long ago when we were young, healthy, and ready to take on the world. First, we had some adjusting to do.

The mountains were covered from bottom to top with shanties, hovels, and shacks, and the poverty was evident. Don Gumm would point to a section on a particular mountain and remark how it might be a place we would want to live, because it was one of the nicer sections. All that was going on outside the sedan window fascinated Ross. Penny had a look of utter despair on her face, and I was beginning to have symptoms of pre-traumatic stress syndrome.

We finally forced our way out of the valley where the airport was located, through a mountain pass, and down into the city proper. Lo and behold, there was a city of wide, palm-lined streets and outdoor restaurants on the Aegean Sea.

Yet another welcome surprise came in the form of a brand new hotel for officers, one located on the waterfront, which included the Officer's Club. The hotel was built in the European style, but the Officer's Club was as American as you could get. The club had slot machines, and the hotel had real American toilet paper.

Our room was spacious with two double beds, a refrigerator, a stove, and cooking and eating utensils. A laundry room was just down the hall, and we had a balcony that overlooked the Aegean. Don and his wife, Terri, had stocked the refrigerator and left a list of available apartments we might be interested in renting. This boy had not had it so good since he had left Barnhart, now some eight thousand miles away.

Don told us that he would leave us alone and that he would pick me up the next morning for processing and that Terri would come later for Penny and Ross to show them around. We were grateful to be alone and hit the bed only to be awakened four or five hours later by the Muslim call to prayer.

We took a seat on the balcony, and I told Penny I was going to call room service for a drink and asked if she would like something. Penny almost never drank, only a glass of wine here and there to be polite. I was quite surprised when she said she would and asked me to suggest something. I decided on a Sloe Gin Fizz, as it was sweet. We drank our drinks, watched the sun beginning to set, and laughed about our arrival and how all was turning out well, and then we had two more drinks. Penny needed to go to the bathroom. As she went inside, she remarked that the room was spinning. She lay on the bed to try to stop it from spinning like one does when they have had too much to drink

Ross was now up and wanting to eat. Ross always wanted to eat. I told Penny we were going to the dining room, and she said she was going to take another nap. Ross and I went downstairs. The dining room was full, and people were checking us out. We were enjoying our meal when Penny came in. Penny, who was quite tall with long legs, was carefully picking her way through the dining room. Her knees were coming up to her chin with each step she took. She was unsteady and quite the mess. All eyes were on her. I helped her to her seat and ordered her a meal. After she ate, she was better and began to agonize over her entrance: "These people are going to feel so sorry for you and Ross having an alcoholic wife and mother. What are they going to think of me? Why did I do this my first night here," and on and on she went, as was her nature. I thought it was funny, and Ross could have cared less.

The first priority was to find a place to live, as there were no quarters except for the commanding general's. All had to live on the economy. Penny and Terri did the looking while I settled into my new job. Ross would stay with the Gumm's maid while they were apartment shopping. Almost all Americans had maids at the US equivalent of two dollars a day. It was illegal to use American dollars in Turkey. We quickly learned the exchange rate, which was nine Turkish lira (TL) for one US dollar in 1965. Later, we discovered that you get eleven TL for one US in Greece. We had a friend, a major and aviator, who flew to Greece quite often, and we would give him our US dollars to exchange for us.

Penny soon found an apartment that she liked. The apartment building had five floors with two apartments on each floor and the proprietor, a Turkish entrepreneur, lived in the penthouse. Our apartment had two bedrooms, a bathroom, a kitchen, and a large, reverse, L-shaped living room. There was a balcony that traversed the entire length and across the front of the building. The bedroom floors were polished oak, and the living room floor was black marble. Yes, marble, as it was cheap in Turkey.

The floor showed dirt easily, but Penny soon had a house cleaner by the name of Sarai. The apartment was located at 7/9 Sehit Neveres Boulevard, a major thoroughfare two blocks from the waterfront, three blocks from the Officer's Club, and four blocks from my office. The American shopping area (commissary, PX, etc.) was five blocks away. The location was quite convenient. I walked to work each morning.

The building came with a *kaopege* (a security person and caretaker) who lived with his wife in an apartment on the ground floor. The doors to the building entrance were locked promptly at 2200 hours each night. If you came in after that time, you would have to ring for the *kaopege* to let you in. The *kaopege* spoke some English and was quite willing to run errands for a tip.

We had no telephone and had to book a call to the States at least two weeks in advance at the Turkish Central Telephone Exchange. Drinking water had to be chlorinated, and fruits and vegetables had to be washed with bleach before we ate them. They were typically packed in manure and transported to the city in large wicker baskets by donkeys or camels. We had a fifteen-gallon plastic container that sat on the kitchen counter to hold our chlorinated drinking water. The water was pure and came from artesian wells in the mountains, but unfortunately, the water flowed through aqueducts dating from the Roman occupation.

It was not unusual to sit on our balcony and see a camel caravan passing down the street or a fellow hawking wares and leading a dancing bear. Our *bachevan* (vegetable and fruit vendor) would come to the apartment each morning and display his wares for our perusal. He soon learned what we liked and would already have it bagged. The vegetables, fruit, and nuts were large and delicious, and every variety was cheap. You could have watermelon year round.

There was a US Air Force dispensary a block from our house, and across the boulevard was the largest and only luxury hotel in Izmir, which was rated five stars and still is today. Again, Turkey was a land of contrast, and this boy from Barnhart was a long way from home.

Now that we had a place to live, it was time to explore ancient Smyrna, modern Izmir, and surrounding environs.

Smyrna is among the pleasant places of the earth. Its sheltered position at the head of a long gulf, at the seaward end of an easy route from the interior, marks it out to be the site of a flourishing port; when to this are added natural beauty, fertile soil and an excellent climate, it is no matter for wonder that a city of Smyrna has existed from prehistoric times.
—George Bean

Izmir is Turkey's third largest city behind Istanbul and Ankara. In 1966, it housed around five hundred thousand people. Today, it has close to three million. It is known as the "Pearl of the Aegean," and it is considered the most westernized city of Turkey in terms of values, ideology, lifestyle, and women's rights.

The city is over five thousand years old and one of the oldest in the Mediterranean. The original city was established in the third millennium BC, at which time it shared the most advanced civilization in Asia Minor with Troy. In the first millennium BC, Izmir, then known as Smyrna, ranked as one of the most important cities of that period. It was during this time that Homer lived in Izmir.

In the fourth century BC, the city was completely rebuilt during the reign of Alexander the Great. Smyrna's Roman period, beginning in the first century BC, was its greatest era. Smyrna, one of the first seats of Christianity, became one of the *Seven Churches of Asia to* which the book of Revelation was sent by John the Apostle.

After WWI, Greece sided with the Allied powers against Turkey and was awarded part of Asia Minor, including the city of Smyrna. Turkish nationalists under Kemal Ataturk declared the Republic of Turkey, defeated the Greeks, and returned Smyrna/Izmir to the Turks. Much of Izmir was burned, and thousands of Greeks left. There is no love lost between the two countries, and the division of Cyprus continues to be a sword in the side of both.

Izmir proper, built around Kultur Park, a large central park, had a covered bazaar nearby for shopping. The bazaar was truly unique with many open-air shops and cubicles offering items from throughout the Middle East: gold and silver jewelry, hand-woven Turkish rugs, brass and bronze from antiquity, marble and alabaster, and locally made crafts of every description.

There was a fantastic museum in Kultur Park where I spent many an entertaining hour, one with marvelous exhibits depicting the history of Izmir and its environs. The old part of the city dating from Roman times was well preserved, and archeological discoveries continued throughout the time we were in Izmir. I have seen many of the historical ruins in Italy, Greece, and Turkey, and the Turkish ruins were by far the most impressive.

In 1966, Turkey had a small tourist industry, so when you visited a site, it was usually just you and the ruins. Several good books provided information for a self-guided tour.

My assignment was to the headquarters of Allied Land Forces Southeastern Europe (ALFSEE), a NATO command. The ALFSEE and its US Air Force counterpart, Sixth Allied Tactical Air Force (Sixth ATF), were a combined force of Greek, Turkish, Italian, British, and American soldiers and airmen working side-by-side to bolster the defenses of NATO's most easterly ground and air assets. It was the largest geographical area of all NATO commands, with much of it bordering on the Soviet Union and her satellite states.

The area included the vital Bosporus and the Dardanelles and stretched from the Caucasus to the western coast of Greece. It was an area the Soviets had aspired to possess, because it would give them warm-water port facilities and ready access to the Mediterranean. The Bosporus and the Dardanelles served as a cork to bottle up the Soviet Black Sea fleet.

Seizure of the Turkish straits by the Soviet Union would enable freedom of passage from the Black Sea for Soviet Naval forces. Allied lines of communication through the Mediterranean would be seriously disrupted or even severed. The Middle East and its vital oil fields and North Africa then would be easily accessible to the Soviet Union.

In the event the Soviet bloc had initiated a thrust toward the western part of the continent, the ALFSEE area was well positioned to serve as a base of operations for a counterattack. In reality, ALFSEE commanded nothing during peacetime. It was a planning headquarters prepared to assume command of Turkish and Hellenic ground forces prior to or upon commencement of hostilities, with the mission of conducting a delaying action until arrival of sufficient NATO forces, primarily from the United States, to push the Soviets back.

ALFSEE was commanded by Lieutenant General William W. Dick, and Sixth ATF by Major General James B. Tipton. The ALFSEE headquarters was located in the Sehir Building on the waterfront in Izmir. The Sixth ATF was located at Sirinyer Garrison on the outskirts of Izmir. The total number of US Army personnel numbered less than four hundred in Izmir. It was a close-knit community, with the officer ranks numbering around forty.

I had the title of COSMIC and ATOMAL control officer in charge of the NATO Registry and the Official Mail and Records Unit. I had a small staff consisting of three Italian warrant officers; an American master sergeant, a sergeant first-class, and four enlisted soldiers; a Turkish NCO, several *askers* (Turkish soldiers), and two Turkish civilians. COSMIC was the preface for Top Secret, and ATOMAL was the NATO designation for documents containing nuclear information. I received, maintained, controlled, and accounted for all classified material in the headquarters. Individual staff offices could store classified material up to Secret, but all documents classified COSMIC or ATOMAL were secured in my vault. The vault housed my office and the office of three of my subordinates. These three individuals all had a Top Secret clearance and were extremely competent and reliable. They were Mr. Sordi, an Italian warrant officer, Master Sergeant Thomas, an American, and Mr. Ali Eralp, a Turkish civilian.

The vault was called the COSMIC Registry, and all official NATO material arrived by courier from our higher headquarters, Allied Forces Southern Europe (AFSOUTH), which was located in Naples, Italy. A US Navy admiral commanded AFSOUTH. We were constantly being inspected by the Central Registry at the Pentagon in Washington, D.C., Supreme Headquarters Allied Powers Europe (SHAPE) in Casteau, Belgium, or AFSOUTH.

Some of what I was privy to remains classified. If made public, it would cause history to be revised, because what is written is simply not the way it happened. In this case, truth is indeed stranger and more interesting than the published fiction.

Duty in ALFSEE was lax and unhurried in stark contrast to a pure American headquarters. Once, my senior Italian warrant officer, who was representing the other two, came to complain about how hard I was working them. He asked, "Captain, why do you Americans work so hard? Soldiers work hard during war but rest during peace."

My response was, "Yes, and how many wars has the Italian Army won?"

We arrived in Izmir just as the summer duty hours were beginning. These were called "NATO hours" and meant we went to work at 0700 and quit for the day at 1300, ostensibly because the Sehir building was not air-conditioned and it became too hot to work.

Throughout the summer months, the wives would have the picnic baskets packed, the beer iced down, and away we would go to the NATO-leased beach at Seferihisar, which was about one hour from Izmir. All the beaches around Izmir were terrific with beautiful white sand, clear, azure Aegean water, and few people.

The NATO beach was special because of the drive. Once you left Izmir, you traveled into and through the mountains, which were covered with spectacular trees and overlooked the Aegean Sea, and then down into this secluded cove and the beach.

Other enjoyable aspects of the assignment were NATO holidays. Not only did we celebrate all America holidays, we celebrated the major holidays of the other nations as well. Altogether, we must have celebrated twenty-five different holidays. A special holiday, such as Independence Day, necessitated a unique gala hosted by the Army contingent from the nation celebrating the holiday.

> *People do not plan to fail; they fail to plan.*
> —Unknown

Living expenses were relatively cheap, and for the first time, we had some extra money that we could save or spend. At the time, the Army had a program that allowed soldiers to place a percentage of their salary into a savings account. The account paid a straight 10 percent and continued through the Vietnam War. Penny and I started our investment program in Turkey and continued the program throughout my military career.

We also had a bit of good fortune. Shortly after our arrival, the Turkish government passed a law dictating that a foreigner could no longer bring a privately owned vehicle (POV) into the country with the intent of selling the vehicle. Our 1964 Ford Fairlane, already driven for over two years, was now in demand, as the Turks had no automobile industry and had to import their vehicles, paying a prohibitive import tax. Rich Turks wanting to buy the car pestered me for months, but I held out until I got the right deal.

Eventually, I reached an agreement with a Turkish businessman. I would sell him the car for three times what I had paid for it new. I would drive the car until two weeks before I left Turkey, and he would pay me one-quarter upfront, 50 percent in equal monthly installments during my assignment, and the remainder upon delivery of the vehicle to him. This enabled Penny and me to have sufficient TL on hand to pay our monthly bills, travel, and buy some Turkish rugs to bring home.

I rarely drove the vehicle in Izmir proper, but I would drive it when we went outside the city. Penny did not drive at all for good reason. The laws of Turkey were unique. The Status of Forces Agreement (SOFA) protected the military somewhat if a soldier broke a Turkish law. The Turkish government could and often did give the military jurisdiction over an offense.

Dependents, however, were strictly held to Turkish law. If someone was involved in a traffic accident through no fault of his or her own, the person was still considered by the Turks to be 50 percent at fault. The reasoning went like this: If you, foreigner, had not been here and had not brought your car to this country, this accident would not have happened. Therefore, the fault was at least half yours. And usually, the Turks found a way to make most of the blame your fault.

The wife of an American missionary had been involved in an automobile accident, one involving a death, and she had been found negligent, at fault, guilty. She was then sent to prison for a number of years. Once a month, the Red Cross volunteers, whom Penny had joined, visited the woman and brought her health and comfort items. Penny would come back from those visits in tears over the appalling conditions in which the woman was incarcerated.

Prostitution was illegal in Turkey—that is, except in the Turkish women's prison. A Turkish woman who had been found guilty of a crime, including prostitution, and had been sent to jail had the option of serving as a prostitute and having her sentence reduced by a certain amount of days for each man she serviced. The Turkish women's prison was quite a popular place for Turkish men and particularly young Turkish soldiers. An *asker* was paid the equivalent of two US dollars per month and was given two packs of cigarettes and two tokens to the women's prison. Those who did not smoke traded their cigarettes for tokens.

I heard but never verified that if a Turkish man became indebted to the government and received a prison sentence, he would be left free to work and pay his debt. Instead, a female family member, wife or daughter, would be placed in prison to help pay the debt, and she was often forced to prostitute herself.

The life of the *asker* was not easy. They were poorly paid, their life austere, and discipline was unduly harsh. Corporal Aritan, an *asker* assigned to me, had a problem getting to work on time. His American sergeant told me that he had discussed the problem with Aritan on several occasions but to no avail. I told him I would take care of the problem. The policy was that if you had a discipline problem with a soldier of another nationality that you could not resolve, you were to take the problem to the senior officer of that nationally in your immediate organization.

The senior Turkish officer in the adjutant general directorate was a major. I discussed the problem with him, and he told me he would take care of it. The next morning, the NCO came to me and asked if I had discussed Corporal Aritan with the major. I told him I had and inquired why he was asking. He told me Aritan had not shown up for work. I went to the major and told him that Corporal Aritan had not reported for work.

He said to me, "You Americans do not understand Turkish discipline! Come, let's go for a ride."

We got in his jeep and drove some distance through the mountains and out into the Turkish plains arriving at a Turkish transportation unit where new soldiers were being trained to drive trucks. The camp had a large parade field, and around the parade field were wooden boxes, which had been buried in the ground. The tops were covered with a metal grate for air and were padlocked. A roving guard opened one of the boxes, and there was Corporal Aritan. The box was not sufficient to stand and too small to kneel. The soldier remained in a crouch. Corporal Aritan's punishment was seven days in the box on bread and water.

When I returned, I gathered my warrant officers and NCOs and told them what I had seen. I told them that from now on, minor disciplinary problems with the *askers* were to be dealt with by them and if they could not deal with it, I would; however, only in the more serious infractions, would I take the problem to the Turkish major. Corporal Aritan returned and was the perfect soldier thereafter. It was a few days before he could stand straight.

Another young *asker* assigned to me was an American. This young fellow was born in Turkey, and his parents immigrated to the United States when he was an infant. Upon high school graduation, his parents bought him a round-trip plane ticket to Turkey to visit his grandparents, whom he had never seen. He spoke little Turkish, and a couple of days after he arrived at his grandparents' home, the Turks came for him. He was a Turkish citizen, and he owed a two-year service obligation. His family flew to Turkey and got the American embassy involved, but the Turks were adamant that he was to serve in the Army, the Turkish Army.

This was one miserable kid, but he was lucky in one respect. He had been assigned to a place where there were Americans. We adopted him and did what we could for him. We use to kid him that when he finished his tour with the Turks, we were going to send him to Vietnam.

The Turks did have a policy that I thought was innovative. They assigned their *askers* from the cities to units in the provinces and their *askers* from the provinces to units located near the big cities. I was always amazed when I went to inspect Turkish Third Army at Erzurum in eastern Turkey. My driver there would be from Izmir, Istanbul, or Ankara, and when at Turkish First Army in Istanbul, my driver would be from some small village in eastern Turkey.

The G2 (Intelligence) Colonel Matthews and I would visit the three Turkish armies every six months to inspect their classified repository and to ensure they were maintaining and accounting for the NATO documents with which they had been entrusted. Colonel Matthews was quite an interesting fellow. He was a debonair man, a talented actor, a brilliant conversationalist, and a damn good intelligence officer. He also liked his booze. One of my jobs was to mix drinks during the flights to wherever we were going. I personally could not stomach a Bloody Mary at 0630, but 0900 was just about right. The Turks would always treat us like royalty and put on a big dog-and-pony show. I did all the work, and Colonel Matthews would *kibitz* with his Turkish counterpart and other general officers. We always had a good time, and I enjoyed traveling with him.

Once, we were flying to Erzurum on an Army fixed-wing aircraft, and we were about forty-five minutes out of Izmir when the plane's radar went out. The pilot recommended turning back, but Colonel Matthews talked the pilot into going on. About fifteen minutes later, we ran into a storm, and the pilot did turn back. The pilot told us he was not sure where we were. The mountains were high, up to fourteen thousand feet in the area, and without oxygen, we could not fly higher than twelve thousand feet. He was flying blind, and we were going to descend to try to break out of the clouds.

Boy, did I pray, as I always do when I am afraid: "Lord, if you will just get me out of this, I will be a good boy from Barnhart from now on."

I expected to see the side of a mountain over the pilot's shoulder any moment. We popped out of the clouds right on top of a railroad and began to follow it. The pilot jokingly said we had it made, so long as the railroad did not pass through a mountain tunnel. We flew the railroad, and it took us to a town where, lo and behold, there was a military airport.

When in Erzurum, we would bunk with the Joint United States Military Mission for Aid to Turkey (JUSMMAT) team supporting Turkish Third Army. The team, which was commanded by a colonel, consisted of a member from each Army branch represented by a lieutenant colonel, although the technical branches, including transportation, ordnance, and quartermaster, were represented by warrant officers. The team had the mission of advising and training the Turks on US Army doctrine and procedures.

The team leased a three-story hotel and had their offices, mess, and living facilities in the hotel. There was a large lounge with a fireplace, pool table, library, bar, and tables for playing card games. There was no TV or American radio. They had their own cook who prepared and served superb meals and a Turkish bartender. The team received their supplies and mail weekly by C-130, although during wintry weather, the plane would often be unable to land.

This was the time of the Peace Corps, and there were several such people, mainly female, in eastern Turkey. Periodically, these young women would come from their villages to Erzurum and head for the JUSMMAT hotel. There was plenty of hot water, American food, and the comfort of home for a few days. The team found the female presence quite pleasant and was always glad to accommodate them. Overall, this was not a bad way to spend a one-year hardship tour.

Colonel Matthews and I were in Erzurum on June 5 and 6, 1967, during the beginning of the Six-Day War between the Israelis and Egypt, Syria, and Jordan. The Israelis had launched a preemptive strike against the three countries on June 5th, and the battle was raging on June 6th.

The commanding general of the Turkish Third Army, a lieutenant general, had assembled his staff and division commanders, and they were war-gaming the battle. He had divided his people into a red team and a blue team, each team representing an opposing force. His signals intelligence (SIGINT) people were pulling in live radio transmissions from the battlefield, and the information was being displayed on a large map board. Each team was using the information to fight the battle against the other and comparing the results against what was actually happening. We sat in on this very realistic training exercise for several hours, and I found it fascinating.

Do not ever underestimate the Israelis or the Turks.

Colonel Matthews sent Captain Jim Davies and me to inspect an Army unit near Istanbul. This unit had a classified mission and belonged to US Army Europe (USAREUR) but would transfer to ALFSEE control upon commencement of hostilities.

We flew to Istanbul, where we remained overnight at the Istanbul Hilton. The next morning, the unit sent a staff car to take us to the unit's location. We were met by the deputy commander, who immediately told us that the commander, a colonel, was too busy to meet with us. He then gave us an unclassified briefing of the unit's mission. Both these actions were setting the tone for the visit, as we were well aware of the unit's classified mission. He then told us the NATO documents were kept with the US classified documents and that we were not cleared for that area. I protested and asked to see the commanding officer, making it clear that we would be unable to accomplish our mission without being allowed access to the NATO documents. The deputy told us the visit was terminated and escorted us back to the waiting staff car. I asked to use the telephone to call ALFSEE, but that permission was denied.

When I arrived at the Hilton, I called Colonel Matthews to tell him what had transpired. He said to stand by the phone and that he would get back to me. An hour or two later, he called to tell me that the unit had a staff car on the way, that there should be no problems this time. He also told me that I was to take them apart and write up everything I could possibly find, and the unit was to receive an unsatisfactory rating.

The staff car arrived, and the deputy commander was in the vehicle. We had a cordial chat on the way to the unit. The colonel met us as we drove up and escorted us into his office, where we had a nice visit over tea and crumpets. We were given the VIP briefing and tour and escorted to the classified area, where we began the inspection. The lieutenant colonel and colonel departed. The unit was in excellent shape, and I had to nitpick to find any discrepancy. We returned to out-brief the commander, and he assured me all gigs would be immediately corrected. He did seem pleased—or maybe it was relieved—that his unit received an overall rating of excellent.

We returned to the Hilton, and I reported to Colonel Matthews that the mission had been accomplished. He had a good laugh about what had transpired, but he was not pleased that I had given the unit an outstanding report. I suspect he was just into his acting role. Both the unit commander and I learned a valuable lesson. When higher headquarter comes to inspect, treat them royally regardless of rank. It was a lesson a colonel should have learned *as* a captain, not *from* a captain. I later found out that General Dick had called USAREUR headquarters and that the colonel had his faced ripped off.

I found colonels the most difficult of all ranks to deal with, even when I was a colonel, especially when I was a colonel. Colonels know everything, and you can tell them nothing. Why that happens is another of life's mysteries. I would rather try to herd a bunch of cats than a bunch of colonels.

Generals, on the other hand, become accustomed to being told where to go and when and then being escorted there. Some are quite unassuming, but when aroused—and they are easily aroused—head for the nearest bunker. They are sprinkled with "holy water" and sent to "charm school," where they are taught to be diplomats and say, "That is very interesting," rather than, "That is bullshit."

Several years ago, an Army chief of staff was welcoming a group of recently promoted brigadier generals before he sent them to "charm school" at Fort Leavenworth. He said, "Gentlemen, I am aware that you are quite proud of yourselves. You should be, but before you get too impressed, remember that if your plane crashes on the way to Leavenworth and you all die, I will select the next thirty colonels on the promotion list and the Army will not skip a beat."

Penny and I made many friends during our stay in Izmir. Captain Jim and Ann Davies, Captain Don and Terri Gumm, Captain Mike and Ann Torrans, Captain Jim and Nancy Flowers, Captain Ed and Carol Buelow, Captain Bob and Ann Boyer, Captain Norm Fuzzell and wife Deloris, and Major Frank Ruggles and his mother, Mae, were all good friends. I still correspond with many of them, if only by Christmas card. These are the people we entertained and who entertained us, ate

Thanksgiving and Christmas dinner with, sat with at official functions, relaxed with at the beaches and at NATO's recreation area in Barakali Park, and traveled with throughout Turkey.

Penny and Herbie on the way to an official function.
(Izmir, Turkey)

Jim Davies retired as a lieutenant colonel and is now a retired teacher in Indianapolis. Don Gumm retired as a lieutenant colonel and is now deceased. Mike Torrans retired as a reserve full colonel and is now deceased. Jim Flowers retired as a lieutenant colonel, and he was the head baseball coach at the US Military Academy at West Point. Ed Buelow got out of the Army and was elected a Mississippi congressional representative. Bob Boyer retired as a major and is now deceased. Norm Fuzzell retired as a major and is a retired postal supervisor. Frank Ruggles retired as a lieutenant colonel and is a retired executive with USAA in San Antonio. They were all good soldiers and friends.

One of our favorite places to visit on a weekend was Barakali Park. The park had been leased by the US Air Force as a recreation area for the military. There were baseball diamonds, an athletic field, a track, a swimming pool, a concession stand, camel rides, and many other activities. The park was located between Cigli Airbase and Izmir, and it was a place for the adults to kick back and the kids to have fun. Ross was constantly begging to go to Barakali: "Poppa, can we go to Barakali?"

Penny, Ross, and Herbie
(Izmir, Turkey)

The Army officer community at ALFSEE was small and close-knit. There were several bachelors in the group, and single females were abundant. The teachers in the Department of Defense School System (DODS) were mostly female, and they were there not only to teach but to travel and perhaps find a husband. They were included in most of our activities.

Lieutenant General and Mrs. Dick lived on a compound guarded by Turkish MPs in a lovely Greek mansion provided by the Turkish government. They entertained quite often and usually invited the junior officers and their ladies.

Penny and Mrs. Dick both did volunteer work with the American Red Cross and bowled on the same bowling team. Mrs. Dick would periodically invite her bowling team and their husbands for a buffet or hors d'oeuvres and cocktails. Everyone knew that when the waiters began to serve ice water, usually precisely at 2100, it was the signal to say thanks for inviting us and good night to the Dicks.

I was promoted to captain on February 1, 1967. Brigadier General William Birdsong and Penny pinned on my "railroad tracks."

Penny, Herbie, and Brigadier General Birdsong.
Promotion to Captain.

Two other officers, a captain and a lieutenant colonel, had recently been promoted, and we went together to host a promotion party. We invited all NATO officers and their wives and many others in the Izmir community. We had the party at the Officer's Club penthouse, and we had a magician, a Turkish belly dancer, an open bar, and several tables of finger foods. I had one heck of a headache the next morning, but the promotion "blowout" was a success.

My three Italian officers often entertained us in their homes, and we included them in parties at our home. The Italians do not eat like Americans. The meal generally started at 1900 and ended when you could barely waddle home. There would be a meat dish followed by *Strega*, a potent Italian alcoholic drink, a salad, more Strega, fruit, more Strega, and finally a fish dish. Lots of toasting, laughing, and good companionship were the order of the day.

Mr. Sordi was married to a tall, light-skinned, blond, blue-eyed girl who had to be a German. She was born in the Italian Alps.

Late one evening, Mr. Sordi and his wife knocked on our apartment door. Mrs. Sordi was holding her two-year old son and crying. Mr. Sordi explained that they had taken their son to a Turkish doctor and he had told them that the son needed an operation, but they were afraid that the Turkish doctor was not qualified. They could not understand what the operation involved because of the language barrier. They asked if an American doctor would look at the child.

The Italians were not authorized to use American medical facilities. Mr. Sordi was well aware of that, but the boy was in terrible pain. I realized they were desperate, so I decided to do what I could.

I took them to the US Air Force clinic and was told by the desk person that the boy was not authorized to be treated. I asked to see the duty doctor, and when he arrived, he inquired as to the problem. I told him, and he examined the boy and discovered a gastrointestinal difficulty that needed to be operated on immediately. The desk person told the doctor that the boy was not authorized medical treatment. The doctor said, "Am I to let this child die? I think not. If anyone complains, send them to me."

The doctor and I became instant heroes in the Italian community. The Italian major general, the ALFSEE comptroller, came to my office to thank me. The Sordis were never billed for the operation or hospital stay. We are called the ugly Americans!

The US Air Force clinic got some more business from the Taylors. I came home from work one evening and told Penny I was not feeling well. We had a party to go to. She wanted to attend, and she implied that I did not want to go. I went and sat in a corner. I really did not feel well.

The next morning, a Saturday, Penny got up, and because she could not stand me staying in bed, she pulled the sheet off. When she saw my face, she was perplexed and softly asked, "What is wrong with you?"

I said, "I don't feel good."

"I guess you don't. Look in the mirror."

I had red spots over my face, so I headed to the clinic. I had the measles and was quarantined for a couple of days with a bunch of little kids. I had missed the measles when they went through Barnhart, and now as a twenty-six-year-old Army captain, I was in a room full of crying kids who were sicker than a snake-bitten dog. The parents were taken aback to find me in the room with their children.

Later, I came home from work and found both Ross and Penny crying. Ross had been throwing rocks at the cats that frequented the trash dumpster behind the apartment. He had been told many times not to do that. One jumped out and scratched him on the face and arms. Penny had taken Ross to the clinic and had been told he needed to take rabies shots, as rabies was quite prevalent in Turkey. It was the same drill as Daddy and Tippe had gone through when we had lived on the Wood place. He was to take his first shot that afternoon. Penny wanted me to be there to help hold and comfort him. It took three corpsmen to hold him. I could barely bear to watch. He would come home from kindergarten crying and wake up each morning crying. It was a difficult time for all.

This incident and others began to wear on Penny. The Turks would periodically hold up our mail over a SOFA dispute, sometimes as long as three weeks. Once, they turned off the electricity to the US Air Force commissary freezer, and the meat spoiled. It was two months before we again had meat. Often, we would go without some necessities in our post exchange because the Turks had stolen them off the supply ship. You could find the stolen goods on the black market. It was difficult to call the States, and Turkish men were more than rude to American women. They loved to pinch their posteriors, and this irritated Penny greatly. Earthquakes, some quite severe, were felt periodically, and they were frightening, especially on the third-floor of our apartment. In addition, the city would be placed under blackout conditions when tensions escalated between Greece and Turkey. I think she was homesick and a little afraid, but she was not the only wife who felt that way. Because of some of the things happening in Turkey, the Army cut the tour from three years to twenty-four months. Our tour was prorated as we had gone to Turkey on a three-year tour. We stayed twenty-eight months. Today, soldiers are not allowed to take their dependents to Turkey.

I loved Turkey and enjoyed myself immensely. The history, the work, the travel, the people, and the atmosphere were all fascinating to a boy from Barnhart. Overseas service can be hard on a family though. I was anxious to get Penny and Ross safely home.

I only had one bad experience with a Turk. As I walked to work one beautiful morning along Ataturk Caddesi, which paralleled the seafront, enjoying the breeze and the ships sailing in the harbor, I saw a young man walking directly toward me with a big smile on his face. He stopped in front of me and saluted. I returned the salute, and he spit in my face and ran. I guess he did not like Americans. I do not think he was a communist. The Turks disliked the Soviets almost as much as they did the Greeks.

One of the highlights of the Turkey tour was the visit of Pope Paul VI to Izmir on July 26, 1967. Pope Paul VI, the Pilgrim Pope, was the first Pope to leave Italy in 150 years, and he was making the first visit of a Pope to Turkey. He was going to Ephesus and then to the House of the Virgin Mary to bless the location and give it the official sanction of the Catholic Church as a holy place.

The name of Ephesus will always be connected with the beginnings of Christianity. The Apostle Paul preached there a number of times and stayed in the town from 55 to 58 AD. It is believed that the Apostle John stayed at Ephesus from 90 to 95 AD. It is speculated that he wrote the Gospel John in Ephesus. A tomb located near Ephesus is said to be St. John's.

A short distance from Ephesus, some four miles up a winding road on Mount Aladag, is the location of the final home of the Virgin Mary. Supposedly, the Apostle John visited the area before the Apostle Paul did, and Mary stayed and died here. The home is a native-rock, two-room structure that is quite small and unimpressive. I visited the site on several occasions, and I was told that people were often healed of their infirmities during their visit. There were crutches and wheelchairs that had been left around the home. I found the site to be serene and peaceful.

Once while visiting the site, we ate a picnic lunch nearby when a small bus of infrequent tourists arrived. In the group were an American and his wife. They saw us drinking Budweiser beer and inquired how we were able to find Budweiser in Turkey. We explained we had picked it up at the drugstore. They then asked where the drugstore was. We responded that it was in Izmir. The drugstore was what we called a small convenience store in the American shopping area. I do not think they were able to understand about the drugstore, but we gave them a beer. It was a hot day. They were grateful.

ALFSEE had been contacted to provide volunteer military personnel to perform crowd control for the Pope within the courtyard of the Cathedral of St. John's in Izmir. This church served the religious needs of all faiths with denominational services being staggered on Sunday. I volunteered for the duty, as it was an opportunity to see the Pope up close and personal. My Italian warrant officers also volunteered.

The big moment arrived, and a large crowd gathered along the Pope's route of travel, both outside and inside the courtyard. He entered the courtyard and began to proceed down the cordon that the NATO soldiers, who were dressed in civilian clothes, had formed for him. Huge men surrounded him—I suppose the Swiss Guards—and the crowd began to surge forward. We had linked arms to keep the crowd back when Mr. Sordi broke ranks and fell at the feet of the Pope and began to kiss his shoes. I grabbed the arms of the next person, and we were able to close the gap. The Swiss Guards were going to forcibly remove Mr. Sordi when the Pope waved his hand across his body, helped Mr. Sordi up, and placed a commemorative coin in his hand. I could have killed Mr. Sordi, as the crowd was now going wild to get to the Pope. I suppose they were thinking that they would receive a similar blessing.

The Pope was tiny, and he had a sweet face—not what I expected at all.

My boss, Colonel Michael Varhol, a Catholic, had a family heirloom, a chair of age that he had loaned to the church for the Pope to sit on. The chair was ornate and high-backed, and it looked like a throne. Some days later, we received an engraved invitation from the Varhols to visit their home and view the chair. The chair sat in a corner with velvet rope around it so that it could not be touched. The guests passed by the chair much as you would in a museum. I was less than impressed.

Pope Paul VI and the colonel's chair.
(Izmir, Turkey)

Colonel Varhol had nine or ten children, some of whom were in college in the States. He looked forward to receiving a letter from his children. Often, he would come to the vault and ask if the mail had arrived, and again, I would explain that the NATO mail had or had not arrived, but that personal mail was delivered at the Army Post Office (APO) in the basement of the building. He would give me a funny look and wander off.

I was at AFSOUTH in Naples and delivering some classified material when I received a call from Varhol. He wanted me to go by the commissary and purchase two cases of instant mashed potatoes for his family. He asked that I not place them in the cargo space of the aircraft but retain them in my possession. This made me unhappy, very unhappy. I had taken a few days leave and had planned to ride the train to Rome while I was having some wine and cheese and enjoying the scenery. I would spend a couple days in Rome and fly back to Izmir. I bought the instant potatoes, went to Rome, and wrestled the two boxes until I got back to Izmir. I did put the boxes in the cargo hold. I figured that if we crashed in the sea, once the water got to the instant potatoes, we would float until we were rescued.

When in Rome either with Penny or by myself, the YMCA was the place to stay. It was cheap and clean, and it had a great dining room and a well-stocked bar. Yes, this was the YMCA. The hotel had floors for single men, women, and families. Baths were communal. There were always many young people around, and it was a neat place to stay.

In Naples, I would stay at the Hotel Vesuvius, a very old European hotel on the Bay of Naples. The room had high ceilings and eighteenth-century furniture, and the bathtub had claw feet. The first time I arrived at the hotel, the door attendant greeted me as Captain Taylor because I was in uniform. Some six months later when I arrived at the hotel in civilian clothes, the same door attendant greeted me as Captain Taylor. I was impressed. I cannot find the hotel on the Internet, so its location now probably has a modern hotel in its place.

Horse-drawn carriages called *arabas* were the primary means of transportation within the city. They were cheap, and some drivers could speak a little English. Six *arabas* parked under trees near our apartment and waited for customers primarily from the hotel across the boulevard. There was one driver, our favorite, we always used if available. One Saturday morning, he came to our apartment and told me his newborn baby was dying and needed American milk. His wife's milk was bad, and the baby could not tolerate Turkish milk. He indicated that he needed the powered milk that we used. Turkish law prohibited Americans from giving or selling any of our imported products to Turks, as did Army regulations. The driver, who was quite distraught and almost begging, had some money with him, but that was not the issue. Did I or did I not give him the milk? Penny and I discussed the situation and decided that if he was going to ask us for something, it would not have been milk unless he really needed milk. We gave him what we had, and he took us to the commissary to get more. The child recovered, and we never paid for an *arabas* ride again.

Bobby Boyer, Ross, the Hagopian boys, and others would play in the vacant lot by the side of the apartment. Ross had a Green Bay Packers football outfit, including helmet, that his grandparents had sent him for Christmas, and we could not get it off him. The lot was dusty, and he and the uniform would get our marble floors very dusty. Sari would walk behind him with a dust mop and rag. We were so glad when he finally outgrew the set.

Bobby graduated from Brown University with a degree in French, married a Norwegian girl, and worked for a German firm with a branch office in Paris for many years. He now lives and works for the German company in Philadelphia.

Ross came home on the last day of the school year, crying. When we asked what was wrong, he said, "Poppa, I plunked kindergarten." He could not pronounce flunked, as he was missing his front teeth. Penny and I had decided he was not mature enough to start the first grade, so we held him back. The other kids were teasing him and telling him he had flunked.

Turkey had many delights, not the least of which happened to be "Turkish delights." The sweet, tasty treats, such as the world-famous baklava, could be bought from street vendors. My favorite, a gummy, sugar-brushed bread cube filled with fruit or pistachios, would make a rabbit slap a bear.

Another favorite delight happened to be a treat of another type, the Turkish bath. Monthly, I along with Bob Boyer and sometimes others would have a few libations at the Officer's Club and then head to the *hamam* or Turkish bath to purify not only the body but also the soul. The bath, a heavenly experience, became a ritual that brought a feeling of well-being and peace and a wonderful night of sleep.

When we entered, we found a room that was lined with changing cubicles and contained a cot covered with a clean, white sheet. The room, which was cold, almost freezing, had a marble fountain in the center and an attendant offering freshly squeezed orange juice or bottled water. After we undressed and wrapped our bodies in a cotton bathing gown, we entered an antechamber for shaving and bodily functions. When we left that room, we found ourselves in a large, domed room constructed of marble and filled with steam. It had a small hole in the ceiling for the steam to dissipate, the *hamam* proper.

Marble benches lined the wall with spigots of warm water and a copper bowl for rinsing as you let the warm, almost-hot, moist steam waft over you while you periodically rinsed yourself from the head down with the warm water. The sweating and rinsing continued for perhaps a half hour, and ever-so-gradually, the waves of total relaxation began to ripple through your body.

Motioned by the bath attendant, you moved to an oval, heated table made from stone in the center of the room and lay down on your stomach. Soon, the heat from the table opened the pores in your skin, and you began to perspire profusely. The attendant then began to vigorously rub the layer of dead skin covering your body, alternating between a lambskin and a coarse raw silk glove. As the skin came off, black filth began to ooze from your pores, and the attendant would wash and rinse you and then rub some more until your skin appeared like a newborn baby's.

The bath was followed by a massage while you were still lying on the heated table. As the attendant kneaded you from head to toe, you began to feel delightfully sleepy and ever-so-blissful. Once finished, you were led back to your cubicle. The support appreciated, you were weak in the knees. Covered in large, warm towels and given orange juice to drink, you remained for fifteen minutes or so to regain your strength. As I walked home, I felt as if I were wearing a new suit of clothes.

The crowning moment of my tour in Izmir took place when, thankfully, Penny was not there. She, Ann Torrans, Ann Boyer, Ann Davies, and some other girls were on a cruise ship touring the Mediterranean. The tour began in Brindisi, Italy, with stopovers in Athens, Cyprus, Rhodes, and Tel Aviv. Ross and I remained in Izmir, as the trip was a girl thing.

I was coaching the US Army basketball team in a NATO league against other services, nationalities, and the "tobacco buyers." The "tobacco buyers" worked for American companies bidding on and buying Turkish tobacco. They were arrogant and overpaid. Their companies paid big bucks to obtain Officer's Club privileges for them, and they were friends with the US Air Force civilian who ran the NATO recreation program. This person favored both the US Air Force and the "tobacco buyers" over the US Army. I repeatedly had problems with him getting gym time for practice and scheduling of games. In general, he was difficult to work with, and I had expressed my displeasure with him on several occasions. We did not like each other.

My team was scheduled to play the "tobacco buyers" on a frigid winter's night at Sirinyer Garrison. When I arrived, I realized the civilian was going to referee the game, and I protested. I felt he could not be impartial based on our past difficulties and his close personal relationship with the "tobacco buyers." He said that he would note the protest and that it would be taken up with the athletic council but that I had to make one of two choices: either play the game or forfeit the game. I was not worried about beating the "tobacco buyers," even with a biased referee, as I had an extremely strong team. I was concerned about my people being knocked around unnecessarily and the game turning into a shoving match. This fellow made numerous bad calls, which I complained about, and on the third technical, he kicked me off the floor. Ross and I took a seat in the stands and watched for the remainder of the game. I had accomplished what I wanted, which was to have the game refereed somewhat fairly. We won by a large margin.

Ross and I were waiting inside the gymnasium for my guys to shower and change clothes when the civilian starting telling me he was going to whip me and challenged me to go outside and fight. I told him I would not fight him on the military installation but that there was an open field between Sirinyer Garrison and Izmir where we could meet and I would accommodate him. A couple of the "tobacco buyers" were egging him on and calling me a coward and afraid to fight. I told him I was leaving. I would stop near the field, and if he were there, fine, and if not, fine.

Ross and I left the gym and walked to our car, and I helped Ross into the front seat. The civilian came out of the gym and was followed by several "tobacco buyers," and then he hollered at me, "Come here. I'm not through with you." I walked toward him with both hands in my coat pockets, as it was an extremely cold night. My right hand was wrapped around a package of Kent cigarettes. When I reached him, he hit me squarely in the face. I could not get my hands out of my coat pockets, as they were now clenched, and he was cleaning my clock. Finally, I was able to get my hands out and began to fight back. My guys and the rest of the "tobacco buyers" arrived on the scene, and a first-class donnybrook broke out. My people were young and strong, and they knew how to fight. The cancer-stick buyers were only young. It was an uneven fight, and the results were not pretty. Some civilian ass got kicked that night.

Ross silently watched through the car window.

The Turkish MPs arrived with a US Air Force security officer. Statements were taken, and we were released. There was not much night left, but what was left was sleepless.

The next morning, I left Ross with Sari and went to work. I had a black eye, a broken nose, and many bruises. My boss met me and told me I was to report to the garrison commander. It was back to Sirinyer Garrison, where I reported to Colonel Lloyd, who was responsible for dispensing military justice to Army soldiers.

I entered his office, saluted, and reported, "Sir, Captain Taylor reports to the commanding officer as ordered."

He did not return my salute and left me at attention. He began to shout, "You are a disgrace to the uniform. You have created an international incident. The Turks are upset. General Dick is upset, and General Tipton is upset. Your behavior can only be described as conduct unbecoming of an officer."

My short army career was passing before my eyes, but my main thought was, How am I going to explain this to Penny? This boy from Barnhart had his ass in a sling, and he knew it. Colonel Lloyd went on to tell me he was offering me an Article 15, and I had twenty-four hours to decide if I would accept the Article 15. If I did not accept the Article 15, an Article 32 investigation would be initiated, and I would be court-martialed.

He stated that he was prepared to take up to one half of one month's pay for six months, confine me to quarters for six months, and allow me only to go to work, visit a doctor, or go to church.

An Article 15 was a career terminator for an officer. I might as well resign my commission, because I would never again be promoted. He returned my salute and dismissed me.

I left his office, my head swimming, when Colonel Lloyd came to his door and called me back into his office. He shut the door, motioned me to a seat, and said, "Tell me all about it. Did you really kick their asses?"

"Sir?"

"That damn civilian and those 'tobacco buyers' have been a pain in the ass, and it was time they got theirs."

"Sir, what about the Article 15?"

He told me to refuse it and that would be the end of it. He had to do what he had to do because General Tipton was involved. He had a file a mile long about the US Air Force civilian and "tobacco buyers," and this latest incident was the last piece of the puzzle. He would brief General Dick, and General Dick would think it was all good stuff and stick it up General Tipton's ass. He went on to quiz me about every blow that was thrown, which I described in detail, assuring him that if he thought I looked bad, he should see the civilian and the "tobacco buyers."

I was Colonel Lloyd's friend from then on. When he saw me, he would say, "Been in any fights lately, captain?"

I would respond, "No, sir."

And he would say, "Well, if you get the urge, let me know."

The US Air Force civilian was immediately reassigned, and I never saw the "tobacco buyers" in the Officer's Club again. My rating chain never mentioned this incident to me. Penny did though, and her remarks were not favorable. I had a lot of explaining to do when she returned from her trip.

My team won the NATO league championship.

ALFSEE had an advanced command post (ACP) in Thessalonica, Greece. Today, the Greeks call it Salonica. Thessaloniki is the second largest city in Greece, second only to Athens, with a population of one million. It is one of the oldest cities in Europe, lying in a bowl much like Izmir, one formed by low hills facing a bay that opens into the Gulf of Thermaikos. It was founded about 315 BC on a site of prehistoric settlements going back to 2300 BC by Cassandra, King of Macedonia, and named after his wife, Thessaloniki, sister of Alexander the Great. In Roman times, it was visited by the Apostle Paul, who preached Christianity and who later addressed his two well-known epistles to the Christians of Thessaloniki.

The modern city is thriving and is one of the most important trade and communications centers in the Mediterranean. This is evident from its financial and commercial activities, its port and special free zone, which provides facilities to other Balkan countries, its international airport, and its important industrial complex. Thessaloniki has a university and many museums and archeological sites from antiquity.

I would visit Thessaloniki periodically on an unannounced schedule to inventory the documents maintained in the COSMIC Registry. A young sergeant who worked for me accounted for the documents. The ACP was an alternate site for ALFSEE to locate during hostilities; therefore, I maintained one copy of the most important documents there, as most documents in Izmir would require burning prior to evacuation.

The sergeant was in the process of submitting paperwork, a tedious affair in view of his security clearance, to marry a Greek girl. The girl had a sister who worked for an import-export firm and who spoke excellent formal English. She had been educated in a British university and wanted to learn conversational English, particularly American slang. It always amazed me that when I was in a foreign country, the indigenous people wanted to learn American slang. I suppose they thought it was cool.

The two Greek girls acted as tour guides, so over time, I became familiar with Thessaloniki and its history. While there, I bought several *flokati* rugs of various dyed colors, as they were the rage at the time. The rugs made from wool have been a Greek tradition for centuries. They originally serviced the shepherds when they were used as beds and clothing. The rugs can be priced up to several thousand dollars, depending on the weight. My rugs are now stored in a closet and have not seen a floor in years, although they were quite nice to have on our marble floors in Izmir.

Headquarters of the Turkish First Army, located at Uskudra, an area of Istanbul on the Asian side, in a complex built prior to the 1850s, is the site of the British Army military hospital, which was made famous by the work of Florence Nightingale during the Crimean War (1854–6). Nightingale's bedroom and work area had been restored, and there was a small display outlining her accomplishments in military health care. The complex was not accessible to the public, but I was privileged to see the site and spend some time there.

Shortly before we departed Turkey, Grandmother and Granddad Farr stayed several days with us in Izmir. We all traveled together for a few days in both Greece and Turkey. They had visited their son, Bill, in Germany, and they were going to visit a cattle rancher in France on their way home.

A day or so before their arrival, one of my folks told me there was a US Air Force general calling me from Ankara. I wondered what I had done to the US Air Force this time as I was not often called by a US Air Force general. It was Major General Benjamin Cassidy, Granddad Farr's Culver Military Academy roommate. He had read in the Culver alumni magazine the Farrs were coming to Turkey and wanted to come to Izmir to visit with them.

We took an overnight trip to Kusadasi to visit Ephesus and stayed a few days in Athens. While in Athens, we visited the Acropolis, and Granddad Farr bought Penny and Grandmother Farr mink stoles in a shop near the Bay of Piraeus. Ross stayed in Izmir with Sari.

Herbie, Penny, Granddad, and Grandmother Farr at the Acropolis, Athens, Greece.

Penny and I had been trying to buy some jewelry in a particular shop at the *agora* (market) in Izmir, but we had not been able to get the price we were willing to pay. The Farrs also wanted to buy some jewelry, so we took them to that shop. We introduced the Farrs to the owner, and you would have thought they were long lost friends. The price on the jewelry we wanted went down considerably, and the Farrs also made some nice purchases. We found out later that the owner was a Freemason as was Granddad Farr. I guess it is all in the handshake. I still find it unusual for a Turk to be a Mason.

On April 21, 1967, a military coup by the colonel's junta led by Colonel George Papadopoulos overthrew the government of Greece and led to the eventual exile of King Constantine and Queen Anne Marie in December 1967. The Greek Army forces were designated for ALFSEE control, so we saw the coup coming several days before, as Greek units began moving from their designated NATO positions closer to Athens. The Greeks were supposed to coordinate or at least advise ALFSEE of major troop movements, but in this case, they did not.

In November 1967, the Turks and Greeks clashed over Cyprus. Until that time, we had Greek officers assigned to ALFSEE, but they were recalled during the conflict. The Turks flew fighters out of Cigli Airbase on intimidation missions over Cyprus, and Izmir operated under strictly enforced blackouts for several nights. I spent some long days and nights at the headquarters as we tried to analyze what each side would do next. I have no position on the Cyprus issue, but in 1967, the Greeks would have been foolish to go to war with the Turks. In my opinion, the Turks would have won easily, and that remains my opinion today. I would not want the Turks as an enemy.

One of the last places I remembering visiting was Hellenic First Army near Larissa, Greece. Larissa is another ancient city located in the central part of Greece. It was the home of Hippocrates, the so-called father of medicine. General Dick called me to his office and handed me a sealed envelope and told me his plane was waiting to take me to Larissa. I would be met and taken to Hellenic First Army, where I was to deliver the envelope to the commanding general.

The Greek lieutenant general, who spoke perfect English, met me at the entrance to his headquarters and proceeded to show me around. The headquarters building was marvelous with lots of marble, paintings, and statutes. He took me to his office suite, where I was given food and drink, while he disappeared into his office. Shortly thereafter, he handed me an envelope hand-addressed to General Dick and thanked me for coming, and then I departed. I wondered what great secret I was carrying. Perhaps General Dick would be passing through Athens, and it was no more that an invitation for the two to get together for lunch at the King George II Palace Hotel.

Our tour in Turkey ended. I now had orders for my next assignment. The destination was Vietnam. *Hot damn, Vietnam, be the first one on your block to come home in a box.* Vietnam was another eight thousand miles from Barnhart in the opposite direction. Colonel Varhol presented Penny and me with an ALFSEE Certificate of Appreciation for our participation in the NATO community, and I was told that I would receive my second Army Commendation Medal in Vietnam.

Colonel Varhol, Herbie, and Penny.

The forwarding of awards to the new command was a bad policy. The thinking was that if the individual received the award in their new command, it would prove what a fine fellow they were getting and start him off on the right foot with his new boss. This sounds good in principle. However, an award was not only tangible evidence of what the soldier had done but also a reflection of the effort of the people he worked with and who had worked for him. I considered my awards to be a group award that I happened to receive on their behalf. I always presented my soldiers' awards in front of the people where they had earned the award.

I did receive the award in Vietnam. There was no ceremony. One of my clerks handed it to me and said, "Sir, here is your award. Nice medal. What did you do to get it?"

There were several friends at the Izmir Airport when we departed. The Italians were lined up at attention as we proceeded to board the aircraft. Each broke into tears as they saluted and hugged me when I stopped to speak to each and say good-bye. Italians are emotional people, perhaps Americans as well. There were tears in my eyes. Ed Buelow put his hand on my shoulder before I stepped on the ramp leading to the aircraft fuselage and whispered, "If you can't cry, you don't care." It was somewhere over the Aegean when my eyes dried. I find it interesting what I remember over the years.

We made plans to take leave in Istanbul and Rome on the way home, but my request was not approved. Pan Am Flight 1 (around the world) was the flight we were to take out of Istanbul. That flight flew over Bulgaria and because of my security clearance, we could not do that. Therefore, we flew by way of Athens, Zurich, and Paris to New York. Bad weather prevented us from an immediate landing at JFK, and we were put into a holding pattern for almost three hours. At one time, I counted over fifty planes circling JFK at various levels. Finally, we landed but had missed our connecting flight to Atlanta and Dallas.

The airline paid for a room at a nearby hotel, but we had a large amount of luggage that I had not intended to drag from one place to another. We finally got to bed, hungry and exhausted in the wee hours of the morning. Our flight left early the next morning, so it was a short night. We flew from New York to Atlanta to Dallas and then to San Angelo, where we were met by our parents.

We were home to the Rocker b for thirty days prior to my shipping out to Vietnam. This boy from Barnhart was glad to have his feet back on West Texas soil. Mr. Blakely had agreed for Penny to live in the Rock House on the hill close to her parents while I was in Vietnam. She ended up staying in the main house in her old bedroom, and Ross stayed in one of the boys' rooms, as Bud and Bill were gone. We stored our household goods in the Rock House. Bill was still in Germany. Bud had married his high school sweetheart, Annis Friend, from Big Lake, graduated veterinary school at Texas A&M College, and was now an Army veterinarian inspecting meat near Los Angeles that was destined for Vietnam.

While on leave, I became ill and spent several days in the hospital at Goodfellow Air Force Base. I had suffered a perforated intestine, the cause of which was never determined. Antibiotics, youth, and the body's self-healing mechanism pulled me through. This problem continued to plague me throughout the years.

Penny, Ross, and I drove to California and visited the Grand Canyon, Las Vegas, and other sites on the way. Grandmother Farr flew to Los Angeles, and we all stayed at Bud and Annis's apartment complex. This gave us a chance to meet the infant, Louis (Lee) Farr V, and visit Disneyland. We attended The Linkletter Show in Culver City. Granddad Farr was president of the Texas Sheep and Goat Raisers Association, which sponsored the annual Miss Wool of America Pageant in San Angelo. Mr. Linkletter was the master of ceremonies for the contest. We visited with him backstage after his show.

Penny, Herbie, Mr. Linkletter, Grandmother Farr, Ross, Annis, and Lee Farr at the Art Linkletter Show in Culver City, California.

On August 4, 1968, Penny, Ross, and Grandmother Farr drove me to the Los Angeles International Airport (LAX), where we hugged and kissed good-bye. I would next see Penny some seven months later in Hawaii. I would not see Ross for a year. They drove back to the Rocker b.

I flew to San Francisco and was met by representatives from Oakland Army Base. I boarded an Army bus with other troops, and I was transported to Travis Air Force Base for the flight to Vietnam.

11

My War

The departure from Travis AFB aboard a US Air Force Military Airlift Command (MAC) contract flight began as one of sadness and excitement—sadness about leaving Penny and Ross and excitement about the journey that lay ahead.

A major and I were the senior officers on the flight. I signed for the troops. The major, the troop commander, and I were responsible for accountability and maintaining order and discipline. We flew to Anchorage, Alaska, for refueling and made another stop in Okinawa.

We were lost in our thoughts as we flew to Alaska. After Alaska, the kidding and horseplay began. Then came fitful sleep and finally the steep descent into Bien Hoa Airfield, South Vietnam, without a word uttered. I thought, What lies ahead, and what is this all about? I am sure I was not alone.

A strong believer in first appearances, I wore a highly starched khaki uniform with polished brass and shoes on the flight. I did my best to keep my legs straight so I would not break the starch, which made the eighteen-hour or so flight even longer. I was certain I would be assigned to the headquarters of the US Army in Vietnam (USARV) located a few kilometers from Saigon at Long Binh or the headquarters of the Military Assistance Advisory Command (MACV) in Saigon. I wanted to make a good impression on my new boss.

What an idiot. I walked off the plane into the baking heat and suffocating, smoldering humidity of Vietnam, and by the time I stepped off the ramp onto the tarmac, my uniform had gone "poof." It was a wet dishrag. So much for appearances. Little did I know I would be wearing that same uniform for almost two weeks.

We were loaded into a big, blue, ugly US Air Force bus with wire screens covering the windows. (I later found out this was done to deflect any grenades a sapper might throw.) We were then transported some thirty minutes to the 90th Replacement Battalion at Long Binh. The 90th, a collection of Southeast Asian huts and GP medium tents outfitted with cots for sleeping, presented a bleak picture. The battalion had few recreational facilities. They did have hot showers, and I should have been grateful because hot water on demand would soon be a thing of the past.

The officers were separated from the enlisted soldiers, our field 201 files (individual personnel records) taken, and a short briefing given explaining that the normal stay would be around two days, at which time we would be given orders for onward movement to our assigned units. I stayed three days, during which I made calls to the USARV officer assignment section and inquired about my assignment. Each time, I was told to cool my heels, as an assignment would be forthcoming.

Other officers were coming and going, but not me. I realized I was an insignificant cog, a replacement part in a very big, green machine that could care less if my pants were creased. I still hoped that my records were sitting on some general's desk, and once he got to them, he would realize I was just the man he was looking for. In the meantime, there was nothing to do except sit on my cot and smoke cigarettes. I did write a letter to Penny to tell her that I had arrived safely.

Finally, I received orders to the 204th Military Intelligence Detachment. Why a military intelligence unit? Maybe it was because of my security clearance. Captains usually commanded detachments, so I asked myself if I would be the commander, and where was this unit? The personnel folks at the 90th told me that the APO numbers on the orders were for DaNang, so it was back to Bien Hoa Airfield, this time for a flight to DaNang on a C-130. The C-130 Hercules, the US Air Force's workhorse during the Vietnam War, was loaded with dead-tired marines in full combat gear and duffel bags, and I was wearing my ever-so-slightly wrinkled and soiled khaki uniform.

The marine sergeant looked me up and down, and from the scowl on his face, he did not care for what he saw. Apparently, this was a marine platoon sprawled out in the belly of the aircraft, butt to butt or cheek to cheek (no pun intended). All were soon sleeping. A marine private motioned he was willing to share a portion of his lumpy duffel bag to use as a pillow. I gratefully accepted.

When I arrived in DaNang, I proceeded to the Army liaison NCO and presented my orders. He fiddled around with some papers and told me he had nothing on the 204th MI Detachment but to hop on the waiting US Navy bus, as it would stop at the Army personnel office and maybe they could help me. They could not help, however, because they had never heard of the 204th, but they assured me that they would get a call through to USARV and told me that I should check back the next morning.

A captain, sensing my plight, told me I could bunk with him, as he had an extra cot in his hooch. The next morning, the personnel folks told me USARV had told them the 204th was in DaNang and suggested I do some scouting on my own to locate the unit. This I did. What I located was a US Navy Officer's Club that served real American food and scotch whiskey. The club would not take American dollars, only something called "military payment certificates" (MPC). In fact, US dollars were illegal in Vietnam.

MPC closely resembled monopoly money. It was the same size, but it had a military or Vietnamese motif in colored pictures. It came in numerous denominations from five cents upward. The purpose of the MPC was to control the impact of inflation on the Vietnamese economy and prevent black-marketing. The "funny money" was used only in US military facilities, but the Vietnamese readily took it. The whole deal was a joke primarily on the South Vietnamese. The MPC script was changed periodically without notice. All military compounds were closed to the locals, and the old MPC was exchanged for new MPC. This caused a clamor outside the wire of the compounds, as the Vietnamese begged soldiers inside to take their old MPC at a reduced rate and exchange it for new in order to salvage something.

I had exchanged my traveler's checks for MPC while at the 90th Replacement Battalion. I drew seventy-five dollars a month while in Vietnam and put a hundred in the 10 percent Soldiers Deposit Savings Program, and Penny received the rcmainder. Cigarettes were a dollar a carton and whiskey was twenty-five cents a drink, so seventy-five dollars went a long way in keeping me supplied with my basic needs.

Penny would periodically send me health and comfort items, such as razor blades, shaving cream, and toothpaste.

I would go to the US Navy Officer's Club each evening and holler over the raucous din, "Does anyone know where the 204th MI Detachment is located?" I would do this several times over the evening, and I would never receive an answer. One evening, I hollered the same plaintive question once more, and a couple of warrant officer helicopter pilots waved me over to the bar. They said that they not only knew its location but that they were assigned to it. They then told me that I really did not want to go there.

I asked, "Where is it?"

One of the warrant officers answered, "Phu Bai and the place 'sucks' so bad we can't fly over it."

They explained that the 204th MI Detachment was being used for personnel accounting purposes as the unit designation for the new corps headquarters, Provisional Corps Vietnam (PCV), that the Army was putting together near Hue. They said that if I really wanted to get there, I was to meet them at the airfield the next morning, and they would fly me up.

Over the years, I have concluded that I could have spent my entire tour in DaNang, not worked a lick, hung out at the US Navy Officer's Club and China Beach, grown a beard, chased the nurses, and had a year-long vacation! It would not have been conducive to career progression, and Penny would not have been pleased. Nevertheless, the "squids" and "jarheads" did have a good thing going for themselves in DaNang. This was a war zone. Hell, it was not that much different from the land of the "Big PX" (Post Exchange-Military equivalent to Wal-Mart) that I had just left!

The two warrants flew me to Phu Bai Airfield, and I got a jeep ride for the short trip to the PCV location and reported to the headquarters commandant, a lieutenant colonel. I explained to him that USARV did not know the location for PCV and that there was no telling how many replacements were wandering around DaNang trying to find the place. He told me my mission was to get with the USARV assignment people and the personnel people in DaNang and get them "clued in" about our location.

Phu Bai, located eight miles south of Hue in Thua Thien Providence, closer to Hanoi than Saigon and very close to the DMZ and Khe Sanh, served as the fulcrum of the Red River Delta and the Mekong Delta. It was Indian country, the home of Victor Charlie (Viet Cong), and the NVA (North Vietnamese Army). This could be a bad neighborhood under any circumstances but especially at night. We Americans may have owned the day, but the bad guys owned the night. It was what had been the heart of marine country, but it was now under the operational control of the Army. This change from an area under marine control to one dominated by the Army resulted in the chaotic conditions I had found when I had arrived at Phu Bai.

The Vietnam War was primarily a land war, and the US Army and Marine Corps were the predominant combat elements, with the US Navy and Air Force in support roles. If national policy is to control territory, boots must be put on the ground, and it is the infantrymen of the US Army and Marine Corps who fill those boots. Unfortunately, these two major combatants, while they were fighting a common enemy, were often in disagreement with how the war should be conducted. This conflict between services, one in which the Army would win, did little in my opinion to further the shared goal of victory against the common enemy.

At the beginning of the Vietnam War, all services wanted a part of the action, particularly the US Army and the Marine Corps. The Army was eager to participate because it had suffered under extreme budgetary constraints and loss of influence during the early years of the Cold War. The national strategy of massive retaliation and mutually assured destruction had resulted in congress being extremely kind to the US Air Force and Navy. The US Army and to a lesser extent the US Marine Corps were almost an afterthought when the money was doled out. Both were chaffing at the bit to gain a dominant role in this new war.

The initial surge of "boots on the ground" occurred on March 8, 1965, when the 3rd Battalion, 9th Marines waded ashore near DaNang and were greeted by a gaggle of photographers, local Vietnam officials, and Vietnamese schoolgirls. This was not an auspicious start for the marines and certainly did not to add to their illustrious history of other landings at places like Iwo Jima and Guadalcanal. Perhaps the landing should have served as an omen that this was not going to be a US Marine Corps war.

In fairness to the marines, their initial deployment mission was to provide security for the DaNang Airfield. As the war escalated and troop movements intensified, the larger Army became the dominant force. Army doctrine, tactics, and strategy prevailed at the higher echelons of command. The Army wanted to pursue a conventional war of "search and destroy" and engage large forces of the enemy, while the US Marine Corps was intent on conducting a pacification campaign.

Reluctantly, the marines, either by direct order from MACV or to save face by doing it on their own, began to move north from DaNang into the DMZ region, establishing bases at Dong Ha, Cam Lo, Phu Bai, Khe Sanh, and the Rockpile. This resulted in the marines fighting two wars simultaneously. One was of counterinsurgency in and around DaNang, and the other, more conventionally, was against NVA regulars in the North. This quieted somewhat the opinion of the Army brass that the marines did not know how to fight a land war, were reluctant to do so, and came in, sat down, and did nothing, which was even more denigrating. The events of Tet 68 were to solidify Army sentiments and change the conduct of the war, not only in the northern provinces but the war as a whole.

On January 31, 1968, some seventy thousand Viet Cong and North Vietnam soldiers launched coordinated attacks throughout South Vietnam. The major battles of the American counteroffensive occurred at Hue and Khe Sanh, and these battles remain two of the defining battles of the Vietnam War. The battle for Hue ended on February 24, 1968, and the battle of Khe Sanh ended on March 25, 1968, with an overwhelming loss of enemy soldiers. However, these two battles and the attack of nineteen sappers on the American embassy in Saigon during the first day of the offensive became the dominant images coming from the battlefield. The resulting media coverage became increasingly critical of military forces and sympathetic to the North Vietnamese.

There are many historians and Vietnam veterans who believe that the victory of US forces over the enemy during Tet 68 was the beginning of the end of American involvement in Vietnam. The biased images and propaganda dispatched by the press convinced the American public the war could not be won.

> *A journalist is a grumbler, a censurer, a giver of advice, a regent of sovereigns, and a tutor of nations. Four hostile newspapers are more to be feared than a thousand bayonets.*
> —Napoleon Bonaparte

A picture truly is worth a thousand words, but sometimes they only project half-truths. One of the most chilling images to come out of the Vietnam War was taken by Associated Press photojournalist Eddie Adams on February 1, 1968, during the Tet Offensive. The photo showed Colonel Nguyen Ngoc Loan, later Brigadier General Loan, the Saigon Chief of Police, executing a Viet Cong prisoner, Nguyen Van Lem, on a Saigon street. This picture, for which Adams won a Pulitzer Prize, horrified and sickened the nation.

Not nearly so well known as that photo was that Nguyen Van Lem, a captain of a Viet Cong assassination and revenge platoon, had just executed the wife, children, and relatives of a police officer serving under Colonel Loan. Innocent noncombatants had been bound, shot, and thrown in a ditch by Lem and his cutthroats. When captured, Lem allegedly was proud of what he had done and boasted of his commitment to Communism and his success at completing his mission to liquidate all persons on his list.

> *This was war. One shot, one kill and the bastard was in Hell. Would you have pulled the trigger on this hot, miserable day when your blood was boiling if the dead had been your friends, your family? Would you?*
> —Herbie Taylor

Adams later apologized to General Loan for the irretrievable damage it did to his honor, and upon Loan's death, Adams praised him as a hero of a just cause. General Loan fled South Vietnam in 1975, the year the Communists overran the country, and settled in Burke, Virginia. He opened a small, indoor pizza/oriental restaurant in a strip mall not far from Lake Braddock. Penny and I often ate in the restaurant before Ross's basketball games. Once when I was in uniform, General Loan came to our table and asked me when and where I had served in Vietnam. We had a pleasant chat, and he mentioned he had been born in Hue and had served in Saigon; however, he did not speak of the photo. General Loan died in 1998 at age sixty-seven, a broken man.

General William Westmoreland, the MACV commander and senior Army general, directed that a MACV forward command post be set up at Phu Bai to monitor operations in the threatened northern provinces of Quang Tri and Thua Thien. General Creighton Abrams, Westmoreland's deputy at MACV, became the commander and arrived in Phu Bai on February 13, 1968. The command post was set up in buildings vacated by the 3d Marine Division rear echelon, which had relocated to Dong Ha. Personnel required to staff the forward site came primarily from the headquarters of USARV and the headquarters of MACV. This makeshift outfit became the forerunner of Provisional Corps, Vietnam (PCV), and later XXIV Corps, and it began the shift of control from the marines to the Army.

With the siege of Hue reduced and the relief of Khe Sanh ongoing, PCV became operational under command of Lieutenant General William B. Rosson on March 10, 1968. The corps had tactical control of the 101st Airborne, 1st Cavalry, 3d Marine, and the US Navy's Task Force CLEARWATER, as well as combat and combat service support units.

The Army activated XXIV Corps to replace the PCV on August 15, 1968. Lieutenant General Richard Stilwell assumed command of XXIV Corps.

My situation as well as others assigned to the headquarters began to improve immediately with the activation of the XXIV Corps, primarily because of administrative and logistical support for the Corps moving from marine to Army assets.

The US Marine Corps believed that if you could not shoot, communicate, eat, or copulate with it, you did not need it. My assessment over the years was that the US Air Force supplied the best logistic support, as they could fly in what was needed. The US Navy could float it over, but that took time. The Army depended on both, and the marines were dead last to all.

Now, I had a place to live, get out of my khakis, and put on jungle fatigues and boots. My quarters or hooch, as it was commonly called, was a rectangular building with plywood walls and floor and a corrugated tin roof. It sat on wooden beams around eighteen inches off the ground to allow water to pass underneath during the monsoon season. The hooch had a door at either end, and it was designed to accommodate eight soldiers, although no more than five other officers ever shared it with me. The interior walls were screened about four feet from the floor to the ceiling to allow air to circulate. Wooden shutters could be lowered from the outside to keep the rain out. Immediately outside, a bunker constructed by my hooch mates and me of sandbags piled on top of each other provided our only protection from incoming mortar fire and 122mm rockets. We worked on the bunker during our spare time to provide as much protection as possible. The hooch furnishings included a large oscillating fan on a pole that we could move around as needed. Each of us had a metal cot with a very thin mattress, a mosquito net to drape around the cot, a footlocker, and a wall locker. That was it. There were neither tables nor chairs. If we wanted to visit or play cards, we used the footlockers. It should be noted that all soldiers from private to lieutenant colonel had the same basic accommodations. Although austere, we were living much better than the soldiers out humping the boonies.

Colonels and general officers, on the other hand, lived in trailer houses and ate in the commanding general's mess on linen-covered tables with china and crystal, and dined on all kinds of delicacies flown in on General Stillwell's personal aircraft from Thailand and the Philippines. Lieutenant colonels and below ate in a large, wooden, tin-roofed mess hall. Officers did have a small, separate area to eat from enlisted soldiers. Our food was not so elegant. Fresh fruits and vegetables were in short supply, and most food came out of cans. I ate two steaks while in Phu Bai. Once, my boss, Colonel George McLaughlin, invited me to dine with him at the general's mess, and another time, I ate steak at a party being held at the Infantry battalion that provided security for the Corps headquarters.

The officers' shower consisted of a wooden building on a concrete foundation with sixteen showerheads, eight on each side. Water came from a metal storage tank on an elevated platform, and it was not heated. The lack of heat did not create a problem during the summer, but it did during the monsoon season in September and October. The nearest latrine facility, a three-seat outhouse some thirty yards from my hooch, provided for the very basic of needs. Fifty-five gallon drums containing used oil were placed under the seats to collect the waste.

Once full, the barrels were removed, kerosene added, and the mixture burned. The delicate aroma of the burning mixture would waft gently in the hot, sultry summer wind and provided one of the unique olfactory memories of Vietnam, and there were many. The latrine facilities, either three seats or one seat, were located throughout the headquarters area. They were necessary, because dysentery was quite prevalent. You were a lucky GI indeed if you did not have a bout with dysentery several times during your one-year tour. The one-seaters were located in the center of elevated roads that ran through the hooch area. The roads were built up several feet to allow vehicles to maneuver without becoming stuck during the rainy season. There was nothing unusual about a deuce-and-a-half passing on either side of you as you went about your morning constitutional.

My first experience with death in a war zone involved a one-seat latrine. One early morning, a soldier was using the facility when a 122mm rocket landed on the far side of the latrine, buried up in the ground, as they would when on a delayed fuse, and exploded. The latrine and the soldier caught most of the shrapnel from the back blast. The soldier was able to stagger a few feet outside before he died with his pants around his boots. The latrine was intact, but it appeared that someone had spent hours sticking it with an ice pick.

The photo of Penny I took to Vietnam.

Now that I had a place to sleep, shower, and shave, things were looking up.

After about a month in Phu Bai, I began to receive mail from home. Mail became our lifeline with the real world in the absence of television, e-mail, and cell phones that soldiers now enjoy, and it was eagerly awaited. I received my first three letters from Penny all at one time. Mail call was the big event of the day, and I lived for it. Letters often arrived out of sequence, which would leave me wondering what Penny was talking about, but the next letter would solve the mystery. Later in the tour, we sent recorded tapes back and forth, and to hear Penny's voice was heaven.

Mother was good about writing, and I received numerous care packages filled with cheese, salami, ham, and other goodies from Pen, Annis, and others. A bottle of Tabasco sauce was a real treat and helped make the Army chow palatable. The arrival of a care package became a community event, as we all shared with each other. Bode and Edith Owens sent back issues of *Western Horsemen* and other periodicals. This boy from Barnhart was lonely, and to hear from home helped ease that loneliness.

He knows little who tells his wife all he knows.
—Thomas Fuller

Penny kept the letters I wrote, and in the process of reading them for this book, I realize how much we changed during that year. Penny became much more independent. She had to make decisions that affected her and Ross's life without my input. It also became obvious with each letter that we were settling into our routines, and we were reluctant to tell each other anything that might upset the other. Only after Vietnam did we share what really went on during our separation. Then we probably shared only part of it.

One thing she did not share with me in detail involved Ross. Ross was a difficult child at best. He was full of energy and unfocused, and he would not or could not mind. No amount of talking or whippings could make him behave. Penny was high-strung, and apparently, she was a bundle of nerves during our separation. She drove 130 miles round-trip for three days a week to attend classes at Angelo State College in San Angelo. She had a doctor prescribe Ritalin for Ross;

however, he was unable to tolerate the medicine, and she took him off it. Penny stayed stressed during that year, and Ross and I were a primary causal factor.

An example of how she typically handled stress occurred when she happened to see Janet Parry Harkelroad at the post office in Barnhart. Janet asked Pen how Ross was doing after his fight with Mickey Tom Owens. (Mickey Tom and Ross were in Mrs. Nunn's first-grade class in Big Lake, and they apparently had a disagreement.) Janet also said that she had heard that Ross had really been beaten up. Pen was not aware of any fight and told Janet there was no visible indication that Ross had been in a fight. Nevertheless, she knew something was not right.

Grandmother Farr took Ross to school each morning and picked him up after school. Ross had told his grandmother about the fight, and she decided not to tell Pen. I imagine the gravel flew as Pen headed to the Rocker b to confront Grandmother and Ross. She threw a "walleyed fit" and accused them of lying and embarrassing her. Apparently, things were quite tense for a few days.

Pen had her wisdom teeth pulled while I was gone. She developed a dry socket, which caused her great pain. The dentist prescribed a sedative, which incapacitated her for several days. Both of these I found out after Vietnam. She did not want to worry me.

We also talked to each other several times by using the Military Affiliate Radio System (MARS). MARS enabled soldiers to talk with their families for up to five minutes using HF radio to contact MARS stations in the United States. The stateside MARS station would run a "phone patch" through the local phone system to the soldier's home phone. Calls had to be booked, and the soldier and family member had to have immediate access to a phone. Military radio/telephone protocol had to be followed, and only one person on the hookup could talk.

During a typical conversation, I would say, "Honey, is everything all right? Over."

She would say, "We are fine. Over"

I would say, "I sure do miss and love you. Over."

She would say something that was garbled.

I would say, "I can't hear you. Over."

The MARS operator would cut in and say, "She says she loves you too," and so it would continue until the time was up. Not much information was passed, but as the phone company says, "It was almost like reaching out and touching someone."

Nothing could beat our R & R in Hawaii. We had seven wonderful days in paradise. We decided to take our R & R the first week in February primarily to get Penny out of Texas during the winter. The Army had a neat system for taking care of the wives while in Hawaii. The wives were met at the airport by the military, taken to Fort DeRussey, which was centrally located in Honolulu, briefed on their husbands' arrivals, and then taken to their hotel.

I flew from Phu Bai to Cam Ranh Bay, where I spent the night, and then boarded a MAC flight with 150 or so other "horny" GIs for the flight to Honolulu. My flight was late, so Penny got to Hawaii seven hours before I did. The Fort DeRussey Welcome Center had a long hall along which the wives and sweethearts were lined. The Army bused us from the airport, and we were all excitedly staring out the window when we drove up to the welcome center. I spotted Penny right away and made a beeline for her as soon as I stepped off the bus. Right before I planted a big juicy kiss on this girl, I realized she was not Penny. Simultaneously, I felt this frantic tug on my arm. I turned around, and there was Penny.

We stayed at the Outrigger Hotel and did the usual tourist things. We rented a car, drove around the island, went to the Don Ho and Kodak Hawaiian Show and the authentic Hawaiian village, and visited the Punchbowl Military Cemetery and Pearl Harbor. We spent time on the beach, ate some wonderful meals, and got to know each other all over again.

You make love to a woman, your wife, over the years many times, but only a few times are etched in your memory. This week was one of those times. I drove Penny to the airport, hugged and kissed her good-bye, and then just held her for a long, long time. I watched her plane depart. It was many years before I felt that lonely again.

One of the hardest adjustments I had to make when I arrived at Phu Bai was to the sound of the guns, the big guns. Initially, the marines had an artillery battery within a hundred yards from my hooch, and later, the Army's 108th Artillery Group had an eight-inch, self-propelled howitzer battery in the same area. Firing usually happened at night.

I thought that I would not be able to sleep through the firing, but I did. The sound of outgoing shells passing overhead became quite comforting. The sound meant the bad guys were having a bad night. Incoming mortars and rockets were a different deal. The sound of incoming would awaken you before the first shell hit. You were awake instinctively and headed to a sandbag bunker or anything that you could get over or around your body by the time of the first explosion. My brain intuitively recognized the difference between "incoming" and "outgoing."

One night, I was awakened by the sound of incoming, jumped out of my cot, and got about three feet when I reached the end of my mosquito net. The net brought my dash to an abrupt halt, flipped me over, and knocked me out. I was still lying on the floor when the "all clear" signal sounded and my hooch mates returned. Looking at me, one asked, "You hurt?" I shook my head to indicate I was not. "You sure missed a damn good fireworks display." That incident and one other was the only time I was oblivious to what was going on around me. The rest of the time, I was fully aware and doing my best to get my entire body inside my helmet. Actually, it is quite amazing how much of your body you are able to get inside a helmet. During attacks, I would sometimes forget (or not take the time) to put on my flak jacket before I started diving and crawling into a bunker, but I never forgot my helmet. I was not afraid of death, and I think most twenty-six-year-olds felt the same way. I was afraid of losing a limb or another part of my anatomy and being a cripple for the remainder of my life. When I was flying on a helicopter, I would often remove my flak jacket and sit on it. I always carried an extra jacket in my jeep to sit on.

Two Vietnamese women came daily to sweep and tidy up our hooch and to wash our clothes. They came from one of the nearby villages and arrived at 0700, when the compound gates opened, and left before 1700, when they closed. They washed our clothes by wetting them with soap and water, beating them with a rock, rinsing them, and then hanging them to dry. Most likely, they were either Viet Cong (VC), VC sympathizers, or people used by the VC. Mortars and especially 122mm rockets made large craters or destroyed buildings, and vehicles when they landed. I often saw these women and other hooch maids stepping off the distance from where a shell had landed to its intended target. This information, I am sure, was passed on so that it could be used during the next attack. Every effort was made after an attack to rid the area of debris and to fill the shell craters before allowing indigenous personnel on the compound, but evidence remained readily visible for their intelligence-collecting activities. The outlines of the craters were quite visible, with the newly turned red dirt standing out prominently. Most attacks occurred at night, but not all. If a large portion of the indigenous workforce did not report for work on a particular day, that was often a sign to be prepared for an attack.

Mortars generally walked through an area, but the rockets would go anywhere without pattern. Mortar attacks were rare, and they only occurred when the VC were trying to breach the perimeter. The rockets were inaccurate as a pinpoint weapon, but they contained large amounts of explosives and shrapnel. Thus, they were quite lethal and effective.

To give you an idea of how difficult it was to distinguish between friend and foe, this short anecdote will illustrate the point: We had an older Vietnamese man who worked as a barber and who would give you a haircut, shave, and massage for seventy-five cents in MPC. I would visit his shop several times a month, as did many others, and get his full treatment. His neck, shoulder, arm, and hand massages were wonderful. I would always have him shave me, and I thought nothing about the razor sliding up and down my throat. One night, mortars and rockets fell on the compound, and the VC tried to breach the perimeter. The story was that the old man's body and several others who worked on the compound were found on the concertina wire the next morning. I did not see the man's body, but I know he no longer worked on the compound.

The third week in Phu Bai, I was told that I would be running the XXIV Corps Area Communications Center and Courier Station, servicing all US Army, Navy, and Marine units from Phu Bai to the DMZ. I was back in the Top Secret business, and I finally had a job.

In addition to my normal duties, I had additional duties, as junior officers always do, serving as the headquarters security officer and MPC control officer. The Communications Center and Courier Transfer Station were collocated in a concrete, log, steel, and dirt bunker located near the commanding general's helipad. The bunker was camouflaged, guarded, and built to withstand a direct hit from a 122mm rocket. The

Corps commander and staff were dependent on the bunker activities and could not afford for it to be destroyed. The bunker was never hit, so I do not know if it would have survived a direct hit, but I believe it could have.

A signal unit from the 1st Signal Brigade was located in the same bunker as my people, but separated from them by a wall with no door. The signal folks called their area the Crypto Bunker, because they had the encryption gear necessary to decode incoming radio-teletype traffic and encode outgoing traffic. The signal unit would receive the message, do their thing, and pass it through a small window in the wall. My people would determine who was to receive copies of the message, reproduce it, stamp it with the appropriate security classification, log the message, deliver it to the proper element, and obtain a signature for the material. Messages were received with four delivery precedents: Routine, Priority, Immediate, and Flash. Sometimes they were received with a "For Eyes Only" or "Personal For" designation. These messages came only for the general officers, and my people delivered them immediately and directly to the general officer concerned. All my soldiers had a Top Secret clearance and had been personally authorized to process the general's messages. Flash and Immediate messages were hand-carried for delivery, as were all Top Secret messages. There were very few routine or unclassified messages received, but if they were, they were pitched in mail bins for staff sections and units to pick up during scheduled courier runs.

Both the Communications Center and Courier Station operated 24/7. At full strength, I had five lieutenants, two master sergeants, and somewhere around thirty-five soldiers. Rarely was I at full strength, and that was especially true initially. XXIV Corps had been put together from people and equipment sent from the headquarters of MACV and USARV. These two headquarters had used this as an opportunity to get rid of their duds, troublemakers, and people with only a short time left in country. Luckily, my people were all good soldiers, probably because they had passed the screening for a Top Secret clearance. Nevertheless, I did get some soldiers who only had a few months left on their tour. One of these was Master Sergeant Murphy.

Sergeant Murphy was the best NCO that could have been assigned to me. Murphy had been a NCO at the Communication Center at

MACV and had wanted to get closer to the war, so he had volunteered to come north. What he really wanted was to get his hands on some war trophies, AK-47s, bayonets, and VC flags and get them back to the States. He was a shyster, hustler, con man, a natural leader, and a first rate NCO who sincerely cared about his troops. He was just the man I needed to help get this outfit set up and operating. He ranks in the top five of my all-time best NCOs.

Captain Taylor and Master Sergeant Murphy, Phu Bai, Republic of Vietnam.

The 3d Marine Division had vacated the building that would be the Corps headquarters, so the first priority was to find office space for my people who did not work in the communications bunker. The headquarters commandant gave me three rooms, which had locks on the doors. The marines had left no keys, so I used a bolt cutter to remove the locks. Inside one room were classified materials consisting of not only documents but also maps. I decided not to pursue the matter with the marines and simply had the material destroyed by burning it in the classified waste incinerator.

In addition to reproducing message traffic, I was also responsible for reproduction services in the headquarters, including all operation plans (OPLANs), operation orders (OPORDERs), and periodic intelligence reports (PERINREPs). Some documents, particularly XXIV Corps regulations, would be reproduced in several thousand copies.

To accomplish this part of the mission, I had been given a worn-out 1250 offset press brought up from MACV headquarters, two expandable communication vans that were in good shape, and two large generators. The offset press would have been unable to handle the high-volume workload, even if it had been brand new.

Apparently, MACV was willing to give up the press because they had a brand new one and spare parts on the way from the continental United States (CONUS). Murphy knew this and told me about it. I told him to intercept it while it was still in the depot and steal it and the spare parts. This was right up Murphy's alley.

We sat down before he left and developed a list of all the supplies and equipment we needed to operate. My guidance to him was to trade for it, beg for it, get it legitimately, and if necessary, steal it, but just get it. Murphy first went to Dong Ha and made a deal with the marines for some AK-47s to use as trading material, which, I found out later, was Hamm's beer, which they gave away in Saigon.

Murphy would get a call through to me as he worked his way down the coast. He hit the depots at DaNang, Cam Ranh Bay, Long Bien, and Saigon, stockpiling materiel as he went. Three weeks passed, and I got a call from him that a convoy with supplies and equipment, including the brand new 1250 offset press, was leaving DaNang and coming to Phu Bai via Highway 1 and the Hai Van Pass. He gave me the bumper numbers so that I could locate the trucks. He told me that the two pallets of beer on one of the trucks were his and to safeguard them for him. He also told me he was still shopping in Saigon and would work his way back to Phu Bai in a few days. Murphy was amazing. Every unit had a Murphy, a scrounger. Murphy ranked among the best.

The Army logistics system was broken during Vietnam. The problem was not a lack of supplies but the manner in which they were distributed. The supplies simply piled up in the depots, and the depot people lost accountability for the materiel. They had no clue about what they had or where it was supposed to go.

The number of messages received by the communications center could only be described as a high volume. My soldiers were humping their entire twelve-hour shift. One particular type of message that bothered me alerted artillery units of defective lots of ammunition. There were an inordinate amount of these messages, and it must have been a real administrative burden on the artillery folks to keep up with them. Someone in corporate America got rich by fudging on quality control. I wonder how many soldiers were killed by defective ammunition because some fat corporate cats did not care about anything but the bottom line. I know of at least one. A short round fired by the battery inside our compound went through the roof of the headquarters building, hitting and killing a lieutenant colonel working at his desk in the G3 (Operations) section. Luckily, the round did not explode, or the loss of life would have been significant.

My duty day started at 0530 and normally ended at 2300 hours. My routine was to wake, shower, go to breakfast, and be at my desk by 0645. My first action would be to thumb through the previous night's message traffic and check to make sure that the correct staff section or unit had been assigned action on the messages and that all interested staff sections had been provided information copies. This also allowed me to keep up with what was happening in the XXIV Corps area of operations (AO). I would then visit each of my elements to ensure all were operating smoothly. Sometimes I would take a courier run, both by jeep and by helicopter, primarily to get away and sightsee for a while. Paperwork usually took up the rest of the morning. I would sunbathe while I napped, shower, and then go back to work, skipping lunch. I would usually break for the night meal around 1800 and be back in the office at 2000, when I would write letters or read. Generally, things were quiet at night unless "Charlie" decided to bring us some excitement. Before I retired for the night, I would again check on my people to make sure all was well.

Life cannot exist in society except by reciprocal concessions.
—Samuel Johnson

Each night, I would visit the reproduction folks who worked out of the expandable vans primarily to make sure the presses were up and running. I only had two operators, and both were outstanding and indefatigable. They each worked a twelve-hour shift and loved their job. Each had been press operators in civilian life, and they knew their business. One was a Hispanic soldier from Chicago, and the other was an Italian from New York. The vans were located in an isolated area between two wings of the headquarters building for protection, and the only people who visited them were my people and me. All documents reproduced were brought to my office, where my people checked them for proper security markings and administrative correctness, and then we delivered them to the reproduction vans for reproduction. These two guys worked by themselves and could have goofed off if they had wanted to do so, but I never caught them if they did. I started noticing a peculiar smell when I would visit the vans, and I soon realized it was the pungent smell of marijuana.

I told Murphy to tell them to stop.

He said, "Sir, do you really want to do that?"

"Absolutely!"

He did, and they did; however, I began to notice that there was a backlog of jobs to be reproduced, and the machines were breaking down quite regularly. I knew a union labor strike when I saw one. Both of these people worked in union shops as civilians. Because they were my only press operators, they had me in a difficult situation. Therefore, I did what any good manager in a union shop would do, I compromised. I told Murphy, "You tell those two yahoos to get those machines running, clear out the backlog, keep it cleared out, and they can do whatever they want to do."

Murphy answered, "Good decision, sir."

What did I do for entertainment in Phu Bai? Not much. The marines did have an officer's club of sorts that they turned over to the Army. I would usually have a couple of drinks before the night meal. Sometimes I would have more, a lot more. Alcohol was the drug of choice for my generation. The younger folks seemed to prefer marijuana and alcohol.

I saw one and a half floor shows while I was at Phu Bai. One consisted of a group of Filipino gals, and the other had some girls from Australia. The night the Australian girls were in the area, "Charlie" decided to interrupt our entertainment and provide a fireworks display instead.

We spent a good part of the night in bunkers. Some guys ended up in the same bunker as the gals. I was not so lucky. Bob Hope and Ann Margaret put on a show in either Dong Ha or Quang Tri that I flew up to attend. I ended up so far from the makeshift stage that I could not see much, but I could hear them. The GIs loved them. A couple of times, I flew up to witness the US Air Force "shock and awe" show, as they now so fondly call it. We called it an *"Arc Light Strike."* B-52s from Guam would be bombing a suspected VC or NVA stronghold, and we would chopper up to watch it from a safe distance on the ground, because if you got too close to a strike, the chopper would be torn apart by the shock waves. The results were a remarkable demonstration of firepower. We could neither hear nor see the bombers. We could only hear the explosions and feel the shock waves as bombs exploded. From the air, a bombed area resembled the craters the astronauts saw outside their window before they landed on the moon.

The Battleship New Jersey also provided interesting visual entertainment. The ship, which was decommissioned after the Korean War, was brought back into service and operated in the South China Sea near Phu Bai. The huge shells she fired looked like small Volkswagens as they slowly arced through the sky toward their destination of death and destruction.

The 8th Radio Research Field Station (RRFS) became the place I enjoyed visiting most while at Phu Bai. The 8th had been at Phu Bai almost since the beginning of the Vietnam War. It belonged to the Army Security Agency (ASA), which had been well funded, so their living conditions were the best by far in the Phu Bai area. They enjoyed a nice mess hall with an officer's club attached to one end, and I believe there was an NCO club on the other. They lived in trailers, had a library, and had an above-ground swimming pool, thus providing a very relaxing place to hang out.

Did these fellows conduct research on radios? Yes and no. The 8th had a secret mission that consisted of pinpointing (research) the location of VC and NVA units by intercepting their communication (radio) traffic, triangulating the coordinates with another RRFS located in Thailand to fix the position of the bad guys, and then providing the information to the B-52, artillery, and naval gunfire units so that they could do their lethal work.

Mike Torrans, who had been with me in Turkey, was the S1 (personnel officer) of the 8th. Mike invited me to eat with him, so I got in my jeep and drove up Highway 1 to his compound, which was located outside Hue City. I parked my jeep next to several others and proceeded to the officer's club, where Mike and I bellied up to the bar. We were talking over old times and were feeling quite convivial as John Barleycorn began kicking in when I heard a strange muffled noise that sounded like an explosion. I looked around. Mike was gone, and I saw people running out the door. I was confused, but as I heard explosions getting closer and began to smell the acrid smell of cordite and the building began to shake, I realized something was not quite right. The club had a replica fireplace that had been built purely for decoration; however, it had been constructed of rock, and it became my place of refuge. Most of my body fit quite well in this sheltered space, and it was where I remained until the shelling stopped and people began to drift back into the club.

As I lay in the fireplace, I thought, *Why is someone trying to kill me? I have done nothing to them. Why is this happening?* That was my introduction to my war. I later found out that the 8th radio antenna field was a prime target for enemy gunners and that this was not an unusual occurrence.

Mike had to attend to his duties, so I headed to my jeep to return to XXIV Corps. I discovered, along with several other officers, that a 122mm rocket had destroyed our jeeps. It was one of three jeeps that I lost while in Vietnam. Two were destroyed by hostile action, and the marines stole the other one.

The marines were woefully short of organic transportation and moved mostly by foot. The Army had plenty of vehicles, especially jeeps, so it was not unusual for them to "borrow" Army assets. After all, we were on the same side fighting a common enemy. Marine jeeps had a rounded hood and were readily distinguishable from Army jeeps, but many of their jeeps looked suspiciously like Army jeeps that had been repainted with marine insignia and bumper numbers.

One morning, I was on my way somewhere, and I saw a squad of marines riding on a mechanical mule, their primary ammunition, supply, and people mover, at the small unit level. The mule was a cumbersome, gangly, flatbed vehicle with a large steering wheel sitting over a two-cylinder engine in an open-air cockpit. The ground they were traversing was rutted with numerous gullies, and the vehicle would overturn about every twenty yards and dump the marines on the ground. I watched this for some time and could not believe my eyes. They could have walked faster than the vehicle was carrying and dumping them and saved time, not to mention the bruises, but they persisted. Later, I watched them coming from the PX, with the mule loaded with cases of Cokes. This time, they were walking, but the same scenario took place. They would go a few yards down a gulley. The vehicle would turn over, and they would reload the vehicle and proceed on their simple, mindless way. I suspect it took them all day to get to their destination; however, by then, I'm sure all the cases of sodas had broken, and each had his pockets full of Coke cans.

This reminds me that sometime during my tour, the PX took a direct hit from a rocket. It caused a hell of a fire and destroyed the building. It was amusing to watch soda cans fly hundreds of feet into the air before they exploded.

In May 1969, Colonel McLaughlin called me into his office, read a citation for a Bronze Star Medal, and fastened the medal on my uniform.

Colonel George McLaughlin, XXIV Corps Adjutant General, awarding the Bronze Star Medal to Captain Taylor.

This is what the Army calls an impact award, and it is given for either valor or meritorious achievement immediately or soon after the accomplishment. Mine was for achievement, specifically for getting the communication center up and running under the most arduous (his words, not mine) of combat conditions. He also handed me a TDY order to proceed to Bangkok, Thailand, to procure vital administrative supplies for XXIV Corps. In reality, he was giving me a free rest-and-recuperation (R & R) trip for a job well-done, as I procured nothing except some jewelry for Penny.

The wife of one of the lieutenant colonels lived in Bangkok and worked in the American embassy. The officer had been in Vietnam for over four years. He would serve his twelve-month tour, take a thirty-day leave in Thailand, and come back for another tour. He told me he would call his wife and ask her to have a car meet me at the airport and make hotel reservations for me. I caught a C-130 flight into Tan Son Nhut airfield in Saigon. While there, Captain Jim Davies, who had been with me in Turkey, came to the airport, and we had a nice visit during my layover before I caught my commercial flight to Bangkok. Jim was serving with MACV headquarters and working in their communication center.

An embassy driver with a staff car met me at the Bangkok airport and took me to the Manhattan Hotel, where I was to stay. The next day, the lieutenant colonel's wife took me to their villa, a two-story mansion located in a walled compound that came with maid, cook, gardener, and who knew what else. The grounds, which were planted with a profusion of beautiful, sweet-smelling flowers and exotic vegetation, were magnificent. I understood then why her husband kept serving in Vietnam. I do not know her position in the embassy—neither she nor he told me—but I am sure she was quite important. We went on a water-taxi tour of the city and ate lunch at one of her favorite restaurants. I do not remember doing much sightseeing. I ate, slept, lay in the sun by the hotel pool, and took several hot showers daily. Being able to eat breakfast by the pool each morning while sipping a Bloody Mary was a particular delight. I was thoroughly relaxed and reinvigorated by the time I returned to Phu Bai.

As the chief of administrative services for XXIV Corps, I had to sign for the property for which I was responsible. Two of the items were large generators. The property book officer (PBO) and I went around and checked serial numbers on various items, but he seemed reluctant to show me one of the generators. I told him that I would not sign for it unless I saw it. He finally agreed and told me that he would pick me up that evening and take me to the generator's location. It was dark when we left the compound, and we traveled a short distance down Highway 1 toward DaNang when MPs stopped us at a checkpoint. They recognized the PBO, and we pulled off to a large clearing where there were several GP medium tents. There, I found the generator providing electricity for this small enclave. Inside the tents, sheets were hung to provide privacy for the Vietnamese prostitutes and the soldiers they were servicing. I did not need the generator at the time and told the PBO I knew where to find it if I did. After all, it was serving a noble purpose by helping improve the morale of the soldier, and I am sure the MPs were donating some of their profits to the orphanage in Hue.

Young men's minds quite often are filled with sexual thoughts, and I found this to be even more pronounced while I was in Vietnam. I would often see young enlisted soldiers standing guard at either end of the opening to a sandbag bunker, a sure clue that a third soldier was inside with one of the hooch maids. God, they were ugly and dirty, but as the old saying goes, "any port in a storm."

One of the majors in the headquarters was my friend, and he had flown to Cam Ranh Bay for a change-of-command ceremony at his previous unit. He called me from the Phu Bai airfield and said, "Come get me, but don't tell anyone that I'm back." He came out of base operations hunched over and could barely walk.

I said, "What happen to you?" He explained he had taken one of the nurses that he had known when assigned at Cam Ranh Bay to her room where they were renewing their friendship. The springs on her bed were squeaking—the medical folks lived quite well, no cots for them—and his friend was afraid the nurse living next door would hear, so they decided to renew their intimacy on the floor. A big mistake, because the floor, which was made of plywood, tended to splinter!

Elements of the 85th Evacuation Hospital moved into the Phu Bai area in December 1968, and we were pleased to see them and have medical support nearby. Moreover, we were delighted to see "round eyes" (American women). The nurses were the first "round eyes" I had seen since I had embarked at Bien Hoa, as the Donut Dollies had not yet found their way to Phu Bai. Prior to their arrival, the typical greeting between soldiers happened to be, "Phu Bai sucks!" After their arrival, the greeting became, "Phu Bai is all right."

One night, I was sitting in the club and drinking when I noticed that one of the nurses who was quite lovely would leave every so often with an officer. I was intrigued, so I pulled up a chair at her table and proceeded to strike up a conversation. We talked, and in her own words, she informed me that she was sitting on a gold mine. Moreover, she was a gold mine, especially at $150 a pop. In 1969, that was a lot of money for three minutes or less of pleasure.

There are no atheists in a foxhole.
—Douglas Mac Arthur

A Sunday morning, I attended a communion service performed by the protestant chaplain. He had his portable altar and communion set arranged in an open area near the mess hall. We all sat on the ground while he preached a short sermon, and then we each knelt at the portable altar to receive communion. Several days later, there was a notice in the *Daily Bulletin* that all personnel who had received communion from this particular chaplain were to report to the medics to receive a gamma globulin shot. The chaplain had hepatitis. The syringe that the medic held looked like it was filled with a half gallon of Karo syrup. It had an attached needle about a foot long. That shot hurt! I never took communion again in Vietnam and often remember that incident when I am walking to the altar to receive communion.

Around 2300, I had taken some documents to the Command Group (where the generals had their offices) and given them to the SGS. He was the only one around, and I asked if I could use the latrine. He said, "Be my guest." The Command Group had three beautiful porcelain toilets just like in the real world. These were the only porcelain toilets that I knew about, and to be able to use one made my day, or so I thought. I had no sooner taken a seat than things began to go to hell in a hand basket. The incoming rockets began exploding, and they were close and getting closer. I pulled my pants up, held them with my left hand, and proceeded to run as fast as possible to the nearest shelter, which happened to be the communication bunker. The bunker entrance was near the end of a long hallway. A door opened to a flight of wooden steps and down to a small area where soldiers waited to receive messages.

I was running so fast that when I went by the door and reached out, I caught the door frame with my left hand, which caused my pants to drop. I pulled myself through the entrance and fell down the stairs and then landed in a heap. I looked up, and several other soldiers had taken shelter there. I was lying on the floor, totally exposed. I gingerly pulled myself and then my pants up and acted as if nothing had happened. No one cracked a smile. I do wonder what they were thinking when I fell among them with my underwear and pants below my knees. This was truly a case of being caught with your pants down. That was the night the rockets destroyed the general's mess and several of the colonel's trailer houses. I seem to remember that one wing of the headquarters building was also destroyed.

I think all of us, as we began to get "short," with seven days or less to go in country, started to take extra precautions. I know I did. I curtailed my jeep and helicopter excursions and stayed close to places with overhead protection.

A portly, older, reserve major in my section reminded me of Major Winchester in the TV series *M*A*S*H*, although he was not that smart. This major's reserve unit had been called up, and he was not happy about being in Vietnam. We had clashed on several occasions, and neither of us was fond of the other. Our primary source of disagreement was my jeep. He had no jeep and asked if he could borrow mine one night to go visit a friend in another compound. I agreed, but the next morning, I found he had trashed it with empty beer cans, breadcrumbs of all things on the seats, and mud. It was generally a mess. Now I was proud of that jeep. I proceeded to tell him he needed to wash it and clean it up. He told me, "I don't take orders from a captain, so go fuck yourself." I decided he would never borrow my jeep again, but he tried. This ended up with the colonel involved, and I lost—that is, until he trashed it again. This time, the colonel told him to clean it up.

One of my lieutenants informed me that the major had moved a cot into the communications bunker and was setting up to spend the night. The major had announced that he intended to stay there until he left Phu Bai to return to the States. My policy was that there was no sleeping in the bunker. It was a work area and was to be used as a work area. I went ballistic when I heard this and proceeded to the bunker, where I threw the major and his cot out. Away he went to the colonel. The colonel said, "Damn it, captain. Leave him alone. It's only a few nights, and he will be gone." The colonel did not like the major any more than I did, but he was pissed at me for creating a hassle. I explained that the major was not the first "short-termer" that had tried to set up housekeeping in the bunker and that I had turned away. If we let one in, especially one of our own, we would have to let others in. And once again, it was a work area, not a sleeping area. The colonel acquiesced, and the major returned to his hooch.

The morning he was to depart, we were eating breakfast when the rockets began to fall. The major jumped or flopped into a slit trench that had sandbags stacked along side. A rocket exploded nearby and covered the major in sandbags and sand. We dug him out, and he was bleeding from his eyes, ears, nose, and throat. I am sure that he had a severe concussion, if not worse. Taken to the 85th Evacuation Hospital, I never heard of him again.

The 108th Field Artillery Group served as the general support artillery unit for the XXIV Corps and had battalions and batteries located at fire bases throughout the AO, including Phu Bai. One of its assigned battalions was a National Guard battalion, the 2d Battalion, 138th Field Artillery from Kentucky, one of the few, very few, Army National Guard combat units to serve in Vietnam. This unit along with most of the National Guard had dug their heels in when they were faced with the prospect of serving in Vietnam. One hundred and fifty of the battalion soldiers had asked for an injunction against the Army for shipping them to Vietnam without an official declaration of war. The US Supreme Court refused to hear the injunction.

The battalion had been located in Phu Bai, but in June 1969, it was supporting the 101st Airborne Division from several firebases with M-109, self-propelled, 155 howitzers. On June 19th, a large group of VC sappers attacked C Battery at Firebase Tomahawk. They repelled the attack, but Bardstown, Kentucky, woke to find that thirteen of its sons had been killed or wounded. I assisted the battalion executive officer as he prepared to escort the bodies of the fallen back to Kentucky. He was quite distraught and explained that most of the soldiers were kin to someone in Bardstown as a brother, uncle, son, or cousin. It was a sad day for a small Kentucky town population of six thousand.

On July 20, 1969, Neil Armstrong became the first man to walk on the moon and uttered the words, "That's one small step for man, one giant leap for mankind."

This was one of the great American achievements of the twentieth century, along with victory in World War II, the GI Bill, and the end of the Cold War, and I have no recollection of the event. My memory banks are empty. I cannot remember what I was doing. There was no TV in Phu Bai, but I am sure the news was broadcast over the US Armed Forces Radio Service (AFRS).

It was not unusual to run into someone I had served with before at various places in Vietnam.

One person I never expected to see was my cousin Jarvis Shaw.

I looked up one morning, and there he stood. Lieutenant Shaw and his men were tired, dirty, and hungry, out of fuel and ammo. They had no place to stay, and they were very glad to see me. I spoke with the headquarters commandant, and we got them fed, showered, refueled, and bedded down. The next morning, they went on their way. Jarvis and I always have a laugh about our chance meeting when we see each other.

Colonel Lytle told me as I left Fort Hood, "Lieutenant, you normally only get one real shooting war in a twenty-year career, so make the best of the one you get. Remember, always think two grades ahead, because in periods of war, you generally are promoted twice. Take care of your men, and they will take care of you. And always tell the truth. Bad news does not get better with age."

Our country in her intercourse, with foreign nations may she always be in the right; but our country right or wrong!
—Stephen Decatur

Vietnam was my war. It was the only shooting war I personally participated in during my twenty-eight years of active service. I did not need another to realize that war squanders the nation's resources through a loss of money, blood, and sometimes honor. War is terribly wasteful, and every effort should be made to avoid war. Politicians should resort to war only after all other efforts have failed. Having said that, I am proud to have served, and if America called again, I would answer the call.

There seems to be a paradox in our country: Soldiers hate war, and politicians love war. It is probably because most politicians have not experienced war up close and personal. To those who have never experienced war, it is an abstract concept. How long has it been since our nation has had a president who has heard the sound of the guns?

I need not write about or discuss most of my Vietnam experience. It serves no purpose.

As a twenty-six-year-old captain, I thought neither of politics nor of such esoteric ideas as whether the Vietnam War was just, unjust, right, or wrong. I was a soldier who simply did my duty the best I knew how. I left the morning of July 28, 1969, from Cam Ranh Bay on a Freedom Bird (the plane that takes you home). I left behind only what little innocence I had left.

I took with me two Bronze Star Medals, the Vietnam Service Medal, Republic of Vietnam Campaign Medal, Republic of Vietnam Cross of Gallantry with Palm, a Meritorious Unit Commendation, and many memories, some good, some bad. With the exception of the Bronze Stars, the other awards were given for the most part for nothing more than simply being there.

The war was to drag on for another six years before it was finally over. By that time, I would be a major.

I believe Colonel Lytle would have approved.

As the plane lifted from the runway and the wheels clanked into the fuselage, a roar vibrated through the cabin as all aboard began to cheer. We had made it.

We were going home.

12

Army Schooling

Tired and lost in our own thoughts of loved ones and good things to come, we had an uneventful flight. It was quiet, so I slept. When the wheels touched down on the tarmac at Sea-Tac (Seattle-Tacoma), another round of cheering and hollering reverberated through the aircraft.

We were home.

When I arrived at the airport terminal, I headed to the nearest latrine. There, I removed my jungle fatigues and boots and dumped them on the floor as did many others. There were several hippies retrieving the clothes. I supposed that they would sell them to buy drugs or maybe even wear them. I did not care. I only wanted the stench of Vietnam gone.

I wished that I had kept the boots. They were new.

I changed into a pair of pants and a shirt that Penny had bought for me in Hawaii. I went to Vietnam weighing 180 pounds; I came home weighing 133 pounds. The clothes were excessively large, and I was a pitiful sight to see. I looked like something out of a POW camp.

I had a connecting flight to San Francisco and another to Los Angles. I was told to take a particular commuter flight from San Francisco to Los Angles, as they had gorgeous flight attendants in skimpy outfits. I think the airline was called Pacific Airways. I did take that flight, and they lived up to my expectations. I settled back with a whiskey and enjoyed the in-cabin scenery on the short flight into Los Angeles.

It was great to be home, but I wanted and needed to feel West Texas soil beneath my feet. I was expecting to be spit upon and harassed by war protesters at the airports. Some were around, but they did not bother me, probably because I looked like I had a terminal illness.

Pen, Ross, Grandmother Farr, Annis, and Lee met me at LAX. Penny, Ross, and Grandmother had driven from West Texas to Los Angeles and were staying with Bud and Annis. I do not remember any of what transpired while we were there. I think we loaded up and headed to West Texas soon thereafter.

Well, I'm running down the road, trying to loosen my load.
—Eagles

These lyrics from the Eagles song "Take It Easy" are etched in my memory. I do not know why. We stopped in Winslow, Arizona, to sleep, eat, and fuel. I walked to the corner, smoked a cigarette, and pondered the past twelve months. There, I knew what to expect—the unexpected. Here, I knew nothing. I do remember that everyone kept their homes too cold for me. I would take a lawn chair and sit in the West Texas sun to get warm, and any loud or strange noise made me jump.

I think we visited my parents in Crane or perhaps Big Spring for a few days, and I know we attended the Miss Wool of America Pageant in the San Angelo Coliseum. Granddad Farr as president of the Sheep and Goat Raisers Association and had good seats for us.

I wonder if other dogs think poodles are members of a weird religious cult.
—Rita Rudner

Pen had bought a dog, a poodle named Gigi. The first night we stayed at the Rocker b, I walked into our bedroom and found the dog perched on the bed like a queen. As I approached, she growled. My fuse was short and did not take much to light. I slapped that dog, and she yelped. So did Penny. That dog slept on Pen's side of the bed that night and every night thereafter until she died. Every time I moved, she would growl. She did not like sharing the bed with me. I grew to love her over time, but it certainly was not love at first sight. Gigi never did take up with either Ross or me.

I had orders to attend the AG Officers Advanced Course, Class Number Two (AGOAC 2), beginning October 3, 1969, with attachment to the AG School until the course began. We headed out to Indianapolis in our 1968 Ford Fairlane that we had bought when we had returned from Turkey and towed a U-Haul trailer.

> *A gentleman is a gentle man.*
> —Unknown

Along the way, we spent a few days with Mammy and Pappy Baucus at their farm near Richmond, Missouri. The Baucus family loved Penny dearly, and it was always a joy to be around them. Penny spent her summers with Mammy and Pappy when she was growing up, and they considered her their child. They were both genteel people with exceptional manners and charm. Pappy Baucus genuinely liked me, and I enjoyed listening to his stories about World War I. We discussed the world situation and especially politics. He was a good man, a bright man with high moral standards and values, and a staunch Republican.

Each evening, Pappy Baucus followed the same routine and included me. We would watch the evening news and then disappear into his walk-in pantry. There, he would pour a generous portion of premium scotch into two glasses, complete filling the glasses with ice and seltzer, light a Camel cigarette, and talk usually about politics and the Army. Two drinks, three cigarettes, no more, no less—and then we would proceed to the dining room at precisely 1900 hours.

Mammy and Penny would have the table set in a formal manner, and Mammy would have prepared a wonderful meal. There would always be an expensive cut of beef and steamed vegetables. Pappy would have all dinner plates placed in front of him, and he would serve each plate and then his own. We would begin to eat after he said grace. All was very formal, simple, and elegant.

As we were leaving, Pappy presented me with the desk where he had toiled for so many years on the Kansas City Livestock Exchange. I have it today in my office.

When we arrived at Fort Benjamin Harrison, our first priority was to find a place to rent. We spent a couple of days at the Holiday Inn while we were looking. Eventually, we settled on a two-story townhouse in Lawrence, Indiana, near Fort Harrison at 8318 Meadowlark Drive.

Fort Benjamin Harrison, which was established in 1903 and named for Benjamin Harrison, the twenty-third president of the United States, had an eclectic mixture of lovely turn-of-the-century architecture and pitifully plain contemporary Army buildings. The home of the Adjutant General and Finance School, the Defense Information School (DINFOS), and the Army Finance Center, it became known derisively or fondly, depending on your point of view, as "Uncle Ben's Rest Home." In the larger Army, it was a laid-back assortment of enlisted and officer students and DACs.

The first few weeks, my duty assignment consisted of working with the directorate of communications in the AG School. I assisted in developing lesson plans and handouts for various courses. In reality, I did not do or accomplish much, but I did develop a rapport with Major Brown and Captain Jim Lawless, who were the effective writing and speaking instructors for the advanced courses.

The mission of the advance course was to prepare and develop career Adjutant General Corps officers to function effectively as field-grade officers (major and above). The main benefit of the course was the contacts I made while in the course. I ran into many of the officers in my class later on in my career, and they were helpful in various ways. Some became friends, although there are only a few with whom I continue to correspond and then only by Christmas card. Time and distance are not conductive to maintaining an "old age" relationship.

There were fifty-five American officers and eight foreign officers in the class. Foreign students consisted of three lieutenant colonels and two majors from the Republic of Vietnam, a colonel and a captain from Thailand, and a lieutenant colonel from Saudi Arabia. The American officers consisted of forty-seven captains and eight majors. Two of the majors were females from the WAC. Almost all the Americans, except for the two WAC officers, had recently returned from Vietnam. Few of the instructors had served in Vietnam, which put them at a distinct disadvantage. They were trying to teach us Army doctrine, and we had been on the ground developing doctrine.

We were a class of irreverent, opinionated, funny, fun-loving, and disruptive individuals. The instructors almost uniformly hated, feared, or envied us. We were just letting off steam after a year in Vietnam—*to hell with everybody else*. We were thinking that the worst they can do to us was send us back to Vietnam. More than once—in fact, several times—the commandant, Colonel Jack Pink, later brigadier general, and Lieutenant Colonel Frank Blake, our class advisor, had a "come to Jesus" meeting with the entire class. Initially, they threatened; later, they begged. They just hoped we graduated before we burned the building down.

Years later when I was a full colonel, I was at Fort Benjamin Harrison as the graduation speaker for one of the basic courses and ran into one of the longtime civilian instructors. We had a "how you doing and where you been" conversation.

Then quite seriously, he said, "Your class was the worst class that ever went through here, and it was your class that the 'eagles' fell on. I did not think you would make major, much less colonel."

I found that to be quite a profound statement, because Colonel Frank Foster, a member of that class and my friend, was the commandant and his boss.

There were no generals that came out of AGOAC-2, but Ken Boegler, Tal Anderson, Bob Asiello, Joe Braccia, Ferruccio Crocetti, Ed Donnan, Gordon Fetkenhour, Frank Foster, Cleve Matthews, Tom Orlowski, and me all were promoted to colonel. I am missing a couple of names, because years ago, I counted thirteen of us wearing eagles.

We did not go without taking a sucking chest wound. One officer was terminated because of plagiarism. All of us probably should have been disciplined for one reason or another, but about twelve of us in particular should have likely been singled out.

The school had enrolled us in a correspondence course that we were to complete prior to arrival. Few of us bothered to open the material, much less complete it. Colonel Pink was unhappy—bless his heart—and gave us a week to complete the course, or we would be dismissed from the class. There were many lessons in the course, so we divided the material up, with each taking a lesson, doing the reading, taking the test, and delivering it to the directorate of nonresident instruction for grading. Each kept the answers for his lesson, sharing it with the others. You can cut it several ways, but this was cheating.

Unknown to us, each had the same questions, but they were all in different order to prevent the very thing we had done. The director of nonresident instruction, Colonel Hornbuckle, apparently was not amused with our ingenuity and made an issue with Colonel Pink. We each had an individual meeting with Colonel Pink, who put us on disciplinary probation, although none of us knew exactly what that meant. Most of us blew it off and went about our business. We felt it was a pissant requirement and got the attention it deserved.

It was wrong. I knew it was wrong. I regret that I allowed myself to compromise my integrity in that manner. It was not my finest hour.

Penny and Herbie, AG Corps Birthday Celebration.

Socializing and partying were major activities. The "Ratskeller" in the basement of the Officer's Club was our hangout. Many evenings were spent discussing politics, sports, the Vietnam War, and draft-dodgers over drinks. The basement was off-limits to senior officers, so it was a place we could do our thing. The music, food, and price of drinks all catered to the junior officer. We were sometimes rowdy. Once the MPs had to come and ask us to go home, but no one went to jail or got their name on the MP blotter, not that I remember.

We also had several formal affairs at the club. We celebrated the AG Corps birthday and attended the Commandant's Reception, and New Year's Day Reception, among others. Penny loved these dress-up affairs. She looked mighty fine on my arm.

AGOAC-2 Basketball Team.

There were cliques in our class, and I belonged to the jock clique. Indiana was a hotbed for basketball, and AGOAC-2 had several good players, some who had played college ball. The wives and kids would attend the games, and we would meet after the game to rehash our win or loss.

The wives got together often and usually had a girl's night out once a month. The guys did the same. We would go to basketball games, both high school and college. The Indiana High School Basketball State Tournament was a happening, and tickets were at a premium.

Penny and I saw one of my all-time favorite movies *Patton* at a downtown Indianapolis theater on opening night.

Another time several couples drove to Ohio to eat a seven-course, gourmet meal at a lovely country home. The meal was prepared in front of us, and the chefs, a man and his wife, sang, told jokes, and entertained us. It was a lot of fun but quite expensive on a captain's pay.

One evening, several of the guys went to a "strip joint" for a little visual excitement. One fellow told his wife he was going to the library to study. The girls had a social the next day, and they were laughing and giggling about the shape we were in when we got home. This fellow's wife proceeded to stick her foot in her mouth down to her "well, you know what" by indignantly stating that her husband went to the library to study, that he would never go to a strip joint, and if he had asked, she would have told him, "No." Almost in unison, the other girls responded sweetly, "Oh, yes, he did."

I did study, but not much. We were given nightly readings to prepare for the next day's class. I read them sometimes, and sometimes I did not. There was to be an honor graduate announced at graduation, and a few folks worked hard to be selected. I do not think they had as much fun as the rest of us did. I realized early on that I was not the brainy type, so I met basic standards, with the exception of speaking and writing assignments in which I tried to excel.

A requirement for graduation was to write a scholarly research paper. The title of my effort was "The Attitude of the Wife: An Important Influence on a Married Junior Officer's Career Decision." I put a lot of time into that paper, not just because of the grade but because it was a subject in which I was interested in finding answers. I developed a questionnaire, mailed it to officers and their wives at other service schools, compiled their responses, researched, and wrote. I concluded what I suspected: The wife was the "key" to deciding on a military career. Penny certainly was in our case.

Penny's role as an Army officer's wife gave her satisfaction, but it did not fulfill her need for accomplishment. Only when she worked did she satisfy that need. She knew I loved the Army, and she wholeheartedly supported my decision and career; however, the Army defined me, not her. Had she not wanted me to make the Army a career, I would have served my time and returned to civilian life. The decision was that simple.

It was a good year for all. Penny enjoyed the time and had a lot of fun with the girls, and we were together as a family. Jim and Ann Davies were at Fort Ben at the time. Jim was attending AGOAC-3 and graduated after I did. We got together several times and shared Turkey and Vietnam memories. In addition, Mike and Ann Torrans arrived just before we were to leave, so we got to visit with them. I seem to remember that Carol Buelow passed through Indianapolis for a short time, and we visited with her. John Wayne Raines, a classmate of mine at Tarleton, was also attending AGOAC-3.

Two months before graduation, the Adjutant General's Corps Officer Assignment Branch from the Military Personnel Center (MILPERCEN), in Washington, D.C., visited the class to discuss our next assignment. Penny and I wanted to go to Germany, but if we could not, we were willing to go just about anywhere overseas. The AG Branch chief, a lieutenant colonel, spoke to the class and indicated some would be going back to Vietnam. This did not sit well with those who had been, because there were several instructors at the school who had not been. We let him know our displeasure individually and collectively.

A month before graduation, the AG Branch chief stood before the class and alphabetically read each student's name followed by their assignment just as I would do many years later. Eight officers before me received orders to Germany. Carl Taylor received orders to the Netherlands, and then it was my turn. The odds were against me going overseas at all. He read, "Taylor, Herbie, Japan."

Penny and I would have preferred Germany, but Japan would do just fine. In retrospect, we could not have received a better assignment. We should have known Japan was going to be a wonderful assignment from the very start.

The post transportation officer called me soon after and said, "Captain Taylor, I don't believe this, but we have received a berth on a ship for you and your family to travel to Japan. We haven't sent anyone overseas on a ship in several years now."

We had many questions: What kind of ship? Was it a troop ship? Could we take a dog? Where would we sail? When would we sail? How long would it take to get to Japan? What should we wear? What were the costs? And the list went on. Most of these questions were not answered until we were back at the Rocker b on leave. It was again moving time to another foreign country that was eight thousand miles from Barnhart and West Texas. We were excited.

Thankfully, the Army packed and shipped our household goods at no expense to us, as they had done before and would do many times again. The consensus among Army wives was that after three Army moves, you might as well junk your furniture, because it would be unusable. In reality, most of our many moves went surprisingly well, although dents, scratches, chips, and rubs were common. Toward the end of my Army career, we could look at our furniture and recall where we had served. We got that scratch in Turkey, that rub in Indiana, and that dent in Japan.

Army wives are known for their lovely homes, decorated with acquisitions from their travels. We were no different. We bought quality furniture and kept our purchases to a minimum. I still have furniture that we bought when I was a lieutenant at Fort Hood over forty-five years ago.

Pilfering became a primary concern when we were shipping household goods. Therefore, one person needed to be inside the home with the packers while another checked items off on the master inventory. Movers were always late in arriving, and consequently, they were late in departing. This move ran true to form. The movers were two hours late, and we were all getting antsy. Penny sent me to a store to buy something that I do not recall. She told me to hurry back, as the movers could arrive at any time. I assured her I would.

The store had *The Godfather* for sale, so I bought a paperback copy. I returned to my car and decided to flip through the book. I soon became engrossed in reading and lost track of time. When I returned home, I found the movers busily loading the moving van. Pen was angry and let me know about her displeasure. Ross and the movers thought it was funny.

I did not!

Graduation ceremonies for AGOAC-2 were held at 1000 hours, April 17, 1970, with Major General Kenneth G. Wickham, The Adjutant General (TAG), the commencement speaker, and the Seventy-Fourth Army Band providing music.

I said my good-byes, and by the time I got to the parking lot, Penny had the engine running, Ross loaded, and we were on our way. We stopped at Mammy and Pappy Baucus' farm for a few days and enjoyed another delightful visit.

Once home, we again stayed with the Farrs on the Rocker b and visited my parents, who were now living in Big Spring. Daddy had finished his apprenticeship with Lewis Evans and had bought the Airport Grocery.

The American President Lines (APL) contacted us and provided a sailing date from Los Angles of May 27, 1970.

Daddy and I decided we would take a trip to far West Texas and Big Bend National Park. We stopped to see the historic San Solomon Spring at Balmorhea State Park, which for eons provided fresh water to prehistoric man, the Apache, and US Cavalry. We drove to Big Bend and the surrounding area by way of Fort Davis Sate Park and McDonald Observatory. On our way back to Big Spring, we decided to take the River Road that paralleled the Rio Grande and visit Ojinaga, Mexico, across from Presidio, Texas. Presidio is the only Texas border town that looks worse than the adjacent Mexican town.

The date was May 11, 1970. We had gone across to Ojinaga to eat. When we returned to our filthy, non-air-conditioned, run-down motel, which was the best in Presidio, Daddy decided to call Mother. She was frantic, as was her nature when any incident involved her family. Lubbock had been hit by a tornado, which had resulted in twenty-six deaths and $125 million worth of damage, although we did not know that at the time. Tippe and her husband, W. D. Martin, and young son, Mike, lived in an apartment near Texas Tech University. Their apartment complex had been hit. Damage was minimal, and they were not hurt.

The three of us drove to Los Angeles, and stayed in the guesthouse at Fort MacArthur, where so many years ago Granddad Farr had been stationed and guarded the harbor from Japanese attack and where we were to ship our Ford Torino to Japan. We had a problem, though. There were now four of us. Penny wanted to take Gigi with us, but I was adamant that we were not going to pay to ship her to Japan.

Pen had checked with APL, and it was going to be quite expensive if we took her with us. I put my foot down, but the closer to departing, the sadder and more despondent Penny became. About three days before we were to leave, I relented and agreed to take the dog. We were drinking cocktails at the time, which probably had something to do with my being so agreeable.

Pen's dad remarked, "That was a real smart decision, Herb."

13

The Land of the Rising Sun

We departed Los Angeles at noon on May 27, 1970, for a fourteen-day voyage to Japan with a one-day stopover in Hawaii aboard the *SS President Cleveland*.

Our departure from Los Angeles was a gala and reminiscent of ship departures seen in the movies—the band playing, people waving, streamers being thrown from ship to shore, and the tugboat straining mightily and spewing water as it pulled the behemoth into the harbor. A shimmer ran through the ship as the huge diesels came to life and the ship crawled slowly out of the harbor and into the open sea, the land fading slowly from view. It would be four years before we saw mainland America again.

The *SS President Cleveland*, originally laid out as the US Navy transport Admiral D. W. Taylor, was redesigned for American President Lines passenger service long before launch and was built in 1947 by the Bethlehem Shipbuilding Company in Alameda, California. She was small in relation to today's gigantic cruise ships, but she was first-class in every respect. No chrome and plastic for this lady. She was all mahogany, leather, and polished brass.

Accommodating 379 first-class and two hundred economy passengers, she was on a three-month round-the-world cruise. She sailed at twenty knots and rode smooth as silk. We experienced no seasickness, and the entire fourteen days were magnificent.

We quickly settled into our daily routine of awakening and eating breakfast as a family, and then Ross was off for the remainder of the day with the youth director, a personable young woman who had nine kids playing games, swimming, enjoying shuffleboard, and participating in other ship activities. We did not see him again until around 1730 hours.

Penny and I checked on Gigi, who also had first-class accommodations, walked her, and then had a morning jog followed by swimming, sunning, reading, and eating a light snack around 1030. Lunch was served at 1300 in the formal dining room. Coat and tie were not required for lunch but were mandatory for dinner at 1930.

The afternoon was spent inside mostly because of the heat. The ship had a wonderful library, and card games and lectures were daily fare. We would have another snack around 1530, usually fruit, and maybe a nap before we dressed for dinner. There were two sittings for dinner, one at 1800 and another at 1930. Ross would eat at the early sitting with his newfound friends, and we would eat at the late sitting.

Tables were assigned, and we had the same table partners and waiter the entire trip. Our partners were three elderly women. In fact, most passengers were elderly, except for the thirty or so military and other government folks on board. These women were on the round-the-world trip. They were extremely wealthy and decorated in huge diamonds and often sick. Almost every meal, at least one would be missing, and sometimes all three. They would either take their meals in their stateroom or not eat at all. They were quite worldly, and we enjoyed talking with them when they were there. It became obvious that their children had sent them on the cruise to get rid of them.

Meals could only be described as superb. I have been on cruises since, and nothing compared to this. There were always five entrees and the obligatory shrimp cocktail, escargot, turtle soup, or caviar. Lobster, filet mignon, salmon, lamb, pheasant, crab legs, frog legs—you name it, and we had it. The service, ambiance, and presentation were all outstanding. Dinner became a happening, and we looked forward to that time.

Our waiter was Mike Lato from the Philippines, and he was there to please. Mike and I developed a routine that worked just fine. After the appetizers, he would bring us a small portion of each entree and allow us to sample and select what we wanted to eat that evening.

Dinner would be followed by entertainment. There would be a band and floorshow, movies in the theater, card tournaments, etc. The ship had an elegant bar, and the passengers would place bets on how far we had traveled the previous night. I got close but never won.

Ross's day with the youth director ended at 2100 each evening, so we usually settled in and spent some time with him before we went to bed.

About halfway to Honolulu, an announcement that there would be a deep-sea fishing trip on a first-come-first-serve basis at 0200 the next morning caught our attention. Ross, of course, wanted to go, so at 0130, we trudged down to get in line with thirty or so other people. I did not know what to expect, but I did not expect to fish for toy fish with a cane pole out of a barrel. They served a wonderful, early breakfast on the deck and presented us with certificates commemorating our deep-sea fishing trip. The Bloody Marys were excellent, but Ross was unhappy and said, "Poppa, I want to catch a fish."

We arrived in Honolulu to a band, hula girls, and leis for all when we left the ship. Bob, Ann, and Bobby Boyer met us and took us to their quarters at Schofield Barracks for the day and that night. Bob was serving with the 25th Infantry Division (Tropic Lighting) at the time. It was good to get our land legs back, and we had a good time reminiscing about Turkey with the Boyers. Gigi had to stay on the ship, as all dogs debarking were required to be quarantined for three weeks before they were released to their owners.

The next morning, we sailed for Yokohama. The remainder of the trip became a rerun of the first leg. What a way to travel, especially for a boy from Barnhart.

We were somewhat intimidated by the wealthy people aboard the ship, although all were very nice. We were the youngest people on the ship and had little in common with others. The federal government subsidized APL, so therein lay the reason we were able to travel on the *President Cleveland*. Apparently, the government had an allotment of staterooms for government employees. There were several DOD civilians and state department employees on board. The military passengers were wives of general officers serving in Vietnam. They were to live in the Philippines during their husband's tour. There was also a US Navy captain and his wife.

An interesting tidbit is that the TV hit *The Gale Storm Show*, which ran from 1956 to 1960 and featured Gale Storm as the social director aboard the *SS Ocean Queen, was actually filmed on the President Cleveland.*

I will always remember that trip. The best part is that Uncle Sam picked up the tab. The Army even reimbursed me for tips and gratuities. Our only out-of-pocket expenses were for Gigi and the bar tab, which added up to a sizeable amount on a captain's pay after fourteen days.

We arrived in Tokyo Bay and the city of Yokohama on the beautiful, clear, sunny morning of June 10, 1970. Lieutenant Paul Stevens and his wife, Kathy, had been assigned as our sponsors and were there with an Army van and driver to meet us. It was always gratifying to be met by someone who knew his or her way around when we arrived in a foreign country. Paul and Kathy were to become fast friends. We were now *gaijins* or foreigners in Japanese parlance. Again, this boy from Barnhart was a long way from home.

As we pulled out of the ocean terminal, I realized something was wrong. We were on the wrong side of the road, and the van's steering wheel was on the right side of the vehicle. Driving on the wrong side of the road was one of many peculiarities of Japan that we would adjust to and find quite normal.

Our trip to Camp Zama, which was about thirty miles from Yokohama, took almost three hours. We traveled along narrow, two-lane roads and passed through many villages, small towns, and numerous stoplights. We quickly realized that Japan was crowded with some 127 million people squeezed into a landmass slightly smaller than California. The road and side streets were filled with cars and trucks, all new. I saw few old vehicles and found out most of them were owned by *gaijins*. Shortly before we arrived at Zama, we crossed under the Tomei Expressway, a modern, four-lane toll road that we would later use to travel to Tokyo some twenty-five miles to the southwest. Outside the main gate of Camp Zama, we saw the bullet train zip by as only a blur at 130 miles per hour.

Distance is measured by time, not miles or kilometers in Japan. If you traveled by car, it would take an inordinate time to go just a few miles, unless you were able to use the Tomei Expressway. The preferred means of travel was by train.

Camp Zama is an oasis in the concrete sprawl of Tokyo and its environs. Located in Kanagawa Prefecture, it is known locally as the "Jewel of the Orient." At first glance, we thought we were entering a vacation resort. Beautiful trees that were primarily pine and cherry lined the streets and grew throughout the post. Rolling hills, small parks, a trout lake, and an immaculately manicured, eighteen-hole golf course awaited us. We were to find that the spring cherry blossoms added immensely to the beauty of the base.

Buildings were a mixture of historic Japanese and post-World War II concrete structures that provided unique but pleasant surroundings. The historic buildings date from 1937 when the Japanese Military Academy, the equivalent of our West Point, moved there. After the war, General Macarthur moved his headquarters from Tokyo to Yokohama, and in 1953, it moved to Camp Zama. Most of the modern buildings began to be built in 1951. The Japanese Military Academy auditorium is now the post theater, and many of the cadet barracks have been modernized and continue to be used for various activities. Monuments abound from the Military Academy days as do the deteriorating bunkers and tunnels burrowed into the hills now covered with trees and other vegetation.

Headquarters of the US Army Japan (USARJ), located in a single, two-story, reinforced concrete building named the "Little Pentagon," offered an exceptional visual effect to the post.

The Stevens family took us to our temporary quarters, which were large and comfortable. The only drawback was that we had to share community baths with other residents who had either recently arrived or were departing. We quickly adjusted and settled into our routine. I believe we stayed there for thirty days, the maximum time allowed, and then I rented a newly constructed Japanese home on the economy, where we only stayed for three weeks.

We took most of our meals in the Officer's Club, a large facility decorated in a florid Japanese motif. We did have cooking and laundry facilities in the transient billets. However, we had no car, which made it difficult for Penny and Ross to get to the commissary located some two miles from Camp Zama in the Sagamihara housing area.

Most families lived at Sagamihara and worked at Camp Zama, Sagami Army Hospital, or Sagami Depot, a large rebuild facility that refurbished damaged military vehicles for return to Vietnam. There were ten sets of spacious quarters located on a hill near the golf course for general officers and colonels, two single houses designated for the

USARJ deputy chief of staff and secretary general staff, and a myriad of two-story townhouses located on Camp Zama.

Transportation became our first priority while we were waiting for our Ford Torino to arrive from the States. I bought a Toyota Corolla sedan from a young specialist fourth-class that was several years old for $250.00. It ran like a top and never gave a bit of trouble. Four years later, I sold it to another specialist four for fifty dollars. The vehicle had to be registered, so the trooper drove me to the prefecture registration office, where we transferred title to the vehicle. I drove back very slowly and very carefully. That was a trying time as I learned to drive on the wrong side of the road with their narrow streets. Penny practiced driving on Camp Zama before she ventured out on the economy.

The Grand Torino finally arrived, and a few months later, I sold it to a soldier returning to the States. It was much too large to drive on the Japanese streets.

I was assigned as the adjutant to the US Army Far East Personnel Center (USAFEPC), a subordinate command of USARJ. USAFEPC, which was comprised of a headquarters element, physical reconditioning detachment, transient detachment, and the Japan R & R Center for soldiers visiting from Vietnam, was an administrative disaster and a haven for lowlifes and never-do-wells.

The commander, a weak officer of limited talent, hailed from Arkansas and fit the mold of the typical redneck. He had a Japanese wife, as did many of the officers and NCOs assigned to Japan. They preferred the subservient, do-as-I-tell-you-when-I-tell-you spouse. We rarely socialized with them and only when mandatory.

The detachment commanders were adequate, and Lieutenant Paul Stevens, who worked in the Japan R & R Center, was an outstanding officer in every respect.

The commander, a major, and I soon locked horns. The first incident involved the daily morning report. These were the days before computers, so daily strength reports were prepared manually. The commander was required to sign the report, certifying that it accurately reflected the status of assigned troops and listed those present for duty, hospitalized, on leave, or absent without leave (AWOL). Each detachment prepared a report, and the morning report clerk consolidated the reports and submitted it to me for review. I submitted it to the commander for signature.

The commander called me into his office and told me he wanted me to sign the morning report, as it had to be at headquarters USARJ rather early each morning and he was often inspecting the troops at that time. I knew that signing the report was his responsibility, not mine, but being new, I did not want to rock the boat, so I agreed.

The reports from the detachments passed across my desk before they went to the morning report clerk, and I noticed that we had a significant number of people AWOL. When I received the consolidated report, there were no AWOLs listed. I questioned the morning report clerk. She advised that the major had directed that AWOLs not be reported until the soldier had been absent seven days.

I confronted him, and he justified his decision by telling me that most of the AWOLs were from the R & R Center and they were usually only a couple of days late in returning once they ran out of money. He also gave me the real reason. If we reported the AWOLs, our statistics would reflect unfavorably on the unit and him. I told the major that I would not sign a false report. He said he would sign them and only report a soldier AWOL after seven days, which is what I did. I now had no confidence or respect for him, and it is difficult to work for a man under those conditions. I also had a moral dilemma. I knew what we were doing was wrong, but what could I do about it?

Loyalty to the commander is paramount in a military unit. Thankfully, the matter was taken out of my hands.

After about a month on the job, I began to have a suspicion that other things were not quite right. I would drive by the USAFEPC headquarters and see lights on at 2230 hours in the offices where my people worked. When I stopped in to see if I could help, I was told that I couldn't, that they were just catching up on some back work or that they were bored and decided to go to the office to have something to do.

One late Sunday night, I went to the headquarters and went through file cabinets, desks, and trash cans. I found two sets of orders on soldiers from the physical reconditioning detachment who were not medically able to return to duty in Vietnam and were being returned to the States. I found one set of orders in the appropriate place in the file cabinets, the set assigning the soldier to a stateside assignment as directed by Department of the Army. I found another order in the desk of a specialist five assigning the soldier to a different stateside unit. There were several of these duplicate orders, too many for DA to have changed that many assignments. It hit me square in the face: My soldiers were selling assignments.

The major could not be trusted, and I thought he might be the leader of this operation. I decided to go to the local criminal investigation detachment (CID) and report what I had found.

The CID surprised me when they told me that they were aware of the situation. They told me they had several soldiers who had purchased assignments and who were waiting in Okinawa and willing to testify against my soldiers. They knew who the ringleader was, but they did not know all those involved. They were still investigating. They would not tell me more than that.

They instructed me to not discuss the situation with anyone and not change any office procedures that would make it difficult for these "dirt bags" to operate or alert them that I suspected them. The next few months were difficult, and I was extremely unhappy; however, I went about my business as usual. Not all was gloom and doom, though. I also had some laughs.

When a detachment commander went on leave or was otherwise absent, I would assume temporary command of the unit. One morning, the first sergeant of the transient detachment called and said he had a situation that needed my help. He was conducting a morning formation, and one soldier had a plastic toy half-track and would not put it down even after he was given a direct order by the first sergeant.

When I took the young trooper aside, I leaned up against a large tree and said, "Soldier, tell me about your half-track."

"Sir, this is my battle wagon. I'm going to take it back to Vietnam and kill gooks. Look at this 50-caliber. I'm going to kill them, and then I'm going to run over them and squash them."

I thought he might be a little "touched," but it was always difficult to tell who was faking and who was not. We got a lot of them coming out of the four Army hospitals (two that had 500 beds and two that had 1000 beds) that would do or say anything to avoid going back to Vietnam.

I quietly explained to him that the vehicle was a death trap. The plastic armor would not protect him from an AK-47 round, much less a rocket-propelled grenade (RPG). He had no driver and no ammunition, so I was confused as to how he was going to do much killing in that vehicle.

He looked at me for a long time, handed me the toy, and said, "I guess I don't want the damn thing. You can have it."

I had a similar situation with a young soldier carrying a toy 747. He called it his "freedom bird," and he planned to fly it home. I talked him into giving the toy up in a similar manner. I asked to see his pilot's license. When he could not produce it, I convinced him that if he did not know how to fly the plane, he would probably crash and die, and it would make his mother sad.

I kept both toys behind my desk for a while just to remind me of the craziness of it all.

The four army hospitals had different specialties. Drake, for the most part, took care of head and spinal wounds in their neo-surgical ward. Ojiie got the orthopedic patients. Kishine got the burns, and Zama got them all.

Once released from a hospital, a soldier was available for immediate return to Vietnam. Alternatively, he might have a condition that did not require further hospitalization but required physical rehabilitation for less than ninety days. Or he might have a condition that required treatment for more than ninety days, necessitating him returning to the States.

Soldiers with ninety days or less would often play on the sympathy of their doctors to give them a profile of more than ninety days so that they would not have to return to Vietnam. That was one problem.

Another was that the doctors would release soldiers for physical reconditioning who had stitches or open wounds or ones who were still bandaged. In checking, you would find that these soldiers had been troublemakers at the hospital and that the doctors were getting rid of them by sending them to the USAFEPC.

I convinced the commander that we should start challenging every case when we thought we had sufficient evidence. The doctors hid behind their cloak of righteousness and said, "I am a doctor. Where is your medical license?" A brigadier general who was also a surgeon commanded the Medical Department Far East, and the hospitals were under his control. Weekly, we would present our case, and the hospitals would present theirs. The general was fair. Sometimes we lost, and sometimes we won; however, it did have the effect of radically reducing the number of incidents. The doctors hated having to attend these meetings, especially when they lost. It was so hard on their egos.

In the interim, Paul Stevens was selected as the protocol officer for USARJ, a job for which he was uniquely qualified by temperament, talent, and demeanor. Paul eventually got out of the Army and went to law school, and many years later, he served as president of the Pennsylvania State Bar Association. He died much too early of lung cancer.

The Vietnam War continued in high pitch, and every congressional representative, general officer, senior government official, or other dignitary wanted a stopover in Japan on their way to or from Vietnam. To justify their shopping boondoggle—stereo equipment was a favorite—they came to USARJ for briefings. Paul had a full-time job escorting and catering to the so-called high-and-mighty.

A new commanding general named Brigadier General Hugh A. Richeson arrived, and his chief of staff, John C. Barney, Jr., was looking for a secretary of the general staff (SGS) for USARJ. Paul told me about the job, and I along with others applied. I interviewed for the job with the deputy chief of staff and Colonel Barney, and I was selected.

This got me out of the USAFEPC. The CID raided USAFEPC a few months later. It was disestablished, and its subordinate activities integrated into other activities. Three enlisted soldiers were court-martialed and sent to prison at Fort Leavenworth, Kansas. The major was not a part of the gang. He returned to the States for retirement, as his sin was one of omission rather than commission. Interestingly, I was never called to testify at the trials.

My new job had visibility, and over time, it gave me great insight into how a headquarters should or should not operate. I had the best job a captain could have in USARJ.

What did a SGS do? My job description follows:

Acts as Executive Officer for the Deputy Chief of Staff. Reviews correspondence for attention of the command group to ensure accuracy, correct format, and accomplishment of necessary staff coordination. Briefs the Commanding General and Chief of Staff on staff actions and correspondence. Maintains suspense control on all correspondence requiring replies either to or from the Commanding General and Chief of Staff. Prepares official correspondence for signature of the Commanding General and Chief of Staff. Controls, schedules, and arranges all briefings and conferences for the Commanding General and Chief of Staff.

No, I was not a secretary. I had a secretary.

This position had a lot of influence, too much for a captain. I could and did control who had access to the commanding general and chief of staff and what they did or did not see. I assumed this position on November 19, 1970, and would remain in the position until I left Japan in May 1974.

On May 15, 1972, the position was upgraded to that of a lieutenant colonel because of the reversion of Okinawa to Japanese control and the transfer of the former high commissioner's position, a lieutenant general, to USARJ.

The colors of IX Corps were transferred to USARJ from Okinawa with most staff positions, including that of the SGS being upgraded by one or two grades. With the arrival of Lieutenant General Welborn G. Dolvin as the commanding general of USARJ/IX Corps, I expected to be replaced by a lieutenant colonel. Brigadier General Ross R. Condit, Jr., who had succeeded BG Richeson as commanding general, stepped down to become the chief of staff upon General Dolvin's arrival, and I stayed on as SGS.

I again remembered Colonel Lytle's sage advice to think two grades ahead.

Me at my desk as the SGS.

Initially, the three of us, after we had lived in the transient billet for thirty days, moved off-post to a recently constructed Japanese house. The home was located in Sagamihara City near Camp Zama. There were no quarters available on Camp Zama at the time. This was a unique and interesting experience for a boy from Barnhart and his family

The house approximated about two thirds of what you would expect of a house in the States. The doors were around five-foot-eight in height, and both Penny and I had to duck as we went from room to room. In addition, the rooms were tiny, covered in the traditional Japanese *tatami* (straw) mats, which meant we had to remove our shoes as we stepped into the house. Sliding partitions with frosted glass or *shoji* paper windows separated the rooms from each other and from the outside. The living room also served as a dining area and a bedroom at night. We slept on sleeping quilts (futons) on the *tatami* floors.

The bathtub appeared to be a shower stall that had been installed in the floor. We had to soap, wash, and rinse before we stepped down into the tub. The tub was chest-deep with a small seat, and it was used for soaking only. Soap was rinsed off before you entered the tub. It was filled with water as hot as you could stand, and I found it to be quite relaxing.

The outside of the house was unpainted wood. The older and more weathered, the better the Japanese liked it; therefore, our house at Suggs Switch would have looked like a mansion in Japan.

We knew we would only be there for a few weeks, so we made the best of the situation and later agreed it was a neat experience.

We moved into Quarters 7-C, a two-story, cinder-block, stucco-covered townhouse built in 1955. The building was a quadruplex with lieutenants and captains residing therein. I do not remember much about the inside of the home, except that it was small, but we did not have much furniture, as we had only been allowed to ship two thousand pounds of household goods to Japan.

We made many good friends in Japan. Brad and Joanne Smith were neighbors living in the quadruplex. Brad, whom I liked, was a captain in the MPs, and Penny and Joanne hit it off from the start.

We also became good friends with Captain Dexter and Shelley Hancock, Captain Roger and Susan Lawson, Captain Danny and Joann Springer, and Paul and Kathy Stevens, who all lived in the Sagamihara housing area. Living at Zama were Jerry and Eva Overgard, who were also good friends.

Jerry was an administrative technician who had been assigned to USARJ shortly before the reversion of Okinawa to Japan and the arrival of Lieutenant General Dolvin. Jerry, a young warrant officer, was to work for Dolvin, and he was responsible for taking care of Dolvin's personal affairs. Because Dolvin had not yet arrived, Jerry worked for me for several months and then moved down the hall to work for Dolvin. Subsequent to my reassignment from Japan and General Dolvin's retirement, Jerry was reassigned to be the administrative technician for General Bernard W. Rogers, the commander of US Forces Command at Fort McPherson, Georgia. Jerry followed Rogers to the Pentagon when Rogers became the army chief of staff and later the Supreme Allied Commander of Europe. I lost touch with Jerry and Eva once they moved to Brussels. It was fun to visit them at their home on Fort Myers, which was adjacent to the chief of staff's quarters. Jerry and Eva were both good cooks specializing in smoked fish, meat, and European salad and dishes, but they both had to take a backseat to Dexter and Shelley Hancock.

Dexter was the head dietician for the Zama Hospital, which was located near the Sagamihara housing area, and his dining facility served the best army chow I have ever eaten. Shelley was also a dietician, and both were gourmet cooks. We enjoyed many a memorable meal with them. Dexter retired from the Army as a colonel, and he and Shelley are now retired in Tuscaloosa, Alabama.

Roger Lawson succeeded Paul Stevens as the USARJ/IX Corps protocol officer. Roger had two brothers, Richard and Warren, who were general officers. Richard, a four-star US Air Force general, commanded several elite US Air Force units. Warren, a two-star Army general, served as the adjutant general for the state of Iowa for many years.

Roger and Susan remain dear friends, and they raised two beautiful and talented women. The oldest, Carrie, came from the same mold as Ross, and I thought I was observing the first female child I knew would wind up with Ross in the penitentiary. What a gorgeous, sweet person she became. Roger retired as a lieutenant colonel and worked as a defense contractor living near Maxwell Air Force Base, Alabama. Today, he and Susan live the good life in Arizona.

Penny became involved in the Officers' Wives' Club and served two years as chair of the Japan-American Red Cross volunteers. She also continued her college studies through the University of Maryland, which offered courses at Camp Zama.

Activities with the American Red Cross involved a lot of her time and energy, and they gave her a sense of satisfaction.

She would visit one of the Army hospitals with her volunteers, and they would write letters for the wounded soldiers, read for them, or just talk to them. I am sure the sight of a pretty, young, sweet-smelling, "round-eyed" girl gave much comfort to these young warriors.

When she came home from these visits, she would often cry and be depressed from seeing so much pain and suffering. Many of the wounded were disfigured and had lost limbs. The sight of these soldiers was both heartrending and gut-wrenching.

Once, I asked her, "If what you see there upsets you so much, why continue to go?"

"Because they need us," she answered.

And she continued to go.

Another rewarding activity came from teaching conversational English to young Japanese executives from the Nissan Motor Corporation. Shelley Hancock had the contract to teach these young men when we first got to Japan, but she decided she wanted to get involved in other activities, so she asked Penny if she would take the class. After much consternation, Penny decided to do it and enjoyed doing it.

There were about fifteen students in the class, which Penny held in our quarters. They had all taken English in school, so they were able to speak some English in varying degrees. Nissan paid for the course, and most were expected to go to the United States at some point in their careers. They were primarily interested in learning American customs and English slang.

Being a good ol' boy from Barnhart and West Texas, I had many colloquial sayings to teach them, such as, "You are a good man to ride the river with," or "That dog won't hunt." They could mouth the words, but I do not think they ever understood the meaning.

It was also funny that they could not pronounce their R's. Clint Eastwood always came out "Crint" Eastwood.

I am sure they found many strange things about us. When asked to describe an American, they would say, "I can't. You *gaijins* all look the same."

Two of these young fellows, Mr. Hara and Mr. Tonomura, and their families became friends. We visited them in their homes and vacationed with them, and for three years, they were very much a part of our lives. They took us places that most Americans never get to see, including exclusive Japanese resorts, beaches, and other sights.

Mr. Tonomura, Herbie San, and Mr. Hara.

I first learned what blacks must have felt during segregation with white-only restrooms and diners. Discrimination is ugly, no matter where you find it. We were sightseeing with another couple in the *Ginza,* Tokyo's renowned, upscale shopping and eating district, and saw a restaurant that looked interesting. Japanese restaurants typically placed plastic replicas inside their front window, ones depicting the different dishes served. We entered the restaurant, and immediately, a waitress rudely and loudly shouted at us, "No *gaijins.* No *gaijins,*" while she pointed at a sign in the window that was written in *Kanji,* the Japanese syllabic writing style using symbols. We were shocked. I could not believe they did not want us there. What had I done to them? Why was my money no good, and how could this be? I burned the image of that sign into my consciousness and never forgot it the remainder of my time in Japan.

This was my only bad experience with the Japanese people. Mr. Hara and Mr. Tonomura could not have been better friends. When we were with them, we could go anywhere, but if they were not, I stayed away from any place that had a sign saying no *gaijins* in Japanese. Mr. Hara is deceased. Mr. Tonomura and I correspond by e-mail.

Ross found himself in Japan. He discovered organized sports. Youth football, baseball, and basketball were all well coached and organized. The kids were able to play both American and Japanese teams throughout the island of Honshu, traveling to Yokota Air Base, Yokohama Naval Base, and Atsugi Naval Air Station, where the US Navy parked their fighter aircraft when the carriers docked at Yokohama. Ross developed into an excellent athlete while he was in Japan and made all-star teams in all three sports. More importantly, he found a release for all his energy while he was developing confidence and maturity, although that remained a problem.

One afternoon, I walked from USARJ headquarters to the baseball field where Ross was playing. I did not always get to see Ross's games, not even on weekends because of my job. Penny saw every one, though. She was a great sports fan and knew the games much better than I did. She was a sports historian who could quote batting, rushing, passing, and scoring averages. She had a myriad of sports knowledge floating around in her gorgeous head.

I sauntered up behind Ross's dugout to watch the game. Ross happened to be catching, and Penny was in the stands behind the backstop. The pitcher was having a difficult time, and each time he threw a bad pitch, Ross would kick the dirt and lazily throw the ball back to the pitcher, which forced him to leave the mound to retrieve the ball.

Penny would then holler at Ross, "Ross, don't work your pitcher. Ross, stop working your pitcher."

They were both getting into a high state of agitation, as they often did, and I knew the explosion was about to come.

Shortly thereafter, Ross turned around, threw his catcher's mask off, and screamed, "Shut up."

I quickly departed the area. First, I was embarrassed, as there were many people around. Second, I could have killed them both, and third, I knew if I intervened, it would only make matters worse, because no one could rationalize with either one when they were mad.

If a child annoys you, quiet him by brushing his hair. If this doesn't work, use the other side of the brush on the other end of the child
—Anonymous

I rarely disciplined Ross; however, when I did, he got a good whipping, and he got one that night. He was not going to talk to his mother that way, especially as a nine-year-old. Gradually over time, Ross learned to control his temper. I never disciplined Ross physically after the fourth grade. I did not have to.

Ross found two great kids to run around with, two kids that we still talk about today, Clayton Kono and Tom Bell. Clayton's dad was a DAC, and they had lived in Japan for many years. His parents were *Nisei*, second generation Japanese-Americans, and fine folks.

Tom's dad, CW4 Bell, a fixed-wing and helicopter pilot and as rough as a cob, was the man you wanted to fly with when the weather was bad and you really needed to get there. He once flew me by helicopter to Yokohoma and then Yokota under those conditions when I was delivering private communications from Dolvin to the US Air Force lieutenant general at Yokota and the US Navy admiral at Yokohoma.

Both Clayton and Tom were outstanding athletes. They were as good or better than Ross, depending on the sport.

Clayton was a good kid, as was Tom, but Tom was tough as nails, rambunctious, and always getting Ross and Clayton to do something they should have not been doing. One afternoon, Penny and I were coming back from Sagamihara, and as we pulled into the main gate of Camp Zama, we saw the three of them at the train station, buying tickets. They had decided to go on a train ride just to see what they could see. They spent many a happy hour together playing sports, swimming in the Sagami River, watching Japanese cartoons on TV, and doing whatever young boys did at that age.

Another key person in our life during this time was *Miki san*. *Miki san* was the maid and Ross's keeper when we were away at night. *Miki san* loved Ross, and she would cook him whatever Japanese dish he wanted when we were away. She taught us all basic Japanese, and she instructed Penny on how to cook tempura and rice the proper way. We loved her, and she loved us. We treated her as one of the family. *Miki* meant "flower stalk" in Japanese, but it should have meant "flower blossom." She was not pretty, but her spirit was lovely.

When I assumed my duty as the SGS, we moved to a single set of quarters on top of a pine-covered hill away from the hustle and bustle of our previous quarters. Penny loved it. Nestled among the trees, it had a nice backyard with a fence for Gigi.

Penny, Gigi and Ross in our backyard at Quarters 8.

Quarters 8 provided more room for entertaining. All official parties were held at the Zama Officer's Club. After these parties, people from captain to colonel would migrate to our house to continue the festivities until the wee hours of the morning. Throw on some Credence Clearwater Revival and Eagles mixed in with "Hey, Jude," Willie and George Jones, crank up the amps, add a lot of scotch whiskey, and it was surefire recipe for a headache the next morning.

I remember Penny cooking breakfast, assisted by a couple of zonked gals, for a house full of people, some asleep on sofas, the floor, or whatever they could find. Most people lived at Sagamihara and did not want to risk being stopped by either the MPs or Japanese police after a night of hard partying.

Quarters 8 also came with upgraded furniture, the same as the colonels'.

Both Penny and Ross were quite happy and content with their surroundings and friends, and so was I. I loved my job, although it was fourteen-hour days, including most weekends.

Damn, life was good for this boy from Barnhart and his family.

I arrived at the office at 0530 each morning and read the electrical message traffic received during the night. I would remove routine administrative cables that the generals did not need to see and separate the remainder into three classifications. The classifications were action, read, and information. The action messages were those that required a response from higher headquarters, and the generals might have wanted to provide guidance to the staff responsible for preparing the response. Read was just that—tidbits they needed to be aware of but required no action. Information needed to be read if you had the time.

Brigadier General Condit would arrive in the office at 0630 sharp, and he expected the cable traffic to be sitting in the middle of his desk. General Dolvin would arrive at 0800, and Condit would discuss any messages he felt appropriate or needed guidance with him. Dolvin would read all the cables but rarely comment on them. Condit would write a question or provide guidance on most of them. These I would "suspense" and "forward" to the staff for response. I had one NCO that did nothing but "bird-dog" suspense items.

I read, proofread, and made changes to every piece of correspondence that came into the command group requiring Dolvin's or Condit's approval or signature. I would return the correspondence to the preparing staff section for retyping or have my secretary retype it if the matter was urgent.

The deputy chief of staff, Colonel Larry Trapp, or I would brief the generals on each document requiring their signature or approval. We would tell them the requirement, a synopsis of the response, and if it had been properly coordinated with other interested staff agencies within the headquarters and, if appropriate, the headquarters of US Forces in Japan, located at Yokota Airbase, the American embassy in Tokyo, or other services.

If the matter was routine, they would ask the question, "Is it okay?" and would sign after they had only given it a cursory glance. If complicated, they would closely read the document, sometimes several times. Occasionally, they would give further guidance and require that information be added or left out. This would hurt my ego, because I took pride in being able to discern what the generals would be looking for and expecting. Each had a different style of writing, and generally, I was good at capturing the essence of their individual styles. This preparation would serve me well in future assignments.

Generals Dolvin and Condit played golf on weekends. I would go to the headquarters around 0645 and assemble the message file and take it to General Condit at the golf course. I remember the Zama course primarily as a walking course, but Dolvin and Condit rode in carts. Rarely did they ride together, but they did usually ride with a Japanese general from the Japanese Ground Self-Defense Force (JGSDF) or an important Japanese government official or businessperson. The Japanese were avid golfers and loved to play the Zama course because of its beauty and its history.

A motor scooter with a Japanese driver would be waiting for my arrival, and we would putter (no pun intended) out to find Condit. I would brief him on the message traffic between swings as he played through several holes. If he decided General Dolvin needed to be aware of a particular cable, I would locate and brief him.

General Condit would invariably ask questions about the cable traffic that would require me to find a subject expert to answer the questions. I would spend the remainder of the day locating someone who could answer the questions, and then I would brief General Condit at the golf course or his quarters. I spent many a weekend just this way.

Thankfully, the generals attended parties on Saturday night, so usually by 1730 or 1800, I was free until Sunday morning.

Sunday morning, I would brief General Condit between him attending Sunday school and church. Rarely did he send me chasing my tail on Sunday. He would usually say, "This can wait until Monday."

No one ever said on his deathbed, "I wish I had spent more time at work."
—Anonymous

My duties often interfered with my attending Ross's games, but neither Penny nor Ross complained. Penny understood that I loved my job, but in retrospect, my life and theirs would have been richer if I had attended more games.

One Saturday afternoon, Ross had a baseball game in Yokohama. I received a call at the office from Penny. She was at the US Naval hospital. Ross had broken his arm, and she asked if I would come get them, as they had ridden the bus to the game and it had already departed for Zama.

I explained that I was still tied up at the office and it would be several hours before I could come get them. Had I called General Condit and explained the situation, he would have told me to get on the road immediately. In fact, he would have sent me down to pick them up in a helicopter. No, I was indispensable and too important to ask. I was a dedicated, motivated Army officer whose job came before family. How wrong could I be! I was a fool! A USARJ physician who happened to be at the hospital brought Penny and Ross home.

Ross nursing his broken arm.

    General Condit and General Dolvin were different both physically and professionally. Condit was a large, heavyset man, a mustang who had come up through the ranks as a logistician. Dolvin was a thin man, a West Pointer, and a war hero. Both were bright, maybe brilliant, and both were serving their last tour before retirement. I liked and respected them. General Dolvin died in 1991, and General Condit died in 2000. They are buried in Arlington National Cemetery.

    General Dolvin had served in World War II, Korea, and Vietnam. He was the last general officer to leave Vietnam and the last commanding general of my old unit, XXIV Corps. He commanded Task Force Dolvin as a lieutenant colonel during the Korean War. He was awarded our nation's second highest award for bravery, the Distinguished Service Cross, for combat while he was operating miles behind enemy lines during the breakout from the Yalu River in May 1951. He had also been awarded four Silver Stars for bravery.

Brigadier General Condit, me, Captain Johnny Castleberry, and General Dolvin celebrating my birthday.
(June 28, 1973)

I worked for Colonel Lawrence "Larry" Trapp, the USARJ/IX Corps deputy chief of staff, during most of my assignment as the SGS. Larry was a special forces officer. He was short, and he inclined to have a paunch. He was "mean as hell," and he was afraid of no man or beast.

He had spent many years in covert operations with special forces and the CIA and served in MACV Special Studies and Observation Group (SOG), a euphemism for a unit conducting clandestine operations during the Vietnam War. He was an undercover operative/observer with the French Army at Dien Bien Phu before the United States was ever officially in Vietnam.

He came from Okinawa, and he was initially assigned as the commander of the US Army garrison at Camp Zama. In that position, he attended the weekly staff meeting each Wednesday with other commanders and staff in the USARJ command conference room.

Responsible for the conference room, Sergeant Gurule, one of my handpicked soldiers, would set the huge, specially built, oval conference table in a formal manner. There would be name tags for each attendee, china saucers and cups for those who drank coffee, crystal glasses for those who drank sodas, silver ice buckets, and always a Japanese centerpiece of some motif. Each attendee would have a notebook with their name printed on it and a conference agenda inside. There would also be pastries or finger sandwiches, depending on the time of the day.

General Condit was very protocol-conscious and would invariably call me into his office and ask, "Is the conference room ready?"

And I would answer, "Yes, sir." I would then stand by the conference room door and announce, "Gentlemen, the commanding general," as General Dolvin walked into the room.

All would rise, and General Dolvin would say, "Take your seats." Then the meeting would begin.

> *If you start a pissing contest with me, expect to be drowned.*
> —Colonel Larry Trapp

The first meeting Colonel Trapp attended, we inadvertently misspelled his name as "Trap" rather than "Trapp." After the meeting, he took me aside and very pointedly told me how to spell his name. Well, he did not know who I was or the power I could wield in the headquarters. I told Sergeant Gurule to put out a correct name tag for the next three meetings and then put out the incorrect name tag on the fourth meeting. In the meantime, I was grading the papers that came from his command rather harshly. Rarely did I find a paper that did not need to be returned for some reason. At the fourth meeting, Sergeant Gurule put the misspelled name tag on the table. Trapp glared at me the entire meeting but did not say anything.

Shortly, it was announced that Colonel Trapp would be assuming duties as the deputy chief of staff. I immediately went to see Colonel Lester Evans, the USARJ/IX Corps adjutant general and asked if he could give me a job. I was quite certain Trapp would not want me. Colonel Evans said he could.

The first morning, Trapp arrived about 0600. The message file was not ready. Again, he glared at me but said nothing. At 0620, I took him the file and said, "Sir, I am sure that you will want to bring in your own people. I have talked to the AG, and he has a job for me. I will stay until you get your own people on board, if you wish."

He looked at me and said, "Captain, you are not going anywhere. I have never wanted anyone to work for me more. I want the message file on my desk at 0600. Dismissed."

The next three months were difficult. I got my ass chewed out repeatedly, consistently, and often. Trapp was an expert at "ass-chewing." I learned well from him and used that experience in later assignments.

Both generals were gone, and Trapp came into my office around 1430 one afternoon and said, "Let's go to the club and get a drink."

I told him, "Sir, the club bar doesn't open until 1630."

He said, "You're the SGS. Call them and tell them to open it."

At the club, Trapp told me he liked the way I operated, he had done all he could to run me off, but I stuck around and he liked that, and we were going to make a good team, and we did. I learned that evening that you did not have just one drink with Larry Trapp. Larry and I shared many memorable occasions as we whipped the USARJ staff into shape.

I once asked Larry what he wanted to do when he retired. He said he wanted to be a 747 pilot or sell cheap whiskey and expensive women to drunk soldiers or be a shyster lawyer. He thought he was too old to fly 747s, so he might be a lawyer.

Larry retired from the Army after I departed Japan. He went to law school and became a lawyer in Salinas, California. He and his wife, Eiko, also bought a motel and restaurant in Salinas near Fort Ord.

I recall the communications and electronics (C&E) officer, a colonel, meeting his Waterloo. General Condit had scribbled out a message and told me to take it to the communication center and have them send it immediately. I told him it needed to be typed in proper format. He told me there was not time to type it. I knew this was going to be a problem. The warrant officer in the communication center told me he would not send it unless it was typed. I told him that General Condit wanted it sent and that he was wasting time. Either he needed to send it or have his boss come explain why he would not to General Condit.

In three minutes, the colonel burst into the command group and hollered at me, "I want to see the general." I walked into the General Condit's office and told him the colonel wanted to see him. General

Condit shouted in an angry, booming voice so the colonel could hear him, "You tell that son of a bitch that message better be gone." I stepped outside, and the colonel was gone.

This was the same colonel that General Condit had procure radios so that he and General Dolvin could talk while either was traveling in a sedan (the precursor to the cell phone) or on the golf course. Only three phones were to be purchased. The third was to remain in the command group for Colonel Trapp's use. Colonel Trapp discovered the colonel had bought four and was using the fourth to listen in on the general's conversations. This, I found, was a very good way to retire early.

What this colonel and the fifteen or so other colonels assigned to USARJ did not know is that I wrote their officer evaluation reports (OERs). Reports were rendered once a year or when the officer was reassigned to a different position or upon PCS. I would prepare typed, double-spaced drafts with comments for both Condit and Dolvin for their approval. Rarely were my comments changed, and then only if the general wanted to include another sentence or two.

The US Army Medical Activity of Japan (USAMEDACT-J) staff had prepared a response to US Army Pacific (USARPAC), our higher headquarters in Hawaii. It was a request to determine the additional resources, people, and equipment that would be required to set up a lab to test urine samples from Vietnam for drugs. General Dolvin wanted to sign the response going to USARPAC.

I returned the document for many, many corrections. It was so poorly written that I could not trust any information contained therein. I also wrote a cryptic note to that effect when I returned the document.

I looked up from my desk to find the MEDACT-J commander an out-of-breath, red-faced, irate brigadier general, shouting at me, "How dare you return a document that I have signed. You take this to General Dolvin," as he shoved the document at me.

I asked, "Sir, has it been corrected?"

He really went ballistic then. "Where is your medical degree? I am a doctor. A captain does not return my work."

I replied, "Sir, I do not need a medical degree to know when words are misspelled, punctuation is incorrect, figures do not add, and sentences make no sense."

He flipped through the document, probably for the first time, wheeled, and departed.

I told General Condit, and he told General Dolvin about the incident. They had a good laugh and instructed me to keep sending the document back until it was perfect. The document went back several times. I do not remember that brigadier general ever speaking to me again.

I also wrote his OER.

Captain Taylor, 1973.

In late 1972 or early 1973, General William B. Rosson, USARPAC commander, visited the headquarters for briefings. Rosson was General Dolvin's boss, so we made a special effort to get all in order. Sergeant Gurule had the command conference room in a high state of readiness, but General Condit came to see for himself instead of asking. Satisfied, he returned to his office while Dolvin and Rosson conversed in Dolvin's office.

I had the USARJ commanders and staff assembled outside the conference room so that General Dolvin could introduce each to General Rosson. They were milling around and chattering when General Condit appeared. He motioned me over and quietly said, "Line them up and inspect them. Pay particular attention to their brass." This, I did. Several had their brass on crooked, which I corrected. This was the first and last time I inspected a gaggle of colonels.

After the briefings, Generals Rosson and Dolvin were returning to Dolvin's office when Mary Middleton ambushed them. The chief of staff's secretary for many years, Mary was a USARJ institution. Some said she was married but had never divorced, and others said she had divorced.

General Rosson was a bachelor, and his wife was the Army, although he did marry after his retirement. He was a big man with a craggy face, imposing and intimidating.

Mary stopped General Rosson in the hallway and invited him to come to her quarters for a home-cooked Japanese meal. I thought Dolvin and Condit would go into apoplexy. They were all to have dinner that night at the Sanno Hotel in Tokyo with the commander of the JGSDF. Mary knew this, and I have no idea what she was thinking. General Rosson graciously told Mary that there was nothing he would rather have done but that his schedule was tight and that if she would give him a rain check, he would do it on his next visit.

The next time Rosson visited USARJ, he and Mary had dinner in her quarters.

Mary, stiff-necked, did not like it that I, not she, controlled who had access to General Condit. Colonels would bypass me and con Mary into letting them in to see him. General Condit would then complain to me about colonels coming in and wasting his time. I would speak to Mary about the situation, and she would go into General Condit's office, sniveling and dabbing her eyes. He would inquire about what was wrong, and with tears running down her cheek and her lips quivering, she would croak, "Captain Taylor."

Condit would dismiss her, call me into his office, and say the same thing each time, "You make that woman cry one more time, I'm going to fire you."

I continued to make her cry.

Both Generals Dolvin and Condit entertained and were entertained by Japanese government officials and businessmen who had a wide range of important contacts. One day, General Dolvin called several members of the command group into his office and proposed we start an investment club. The president of the Japanese Railroad, a golfing friend, had been giving him tips on stocks to buy on the *Nikkei*, the Japanese stock market, and General Dolvin thought we could all benefit from that relationship.

Each participant would put in an initial investment, and if desired, each could make additional contributions monthly. Each would share in the profits or losses based on the percentage of their contributions. The club would be open to all members of the command group—enlisted, officer, and civilian—but upon reassignment, we would have to cash out.

General Dolvin's Japanese friend attended our first meeting to give us suggestions on stocks to buy. In the typical Japanese way, this man craftily guided us into buying ball bearings. We all left the meeting mumbling, "Ball bearings."

A few days later, the headlines of the English language version of the Tokyo newspaper read, "Japan Signs Trade Agreement with China-Ball Bearings."

I had invested a thousand dollars initially and immediately started investing monthly. Penny and I made a little over a 100 percent when we departed Japan.

Grandmother Farr came to visit in the summer of 1973, and we were all elated to see her, especially Ross. He and his grandmother had a special relationship that went back to the days when she raised him while we were at Tarleton.

We took her to see all the sights in Tokyo and the surrounding area, and then the three of us flew to Hong Kong for a few days and left Ross with Miki. While in Hong Kong, we bought a beautiful, hand-woven Chinese rug from Beijing, China. I later returned to Hong Kong on a US Air Force training flight and brought the rug back to Japan as military cargo.

Grandmother Farr, Herbie, and Penny at the Hong Kong Hilton.

We stayed at the Hong Kong Hilton, and the girls had a marvelous time seeing all the sights. We toured the Chinese border, took a ride in a Chinese *junk*, and ate many good meals.

The shopping was fabulous, and Penny and Grandmother bought several antique porcelain items made in China. I bought a copy of Chairman Mao Tse Tung's *Little Red Book*, which is now probably a collector's item, even though millions were published in China.

Penny, Grandmother Farr, and me sightseeing in Hong Kong.

Penny was in the market to buy some antique Japanese furniture from the day we arrived in Japan. She had bought a *hibachi* table and several other small pieces, but she was set on getting a Japanese chest. We would go to the Sanno Hotel in Tokyo when the generals were gone and shop in antique stores but could find little in our price range.

After World War II, Americans bought or confiscated most Japanese heirlooms. In addition, when the Japanese began to prosper after the war, they wanted modern furniture of chrome and plastic. Accordingly, the pieces that remained brought a premium price.

We would usually spend the night in the Sanno Hotel. The Sanno, which was built in 1932, was one of three world-known hotels in Tokyo, with the Imperial and Daiichi being the others. The hotel was located near Rappongi, the infamous nightclub district, and the National Diet Building, which then and today is the center of the Japanese government. Originally used by Japanese legislators, the building was a burned-out hulk after the war. The American Army renovated the building and turned it into transient billets for VIPs and senior officers. Later, it became an all-service officer's club and hotel.

USARJ, the executive agent, ran the Sanno through a joint-service board of directors, but the manager had his report card written by General Dolvin. Naturally, Dolvin and Condit received special treatment while at the Sanno. Both had private suites decorated by their wives. The suites were not to be used by others without permission. If the Sanno wanted to use the rooms for other VIPs, they called me. Penny and I, with the general's permission, would stay in one of the suites, if the generals were not using them. Mrs. Dolvin often stayed in their suite when General Dolvin played golf on weekends.

We also stayed there for various official functions. Centrally located, the hotel offered all the amenities you would find in a first-class Las Vegas casino and hotel. We spent many an evening there playing the slot machines and watching a floorshow when the generals were out of the country or otherwise engaged.

Captain and Mrs. Taylor, Christmas Formal, Japan.

We were told to go to Korea if we wanted Japanese antique furniture. Korea had been occupied by Japan during WWII, and the Japanese had left furniture that could be found in secondhand stores and back alleys if you looked.

Dexter Hancock and I caught a flight out of Yokota Airbase to Osan Air Force Base some forty miles from Seoul. It was relatively easy to catch a military flight out of Yokota, as Paul Stevens and later Captain Roger Lawson, the USARJ protocol officers, dealt daily with the protocol office at Yokota. We scratched their backs, and they scratched our backs.

We stayed in Seoul for two days and searched the back alleys for treasure. I found two Japanese chests that met Penny's specifications and bought them for less than a hundred dollars. I shipped them to Japan on a US Air Force C-130 as cargo. Penny was pleased with my purchases.

Penny and I were all set to catch a US Air Force training flight to Taipei, Taiwan, and Hong Kong, but the protocol officer at Yokota called to say that their commanding general had directed that wives were no longer to fly as passenger on training flights. Therefore, Penny could not go. I boarded the plane with probably five pilots and a couple of other US Air Force officers. We taxied out to the runway, did a hard right, and pulled close to a hanger. Waiting were six or seven US Air Force wives who quickly boarded, and away we went.

I had a newfound respect for US Air Force officers. Hell, they broke the rules just like the Army. Maybe they learned it from us when they were part of the Army.

USARJ was one social function after another. General Dolvin had unlimited representational funds he could use to entertain Japanese dignitaries. One night, we had a Western night at the Zama Club. We ordered cowboy hats, vests, kerchiefs, toy pistols, and scabbards from the Sears catalogue for each attendee. The Japanese VIPs loved it.

Because we traveled quite extensively during our stay in Japan, we visited Tokyo, Kyoto, Osaka, Nara, Sapporo, Kamakura, Nikko, Hakone, and Mt. Fuji.

Penny—Tokyo Gardens.

Usually, we traveled with the Haras and Tonomuras or other friends staying in a Japanese *ryokan*.

Ryokans, Japanese-style inns, have rooms with *tatami* floors and low tables with no chairs, which made it necessary to sit on the floor. Shoes are removed at the front entrance, and you are issued slippers, which are removed when you enter your room, and a *yukata*, a type of robe that can be worn both inside and outside the *ryokan* while you are viewing their magnificent gardens and grounds. Breakfast and dinner are included in the price, and meals are taken in your rooms, which resemble suites. In addition, you would sleep on futons.

Once, we went to an exclusive *ryokan* near Mt. Fuji with the Haras and Tonomuras, including Mr. Tonomura's father and grandmother. This *ryokan* was known for its hot spring baths.

Our bath, which was located in a small garden surrounded by shrubbery, could be entered by merely stepping out of our room. Naked is the way you bathed. Bathing suits were not allowed.

Penny, Ross, and I were leisurely soaking in the hot spring-fed water as a gardener trimmed the shrubs. We ignored him, and he ignored us, I think. I bet he sneaked a peak at Penny when we were not looking. I was amazed that Penny would bathe naked, but she did.

When we were staying at a *ryokan*, we always took our own liquor, as Japanese liquor was quite expensive. Kirin beer was cheap though and quite good. It was on this trip that Mr. Tonomura's father, who spoke excellent English, and I were drinking scotch, and he began to tell me about his military service during World War II. He had been a major serving in China and had seen extensive combat. He had a picture of himself in uniform standing by his staff car, a 1936 Buick. He was proud of that car and told me that he knew if Japan went to war with the United States, Japan would lose, because no country that could make a car as fine as that Buick could be defeated.

The grandmother also told me of watching B-29s flying over her home and looking into the eerie but mesmerizing light emanating from the open bomb bays and the silver belly of the American planes as searchlights silhouetted them and the planes descended over Tokyo. She would cover her face with her hand and weep gently as old memories flooded her mind.

One of our favorite trips was to Sapporo, which hosted the 1972 Winter Olympics. We flew up for their Ice Festival and viewed beautiful, sculpted ice carvings up to two stories high of animals, famous buildings like the Eiffel Tower, trains, planes, and many other wonderful scenes.

I have never been so cold in my life. Temperatures were subzero, and even the borrowed US Air Force arctic parkas could not keep out the cold. Much of the shopping in Sapporo was underground because of the cold and serviced by the subway. The king crab legs and salmon were delicious.

There were many unusual sights, sounds, and places to visit in Japan. The Tokyo fish market was the most unique—several hundred yards of covered area containing fish of every size and description imaginable, fish caught that night and sold the next morning. More fish to view in one morning than I thought the oceans could hold.

Another unique experience was the love motels, rooms for rent for short periods, usually two hours. All were very anonymous, as you paid the attendant through your car window and pulled a partition behind your car. The rooms were quite nice. They contained a double bed, mirrored ceiling, a minibar, some unusual toys/vibrators, and a television offering erotic programs. Some Americans took their wives there on their wedding anniversary or other special occasions or no occasion at all—or so I am told.

Penny climbed Mount Fuji, Japan's highest and most prominent mountain. I do not remember why I did not. She started at night and reached the summit in time to see the rising sun spread its majestic rays over the "Land of the Rising Sun." She did this during early July, as most of the snow had melted.

Ross climbed the mountain with his school class. Both returned home with skinned knees and sore muscles, but they were quite proud of their accomplishment. They agreed that they did not need to do it again.

All three of us became great fans of sumo wrestling. Sumo is Japan's national sport, and it is more popular than baseball. Although the fights are short, always less than a minute and usually only a few seconds, the rituals leading up to the conflict builds the suspense. Several times, we went to *Kokugikan*, the sumo stadium in Tokyo, to watch tournaments. Most of the time, we watched them on TV. When the tournaments were held (six per year), we were watching along with most of Japan.

When we first arrived in Japan there was a young wrestler, an American named Jesse Kuhaulua from Hawaii, who rose steadily up the sumo ranks. Jesse went by his Japanese name of *Takamiyma*, and in 1972, he won the Emperor's Cup, the highest prize a sumo wrestler could win. Jesse became our favorite, but we had others. Such a simple game of pushing and shoving the opponent out of a small ring should not have been so enthralling, but we were hooked.

Takamiyma did not achieve *yokozuna* (grand champion) status until after we left Japan. After one tourney, which he did not win, we visited him, and he gave us a print of his right hand, which was two and one-half times the size of mine, and signed the print. We thought it a big deal at the time.

In Turkey, I visited the public baths, and I did the same in Japan, although the bathing ritual changed somewhat. The Officer's Club at Atsugi Naval Air Station, which was about twenty-five minutes from Camp Zama, had a family bath in the traditional manner. We would have our bath, eat a nice meal, and return home.

When we entered the bath, we removed our clothes and remained naked throughout, although we had a small towel to hold in front of our privates. The female attendant took us to a steam room where we sweated for about fifteen minutes.

We were then taken to a large room containing the bath, which was ten yards long and three-foot deep, almost deep enough to swim but not quite. The bath was filled to the brim with warm water. Before we entered the bath, an attendant would take a cloth and soap, wash, and rinse us several times as we sat on a small wooden stool. When she reached our private parts, she would hand us the cloth, and we would perform that task ourselves. We would enter the bath and soak for thirty minutes. The attendant would bring Penny a glass of plum wine, me a scotch whiskey, and Ross a Coke while we soaked.

We were then taken to an air-conditioned room and given a massage. The masseuses were women, one tiny and the other the size of a sumo wrestler. Their final act was to walk on our backs. Each time, the tiny woman walked on me, and the huge woman walked on Penny. We thought it great fun and so relaxing.

Our tour in Japan was originally for three years, but we enjoyed the assignment so much that we extended for a fourth year. Penny and I agreed that Japan had been the best assignment we had had as a family. I loved my job, and Penny and Ross were happy. The "Land of the Rising Sun" had cast a beautiful spell upon us, and we hated to break it.

In February 1974, General Condit asked me if I had received orders for Command and General Staff College (CGSC). I told him I hadn't and that I did not know if I would be selected. Only 50 percent of Army officers are selected for attendance at CGSC; therefore, selection was imperative if you had aspirations of being a lieutenant colonel or higher.

I had been selected for promotion to major but had not yet been promoted. Accordingly, I felt good about my selection for CGSC, but I could not be sure. At that time, selection for CGSC was made by an officer's assignment branch in Washington.

General Condit directed me to prepare a back-channel message for General Dolvin's signature to my branch chief supporting my selection. Back-channel messages were unofficial, private cable traffic that general officers used to communicate with other general officers and senior government officials. The messages were sent through special intelligence circuits and were treated as classified. A general could express his opinion without it becoming a matter of official record. I wrote many "back channels" for Dolvin and Condit. Several days later, a response was received. I had been selected to attend CGSC, and orders would be forthcoming.

It was now time to do our last-minute shopping. When we had arrived in Japan, one US dollar would buy 365 yen. When we left, however, one US dollar would buy only 135 yen. Thus, our purchasing power had been drastically reduced. Still, we bought a quadraphonic stereo receiver, tape deck, Asahi-Pentax camera, and other assorted items. I also had a couple of suits and a cashmere overcoat hand-tailored, and Penny had some clothes made. In addition, we ordered a new car through the post exchange (PX) for delivery in Dallas, a 1974 Ford Grand Torino.

The Vietnam War was swiftly coming to an ignoble end, and the large Army hospitals had closed or were closing. However, an excess of doctors and dentists remained, and they were bored. Consequently, if you desired elective surgery or a procedure of any type, they were more than willing to accommodate to maintain their skills. I had several teeth extracted, a new bridge installed, and teeth crowned. Each time I visit my dentist today, he tells me to take care of my mouth, as I have at least twenty thousand dollars worth of work inside.

We departed Japan on May 29, 1974, and flew in the first-class cabin of a Northwest Airlines 747 to Hawaii, where we spent a few days before we flew to the continental United States. The USARJ/IX Corps protocol folks worked closely with Northwest Airlines and were able obtain three first-class tickets as a farewell gift.

There were several parties for us before we left, and several friends, including Mr. Hara and Mr. Tonomura and their families, saw us off at the airport. Mr. Tonomura's father hosted a lavish buffet in Northwest's executive suite before our departure.

I was awarded two Meritorious Service Medals while I was in Japan—an impact award for the work I had done on the planning for the reversion of the Ryukyus Islands (Okinawa) to Japan and the other for my overall service.

We were worn out from all the parties, so we slept most of the way to Honolulu. As soon as we settled into our hotel room, we hit the beach. Our stay in Hawaii was pleasant, as is any stay in paradise. We did the usual tourist things, and Ross and I ended up with bad sunburns.

The one item that stands out in my mind of all things is going to a Ponderosa restaurant for the first time. Ross trailed behind Pen and me in the line, and I was not paying any attention to what he was doing. When I arrived at the cashier, I discovered he had ordered two different steaks with all the fixings. I paid for them and made him eat it all. I may have helped him some. I think he thought it was similar to a school cafeteria.

The Farrs were now living in Austin, so that was where we went first. Granddad Farr had a ranch management and real estate partnership with Wayne Connally, a state senator and the brother of Governor John Connally. We then headed to Big Spring for a few days to visit my parents.

The Ford dealership in Dallas called while we were in Big Spring to let me know our new Grand Torino was ready for delivery. Daddy had never flown on an airplane, so I shamed him into going with me. He really did not want to go, but away we went to the Midland-Odessa Airport for the short hop to Dallas.

It was a clear day, so we could see the ground, and we tried to determine the towns we were flying over; however, it became cloudy the closer we got to Dallas. Daddy liked that, but he did not like the sounds or sudden movements the airplane made. With each creak, he would whisper, "Herb, what's that?"

We arrived in Dallas and were preparing to land at Love Field when the pilot came on the intercom and announced, "Folks, Love Field is socked in with weather, and we are being diverted to an alternate airfield, which happens to be the one we just left, Midland-Odessa." Back we flew to Midland, where we landed and taxied toward the terminal.

When we arrived at the terminal, but before the stewardess could open the doors to disembark, the pilot's voice once more came over the intercom and said, "Folks, the weather is now clearing in Dallas, so we will be heading back that way." Daddy had had more than his fill of airplane rides.

My promotion to major on July 1, 1974, occurred while I was on leave, the first and only time I did not have a formal ceremony. We were in Austin at the time, so Penny and I drove the ninety miles to San Antonio and Fort Sam Houston. I bought my field-grade cap with the scrambled eggs on the bill and some rank insignia for my uniform. That hat sure did look fine. We went to the Fort Sam Officer's Club that night to celebrate.

Command and General Staff College began August 12, 1974, and lasted until June 6, 1975. I did not want to use all my accrued leave, so we started for Fort Leavenworth, leisurely motoring along in our new Ford.

14

Command and General Staff College

Arriving at Fort Leavenworth, Kansas, the home of the Army Command and General Staff College (CGSC), and the oldest military installation west of the Mississippi, I signed in at the school and drove to the post housing office. I was handed the keys to quarters 520-8, Kearny Avenue, better known as artillery barracks, and we proceeded to our new home.

Built prior to the Civil War, artillery barracks had served as both billets and battery orderly rooms for artillery troopers. Around 1910, the barracks had been converted into apartments for officers and their families.

A huge living room, kitchen, and three small bedrooms, one bath, no air-conditioning, radiators for heat, and twenty-foot ceilings greeted us. The living room and its high ceilings resembled the inside of the Barnhart gym.

We were on the second floor of the old three-story, historical, brick building along with eight other families. The basement had been the location of the battery orderly rooms, but it now served as a storage area for excess furniture not needed by the tenants, such as lawn mowers, camping equipment, and refrigerators. Behind the barracks, the stables had been converted into garages.

Rank has its privileges.
—Army maxim

I was one of the least senior officers in the class because I had recently been promoted, and the Army determined seniority by date of rank. Therefore, we lived in artillery barracks rather than in the nice but small, single-family homes other students lived in on post.

When we opened the door and walked into the quarters, the crushing heat of probably 140 degrees hit us, and we wilted. Penny and I looked at each other. We knew there was no way we could stay there without air-conditioning.

We loaded up and returned to Lawrence, Kansas, where we had spent the previous night. There, we devised our battle plan to make our new quarters livable. We stayed the weekend in Lawrence, and while there, we toured the University of Kansas and took Ross to see Allen Field House, named for the legendary basketball coach "Phog" Allen.

Monday morning, we bought and installed two large window air conditioners, and our household goods were delivered soon after. Artillery barracks turned out to work just fine. It was roomy, and best of all, it was filled with kids for Ross to play with.

Major Al Wissinger and his wife, Kathy, lived next door in two apartments with four bedrooms in each apartment. They had eleven children ranging from Janie (five) to Allen, Jr., (fifteen) and an infant.

All the other families except Captain Cleo and Glynna Hogan had children. Thankfully, the Hogans liked children, because there were plenty of them to like along with their bicycles, tricycles, and assorted toys. It was an obstacle course to maneuver up the stairwells.

Weekday afternoons and weekends were quite chaotic with the sound of children echoing through the hallways between apartments. The guys had to study each night, so we had a standing rule that children would not play outside or in the hallways after 1900.

Penny's photo for the CGSC annual.

The CGSC was designed to equip an officer with the knowledge and skills needed to plan military campaigns and maneuver large formations of troops, divisions, and corps in battle, but also taught the bureaucratic procedures necessary to maneuver in staff jobs at the Pentagon. The lessons were intense, and reading assignments amounted to around three hours each night. There was no goofing off, and the competition among students was brutal. I disliked every minute of the course and studied longer and harder there than at Tarleton, the War College, or Shippensburg State.

A new commandant, Major General John H. Cushman, whom we quickly named "Cush Person," had arrived shortly before the students. He had initiated a massive revamping of the curriculum that continued as a work in progress throughout the school year. Consequently, instructors were working as hard as the students, trying to revise and learn new lesson plans. It was not unusual to have an instructor who had not slept that night teaching an 0800 class.

Cushman's idea to revamp the course in view of lessons learned in Vietnam was admirable. The emphasis on ethics, values, common decency, and morality was needed, but his mistake was to attempt to do it all at once rather than in a phased, orderly, and methodical fashion.

Instructors, students, and wives were all frustrated. Cushman almost ended up with a mutiny when he dictated that we would go to class at night until 2100 the last eight weeks of the course. Most of us said to hell with it and cut back on our study time, resigning ourselves to a "Leavenworth B." Only those who thought they had a chance to be the distinguished graduate or get on the commandant's list continued to burn the midnight oil.

The class consisted of 896 regular army, eight-four US National Guard and Reserve, fourteen US Air Force, ten US Marine Corps, four US Navy, and ninety-seven foreign officers from fifty-two countries. The class was divided into twenty-three sections of approximately fifty students and further subdivided into work groups of thirteen students.

I knew the students in my section, but not necessarily well. I knew those in my work group extremely well, as they were the ones we socialized with for the most part. I also knew a few other students well. Each of us had a tablemate with whom we sat, studied, made presentations, and worked on projects. Major Paul Ware, an infantryman and aviator, was my tablemate. Paul saved my bacon many times, particularly on map exercises. He knew the war-fighting business.

Paul had served two tours in Vietnam but had finished neither. His first trip, he flew a Huey into a hot landing zone, and because of the intense small-arms fire, he could not land. He hovered about five feet off the ground as the soldiers jumped from the helicopter. When he looked over his right shoulder to check that all were out, he saw the last soldier catch a grenade on the door frame of the chopper as he exited.

He told me everything went into slow motion as the grenade rolled around on the metal floor before it exploded. The chopper crashed, and Paul suffered extensive burns over his arms, hands, face, and torso as he tried to pull his co-pilot out of the burning chopper. He was unable to do so, and the co-pilot and door gunner perished in the flames. Paul spent many months recovering in the burn ward at Brooke Army Medical Center in San Antonio.

His second tour, he was flying fixed-wing aircraft, ferrying VIPs to various locations. He had flown a general to an airfield, landed, and discharged the general and his aide, and he was taxiing to park his aircraft. He looked up, and a fighter/bomber ran into him. Again, he was medically evacuated to the States for an extensive hospital stay.

Paul was severely scarred. He suffered pain but never complained. After graduation, the Army assigned him as the professor of military science at McNeese State University. Over time, we lost touch with each other.

Many well-known soldiers have graduated from CGSC with top honors. Eisenhower, Bradley, and Patton were three who went on to become great battle captains. Our distinguished graduate, Captain Wesley (Wes) K. Clark, also did well, becoming a four-star general, the Supreme Allied Commander Europe (SACEUR), and a presidential candidate in 2004. Wes graduated the USMA and attended Oxford University as a Rhodes scholar. He was awarded the Silver Star and severely wounded in Vietnam. He was bright and intense, and everyone knew Wes Clark. Most of us expected him to make it to the top.

Classes were held in Bell Hall. This modern school building contained a large auditorium seating around 1,500 people. It was known as the world's largest bedroom because of its comfortable seats and dim lighting. Often, there would be few open eyes as we listened to speakers from academia, business, government, and the media, as well as the many general officers that passed through.

One speaker we did listen to—and listened closely—was Secretary of Defense James Schlesinger. Schlesinger was brilliant, and one of the most dynamic speakers I have been privileged to hear. A friend of the Army, he supported a strong national defense, no amnesty for draft-dodgers, and the A-10 Thunderbolt (Warthog), which became the only close-combat support aircraft our friends in the US Air Force were able to offer, and then reluctantly.

President Ford fired Schlesinger because of his aloof and arrogant manner, or so the story goes. Actually, his demise resulted over his insistence on maintaining a large defense budget.

He was cold and egotistical, as was General Cushman, and the day they clashed in Bell Hall was a hoot. Schlesinger, involved in a mutually beneficial question-and-answer session with the student body, was on a roll. He had a plane to catch, and General Cushman interrupted him twice to say, "Sir, you need to depart now."

Finally, Schlesinger, exasperated, very haughtily and pointedly said, "General, the last time I checked, I outrank you; therefore, I will leave when I am ready to leave." A tittering drifted across the auditorium as the general disappeared behind the stage curtains.

One of the most moving and memorable experiences in my military career took place in Bell Hall, and General Cushman was in the forefront. In early May, we had gathered in our section rooms along with a few journalists, academics, and general officers to ask, ponder, and answer some hard questions. The questions included the following: "Is the individual first a military officer responsible to the dictates of the system or first a human being answerable to personal conscience? What happens when the mission and one's own value system come into conflict? What sort of compromises can decently be made? And what cannot?"

These were weighty, difficult, and important questions that most of us had thought about but had not resolved. For two and a half uninterrupted days, we considered these questions. Discussions were heated, introspective, cerebral, and often painful.

An attendee at the symposium was C. W. Gusewelle, an editorial writer for *the Kansas City Star*. Gusewelle wrote an article in the May 11, 1975, edition of the *Star* titled, "Remarkable Military Maneuver at Ft. Leavenworth." In the article, he offered his reflection of what he had seen and heard during his visit. He wrote about how young the officers were, mostly in their early thirties, and how the majority had served a combat tour. He wrote of their level of skill, sophistication, and education, many holding master's degrees. He wrote of their willingness to intellectually challenge the general officers in attendance, and in his opinion, their constructive self-examination could not help but lead to a better led Army with a refined sense of duty. He wrote that on the last morning of the symposium, classroom TVs flickered with the excruciating images of the last American being plucked from the American embassy in Saigon and the surrender of the South Vietnamese government to the Communist North. Moreover, he wrote that someone had written on a chalkboard in one of the classrooms: "It's all over, over there."

He wrote of all filing into a huge auditorium and journalists, professors, generals, and students speaking, and lastly, he spoke of General Cushman rising to close the symposium. I quote from his editorial:

> Finally, it was the turn of the commandant of the college, a major general, who, after some summarizing comments, seem to hesitate just an instant and then asked them all to stand.
>
> It must be a hard thing to say a public prayer from the lighted stage in an auditorium of 1,000 professional soldiers of many backgrounds and several faiths, or none at all. In the Army, praying is the chaplain's job. But this obviously was something that had occurred to the general spontaneously in that moment to do.
>
> The long habit of command had shaped his manner. So that when he spoke to God, he still sounded a little like a man addressing troops. But his sincerity was not to be doubted, nor the plain decency of what he asked.
>
> He prayed for all those who had suffered in the war just ended, and those who might yet suffer after it. And for the country. And for the wisdom to understand duty. And for the courage to do it. And finally he prayed for the friends and comrades that all of them—every single man there—had left behind on that bloody field.
>
> It was a moment very full of emotion.
>
> Somehow reluctant, then, to pronounce an amen, which seems more a preacher's word than a general's, he simply stopped, having said what was in his mind.
>
> And after a pause he told them, "Now just go quietly out of here."
>
> They did. And it was a little time before some present could comfortably speak.

I still get a lump in my throat when I think about the emotions I felt that May morning—the sadness and the futility of it all.

About this time, I received orders for my next duty assignment, the US Army Military Personnel Center (MILPERCEN) located in Alexandria, Virginia. Neither Penny nor I were pleased. We had no desire to be located in the Washington, D.C., area with its horrendous traffic and high living costs. We wanted to go to Germany. However, the corporate office had called and I now had to answer.

Penny and I decided that we would be better off financially if we bought rather than rented a house. We also knew we would have to cut some corners, but we thought the sacrifice would be worth the effort.

Realtors had their own intelligence network, and they knew which students were going where before the students did. They descended on Leavenworth, Kansas, like locusts swarming, setting up shop in hotels and motels with their liquor and hors d' oeuvres, ready to devour the naïve and uninitiated. We were both.

Luckily, we found a good and honest realtor in Bill Bisson. Bill specialized in military sales in the D.C. area, traveled to most of the service schools, and went overseas to obtain clients. He knew what we could afford before we did, and he knew what we would be satisfied with within our price range.

Bill quickly dissuaded us of our desire for a four-bedroom, three-bath, two-car-garage home with a large kitchen and yard when we told him our price range was $40,000 with $55,000 tops. Bill pointed out, quite seriously, that for 35K, he could probably get us an apartment over a two-car garage.

Bill and I agreed that I would fly to D.C. over Memorial Day weekend and house hunt. Penny would have gone, but we did not think we could afford two tickets. When I arrived in D.C. at National Airport, now Ronald Reagan International, Bill met me, and we began to look.

Around two in the afternoon the next day, Bill said to me, "I have shown you different neighborhoods, price ranges, and types of homes, but the place I am taking you to next is where you will buy." And he drove me to the Townes of Orange Hunt situated in the Orange Hunt subdivision, city of Springfield, Fairfax County, Virginia.

There were four townhouses left, and the models were all decorated with wallpaper, drapes, finished basements, and upgraded appliances. Each was lovely, but I knew Penny would fall in love with 9140 Conservation Way, which was decorated in early American style with lots of blues and whites, her colors. With three bedrooms, three and a half baths, a formal living and dining room, plus the finished den in the basement, it was neither the largest nor the fanciest. It did not even have a garage. The largest, an end unit, would have been a better buy, but it was not Penny.

An open house was taking place, and the owner wanted to deal. I figured that if I thought about the purchase and called Penny and if she wanted to see pictures, we would lose the opportunity to buy the home. I put two thousand dollars down as earnest money and agreed to a thirty-year mortgage, with the seller paying closing costs. I do not remember the interest rate, but I think it was around 6.5 percent. This was a big purchase for a boy from Barnhart, the biggest he had ever made, and it frightened him. I took many pictures, and Penny seemed pleased with my purchase, but until she actually saw the home, I would not be sure.

That year turned out to be a good one for both Penny and Ross. Ross went through the seventh grade and had excellent teachers. Many were spouses of officers in CGSC and understood the military child. It became easy for him to adjust to his new surroundings, as all his friends were the new kids on the block. He continued with his sports, and again, he had good coaches. And the competition was keen.

That winter, it snowed and snowed. Kids descended on a steep, treeless hill near artillery barracks to slip, slide, and ride various contraptions down the slope. Trash can lids, boards, and bodies went flying and tumbling down the hill.

Ross had a fancy sled that we had bought in anticipation of such an occasion. He had made several perilous runs without serious mishap, and he was enjoying himself immensely. I could not resist joining in the fun. After I climbed aboard the sled, Ross and I sped down the slope and over a rise. We became airborne, landed hard, flew off, and rolled down the hill as the sled remained where it had landed. The runners were crushed from our combined weight, and the sled was ruined.

Penny stayed busy with her activities and took college courses at night. We hosted one work-group social function in our gymnasium, and the girls who did not have the pleasure of living in artillery barrack were quite envious. Me? Well, I was just glad to get it behind me and move on.

Penny at home at Fort Leavenworth.

Daddy drove up to see us at the end of May and brought a 1969 Ford Mustang that he was willing to sell us as a second car. We chauffeured him around to see all the sights. We all had a good time. I believe he rode the bus home.

I graduated the morning of June 6, 1975. My old boss in Vietnam, Richard G. Stilwell, now a four-star and the commander of US Forces in Korea, gave the graduation address. We had shipped our household goods the day before, and we were set on beating the moving van to our new home so that we could have a door-to-door move. Again, Penny and Ross had the engine running, and we were off on a very fast trip. We were returning to the land of my ancestors, where it had all started almost four centuries ago, the Commonwealth of Virginia.

15

Mother MILPERCEN

The eastern United States is a forest-covered wonderland of streams, beautiful valleys, large rivers, and mountains. Almost every village or town has a conspicuously posted sign proclaiming its significance as a historic area. Revolutionary, French-Indian, and the Civil War touched part or all of this land. It is paradise for a military history buff.

It is also a land of large cities. Fortunately, the Eisenhower Interstate System allows one to get around or out of most of them. On this trip, we were not sightseeing or enjoying the scenery. We had a long way to go and a short time to get there. We were traveling hard, and we were traveling fast. After we spent the first night somewhere east of St. Louis and the second night in a quaint village off the Pennsylvania Turnpike, we dropped down through Maryland and hit the Washington Beltway. This boy from Barnhart knew he was a long way from home and his comfort zone.

After we had weaved, dodged, came to full stops on the Beltway, and lost our way on the streets of Springfield, Virginia, we arrived at 9140 Conservation Way. Penny could not have been more pleased with her new home. For that, I will forever be grateful, for unknown to either of us, it would be her home for ten of the next twelve years. The moving van arrived the next day, so we had our first and last door-to-door move.

Ross had a choice between attending West Springfield High School or Lake Braddock. We decided we liked the facilities at Lake Braddock, particularly their sports facilities. Braddock had recently been built, and we felt Ross would have an easier time adjusting to a school where most of the kids were new rather than at West Springfield in an older, more established school and community. The school, huge and intimidating, served kids from the seventh through the twelfth grade. Ross's senior class had 873 graduates.

Moreover, it had open classrooms. Students often sat on the floor and could leave the classroom at any time to go to the restroom or walk around without the teacher's permission. We worried that Ross would not find this conducive to learning, but he loved the freedom and thrived athletically and academically.

My tour was spent with "Mother MILPERCEN," so called because she was responsible for managing the careers of all soldiers, both officer and enlisted, from initial entry into the Army to ultimate separation or retirement. It was a career-enhancing move similar to a midlevel executive being assigned to the home office of a large corporation. Assigned to the personnel management support division, I originally had been designated as the executive officer to the director, a brigadier general whose name I no longer remember.

When I arrived, he told me his chief of the service retirement section had retired unexpectedly. It was a critical vacancy that he had to fill immediately, and he planned to assign me to the job. I was disappointed.

My job description read:

> Chief of the Service Retirement Section, responsible for processing all officer and warrant officer retirements, both voluntary and mandatory, based on age and service in accordance with the provisions of United States Code, Title 10. Advises higher authority of laws and policies pertaining to retirement. Approval authority for requests to exception to HQDA policy for both officers and enlisted soldiers. Responsible for General Officer retirements from initial notification by the Office Chief of Staff, Army (OCSA) through final administrative processing.

The job, piecemeal assembly-line work, required a concerned and caring attitude, as we were dealing with senior people who had served their nation faithfully for many years. They either were leaving the

Army voluntarily or were being put out to pasture because of age or length of service.

I arrived to find the Army as well as the other services experiencing a large influx of retirement applications as a result of a phenomenon known as "retired pay inversion." This aberration adversely affected readiness because of the large number of senior officers bailing out.

Retired pay inversion penalized a soldier eligible for retirement (minimum twenty years of service) for remaining on active duty. Simply put, cost-of-living allowances (COLAs) were greater (significantly greater) than active-duty pay raises. Retired soldiers have their military retired pay increased at the same percent as social security recipients with each year's COLA increase. If, for example, the active-duty pay raise is 2.0 percent and the COLA is 3.5 percent, a soldier with at least twenty years active service loses money by remaining on active duty.

Why would anyone want to remain on active duty under those circumstances? Initially, soldiers did not understand this aberration and went blissfully on their way, but once it became general knowledge, they began to retire in droves.

Something had to be done, or the entire military leadership would disappear. The Department of Defense's (DOD) answer was to submit to congress a fix that eventually became Public Law 94-106. This law allowed soldiers to either have their retired pay computed using their basic pay at the time of retirement or have their retired pay computed using their basic pay plus COLA increases when they first became eligible to retire.

This fixed the problem, and in fact, some three-and four-star generals ended up making more money in retirement than they did on active duty. Was this fair? Hell yes, it was fair as long as military retirees benefit from COLAs, and they do. That is the law.

> *The only thing that saves us from the bureaucracy is inefficiency. An efficient bureaucracy is the greatest threat to liberty.*
> —Eugene McCarthy

The DOD bureaucracy moves slowly, and the congressional bureaucracy even slower. In the meantime, while PL 94-106 meandered like molasses through these bureaucracies, we were being inundated with retirements. In addition, I was being asked for reports from DA,

DOD, and congress to provide data on how many people were retiring, what grade, what amount of service, what race, what branch of service, etc. The requests were endless and came by telephone and letter for several months.

The upside of this was that I received a fair amount of visibility within the general officer community. Each Monday morning, I rode with the MILPERCEN commanding general, Major General Robert Gard, to brief Lieutenant General Harold G. Moore, the Army's deputy chief of staff for personnel (DCSPER) at the Pentagon. I was also a backup for Moore and the secretary of the Army when they appeared before congressional committees.

Initially, I happened to be one of the few who knew how to compute retired pay under the proposed provisions of PL 94-106, which resulted in my visiting many of the three-and four-star generals in the Washington area to explain their possible pay upon retirement. On August 31, 1976, over one thousand three hundred senior officers retired, the most ever retired in one month in the history of the Army. I am sure that's a record that still stands today.

Congress passed Public Law 94-106 on September 6, 1976. It was not retroactive. There were a number of those who had retired that wanted me to revoke their retirement after the law had been passed. Title 10 of the USC specifically states that once an officer retires, he remains retired, although he may be recalled to active duty; however, his pay remains the same once he reverts to retired status. There were no officers recalled because of retired pay inversion, but it did not stop my phone from ringing.

When I first arrived at MILPERCEN, my recollection is that Hal Moore, then a major general, served as the commanding general for a short time. I remember briefing him on at least one occasion at either MILPERCEN or the Pentagon and thinking he was a somewhat morose and lonely individual. I do recall him showing a large diagram depicting the Ia Drang Battle (LZ Xray) and discussing the battle.

Upon retirement, General Moore wrote a book titled *We Were Soldiers Once . . . and Young* with his co-author, Joe Galloway, then of *US News and World Report*, covering this first major battle of the Vietnam War. Mel Gibson and Barry Pepper portrayed Moore, the battalion commander, and Galloway, a UPI correspondent, in the subsequent movie, *We Were Soldiers*.

General Gard, who was promoted to lieutenant general, served his final assignment as the president of the National Defense University. While at MILPERCEN, we referred to him (behind his back) as "Bobby Blue Eyes" for his penchant to flirt with any skirt that happened to be passing by. I liked him, and he always treated me right.

The civilians working for me were primarily female and black. Most were longtime government employees, several of whom started to work for the government on December 8, 1941. They were quite capable for the most part, and all knew their jobs. Their sense of urgency could have been better defined, especially during the hectic days of retired pay inversion. They were eight-to-five employees with one exception, Mr. Burrell.

Mr. Burrell, one of the finest gentlemen and hardest working individuals I have known, served as my deputy and processed all general officer retirements. His expertise and knowledge of the complicated retirement laws served me well. Mr. Burrell died of a heart attack, and Colonel James Windsor, my boss, and I attended his funeral at a black church somewhere in D.C. We were the only white people there.

One morning about 0300, I awoke with excruciating pain in my back and told Penny that I would drive to the office and get Mr. Burrell to drive me to the Pentagon clinic. I knew Mr. Burrell arrived at his desk at precisely 0530 every morning.

Somehow, I made the drive to MILPERCEN and waited until Mr. Burrell arrived, at which time he drove me to the Pentagon. The Pentagon clinic was staffed for emergencies only, and the on-call physician suspected that I was having a kidney stone attack. They loaded me in an ambulance to be taken to DeWitt Army Hospital at Fort Belvoir just as a blinding snowstorm blew into town. The thirty-minute drive to Belvoir took four hours, and I wanted to die the entire time; however, I hurt too badly.

When I arrived at the Belvoir emergency room, the doctor took one look at me and immediately gave me a shot to relieve my pain.

My next recollection was wakening in a hospital room and hearing crying, moaning, and wailing coming from outside the room. I climbed out of bed to discover that I was attached to an IV, which was attached to a pole with no wheels. I wanted a cigarette. I found my clothes in a closet, got my cigarettes, and dragged the IV pole into the hallway. I was clothed in a hospital gown that had no buttons, and my butt was showing. To my dismay, I realized I was in an open-bay hospital room with a bunch of women who were in various stages of labor. I needed a cigarette badly. I dragged the IV pole down a hall when I spotted a conference room and decided I would slip inside and smoke.

I opened the door and stepped inside to find a gathering of Army nurses sitting around a conference table. At the head of the table was a big, ugly, full-bull colonel of the female persuasion who was chewing ass and taking names. Before I could exit the room, she screamed at her nurses, "God damn it! That is what I am talking about. Look at him. No buttons on his gown. Why does he have an IV without rollers? I told you to turn those in months ago." She looked at me quizzically and then looked at her nurses and again at me and bellowed like an old cow, "What the hell are you doing on my maternity ward?"

Apparently, when I arrived, there were no beds available except the one I happened to be occupying. It did not take long until that colonel had me moved, but I went with an IV pole with rollers and a gown that buttoned. I stayed in the hospital for nine days before I passed the kidney stone. Apparently, the doctors did not want to operate because of its large size. Thankfully, they were generous with the morphine when I needed it.

I hired a young teenybopper who had just graduated from high school as a GS-3 control clerk. A cutie, Sindy was quite fashionable in her miniskirts, which were the style at the time.

One morning, I looked up from my desk, and several of my ladies were standing in my doorway.

Miss Grover, the senior analyst, emphatically demanded, "What are you going to do about that girl?"

"What are you talking about?"

She answered, "Just go look at her, and you'll see."

I was sure that she was speaking of Sindy, so I walked to her desk. Sindy had on a sheer, silk blouse but no brassiere. I looked long and hard to make sure she had no brassiere, because I would not want to accuse someone falsely. I was able to determine that Sindy was indeed not wearing a brassiere. Sindy and I along with Miss Grover had a chat about proper office attire, and a crisis of major proportions was averted. Sometimes it is hard to be a leader, especially with so many difficult decisions involving life-and-death issues.

Sometime later, Sindy came into my office and asked if she could talk with me. She asked if she could close the door, and I told her that she couldn't. My secretary could see into my office, so I felt okay to talk to Cindy alone but not with the door closed. She came right to the point and bluntly asked, "Why do you not like me?"

I responded that I did like her and that she was a good worker, and I asked what made her think that I did not like her.

"You have never asked me out."

Well, that caught me off guard.

After some thought, I told her, "Sindy, first of all, I am married and have a son almost your age. Second, I am almost twice your age, and third, it is a no-no to get your honey where you get your money."

Sindy looked at me sweetly, smiled, and said, "So!"

He knows little who tells his wife all he knows.
—Japanese proverb

All the way home that evening, I thought to myself, "Herb, old buddy, you still have it," and could hardly wait to tell Penny. Dumb! That was a colossal mistake. Penny did not see the humor of the situation. I later discovered that some of the single officers had taken Sindy out, and a couple who were not single did as well. I had one full colonel who spent more time at Sindy's desk than his own. After I told him he was interfering with her work to no avail, Colonel Windsor had to tell him to stay away from her.

Sindy was a good worker. I was glad when she found another job.

One evening, after duty hours, I heard the phone ring. I knew that one of my employees happened to be waiting on a ride, and I wondered if she would answer the call. The phone rang for a long time and then stopped. In a few minutes, it began to ring again, and I proceeded to pick up the receiver. I heard my employee say, "I'm sorry, sir. I am the cleaning lady, and everyone has gone home. Please call back in the morning."

We had lived in northern Virginia for around four months when Penny decided she wanted to return to the workforce. First, she was bored. Ross, who was now in the eighth grade, could take care of himself, and in her words, "I need to feel productive, useful, and make a contribution." Second, we could use the money.

I had felt badly for a long time about her having to work to get me through college, sacrificing her own education goals. But quite selfishly, I enjoyed having her home. It gave me some degree of pride to say that my wife did not work, a throwback to my macho West Texas upbringing. Nevertheless, we did need the money.

Penny managed our checkbook throughout our married lives. We would decide at the beginning of each year how much we would invest monthly and how much we would place into a contingency fund. Over the years, the contingency fund had grown to include six months' salary for emergencies plus yearly expenses for vacation, taxes, and any unexpected expense. This money was placed in a money market account with the Pentagon Federal Credit Union and drawn on as needed. The investments were left alone and never drawn on. The remainder remained in the checkbook, and it was used for monthly expenses.

Insistent that she wanted and needed to work, she soon found a position with a dentist. He paid well and proposed to teach her to be a dental hygienist. A man of little patience and a short temper, he and Penny were too similar to get along. Besides, she hated to put her hands in other people's mouths. The job lasted only a short time before she quit. She then found her niche with the Woodburn Mental Health Center in Annandale, Virginia, a thirty-minute drive from the house on a good day.

Fairfax County has one of the most affluent and educated populaces in the nation with a median household income twice the national average. Woodburn served all youth (age twelve through seventeen) who had problems with truancy, drugs, alcohol, sex, or other issues. These kids were not your usual delinquents. Their parents were bright, financially comfortable, success-driven, and therein lay the reason for most of the children's problems. They were spoiled, bored, and undisciplined.

Penny was initially hired as a receptionist, but she soon caught the attention of the doctors, psychiatrists, and social workers. More importantly, she developed a rapport with the children and their parents, thus catching the eye of her boss, Martha Ragagli, and the center director, John Defee.

Penny was smart, organized, efficient, and willing to do whatever it took to get the job done. She was of solid West Texas and Middle America stock with a finely tuned work ethic. Soon, she received a promotion as an intake counselor, and she eventually became a program coordinator. In reality, I believe Martha Ragagli and John Defee would have admitted that she ran the place.

She loved her job much the same way I loved the Army. The money, while nice, did not provide the reason for her satisfaction. She felt useful and needed, and she was damn good at what she did. Again, we did not know it, but she would work for Woodburn for ten out of the next twelve years.

It was during this time that Penny started her running program. She and Rosalee Hufnagel, a neighbor, began by walking and then jogging short distances, and they finally worked up to two miles. Each morning, Penny would rise at 0530 for her two-mile-plus run.

Required to take a semiannual PT test that included a timed, two-mile run, I would begin to train a month before, so initially, Penny would embarrass me on our early morning jogs. I gave her the Army standard for females, and her goal became to run the two miles at the standard for a female one age group less than her age. And she consistently did just that.

Penny never smoked, rarely drank, and even then, she only had a glass of wine. She watched her weight and jogged almost every morning for the rest of her life. I would jokingly kid her that she would outlive me by twenty years and would be very lonely in the nursing home without me.

Ross entered the eighth grade and played football, baseball, and basketball in Fairfax County Youth Leagues, achieving success in all his endeavors. A successful businessman and his basketball coach, Mr. McClendon could have been a success as a college coach. He was the best bench coach I have known, probably in the same manner as the great Marquette University coach, Al McGuire. Ross's teams did well, but his basketball team did particularly well when they won the Fairfax County Championship for their age group.

The other kids had been together for a number of years, and although Ross was at least the second best, if not the best player, the coach rarely started Ross and would remove him from the game if his team was winning. Being a typical parent, I questioned Mr. McClendon about Ross's lack of playing time.

McClendon told me, "Mr. Taylor, this will be the last chance most of these kids will have to be star players. Most will not grow much more, and some have reached their highest skill level. Ross will go on to be a star in high school, play before large crowds, get a lot of press time, and play college ball. A couple of these kids will start in high school, but none will be a star. This is their last chance. This is it for them."

Ross could have been a good high school football player, but his high school basketball coach, Carl (Hooks) Hensley, had a rule that if you played football, you did not play basketball. Hooks started practice in the middle of football season, and he insisted his kids play in a summer league as a team. The D.C. area had great summer leagues.

Hooks had won the Virginia State Championship in the big school classification at Edison High School, which was also in Fairfax County, and had moved to Lake Braddock with its opening as the new school in the area. He was a tough taskmaster and a defensive specialist who taught a full-court, man-to-man press. He was old school: "Play tough D and pass the ball at least three times before you shoot." He did have one idiosyncrasy: His offense revolved around one person, the shooting guard, and Ross became his shooting guard.

During Ross's first year, he played on the freshman team. I thought that a mistake, especially because Hooks had a kid playing on the junior varsity that I had seen play in the youth league and Ross was better. As I sat in the stands at West Springfield and watched a freshman game, I overheard the West Springfield varsity coach tell another coach, "See the Taylor kid? Hooks made a mistake leaving him down here. Hooks will start him on the varsity next year as his shooting guard." That was the way it turned out.

Each summer, we sent Ross to a basketball camp. His junior year, he went to the Five-Star Camp in Philadelphia, Pennsylvania, a by-invitation-only camp for the best high school players in the Northeast.

Ross made many good friends in high school, but one stands out in particular, namely Gregory (Cag) Cagnassola, the "Old Tom Cat," so named for his habit of staying out all night and sneaking into our house after a night of carousing. Cag's father was an FBI agent, and during Greg's junior year, his father became the agent in charge for the Midwest Region stationed in Indianapolis. Greg returned that summer to stay with us, as he had already become one of the family.

Gregarious, a people person, extremely intelligent, short-tempered, and funny, Cag was not an athlete. Ross and Cag could not have been better friends, probably because they were so different. Cag competed against Ross in everything, including pick-up basketball, foosball, tennis, running, and wrestling, and though he became frustrated when he lost, he never quit.

When it came to games, Ross could not compete with Cag, an expert in word games and sports trivia, but Penny could. Cag and Penny would often see who could outdo the other by reciting the batting and scoring average of sports figures. Penny loved Cag like a son. She taught Cag how to drive in the standard-shift Ford Pinto we bought after the Mustang died. Penny's patience could be easily tried, but teaching Cag to drive a stick shift took remarkable patience.

Today, Greg and his wife, Carrie, are both attorneys in Indianapolis, and as good Catholics, they have a house full of kiddoes. The summer of 2004, Cag flew to Texas, and he and Ross came to Salado to visit on their way back from watching the Final Four men's college basketball tournament held in San Antonio. We had a good time.

The one thing Ross did not make, much to my chagrin, happened to be girlfriends. Ross did not figure out that girls were not soft boys who could not throw a baseball until he got into college. One night after a basketball game his sophomore year as we walked out of the gym, a bubbly, sweet, young thing came bouncing up in her cheerleader uniform and asked Ross to take her to a party the next night. Ross told her he did not have his driver's license, and the girl breathlessly exclaimed, "That's okay. I have a car and will pick you up at six."

The next night, I jokingly told Ross as he prepared for his first date, "I am going to be quite upset if that girl drives up and honks the horn. I want her to come in and meet your parents." Actually, I did want to see her. She was a knockout.

We shipped Ross off to his Uncle Phil Farr in Hereford, Texas, for at least a month each summer. I could have gotten him a summer job working for the government running a Zerox machine or delivering interoffice memos, but both Penny and I wanted him to get a taste of the way we had grown up. Phil Farr could give him not only a taste of ranch work but also a full seven-course meal. It was daylight-to-dark, hard, dirty, sweaty, backbreaking work seven days a week with lots of good food prepared by Aunt Billie and little pay from Uncle Phil.

I will forever be grateful to Phil for giving him that experience, and so will Ross. It also gave him a chance to get to know his cousins, Jeff and Zack. They are all close today. Ross looks up to Phil as a big brother. Perhaps Jeff and Zack do the same with Ross.

When he played in a summer league, Ross had a game in D.C. at one of the all-black high schools. Penny and I were walking into the gymnasium, and some black kids were in front of us.

One said to another, "Hey, man, what you doing here?"

The other responded, "I comes to see that white boy that plays like a black boy."

Ross gave them a show that night, dunking and shooting the lights out. Ross would dunk in summer league games, but Hooks did not like his players to dunk during practice or the regular season. Ross did it anyway.

That same evening as Penny and I drove home, we had to travel along 14th Street to cross the 14th Street Bridge over the Potomac into Virginia. This street, only four blocks from our nation's capital, is known for its bars, streetwalkers, porn shops, and drugs. We were caught by a stoplight, and while we were waiting, a streetwalker walked up and tapped on the window.

Penny shouted, "Let's go." However, the light was still red. I cracked my window just a bit to tell her to go away, and she said, "Hey, you want to party."

I said, "Lady, I've got my wife in the car."

And she said, "Bring her along."

Washington, D.C., has much to do and see. In all the years we were there, we never saw it all. Early on, we joined the Smithsonian Institute primarily for their members-only dining room in the basement of the

Museum of Natural History. It was a great place to rest in the middle of sightseeing. They served a fine buffet, including a steam ship round of beef, and mixed a good martini. Penny's favorite place was the Museum of Modern Art, which was my least favorite. My favorite place was the Air and Space Museum. They were across the mall from each other, so we would usually visit both.

We both enjoyed the Kennedy Center, which was across from the Watergate Apartments and overlooked the Potomac. We went many times to watch plays with stars, such as Charlton Heston and Jason Robards, Jr. Penny particularly enjoyed the musicals and the opera. I went, but I cannot say I enjoyed them.

We would take overnight trips to Annapolis, the Chesapeake and Eastern Shore, the Civil War battlefields, and Skyline Drive in the Blue Ridge Mountains and stay in the National Park accommodations.

Once, we floated in the Shenandoah River on tubes. We were young and healthy, and life was good for a boy from Barnhart and his family.

My job became routine, and while not much fun, there were times that made it interesting.

Often, a chief of staff or a general's aide-de-camp would call and ask if I could send their general a copy of the Green Book. The Green Book, prepared by Mr. Burrell, contained a plethora of information that a general could use to prepare for and use after retirement. It contained his retired pay computation and information about social security (yes, the military pays into and draws social security in addition to their retired pay), military, VA, and other government benefits tailored to the general's personal situation.

The person calling would always preface their call by saying, "My general is not planning on retiring, and he would just like some information." I, of course, knew the general had to be thinking about retiring—if not soon, then at least later—and in most cases, it was soon.

General officers normally received the book from the General Officer Management Office (GOMO) in the OCSA once they had submitted or announced their intention to retire. GOMO would call and direct that we prepare the book and give us certain information, such as his grade and length of service, but not his name. General officers' retirements were kept "close hold" until released to the press by the OCSA.

I took great delight when they would call for a Green Book by asking them, "Oh, General Halftrack has decided to retire, has he? We have his Green Book ready. Actually, he already has one. You will get it this afternoon." They never learned how I knew, but I knew they knew I knew.

GOMO knew neither that I dealt directly with the general's command nor that Mr. Burrell had a worksheet on every Army general that he continually updated. If given their grade and length of service, we could narrow it down to the name of the general who was retiring.

Over time, word got around that I would keep my mouth shut when I was talking with generals about their retirement. There were those who did not want anyone to know they were contemplating retirement, including their aide-de-camp and chief of staff. MILPERCEN had a policy that anytime you were called or visited by a general officer, a record of the contact, including a synopsis of the discussion, had to be forwarded through channels to the commanding general. I ignored the policy, but I suspect my bosses knew I did.

Officers are retired mandatorily for age and service through the grade of major general. Major general is the last grade for which an officer is selected by an Army-centralized promotion board.

Lieutenant generals and generals are "political appointees" serving at the pleasure of their service chief, the secretary of defense, and the president. Upon promotion to lieutenant general, these officers submit their retirement papers with the date of requested retirement left blank. This date GOMO completes when the general falls out of favor with the secretary of defense or the White House, completes his/her statutory tour, or requests voluntarily retirement.

Title 10 of the USC also allows the Army to convene boards to select lieutenant colonels through major general for retirement called Selective Early Retirement Boards (SERBs). These boards are used to draw down the Army, as it is done after every war. Korea, Vietnam, and the first Gulf War are all examples of when they were used.

Some officers being mandatorily retired are not ready for retirement. They feel there is a stigma attached to mandatory retirement, or they simply cannot accept they will no longer wear the uniform. Many become ill. Some suffer heart attacks. The law allows them to remain on active duty as long as they are in medical channels, but eventually, they all retire. During the time I served in the retirement branch, we pursued a regulatory change that would allow an officer to submit a voluntarily retirement for the same date as mandatory retirement. Upon approval of the change, officers were able to say they had voluntarily retired, thus removing any stigma attached to mandatory retirement.

Retirement often became an emotional issue and needed to be treated with kid gloves by my people. I told myself I would be prepared when my time came, because I had seen too many that had not been. However, at that time, I did not know if I would even make it to retirement.

I dealt with one four-star who had been placed on the temporary disability retired list (TDRL). The TDRL was used for those who had not yet reached mandatory retirement, had a medical situation that would not allow them to perform their duties, and could possibly return to active duty. This general had cancer, and after five years, we placed him on the retired list. He threw a walleyed fit. He wanted to come back on active duty. He had forgotten the retirement application he had signed long ago.

One morning, I received a call from Major Art Dean, the assignment officer for majors in the Adjutant General Officer Assignment Branch, which was located two floors below me. He told me he had received a requirement from OCSA to provide the best available AG major to serve on a special task force in the Washington, D.C., area and that I had been selected.

I knew that a reassignment was imminent, but I had been assured previously by Major Dean that my next assignment would be to the Pentagon and the Army staff. Major Dean and I had words, and he reluctantly told me he would send someone else to fill the requirement. A few days later, when I returned from the Pentagon, I found a message on my desk to call Major Dean's boss, the chief of the Adjutant General Officer Assignment Branch. This lieutenant colonel told me he had a hot assignment with the 2nd Infantry Division in Korea and that I needed to shut up and suit up, because I had to be there in two weeks.

This meant I would miss Ross's junior year in high school, but I figured it would be better to miss his junior year than his senior year. I also realized the AG Branch would move me regardless, so I shut up, suited up, and prepared to ship out.

I found out later that Art Dean took the special task force assignment. The Army promoted Art to major general years later. Perhaps I should have kept my mouth shut and accepted the assignment.

Thus, my tour with MILPERCEN ended on March 16, 1978, and I departed with my third Meritorious Service Medal. All in all, it was not a bad assignment, but quite truthfully, I looked forward to getting back to the real Army and soldiers and wearing fatigues and boots.

16

Land of the Morning Calm

Again, I flew out of Travis Air Force Base on a chartered MAC flight, this time arriving at Kimpo Airport in Seoul, Korea, on March 30, 1978. Met by representatives of the Military Personnel Center-Korea (MILPERCEN-K) and whisked through Korean customs, I was met by Captain Malcolm G. Weaver and my jeep driver, Specialist Four Wanda (Wicked Wanda) Matlock for the drive to Camp Casey, which was thirty-five miles north of Seoul and eleven miles south of the demilitarized zone (DMZ), better known from the Korean War as the 38th Parallel.

I had met Captain Weaver before at my office in the retirement branch about a week prior to my departure for Korea, when he came to tell me he was being reassigned to the 2nd Infantry Division and wanted to be my chief of enlisted management. I told Malcolm I would consider his request but would make no decision until I arrived at the 2nd Division.

Malcolm had arrived in Korea first and convinced Lieutenant Colonel Ralph Bilberry, my new boss, that he should have the enlisted management job, so when I arrived, it was a done deal. As it turned out, Malcolm was the right man for the job, and we made a good team.

"Wicked Wanda," a tiny, black-haired, bundle of fire, "coon-ass" Cajun from Dubach, Louisiana, served as my secretary, driver, and gatekeeper, taking no sass from anyone, especially other females. She did an outstanding job. Married to Specialist Four Jay Matlock, a mechanic assigned to the 702nd Maintenance Battalion, Wanda drove one of the best-maintained jeeps in the 2nd Division. Wanda, Jay, and I became good friends and shared several fine Cajun meals in their small apartment in Tong Du Chon, the village located across the main supply route (MSR) or highway from Camp Casey.

When I arrived at Camp Casey, my new home for the next twelve months, I found a scraggly succession of World War II Quonset huts stretching up a long, narrow valley and climbing the surrounding hillsides. This was pure war zone much like what I had left in Vietnam. It had few of the amenities of a stateside post, and it became readily apparent the 2nd Infantry Division was all business and that business was war.

The 2nd Division, the "Indian Head" Division, so named for its unit patch, had the official nickname of the "Warrior Division" and the motto of "Second to None." The division existed for one reason only, namely to serve as a trip wire when and if the North Koreans crossed the DMZ. The division was there to provide a buffer of American blood and guts until other American units could arrive. Consequently, there was no reason to build costly buildings or provide wasteful frills.

The second day of my arrival, after I drew my TA-50 (helmet, rucksack, web gear, holster, .45-caliber pistol, gas mask, etc.), I attended a briefing for newly assigned officers that was given by the commanding general, Major General David E. Grange, Jr.

Because I sat in the front row, I must have been conspicuous, as General Grange began by asking, "Major Taylor, how much warning do you think this division will have to prepare for a North Korean attack?"

I guessed, "Twenty-four to thirty-six hours, sir."

Grange said, "None, if your unit is on the DMZ, and three minutes if you are here at Camp Casey. Three minutes is how long it will take their MIGs to arrive and began to strafe and bomb. Therefore, you'd better be ready now." He then said, "I do not ever want to see tanks or tracks lined up in motor pools like battleships at Pearl Harbor. Get them out of the motor pool, live on them, fix them in the field, and be prepared to fight them without notice."

General Grange went on to say that across the DMZ was one of the world's largest armies, well-trained, equipped, and completely unpredictable. He explained that the North Koreans periodically assembled large troop concentrations near the DMZ, rolled out their big guns on railroad cars from hidden mountainside bunkers, and ran their MIGs up to the DMZ. Hence, his admonition that there would be little warning of an imminent attack, and the "Land of the Morning Calm" could become chaos in a very short time.

My quarters consisted of a room in a two-story, cinder block building, a stone's throw from my office. As the senior officer in the building, I made all room assignments and became responsible for overseeing all the housekeeping requirements, including discipline of the occupants.

There were twenty-four rooms in the building. Most had two or more officers to a room but not all. I had females working for me for the first time, and there were six or seven female officers who lived on the first floor. The female latrine facilities were on the first floor, so the guys who lived on that floor had to come to the second floor to shave and shower.

The accommodations were adequate. There was a small dayroom on the first floor with a pool table, card tables, and a TV set with very poor reception of Armed Forces Radio and TV (AFRT) programs. We had several maids who were paid to clean our rooms, wash our clothes, and polish our boots for twenty dollars apiece each month.

Over time, previous occupants of my quarters had made them quite livable with an easy chair, a couch, a small refrigerator, hot plate, cooking utensils, cabinets, shelves, and a window air conditioner for the summer and a space heater for the winter. I purchased these items from the fellow I replaced and sold them to my replacement. Unfortunately, the other rooms were not as comfortable.

The 2nd Infantry Division was a twelve-month, unaccompanied tour, so we were not encumbered with family responsibilities. There was little to do except train, work, and if so inclined, "run the whores" in Tong Du Chon. A few soldiers brought their wives over at their own expense and found living accommodations for them in Seoul or Tong Du Chon.

There was an officer's club near the billets that we shared with the 2nd Aviation Battalion, and where we enjoyed many a memorable evening. The aviators called the club "the Mile High Club," so named for consummating the act of love while flying. There were many claimants of membership from the aviation battalion but few who could provide credible evidence of their achievement. The AGs called the club "the 2-2-0 Club," which stood for "second to none."

The duty day started each morning at 0530 hours with a mandatory physical training (PT) formation that included a four-mile unit run in combat boots to be completed in thirty-two minutes or less. We started our workday exhausted. Running in combat boots along and on the asphalt of the main supply route (MSR) and its many hills messed up many knees. After I left Korea, the Army got wise and allowed PT to be conducted in running shoes.

I was in the office by 0730 and rarely left the office before 2130, and often much later. I usually worked until noon or later on Saturday and then watched our unit play various sports against other units on Saturday and Sunday afternoon.

Occasionally, on a Saturday, I would take Captain Weaver and Master Sergeant Wallace and have Wanda drive us to a brigade headquarters at Camp Hovey, Howze, Stanley, or Essayons to brief the brigade commander and his staff. Afterward, we would lunch with them and return to Camp Casey, sightseeing while driving through the old mountain trails used during the Korean War. It provided a brief respite in an otherwise hectic week.

I had a way of operating that I think was unique, but it worked for me when I was assigned to a combat division. I did not do business with battalion commanders, the lieutenant colonels. There were too many of them. Most were prima donnas wanting something at the expense of their fellow battalion commanders. I dealt with their bosses, the colonels commanding the brigade-level units. There were only five of them, and if I could keep them pleased, they, in turn, would keep their subordinates off my back. This did not endear me to the battalion commanders.

Sunday, I rested, actually sleeping a good part of the day. I rarely went to Seoul, and then only for a meeting or social function. In fact, I can remember only going to Seoul once for anything other than business. I would go to the Mile High Club on Sunday morning have a couple of Bloody Marys, orange juice, steak, and eggs, read the *Stars and Stripes*, and then take a nap.

This photo was taken outside my complex of buildings at Camp Casey, Korea in 1979.

Assigned as the chief of the personnel services division, my job description read:

> Responsible for supervising and managing a large and diversified organization in providing personnel services support to a 15,000 man Infantry Division deployed over a 500 square mile area. Authorized 8 officers and 164 enlisted soldiers. Supervises operation of the 5th Adjutant General Replacement Detachment.

In addition to the fifteen thousand American soldiers assigned the 2nd Division, unlike any other division in the army, we had assigned approximately 2,100 Korean soldiers called KATUSAs (Korean Augmentation to US Army). KATUSAs began serving with US Forces at the direction of South-Korean President Syngman Rhee during the Korean War and continue to serve to this day. These soldiers were the pick of the litter from the Korean Army. Generally better educated and motivated, they worked, slept, ate, and partied alongside our soldiers. Rarely did KATUSA soldiers present a discipline problem, for they knew that meant going back to their own army, where treatment could not only be harsh but often cruel. They performed the full gamut of duties from rifleman to mechanic to cook to clerk.

The 2nd Infantry Division also had female soldiers, as the army integrated the WAC in 1978. No one was supposed to be assigned below brigade, so there were probably sixty-five at Camp Casey. To this day, I have mixed emotions and have not resolved my opinion about women in the Army. If I had a daughter and she told me she wanted to serve her country by joining the armed forces, I would wish that my little girl had made another career choice. Nevertheless, she would go with my full blessing and support and the advice to join the US Air Force because they always have clean sheets to sleep on as well as hot chow.

My concern then as now revolves around body strength and the natural inclination for the male to protect the female. I simply feel that there is a real danger in ground combat, from women not being able to perform, resulting in needless deaths by males attempting to assist them. Today, war is asymmetrical with no front lines, resulting in difficulty in distinguishing the good guys from the bad guys. Consequently, females assigned to a combat area, regardless of duty position, face the same dangers as the combat soldier. No one is just a cook or a rifleman or a clerk. They are simply soldiers going into harm's way in varying degrees.

The reality is that manpower considerations dictate that females be placed in harm's way. Our Army would indeed be a hollow shell without the female soldier.

My unit, the 2nd Adjutant General Company, performed a twelve-mile road march with full combat gear and crew-served weapons quarterly. As I traveled through thatch-roofed villages, small vegetable farms, rice paddies, and the ever-present oxen, I always looked forward to the exercise. It was not West Texas, but it would have to do.

The unit, large with over three hundred soldiers, would be staggered at five-foot intervals on both sides of the road. Captain Weaver and I would walk the length of the formation, give encouragement, speed up the slow ones to maintain proper intervals, and make our presence known.

Invariably, I would find a female without her weapon, look to her rear, and find a male soldier with a rifle slung over each shoulder.

My mortar squad would not only carry their individual weapons, but each carried a part of the mortar. There were few females—maybe none—who could carry the base plate for more than a few minutes. Combat requires teamwork, and if a person could only contribute for a few minutes, the cohesion of the team was broken.

I had one Hispanic female who could only be described as tiny. She was maybe four-foot-ten and eighty pounds, with the smallest feet I have ever seen. How she got into the Army and where boots were found to fit her remains a mystery. Her legs were so short that she literally had to run to keep up with the formation. She tried hard, but she eventually fell so far behind I would have the medics pick her up in a jeep.

When we arrived at our designated defensive area, two-man foxholes and slit latrines were dug. The latrines would be surrounded with canvas for privacy, and we would go on an even-odd schedule by gender for use of the latrines.

The fox holes on our perimeter were manned throughout the bivouac, not only to use for training purposes, but also to keep the Korean "slicky boys" out. I do not know how they knew we were coming, but on arrival, they were there, wanting to sell Cokes, souvenirs, cigarettes, and just about anything we might want. We would run them off, but at night, the folks in the foxholes had to be alert to keep them from coming back to steal whatever they could find. I would sleep with my .45 tucked in the bottom of my sleeping bag. They were that good at relieving you of your possessions.

During the Korean War, they were so bad about stealing that our friends in the Turkish Army came up with an ingenious solution. When they caught one, they would take a rifle-cleaning rod, run it through their ears, and hang the unlucky chap in front of their area. The Turks did not have many problems with Koreans stealing; however, that was not the American way.

The foxholes were manned with males in one and females in another. NCOs and officers would find the arrangement changed as they made their nightly inspections. The foxholes would now have males and females paired up. We even caught one couple performing the act in a sleeping bag. It is difficult to get two people in a sleeping bag, much less perform sexual calisthenics. Again, never underestimate the ingenuity of the American soldier.

There was always at least one female who did not come prepared for her monthly misery, which required our medics to stock their medical kit for unexpected emergencies.

PT formations had to be broken into two groups—one for the slow runners or the new people in the unit who were not yet acclimated, and one consisting of those who could run an eight-minute mile for four miles. Females made up the majority of the slow group, but we had some women who could run with the best of us.

Master Sergeant George Wallace, my senior NCO, came into the office one morning after PT and told me several of the females wanted to talk with me.

I asked, "About what?"

"Their sex life."

Flabbergasted, I blustered, "Christ, George, you got to be kidding."

"Nope," he said.

George Wallace was a man of few words.

They indeed wanted to talk about their sex life or, more accurately, the lack thereof. It seems the guys preferred the Korean prostitutes or *yobos* to them. Any pimple-faced eighteen-year-old who had trouble getting a date in high school could have an apartment and a girl, a *yobo* of his own in Tong Du Chon for around $120.00 a month. Alternatively, he could have a "quickie" for ten bucks.

The apartment arrangement from a health standpoint was much preferred, as VD was rampant among the short-time hookers. In fact, as a soldier walked out of Camp Casey to cross the highway and enter Tong Du Chon, he saw a large wooden sign that listed the top ten clubs in town. The clubs listed were not the most popular clubs but the ones with the highest VD rate.

There were several large boxes filled with condoms for soldiers' use at the MP gate. I often saw soldiers grab a handful as they walked by, and I wondered if they planned to blow them up for balloons, as the division VD rate indicated they were not using them for their intended purpose.

Tong Du Chon was a one-industry town, and the Army was the industry.

My advice to these deprived soldiers was, "Try harder."

Actually, I felt little sympathy, as I had taken my own vow of celibacy.

Try, they must have, because some became pregnant.

I asked Captain Joyce A. Lewis, one of my female officers, to clue me in: "What the hell is going on? Two months ago, they were crying because no one would screw them, and now they are knocked up."

"They don't like PT."

"They don't like what!"

"Sir, they don't like PT. They don't like all the training, and they don't like the living conditions."

"So they get pregnant?"

"Yes, sir."

Captain Lewis went on to explain that the division did not have the medical personnel or facilities to take care of a woman after her third trimester, so she was reassigned to Seoul, where she could be treated at the 21st Evacuation Hospital. In addition, they did not have to do all the soldier stuff in Seoul.

That stumped me, and I never did find a solution. I simply could not fathom a woman bringing a child into the world to get out of PT. Moreover, I sure as hell was not going to excuse them from PT.

If a soldier does not learn morals, ethics, and right thinking at home, our schools and our Army will not be able to teach them, no matter how much we try.

Captain Weaver had a female second lieutenant who presented problems, and therefore, she became my problem.

I shall call her Lieutenant Naïve. Lieutenant Naïve had been an NFL cheerleader, and her boyfriend was an Army recruiting sergeant. Apparently, the sergeant was having trouble meeting his enlistment quotas and talked Lieutenant Naïve into joining the Army with the same promises as depicted in the movie *Private Benjamin* starring Goldie Hawn, namely a condominium on the Rivera, good pay, and little work.

Prior to starting basic training, the Army discovered she had a master's degree from a local university and offered her a direct commission, which she accepted. Unfortunately for Captain Weaver and me, this lieutenant did not have the sense to pour piss out of a boot. She wanted to be a clerk-typist, not an officer.

Sergeant Wallace came into the office and asked, "Have you seen Lieutenant Naïve this morning?"

"No. Why?"

"You should."

"Damn it, George," I said. "Why?"

"Call her in, and you'll see."

"Have her report to me."

When she reported, I looked Lieutenant Naïve over from head to toe. She was nice-looking, but I did not see anything wrong with her. I made some small talk and dismissed her. As she walked out of the room, it hit me. Fatigue pants are bloused by either tucking them in your boots or using a blousing garter that makes them appear they are tucked in. Lieutenant Naïve had decided that was too much trouble and had hemmed hers.

Specialist Matlock had taken me to division headquarters late one afternoon for a meeting. I told Wanda to turn in the jeep and go on home because it would be late when the meeting was over, and I would catch the post-shuttle bus back to the office.

As I rode the shuttle bus, I sat behind two young enlisted troopers, and I happened to overhear their conservation.

One said, "You're all dressed up. Where you going?

The other replied, "I've got a date with Lieutenant Naïve."

"You ain't supposed to be dating officers."

"I know that, but she don't."

Captain Weaver and I made sure that Lieutenant Naïve harbored no thoughts about making the Army a career.

Supervising female soldiers was generally a pain. They were manipulative and used their wiles to get their way. I particularly disliked the whining and the crying. When a female cried on me, I would bore in and give her something to cry about. The word soon got around, and few tried to pull the crying tactic.

Occasionally, they gave me a good laugh.

We had an old mongrel dog that the officers had adopted. She hung around the billets. We would feed her, and one of the male officers let her sleep in his room. He even carried her down to Seoul to have the Eighth Army veterinary give her shots.

One evening, I walked into the billets, and four irate female officers were lying in ambush. It seems the male officers had decided that the dog needed a bath, and because she happened to be a female, they had bathed her in the female showers, leaving quite a mess of dog hair and mud.

"You didn't expect them to bathe a female in the male shower, did you?" I said.

They did not find my response humorous.

In fairness to the ladies, I got some guys together, and we had a GI party and scrubbed the female latrine. Even the girls joined in, and later, I bought a round of drinks at the 2-2-0 Club.

I do not think that old dog got another bath while I was there.

Weakness of character is the only defect which cannot be amended.
—Francois de La Rochefoucauld

Korea, while a superb place to soldier, had its drawbacks. Drugs, sex, black-market activities, and alcohol were all available in abundance. If a soldier had a character defect, it surfaced in Korea. Thus, the devil had a target-rich environment to do his work. Boredom and the unaccompanied, short tour added to the problem.

Cigarettes, whiskey, perfume, jewelry, coffee, and other items desired by the wealthier Koreans were rationed to preclude black-marketing. Regardless, the black market was profitable. Some soldiers tried it, and some got caught. Each soldier had a monthly ration card, and each time a rationed item was purchased from the PX or Class VI (beverage alcohol) store, the card was punched to reflect the purchase. Four cartons of cigarettes and four bottles of whiskey could be purchased monthly. Neither was sufficient for my addiction. Therefore, I would ask Malcolm Weaver to purchase additional cigarettes and liquor using his ration card, as he did not smoke and rarely drank.

After Wanda and Jay Matlock reenlisted for a second tour in Korea, this time in Seoul, I needed a new driver and asked Sergeant Wallace to find one out of the replacement detachment. The 2nd Adjutant General Replacement Detachment, which processed all soldiers arriving and departing the division, belonged to me, so it became a simple matter to find a good soldier, as around three hundred arrived while an equal number departed each week.

Wallace found a tall, sharp-looking, young infantry private from Tennessee and brought him to me to interview. I liked the kid and decided to try him.

The next morning at PT, Wallace sidled up and whispered, "I had one hell of a night."

"Drank a little too much joy juice, did you, George?"

"Hell, no, sir! I had to get the private out of jail."

"For what?"

"Black-marketing!"

The kid had only been in the country for three days, and he had already gone to the PX, bought everything he could purchase on his ration card, taken it to Tong Du Chon to sell, and had been apprehended by the MPs. Thankfully, the MPs caught him rather than the Korean *gendarme*, or else he would still be in jail. All soldiers were briefed about the penalty for black-marketing at both MILPERCEN-K and the 2nd Replacement Detachment. It was often not enough to tell them not to piss on an electric fence. They had to go find out for themselves if it would shock them.

These eighteen- and nineteen-year-old soldiers that were full of vim and vigor were easy prey for the bar girls. They would have their first sexual experience with a woman and think they were in love, and the girls would encourage their infatuation. The fondest dream of the working girls was to find a GI who would marry them and take them to a better life in the land of the big PX. Some had their dreams realized.

A soldier who wanted to marry a Korean had to be interviewed by a field-grade officer, a chaplain, and the staff judge advocate (SJA) and then complete a ton of paperwork, all designed to prevent them from making a mistake they might regret.

Master Sergeant Wallace would pop his head in my office and say, "Sir, when you get time, I got another one who wants to get married."

The soldier would come in, salute, and report, "Sir, Private Lust requests permission to speak to the major."

I would return the salute and ask, "What's on your mind, Lust?"

"Sir, I want to get married. I met this wonderful girl, and we're in love."

"How long you been in country, Lust?"

"A few weeks, sir."

"Where did you meet the girl?" I would ask.
"The Vil sir."
"One of the bars?"
"Yes, sir, but she's a really nice girl."
"Tell you what, Lust. Let's let this romance blossom for a while. Come back in three weeks, and if you're still in love, we'll talk."
"But, sir!"
"Dismissed."

Later, I would see Private Lust and ask, "How's your love life, Lust?"
"Great, sir."
"Same girl?'
"No, sir, I got a new one. You ought to see what she can do."
"I'll bet!"

The majority of Korean girls were not working girls, but around Tong Du Chon, many were. Some soldiers went home with Korean wives, and some remain happily married. Most simply screwed 'em and forgot 'em.

The captain who honchoed my Standard Installation Division Personnel System (SIDPERS) branch was engaged to a beautiful young woman, the mayor of Tong Du Chon's daughter. Because he departed Korea before the paperwork had been finalized, he would mail me letters to deliver to her at the PX, where she worked.

One of the more interesting duties that I performed in the 2nd Infantry Division was field officer of the day (FOD). This duty came around about once a quarter, and consisted of coordinating with the MPs and patrolling the streets of Tong Du Chon, where the myriad of bars and *yobo* rooms were located. The FOD's role was to bring some adult leadership to the situation when required and to issue direct orders when necessary.

Two operable factors existed in Korea in 1978. First, Korea was under martial law with a strict 2300 curfew on weeknights and 2400 on weekends. If anyone moved after that time, they were considered a North Korea infiltrator and shot.

Second, while racism had improved tenfold since the Vietnam War, the tendency for the races to polarize when they were socializing remained.

Therefore, the job of the FOD and the MPs was to sweep the area about fifteen minutes before curfew went into effect, ensuring that all soldiers were safely back on Camp Casey or ensconced with their female companions. We also walked the bar area from 1730 until curfew and broke up fights, trying to maintain law and order.

A particular area of interest was the Crack.

White troops gravitated toward bars in one part of town to drink and listen to rock-and-roll and country-and-western music and the blacks gravitated to the other to drink and listen to soul music. Both smoked "wacky weed."

The area frequented by the blacks was known as the Crack, and whites were not welcome.

When I entered the Crack for the first time, the MP sergeant asked me to roll my sleeves down. When I asked why, he told me, "You'll see."

The clubs were filled with people dancing. The Korean girls wore Afro wigs and the style of clothes worn by black women at the time. The duds worn by the soldiers were a remarkable sight. As I pushed through the crowd to spot-check the girl's health cards to ensure they had been checked for VD within the past two weeks, lighted cigarettes would inadvertently (or maybe intentionally) press against the sleeves of my uniform.

The Crack had to be seen to be believed, but I found more trouble in the white area with drunken soldiers fighting or beating up whores.

One night, a drunk came up to me complaining that another soldier had stolen his girl and that the girl owed him for services not yet performed. I asked to see his military ID card and discovered that he was a captain. I escorted the captain back to the club where the girl worked and found her drinking with four soldiers. After some discussion, it was apparent that the girl was the captain's *yobo* and that she had been cuckolding while he had been in the field. When he returned unexpectedly and found her at the club with another soldier, he asked the soldier to leave. Both being drunk, the soldier flipped the captain off. Thus, the captain came to see me.

I took the captain aside and told him, "I am not pleased to find an officer arguing with an enlisted man over the favors of a whore. You have two choices: Either go back to Casey now, or stay, and I will have you handcuffed, thrown in the drunk tank, and your battalion commander called to come get you. Which will it be?"

He left quietly.

Lieutenant Colonel Ralph Bilberry, my first boss, had a policy that officers and NCOs were not to fraternize with bar girls. I personally had no problem with them getting a little strange leg as long as they were discreet. They were big boys and could consult their own consciences and make their own decisions in that regard, but if their extracurricular activities got them into trouble, they were on their own. My concern was operational readiness, not morals. Morals were the chaplains' worry.

Alerts were called at random, and if you did not have 70 percent of your people formed up within fifteen minutes and 100 percent in thirty minutes, you failed the alert. And it was not good for your career to fail an alert.

I made it clear that if they were shacked up and did not hear the alert siren, I would have their asses. To ensure all who were *yoboing* responded to the signal, I had Sergeant Wallace make a map of the location where each lived and send runners to wake them up.

Even the PX had working girls (as they were called). The Koreans do not attach the same stigma to selling one's body that we do. I found this out inadvertently when I was visiting the PX for a massage.

Because I had completed a hard day, I decided a steam bath and massage might work out the kinks. When I finished in the steam room, the attendant led me to a sheet-covered table and began to massage my neck, back, arms, and legs.

She asked, "You Christian?"

"Yes," I said

"Me too," she said, and then she began to quietly sing "Just a Closer Walk with Thee," one of my favorite hymns.

As I drifted off in my thoughts, she gently rolled me over and began to massage a portion of my anatomy that I did not want stimulated, still singing her hymn. I was no longer calm in the "Land of the Morning Calm."

The Mile High or 2-2-0 club provided ample opportunity, especially after too much to drink, for some high-spirited high jinks between the two units.

One wall of the club contained bronze aviator wings with the officers' name etched thereon, while another wall contained bronze shields with the AG officers' names on them. When an officer rotated back to the States, a ceremony would be held, and the wing or shield would be presented to him. And the man would be expected to buy all in attendance a round of drinks.

Soon, the shield with my name disappeared from the wall. Once the club filled up that evening, I got people's attention by announcing that my folks who handled port calls were having problems obtaining space on flights returning to the States, particularly for aviators. This indeed piqued the interest of the aviators, as there was a fourteen-day window for each soldier completing their normal tour in Korea. Based upon seat availability on MAC contract flights, a soldier could be manifested on a flight up to seven days before the end of their one-year tour or seven days after. Most soldiers wanted to go home early. I declared that if my shield returned to the wall, this problem with flights might be resolved. The next day, my shield had been returned.

Once, my boss called to inform me that the fixed-wing aircraft propeller that the aviation folks had mounted at the front of the club had been stolen and that the aviation battalion commander had accused my officers of being the perpetrators. He ordered me to conduct an investigation to determine if my folks were guilty. I went through the motions of interviewing each AG officer and dutifully reported that all denied any knowledge of the incident. Later, I entered the storage room of the billets to retrieve my suitcase prior to returning to the States. I discovered the propeller at the back of the storage room. The propeller is probably still there. I have no idea which one of my people did the deed, but I applaud their effort.

The aviation battalion commander was a pistol. A hard drinker, first-rate aviator, and commander, he was genuinely respected and liked by his soldiers. Some of the things we did would have resulted in a court-martial in today's Army, but in 1979, it was a different Army. His and our antics were simply the misbehavior of lonely, bored men letting off a little steam. Some specific incidents stand out.

I had one lieutenant, a West Pointer, who backed down from no one. One evening, he and the aviation battalion commander were drinking at the club bar when they decided they did not like each other. Some words were exchanged, and a shoving contest initiated, with the two of them deciding that they would adjourn to the club patio and decide through fisticuffs who was the better man. Fortunately, some of my officers and some of the aviators separated the two, and the puerile caper ended.

The first female aviator, a chopper pilot, was soon to arrive at the 2nd Aviation Battalion, and the club was abuzz with grousing. It seemed that no self-respecting aviator wanted to fly with a female. Upon arrival, this petite, attractive, young warrant officer generated even more comments. The prevailing attitude appeared to be, "I'd sure like to fuck her, but I'll be damned if I want to fly with her."

The battalion commander dealt with the problem directly and announced he would fly with her on her initial checkout flights as she learned the unique difficulties of flying in the valleys and mountains of Korea. Soon, the battalion commander reported that she was one of the best pilots he had ever flown, which resulted in the entire aviator contingent wanting to fly with her. The word was that her hand, eye, and foot coordination on the hydraulic controls were outstanding, giving her a sense of touch that could not be duplicated by the male aviators. Moreover, she was an easy looker, a very easy looker.

A freelance prostitute who was named the Indian Princess for the Indian costume she wore was a legend in Tong Du Chon. This young lady only "short-timed" officers generally in the rank of major or above. She was a hell of a dancer and could perform unbelievable gymnastics on the dance floor—and I am told she did the same in bed as well. The officers of the aviation battalion rented the woman for a night and presented her to the battalion commander as a going-away present at his farewell party. I believe his virtue remained untarnished, as he left the club in a high state of inebriation.

Photo of Penny and Ross I took to Korea.

Korea was a great improvement over Vietnam in maintaining contact with Penny and Ross. Mail arrived on time and in sequence, and I talked with them periodically by booking a call through the Eighth Army switchboard in Seoul. I would "sweet talk" the Pentagon operators into connecting me to our house.

Soldiers serving an unaccompanied tour were authorized a thirty-day, midtour leave, and I took mine at seven months, which allowed me to watch a couple of Ross's basketball games.

Leaving Penny and Ross after my short time home became harder than when I had said good-bye to Penny in the Honolulu airport on my way back to Vietnam. Then I was twenty-six and still on an adventure, and Ross was only a small boy. Now I was thirty-five. Ross was a teenager tearing up the basketball court, and I was missing it. Moreover, I knew what I was missing, resented it, and probably resented finding out how well they were doing without me.

Penny was happy in her job, and Ross enjoyed basketball and school. They had no crises and had done just fine. As time swiftly passed, I got a sinking feeling when I thought about returning to Korea and particularly the loneliness that set in late at night; however, we all went to National Airport, now Ronald Reagan National Airport, with a smile on our faces, and away I went.

As I flew back, I began to get excited about being in the thick of things. I had the best job an AG major could hope for, as fine a group of soldiers a man could want, and a great mission to perform. I was leaving the ones I loved, but I was going back to what I loved.

Convoluted and conflicted thoughts remained until I walked out of Kimpo Airport and Malcolm and Wanda were there to meet me and bring me up to speed on what had happened during my absence. It was time to go to work.

Several weeks after mid-tour leave, I received a message through the American Red Cross that I needed to return to the States. A lump had been found in Penny's breast. The physician recommended an immediate mastectomy. This hit me like a sucker punch in the solar plexus. Dazed, I found it difficult to function. I was scared.

My port-call people began arranging for a return flight while I tried to get a call through to Ross or Penny. When I reached Penny, she gave me great news.

The young doctor had overreacted by having the Red Cross message sent. Further tests, after Penny asked for a second opinion, revealed that the lump was benign. It still had given me quite a scare. I realized how much Penny meant to me and how much I hated being separated from her.

I had two rating officers during my tour in Korea, Lieutenant Colonel Ralph W. Bilberry and Lieutenant Colonel Dennis J. Flynn, and one indorsing officer, Colonel John W. Nicholson. Both Bilberry and Flynn served as the 2nd Infantry Division adjutant general (AG), with me as their deputy, and both were promoted to full colonel after their departure from Korea. I served with Colonel Flynn several years later in the adjutant general office at the Department of the Army (DA). Colonel Nicholson was the chief of staff of the 2nd Infantry Division and retired as a brigadier general. Today, Brigadier General (Retired) Nicholson is the Undersecretary for Memorial Affairs at the Department of Veterans Affairs (VA). Major General David E. Grange, Jr., the division commander, was the senior rater on my officer evaluation reports.

Ralph Bilberry was a small, articulate, handsome, soft-spoken, easy-going, black officer. I found him to be exasperating to work for because of his difficulty in making decisions. Technically competent, he knew his business, but I often went around him to accomplish the mission.

Too often, I would receive a call from the SGS informing me that Colonel Nicholson was looking for a response to one of his requirements. I would inform the SGS that I had sent the response to the AG several days ago and that it should have been in the command group by now. After I waited until Colonel Bilberry had gone to lunch, I would search his desk, find the paper, sign it for him over my signature, and carry it by hand to the SGS.

When Colonel Bilberry returned from lunch, I would inform him of what I had done, and he would invariably ask, "Do you think the paper answered the chief's questions, or do you think it was what the chief wanted?"

I would respond, "Sir, I would not have sent it to you unless I believed it did," and usually, it did.

A man of few vices, Bilberry kept to himself and generally dined at the general's mess rather than the 2-2-0 Club or the unit mess hall with his officers. Once, though, he let his hair down and became one of the boys.

To set the stage for this occasion, a short history of the Adjutant General's Corps follows: The Corps dates back to the formation of the American Army, which it has served for over 230 years. Horatio Gates, a former British Army officer, is honored as the father of the Adjutant General's Corps. On June 16, 1775, the Continental Congress appointed him as the first adjutant general to George Washington, with the rank of brigadier general. Historically, he was the second officer to receive a commission in the Continental Army, preceded only by Washington. With that appointment, the second oldest branch of the Army was born.

General Gates' primary duty was to serve as key advisor and principal assistant to General Washington. He organized the state militias into what became the Continental Army. General Gates proved himself an able assistant as well as a competent field commander. Under his leadership, the Continental Army won the Battle of Saratoga, considered by many to be the turning point of the Revolutionary War. Following this important strategic victory over the British, the Continental Congress awarded General Gates what was then our nation's highest honor, the Congressional Gold Medal.

Today, the Horatio Gates Bronze and Gold Medals, which recognize superior achievement or service to the AG Corps, dates from this important event. The medals are struck by the US Mint from the original die used in making the gold medal awarded to General Gates. I am a proud recipient of both the bronze and gold medals.

Over the years, the mission and duties of adjutant generals have morphed, but AG officers continue as the only officers vested with the authority to speak and sign official correspondence "For the Commander."

Annually, Adjutant General's Corps officers gather worldwide on June 16th to celebrate the anniversary of the Corps, and June 16, 1978, was no different. Colonel Bilberry had intended to take a staff car to the celebration held at the Eighth Army Officer's Club on the Yongsan compound in Seoul, but we chided him into traveling with some of the officers. We loaded my SIDPERS supply van with a couch from our billet dayroom, put on our dressy blue formal uniforms with bow ties, and added a cooler of beer and some whiskey, and away we went to Seoul.

The function in Seoul was a formal affair with several toasts, a dinner, cutting of the birthday cake by the senior and junior officers present, followed by dancing. Because we were from the combat division, we felt the need to uphold our wild and woolly reputation with the rear echelon folks stationed in and around Seoul, many of whom had their wives with them.

When we arrived in Seoul, we were well lubricated and in fine form to make fools of ourselves. We tried dancing with the wives in attendance during the cocktail hour, made an inappropriate toast, threw dinner rolls across tables during the dinner, and generally became somewhat more than obnoxious. With martial law and a midnight curfew in effect, we needed to leave Seoul by 2300 to be safely ensconced at Camp Casey prior to 2400 hours. We did not need to worry. We were politely asked to leave the premises around 2200.

I had never seen Colonel Bilberry drink more than one drink at a time; however, by the time we arrived back at Camp Casey, he was well "oiled," actually "boiled," and he had a bad case of the giggles, as did we all. One of the officers escorted him back to his hooch, as he was in no condition to proceed without an escort.

We did not see Bilberry for a couple of days; however, when we did, he had a sheepish grin, and from then on, he had become one of the boys, or as much as a lieutenant colonel could be one of the boys. How our conduct did not get back to Colonel Nicholson and General Grange I will never know. Maybe it did.

Ralph Bilberry took care of me on my OER, recommending me for promotion to lieutenant colonel and selection for senior service college ahead of my contemporaries.

Colonel Flynn replaced Colonel Bilberry, and the difference between the two was pronounced. Because of the one-year tour, an assignment with the 2nd Infantry Division compared to trying to catch a moving train. You caught it on the first try, or you were left behind. Malcolm Weaver and I had caught the train and were in the cab, engineering it down the track. Consequently, Colonel Flynn was content to give us a loose rein to run our own show. Further, he returned to the States to deal with a family problem at least twice. Thus I became the de facto adjutant general over long periods.

One of Colonel Flynn's first actions was to have all officers participate in a transition training exercise conducted over two days, one utilizing the Jung Myers-Briggs personality model. The Army like the corporate world quickly latches on to the latest management fads, such as zero defects, role-playing, and total quality management (TQM). In my opinion, all were a waste of time and resources. In lieu of developing and improving management skills, the focus should have been on developing and improving leadership skills. Again in my opinion, the emphasis on fads resulted in the Army having too many managers and not enough warriors.

The Myers-Briggs exercise was enlightening in that career military officers had a natural inclination or preference for certain ways of thinking and behaving. Most, such as me, prefer to deal with ideas, information, and facts, making decisions based on objective logic in a planned, stable, and organized environment. Some prefer to deal with people, things, and ideas while they are looking into what is not obvious, basing decisions on feelings while going with the flow and responding to situations as they arise. A few prefer a combination of the preceding.

This information is particularly helpful when you are working with or for people who do not share your particular personality style.

The most visible time for my staff and me was the monthly "unit status report" (USR) briefing held in the command conference room over a two-day period. Each brigade, battalion, and separate company commander would brief the status of their unit with regard to personnel, training, equipment, maintenance, and overall capability to go to war. This briefing would be presented to the commanding general (CG), assistant division commander for maneuver, (ADC-M), assistant division commander for support, (ADC-S), chief of staff, and the assembled division staff. Often, this monthly gathering became a bloodletting for the staff, particularly the adjutant general.

The 2nd Division, as a forward deployed division, had an assigned combat rating of C-1. This meant the division was expected to report a personnel readiness between 98 and 100 percent, and through my tenure, the division did so in the aggregate. However, there often were shortages of NCOs and certain key specialties. Accordingly, a commander with maintenance or training problems would blame the AG for not providing the requisite number of soldiers in the required grade and skills as the contributing factor for their own inadequacies. I never once heard a commander admit that his maintenance or training program was screwed up because of his own internal problems.

General Grange did not buy the commanders' excuses, and more than once, he told them that never before had he served in a unit that had as high a personnel filled as the 2nd Infantry Division. He had fought most of the Korean War with units that were less than 60 percent filled. He further reminded the commanders that they were responsible for training their people to perform at a level two grades higher than their current ranks, and there were 2,100 KATUSAs assigned to the division that possessed critical, hard skills that other divisions did not have.

The ADC-M, whom I shall call Brigadier General Hardass, specifically disliked staff officers and adjutant generals in particular. He took great delight in harassing and embarrassing my folks and me during USR briefings. When a commander would brief that he was short a particular NCO or soldier, the ADC-M would holler, "AG," and either Captain Weaver, Chief Warrant Officer Three (CW3) Tony

Eclava, Sergeant First Class (SFC) Ed McGlynn, or myself, depending upon who had the information at his fingertips, would rise and respond to the ADC-M. We would report the number of people in the replacement stream in that grade and skill, when they were due to arrive, and the unit where they were expected to be assigned. If there were no soldiers in the replacement stream in the particular grade or skill, we would report what we were doing or had done in order to have a requisition filled. Our report never once satisfied the ADC-M, and he would continue to press until he got the look from General Grange to shut up.

Preparing for the USR became an eighteen-hour session, as the unit reports habitually were not received until the day before. Therefore, we would work until the wee hours of the morning and review the unit reports and anticipate questions and remarks from the ADC-M and commanders. Colonel Flynn, sitting in on one session, remarked, "This is as bad as trying to prepare to defend a master's thesis."

We were always glad to get the monthly USR out of the way, particularly if we had not been bloodied too badly.

One afternoon when I was leaving division headquarters, General Hardass saw me and asked if his OER had been received at MILPERCEN. I had no idea but told him I would check. He went ballistic and informed me that General Grange had written a special OER on him for the upcoming major general selection board. The report had been given to Colonel Flynn, who was to take the report to MILPERCEN upon his return to the States on leave.

Flynn had said nothing to me about the report. When I returned to my office, I checked with CW4 Bob Kormelink, whose folks were responsible for processing and forwarding all OERs rendered on officers assigned to the division. Bob, an aviator grounded because of eye problems, told me that Flynn had given him the report for processing but had not said anything about carrying the report by hand.

Flynn had departed on leave, so I deduced I probably had a problem.

"Where is the report?"

Bob responded that his people were getting it ready for mailing.

"When does the major general board meet?" I asked.

"In a couple of weeks, sir."

I knew that it would take several days for the report to reach MILPERCEN by mail and several more days for processing at OER branch, so the schedule was tight. I told Kormelink to take my jeep and go to Seoul to mail the OER, go to MILPERCEN-K, find out who was going TDY to Washington, and ask them to take a Zerox copy to OER branch.

Remember, this was before the days of faxes.

When I called OER branch, I informed them of my problem, and they assured me that they would immediately take the report to the selection board when they received it.

Wanda informed me that General Hardass was on the line.

I explained to Hardass the situation and received one of what would be many ass-chewings over the next few days and, in fact, the rest of my tour. Several times, Hardass ordered me to his private office in the headquarters building and left me at attention while he berated me in a belligerent manner. His point was that I was in the people business and if I treated a brigadier general in the way he thought I had treated him, how did I treat a private. I could only stand and take his abuse, knowing he was dead wrong.

The report got to the selection board on time.

Colonel Nicholson called me one morning and started our very short conversation by asking, "How long does it take to process a soldier out of the division?"

"About an hour, sir."

"Good! You now have fifty-nine minutes. General Grange's sedan should be pulling up to your door. Inside is his military secretary. I want her processed out of the division and out of the AO and delivered to the front door of MILPERCEN-K. The commander will be waiting for her. I will explain later. You now have fifty-eight minutes. Got it?

"Yes, sir," I said.

It turned out that this attractive, young stenographer had visited the division surgeon and had told him she had had a problem and could not sleep. Apparently, she had set a goal of sleeping with the entire division staff; however, one officer wanted her just for himself, and she just did not know what to do.

In an attempt to maintain division strength at 100 percent, I would badger MILPERCEN-K and MILPERCEN anytime strength projections indicated a shortfall in the aggregate, MOS, or grade level. The division consistently had critical shortages of senior NCOs and master tank gunners. I would also prepare back-channel messages for General Grange to send to the commander of MILPERCEN, outlining our needs.

Sometime near the end of my tour, I received a call from the chief of the Infantry Branch, Enlisted Personnel Management Directorate at MILPERCEN, informing me that the division would be brought over 100 percent strength and would be receiving the next two classes of infantry AIT graduates consisting of several hundred privates.

Once they started arriving, I began to receive calls from battalion commanders saying, "Do not send me any more troops." It was the first and last time I heard a commander say he did not want any more soldiers.

Commanders complained at the next USR meeting and stated that the influx of privates exacerbated their NCO shortage, as they did not have enough leaders to train and supervise such large numbers. General Grange cut them no slack and told them they had better get busy training their young NCOs to do the job of the more senior NCOs.

In retrospect, sending so many soldiers to the division at one time was a mistake, as most would leave at the same time the following year, truly complicating training and strength problems. Such was the fast-moving train of the 2nd Infantry Division.

Piss poor planning results in piss poor performance.
—Unknown

When I attended a meeting at MILPERCEN-K, the commander announced that a recall of KATUSAs would take place within the next couple of months. All KATUSAs would need to be transported to an undisclosed location, released to ROK (Republic of Korea) control, and then returned to their US unit. The drill was strictly for accountability and contingency purposes, but because the ROK Army would be involved, we needed to have our act together, as the recall would be unannounced. We would only have six hours to have all assembled at the undisclosed location.

Moving 2100 soldiers located throughout the division AO in a short period is difficult without a plan. When I returned to Camp Casey, I visited the Division G3 (Operations), Lieutenant Colonel James Terry Scott. I solicited his support in developing a division OPLAN (Operation Plan) notifying division units of the upcoming exercise and outlining responsibilities. Scott told me to get out of the net, as his people would develop the plan, and he saw no need for the AG to be involved.

At a subsequent command and staff meeting and after I had not seen an OPLAN, I slipped a note to Terry Scott, one reminding him of the pending requirement and suggesting he mention it in the meeting, which he did.

Several weeks later, the division duty officer received a predawn call from USFK operations announcing the recall. Terry Scott was on leave at the time, and neither the deputy G3 nor the G3 plans officer knew anything about the requirement, so the duty officer called me and asked if I knew anything about the recall. I said I did, but the G3 had assumed responsibility. He said, "Wrong! The G3 folks know nothing, and because you are the only one who knows anything about it, you got it."

When I called Colonel Nicholson and got him out of bed, I advised him of the recall and offered him my best recommendation: Get each major subordinate commander on the line and give them the mission of assembling and transporting their KATUSAs to the now-known location. I explained only a call from him or General Grange would sufficiently energize the commanders to react in time to meet the requirement.

Colonel Nicholson was not pleased and took his frustration out on me; however, he did as I suggested, and the brigade commanders came through. The 2nd Infantry Division met the requirement, but commanders were put through an unnecessary "jump through your hoops" drill.

I do not know if Nicholson discussed the matter with Terry Scott upon his return from leave, but if he did, he apparently did not mention it in Scott's OER and certainly not in mine.

Today, Lieutenant General Terry Scott is retired and recently served as the chairman of the Veterans Disability Benefits Commission. The commission, which was established by congress in 2003, was charged with examining the appropriateness and the level of veterans' compensation for service-connected disabilities and survivors' benefits. Congress passed legislation implementing some of the commission recommendations, but most remained in limbo because of budget constraints. In defense of congress, a significant amount of money has been appropriated for the VA to eliminate the tremendous backlog of soldiers awaiting a decision on eligibility for benefits. This backlog is a result of the two wars our nation has been engaged in for over ten years. Sun Tzu's axiom on waging war comes to mind: "There has never been a protracted war from which a country has benefited."

When I entered the Army, I asked a senior officer what he considered a successful career. His response was retirement in the grade of major. He went on to say retirement as a lieutenant colonel was evidence of an extremely successful career and anything more was a matter of luck and timing. True then, and I believe true today.

I resolved to do the best job I could regardless of the assignment and let the chips fall where they may. I never stewed over whether I would or would not be promoted except for one time. That time was when I became eligible for promotion to regular Army (RA) major. That promotion would guarantee that I could remain in the service for twenty years and thus reach retirement eligibility.

In 1978, the Army, which was then called the Army of the United States (AUS), had a dual-component promotion system with both RA and US Reserve officers serving on active duty. Officers held a temporary grade in the AUS and a permanent grade in either the RA or the US Reserves. Officers served on active duty in the highest grade they held, generally their AUS grade. However, continuance on active duty was dependent on the officers' permanent grade. Officers with a permanent grade of major were permitted to remain on active duty until the completion of twenty years of active service.

At the time, I served on active duty as an AUS major; however, my permanent grade was RA captain. It was imperative that I be selected for RA major if I held any chance for a successful career and eventual retirement. My concern about being promoted in the RA stemmed from the simple fact that the criterion for promotion in the RA was much more competitive and stringent than promotion in either the AUS or US Reserves. Fortuitously, I was selected for RA major and promoted on July 20, 1978. I was now a career soldier, or in the jargon of the day, a "lifer." Today, the confusing dual system has been replaced by a single active duty promotion system.

> *The man who gets the most satisfactory results is not always the man with the most brilliant single mind, but rather the man who can best coordinate the brains and talents of his associates.*
> —W. Alton Jones

The officers and NCOs who worked for me in the 2nd Infantry Division were first-rate as were the enlisted soldiers. Captain Malcolm Weaver, Master Sergeant George Wallace, Sergeant First-Class Ed McGlynn, and CW3 Tony Eclava were all in the top five of their grade and rank who served under me during my career. Malcolm Weaver retired as a lieutenant colonel, and both George Wallace and Ed McGlynn retired as sergeant majors, the highest enlisted rank. Tony Eclava was one of the first in the Army to be promoted to the new master warrant officer grade of CW5. I am deeply indebted to these folks along with Wicked Wanda Matlock for their outstanding performances, loyalty, and dedication. Without them, it would have been a much longer twelve months in Korea.

In December 1978, I received notification that my next assignment would be to the Pentagon, serving in the office of the deputy chief of staff for personnel, now the Army G1, with a report date of April 16, 1979. This news pleased Penny, Ross, and me. We would not have to move. Penny could continue to work in a job she loved. Ross would graduate from Lake Braddock, and I needed to get my "ticket punched" working on the DA staff. I did not look forward to working in the Pentagon, but I knew it was necessary for career progression.

The day prior to my departure from Korea, Colonel Nicholson presented me with my OER. Both he and Colonel Flynn had given me a numerical rating of a hundred points out of a possible hundred points, and both had recommended me for command, the adjutant general of a combat division, promotion ahead of my contemporaries, and early selection for attendance at a senior service college. I could not have received a better report if I had written it myself.

As we left Colonel Nicholson's office, we proceeded to the command conference room, where General Grange awarded me my fourth Meritorious Service Medal. In attendance at the ceremony was Brigadier General Hardass. After the ceremony, General Hardass approached, and I thought, "Oh, no, here it comes again."

As he poked a finger in my chest, he looked me hard in the eye and said, "I don't attend ceremonies for staff pukes. First one I have attended. You can work for me anytime." He then wheeled and departed.

When I flew out of Kimpo Airport on March 25, 1979, I felt this boy from Barnhart could handle any mission the Army gave me. It was good to be going home.

17

The Pentagon

The first couple of months after my return became a period of adjustment for the family as we attempted to transition to our traditional roles. Both Penny and Ross had become independent during my absence, Ross as the man of the house and Penny free to devote her energies to her job without having to attend to my needs. Ross had matured and become a young adult, and they had developed a close relationship and depended on each other for support. This was good and right, and I was the one who needed most of the adjustment.

Unfortunately, ego and pride do not allow me to adjust easily. Once a situation changes and has time to solidify, it is impossible to go back. It was no different in our case, which resulted in three adults now occupying the same space. It became a seminal moment in our family life. On reflection, I was jealous of their relationship and had been for years. I did not want to share Penny's love or attention with anyone, not even my own son. Selfish, psychologically immature and needy are not my best traits.

Proud of them both for their accomplishments, I especially reveled in Ross's success on the basketball court. While in Korea, Ross had been selected as his team's MVP and had made first team all-district and second team all-regional in a very competitive region. This resulted in a lot of press coverage in area newspapers, and along with his exposure at the Five-Star Camp in Pennsylvania, contacts from various college and universities were now showing up.

Because I had missed his games the previous year, Coach Hensley loaned me videos, and I spent several enjoyable evenings reviewing them. Ross could indeed play basketball.

Ross shooting his patented jump shot in a game against Garfield High School his junior year.

My assignment officer told me I would be an assistant executive officer (XO) in the office of the deputy chief of staff for personnel (ODCSPER), now the Army G1, headed up by a lieutenant general. I thought, "Here come the horrendously long hours, but the hours would be balanced by having a general's signature on my OER." I figured it would be a piece of cake after my experience as the SGS of USARJ/IX Corps.

When I arrived at the ODCSPER, I found the job not quite what I had expected. My job title included assistant executive officer, but it included other things as well. It read:

> Duties include serving as Assistant Executive Officer, ODCSPER; Chief, Personnel and Administration Team; and Security Manager. Responsible for a wide variety of administrative and logistical support functions for military and civilian personnel assigned to ODCSPER. Functions include the broad spectrum of military and civilian personnel support, office management, information security, physical security and special projects in support of the DCSPER/ADCSPER.

I was the "head flunky," and the assistant executive officer title was a sham. If it did not fit anywhere else, give it to Taylor.

There were three real assistant executive officers and me. I had the title of assistant executive solely to serve as "late man" for a week each month.

Lieutenant General Robert G. Yerks, the DCSPER, would not depart the Pentagon at night until he had received a call from the XO to the Army vice chief of staff (VCSA), General Frederick J. Kroesen (and later General John W. Vessey), that he would not be needed. Rarely would he be on-call to see the Army chief of staff, General Bernard W. Rogers, although that happened on occasion, as Rogers had been the DCSPER prior to Yerks. Late-man duties required one of the assistant XOs to stay with General Yerks to close his safe and assist him if needed. Pulling late-man duty meant many long nights, but it was only once a month for one week.

A fine, kind, and Christian man, Yerks, a West Pointer, had a distinguished combat record and eleven or twelve children, most whom were still at home. I marveled at the old cars his kids would drive to pick him up at the heliport entrance of the Pentagon. I think he bought a clunker for each one.

General Yerks, unique among the DA staff principals, allowed ODCSPER action officers to coordinate on staff actions prepared by other DA agencies. Consequently, an ODCSPER major could sign a paper from another staff agency concurring in the proposed action if, in the opinion of the staff officer, the paper was correct and reflected the views of General Yerks. A proposed non-concurrence had to be referred to the next higher level.

Bureaucrats write memorandum both because they appear to be busy when they are writing and because the memos, once written, immediately become proof that they were busy.
—Charles Peters

The policy of deputy chief of staff for operations (DCSOPS), now the Army G3, stipulated only a general officer could concur on a staff action being circulated by another staff element. Accordingly, obtaining an ODCSPER "chop" became easy, but trying to staff a paper through ODCSOPS was difficult at best. A typical sequence of coordinating an

ODCSPER staff action involved obtaining a preliminary concurrence from your ODCSOPS counterpart, usually a major, another preliminary chop with his boss, a lieutenant colonel, and then an appointment with an ODSOPS colonel. If you survived the gauntlet, you eventually got to appear before an ODCSOPS general.

This whole sequence could take days, even weeks. Each ODCSOPS officer wanted to "wordsmith" your paper and change "happy" to "glad," which would necessitate the paper be retyped usually by the action officer, as secretaries and clerk-typists were in short supply. Finally, the paper would get to an ODCSOPS general, and a concurrence would be obtained. (They usually only wanted to know where to sign, and then they wanted you gone, as they had too many other alligators chomping on their butts.) If not, it was back to the drawing board. This was the epitome of bureaucracy, and it did not leave an action officer with the gut feeling he was doing great and wonderful things for his country.

The contacts I had made at Command and General Staff College and elsewhere served me well during my Pentagon tour. Having a friend in another staff element, particularly ODCSOPS, allowed me to turn my action over to them to shepherd through the bureaucratic maze of their staff element. I would, of course, return the favor in a quid-pro-quo arrangement or "you scratch my itch, and I will scratch yours."

As the ODCSPER flunky, I cannot count the times that I received calls from menopausal women complaining that their office was too hot or too cold, and they were right. The Pentagon heating and air-conditioning systems were antiquated, and some people remained hot in the summer and cold in the winter; however, they had someone on whom they could take out their frustrations.

Space in the Pentagon was at a premium with the exception of the E-Ring, where lieutenant generals and above and high-level civilians (political appointees) resided. Action officers shared open rooms with metal desks pushed together and little space to walk alongside them. There were usually six to eight action officers to a room, each sharing one clerk-typist with their lieutenant colonel branch chief. Most colonels had a very small but private office.

General officers arriving at the Pentagon, usually from a field assignment and expecting large offices and nice furniture were sorely disappointed. The General Service Administration (GSA) controlled the Pentagon, and it had specific guidelines as to the size of the office and type of furniture that each political appointee, general, and senior executive service civilian could have. This is not to say they did not have nice, large offices, but it was generally not what they had as a field commander.

Major generals and brigadiers were the ones primarily disappointed. When they came from an assignment as a division or installation commander, they were used to having what they wanted. I experienced the displeasure of one major general who unhappy with the size and amount of furniture in his office ordered me to get him additional furniture and have his office enlarged. When shown the GSA schedule depicting what a major general was authorized, he relented, but he never did like me, nor I him. Thankfully, he was not in my rating chain.

I have not written on this manuscript for months, primarily because of illness, travel, and simply writer's block. I must write today. Daddy died at 2352 hours on August 4, 2007, and went gentle into the night to his heavenly reward. I miss him! He was a remarkable man who lived quite a life. His obituary was published in the *San Angelo Standard-Times,* and it succinctly sums up his life below:

Daddy's Obituary Photo

"Norvel Ross 'Shorty' Taylor," 97, of Slaton went to be with his lord on Saturday, August 4, 2007.

Shorty was born April 9, 1910, in the Bethel Community, San Saba County to Emmett O. and Mamie Wood Taylor. He attended school in the Bethel Community and graduated the eighth grade. He went to work for his Uncle Herbert Taylor as a rancher and later as a youth of sixteen worked in the oil fields of McCamey.

Shorty married Elanor Alyene Shaw on September 30, 1939, in Kerrville and soon after they moved to Maryneal, where Shorty became a full time cowboy. Later they moved to Suggs Switch east of Barnhart working for Cotton Brooks and running some livestock on his own lease. In 1956, they moved to the Murphey ranch between Barnhart and Big Lake, leasing a portion of the ranch, and working for Teddy Russell.

Shorty made the big life change move in 1962 when he left the ranching business and became a grocery man first in Crane and later in Big Spring. He owned the Airport Grocery in Big Spring until his retirement in 1973. Shorty often remarked that he should have gotten in the grocery business sooner since it was less work and more profitable than ranch work. Today most folks only remember Shorty as a cowboy or as grocery man but not both.

Upon retirement, Shorty became a man of leisure gardening and piddling with his yard. Several times, he was awarded Yard of the Year in Big Spring.

Shorty was active in the Baptist Church from his baptism in Barnhart, Texas, in 1954, serving as a deacon or Sunday school teacher. He was always eager to do the work of the Lord and lend a hand to his fellow man.

Survivors include his wife Alyene; daughter, Norvel Nantippe Cox and husband Jackie of Ransom Canyon; son Herbie Ross Taylor and wife Janice of Salado; grandsons, Michael Wayne Martin and wife Melanie of Austin and Herbie Ross Taylor, Jr and wife Kristi of Frisco; great-grandsons, Ryan, Reed and Riley Martin of Austin and Micah Jeb and Jared Ross Taylor of Frisco; brother Carmen O. 'Billy' Taylor of San Saba; and half-sister Lavon Clark of Rockdale, Texas.

Shorty was preceded in death by his parents, his brothers, Bernard and Willard, his sisters, Verma Telecamp and Roxie Grumbles; and daughter-in-law Penelope Ann Farr Taylor."

Services were held at 2:00 pm, Tuesday, August 7th, at Bible Baptist Church in Slaton with the Reverend Chris Donner officiating, and the burial took place at Resthaven Cemetery, Lubbock, Texas. Pallbearers were Travis and Jarvis Shaw, Mike and Ryan Martin, Ross Taylor, and J. R. Landry.

I realize that my daddy is in a far better place than we can hope to imagine. He is now singing with the angels, clearly hearing the voice of the Lord, and seeing plainly the most magnificent sights in the Lord's realm. This man, my father, taught this boy from Barnhart right from wrong and how to be a man. It is a debt that I am not sure I can ever repay.

Here are some reminiscences from my time as the assistant XO:

Army custom is that an Adjutant General's Corps officer read award citations when presented by an organization's senior officer or his deputy. This task fell to me when General Yerks presented an award in the ODCSPER conference room. I had done this duty in prior assignments, but I did not particularly like to do so. Reading citations is stressful, particularly in the ODCSPER conference room because of its rather small size. The room would accommodate only a hundred folks standing shoulder-to-shoulder, with some usually standing outside in the hallway.

General Yerks would have the recipient and his family in his office for a few minutes. They would proceed to the conference room and take their position at the front of the room. I would already be at the podium, awaiting their arrival. The room would be uncomfortable because of body heat, and I would be tense.

General Yerks would give a small talk of gratitude or whatever was appropriate for the occasion and then turn to me to read the citation and say, "Publish the order."

It is a time when you have no warning. There is absolute silence. You are the only actor on the stage. It is very important that you read the order and especially the citation with real meaning and pronounce the words correctly.

Shortly after arrival at ODCSPER, I was informed that I was to read a citation. Given the citation, I had no time to rehearse before I was to perform. I was quite nervous by the time General Yerks and the award recipient arrived. When he turned to me, I announced, "Attention to Orders," and began to read the citation, stumbling over a word, losing my composure. My voice cracked. I received a piercing look from the XO and immediately regained my poise and completed reading the citation. However, I was embarrassed, and that memory lingers still.

I determined that if I were to do this, I would thoroughly study each citation beforehand. Some citations had words that were difficult to pronounce or sentences that did not flow smoothly when read. I would change the word or revise the sentence. No one knew the difference. I would read the citations aloud before I read them officially, and I got good at doing this. Even so, it remained stressful.

When I arrived at my desk one Monday morning, I found the DA director of civilian personnel waiting for me. This civilian leader, who should have known better, had some of his folks work over the weekend to rearrange the desks and offices in his area. He was quite proud that his people had done the heavy lifting, and all he wanted me to do was get the phones rearranged. I knew he (and now I) had a problem, and I told him so; however, I agreed to see what I could do. When I contacted the office responsible for providing telephone service within the Pentagon, I was told there was a major reorganization in the US Navy offices within the Pentagon. Their assets were tied up. They were behind on their usual work and service orders, and it would be at least a month, if not more, before they could get to me. When I repeated this to the civilian, he was incensed and directed me to have his furniture put back in its original place.

This prima donna and I had words before, and I did not like him. His status in the senior executive service (general officer equivalent) did not impress me, and I did not intend to take orders from him, as he was not in my rating chain. I understood he might go to my boss, but I deduced that he was too embarrassed to admit he had not coordinated the move with me, as I was responsible for all moves within the ODCSPER. I took perverse delight in seeing his people move their desks back to the places whence they came. Boy, they were upset at him!

I had been told that my assignment as an assistant XO would be for eighteen months and that I could then transfer within ODCSPER to be an action officer. I was determined to get out of the job as soon as I could, and an opportunity presented itself when Colonel Bill Gourley, later major general, was selected to be General Yerks's XO. Gourley had been the chief of the enlisted division for the Directorate of Military Personnel Management (DMPM), and he was an Adjutant General's Corps officer. I knew he was on the fast track to general officer, and I wanted to develop a good relationship with him. Periodically, as chief of the enlisted division, he would visit and try to get me to assign him an officer or two above his authorization, as I was responsible for officer assignments below colonel within ODCSPER. Actually, he hustled me by telling me I needed to get out of the assistant XO job and work for him as an action officer. I never assigned him an officer above authorization; however, I did make sure there was overlap with any officer he had departing, and if he asked for an officer by name, which he often did, I worked to make sure that happened.

Once Gourley assumed duties as the XO, I reminded him of our previous talks about me becoming an action officer, but he began to "crawfish." Finally, he agreed, provided I find an officer to replace me that he found suitable, and he gave me a couple of names. I did this in short order.

Moving to the distribution and readiness branch of the enlisted division for DMPM, I became an action officer. I had spent six months as an assistant XO. Little did I know that I only had six more months in my assignment in the ODCSPER and the Pentagon.

My job description read:

> Responsible for enlisted MOS development, preparing and coordinating directorate input to accomplish enlisted personnel interface on force modernization actions pertaining to the budget/POM within the purview of the branch, insuring proper personnel support to the Training and Doctrine Command (TRADOC) to accomplish the FY80 training surge and the Space Imbalanced MOS Incentive Program.

Mumbo jumbo to you and somewhat to me, but I did this, writing numerous papers to be coordinated with staff agencies and presenting briefings to decision makers. Most of my effort, which was not in my job description, was preparing for and participating in the close-combat cell, developing the Army's budget for FY80. The cell consisted of action officers from all DA staff elements headed up by an ODCSOPS colonel, with me representing the ODCSPER. Our job was to develop the right mix of close-combat soldiers (i.e., infantry, armor, and special forces) needed by the Army within the total force structure to meet mission requirements during FY80 and beyond. We were also to determine the personnel and training costs for the mix and to defend our decisions before a panel of general officers against the combat support and combat service support cells. In short, we were to justify as many "trigger pullers" as possible within the overall Army budget.

The budget cycle drives the train in the Pentagon, with all services competing for more than their fair share of the overall DOD budget. The US Navy fought internally over surface ships versus submarines, the US Air Force over fighters versus bombers, and the US Army over tanks versus helicopters. Once the internal battles had been fought and decisions made, the competition between services for more dollars began.

This process within the Army took some fifteen weeks of long, hectic hours. The close-combat cell met each morning at 0630 and ran until approximately 1830 hours for six days a week. I still had routine actions to accomplish within my branch. Usually, I would arrive at the Pentagon around 0600 and leave around 2000 hours. These hours along with horrible Washington traffic made for a long day and a short night.

Normally, I would ride a metro bus to and from work, but during the budget cycle and when I was pulling late-man duties, I would drive. I drove simply because I had no idea when I might be able to leave the Pentagon. Bus service to Orange Hunt began at 0530 and ran every thirty minutes until 1900, when service was hourly until 2400.

One of my vivid memories is the bus rides. Whenever I would get on the bus at the Townes of Orange Hunt on a Monday morning, all riders would have their heads in the *Washington Post* or a book. There would be no conversation between riders, and all would have an unhappy demeanor. It would be dark when we arrived at the Pentagon, where we would toil without seeing the sun and then return home in the dark. All suffered from light and sun deprivation. Come Friday evening, though, all would have a smile, and folks would chitchat on the ride home. There was no joy or happiness working in the Pentagon.

Around the end of February 1980, I received a call from the chief of the Adjutant General Officer Assignment Branch asking if I could be released from ODSCPER if I was accepted for an assignment as the AG of the 5th Infantry Division (Mechanized) and Fort Polk.

The position of adjutant general in an Army division was a nominate position. The procedure was for AG Branch to submit the files of three of the branch's best and brightest to the division commander for selection. The position called for a lieutenant colonel. Although I had been selected for promotion to lieutenant colonel, there was no way I would be promoted by the time I had to meet a May report date to Fortress Polk.

I went to my boss, Lieutenant Colonel R. J. Wooten, and asked if he would release me for the assignment. He said that he would but that I should not get my hopes up, as a division commander was not likely to select an officer who would arrive as a major in this important and highly visible position. In fact, Colonel Wooten felt the division commander would want a senior lieutenant colonel. I believed he was right, but I was pleased to know that AG Branch considered me competitive.

Penny was not happy about me possibly being reassigned, certainly not to Fort Polk, which was known as "Camp Swampy" in Army circles at the time. The normal tour in the Pentagon was three years, and she hoped that I would serve the three years and be reassigned within the Washington area for another tour. She loved the area and her job, and she was not ready to move, though she understood the favorable impact a division AG job would have on my career.

I held no illusions about being selected for the job, and because I had not heard from the branch, I did not prepare for a move. Around mid-April, the AG Branch chief called to inform me that I had been selected and to get my bags packed, because I needed to be at Polk in early May.

This presented several problems. First, I had to break the news to Penny. Second, Ross would graduate from high school at the end of May. In addition, I needed a year in the Pentagon to be eligible for the Army General Staff Identification Badge (AGSIB) so that I could validate my time in the Pentagon and fill another space on my Army resume, the officer record brief (ORB).

Penny did not take the news well, but after a couple of days, she became resigned to the fact. We decided to rent the house rather than sell, as I would probably be reassigned to Washington after my two years at Polk. We also decided that I would not fly back for Ross' graduation, as a plane ticket would only add to the moving expenses, which were always high, and it would not be wise to ask for leave so soon after I arrived at Polk.

I immediately took leave to get ready for the move. I returned to the Pentagon on the morning I departed for Polk, signing in from regular leave, and then signing out again on PCS leave. This gave me one year exactly on the DA staff, qualifying me for the award of the AGSIB.

One problem remained. What were we to do with Ross? Ross had received a presidential appointment to attend the US Naval Academy at Annapolis to play basketball and had made his visit to the campus. A staff car had picked him up and transported him to the academy, where he roomed, attended classes, and ate with a first-year basketball player.

When he returned from the trip, Ross told me, "Poppa, I have been in the military for eighteen years, and I am tired of it. Those people cannot even watch television at night and are hollered at day and night. I'm not going!"

I was crushed! I am not sure about Penny. A great education, a free education, and the promise of a career in a noble profession were being thrown away. I realized that there was no justification in convincing him to go, if he would be unhappy, so I resigned myself to the idea that he would go elsewhere.

But where would he go? Ross had received serious attention from universities in Virginia, Maryland, Pennsylvania, and elsewhere; however, once he had verbally committed to the US Naval Academy, they had quit calling, and Ross would not tell us which universities he was interested in attending. Thus, his college plans remained in limbo.

Ross had done quite well in basketball his senior year, setting the Lake Braddock scoring record and making the all-district and all-region teams. I thought his selection for the Virginia all-star team to play the Maryland all-star team in the McDonald Classic at the Capital Centre in Landover, Maryland, was a big deal.

This created some dissension in the family, as Virginia had a rule that if a student played in an all-star game, they could not play another sport. Ross was a good baseball player. He wanted to play baseball, and Penny wanted him to play baseball. Ross had not yet committed to Annapolis, so I felt that playing in the all-star game would give him additional exposure to college coaches. I badgered Ross into playing, and it was a mistake. The Lake Braddock baseball team was exceptional, and had they had Ross's bat and glove, there is no doubt they would have won the Virginia state championship. Ross, Penny, the Braddock coaches and players, and their families were all mad at me, and Ross may still be. I regret influencing his decision.

Ross graduated Lake Braddock along with over 873 other seniors. He received scattered applause when he walked across the stage to receive his diploma. Ross had touched many lives by shooting a jump shot. The large number of graduates necessitated only parents being allowed to attend the graduation ceremony. However, the kids knew.

Notable graduates of Lake Braddock over the years include Mia Hamm of Olympic soccer fame; Michael K. Powell, the former chairman of the Federal Communications Agency and son of General Colin Powell; and Hubert Davis, who broke Ross's scoring record in basketball and played in the NBA for fourteen years, including a stint with the Dallas Mavericks during the 1997–2001 seasons.

I received max OERs while I was assigned to the ODCSPER, along with the right words in the narrative, so I considered the assignment a success. Nevertheless, I was glad to get away from the hustle and bustle of the Washington metropolitan area and put on fatigues and get back to soldiering.

18

Fortress Polk

When I signed out from the Pentagon, I hit the road for Fortress Polk and stopped only for sleep, food, and gas. I made the trip in our Ford Pinto, which I had loaded to the gills, as I would be "batching" for a month or so. Hard driving in a Pinto is not a pleasant experience, especially with no air-conditioning.

The officer I was replacing, Lieutenant Colonel Bill Ross, had a BOQ room waiting for me. I had dinner at the Ross's quarters that night and was processed the next day, spending a couple of hours visiting with Bill in my new office. Bill was to move up to be the deputy chief of staff, and neither he nor I felt a need for further discussion.

I was confident I could be a success as the adjutant general based on my time in Korea and de facto status as the 2nd Infantry Division adjutant general. This boy from Barnhart had the job that he had worked for his entire army career, and he planned to make the best of the opportunity.

Fort Polk, which was located some seven miles from Leesville, a town of around seven thousand, eighteen miles from DeRidder, another small town of nine thousand souls, and fifty miles from the nearest town of any size, which was Alexandria (population fifty thousand).

Leesville, the parish seat for Vernon Parish—parishes equate to counties in other states—was a typical southern Army town of cheap motels, fast-food restaurants, pawnshops, bars, and used car lots. Payday weekend, you could not find a hotel room in Leesville, as the whores had them all rented. They would sit in chairs outside their rooms and entice the soldiers and then relieve them of their hard-earned dollars.

DeRidder did not have the affect of a military town, and mostly officers lived there.

Alexandria was enjoyable, but it was still another military town, as England Air Force Base was located nearby. Even so, if you wanted to shop, Alexandria was the place to go. Unfortunately, you had to travel fifty miles over terrible roads to get there. In fact, there were no good roads in Louisiana except for the interstate.

Established in 1941 after the famous Louisiana Maneuvers and named in honor of the Right Reverend Leonidas Polk, the first Episcopal bishop of the Diocese of Louisiana and a Confederate general, the post consisted of 198,555 acres, 98,125 acres of which were in the Kisatchie National Forest. After the Louisiana Maneuvers, the post closed. It then opened for the Korean War and again closed. It was not until the 1961 Berlin Crisis that Fort Polk reactivated on a more permanent basis and became an infantry-training center in 1962. Subsequently, it was selected to conduct Vietnam-oriented training.

The 5th Infantry Division (Mechanized) became Fort Polk's major unit in 1976, initiating the start of a massive construction effort that resulted in one of the most modern installations in the Army. I then arrived at the new, modern Fort Polk, not the "Camp Swampy" of the past. A new hospital, post exchange, commissary, enlisted barracks, motor pools, dining facilities, orderly rooms, chapels, officer club, BOQ, senior officer housing, and enlisted housing all added to the image of the new Polk. Remaining were many WWII wooden buildings, which were used for various purposes. Housing for company and field-grade officers was limited. There were no quarters for married junior enlisted soldiers. Thus, they had to live off-post, as did many officers. I was one of them.

Satisfactory rental property in the area was in short supply. I had arrived prior to the normal summer rotation, so I ended up renting a house at 401 Davella Drive in DeRidder, making the twenty-mile trip each morning for the 0545 PT formation. The house was a brick rancher, old and outdated. It consisted of four bedrooms, three baths, den, living room, dining room, kitchen, storage building, and carport. It sat on a large lot that became a chore to mow, but it had many large trees and was located on a quiet dead-end street. Our neighbors were schoolteachers. The owner was a DAC working at Forces Command

(FORSCOM) headquarters in Atlanta. He was easy to deal with and did not gouge me on the price. I only had to pay fifty dollars over the housing allowance for a lieutenant colonel, even though I was not yet one.

I had work areas and billets located in various places on post, including "Eagle Hall," that provided centralized in and out-processing for the division and installation. I was responsible for a replacement detachment that housed all arriving soldiers and provided command and control of the soldiers during their three days of in-processing; the 5th Adjutant General Company, including orderly, supply, and weapons areas and the billets where all my single soldiers were housed; and the 5th Infantry Division Band area, where my "blowers" and "bangers" practiced. My troops were fed, and my mechanics worked in a consolidated Division Support Command (DISCOM) facility. The installation post office housed my postal officer and a couple of enlisted postal inspectors responsible for coordinating mail service to both troop and housing areas as well as inspecting unit mailrooms for compliance with Army postal regulations.

Soldiers do well what the boss checks.
—Army maxim

Sergeant Major Bill Gravitt, my senior NCO and right-hand man, and I visited most of these areas daily or at least weekly to ensure they were performing to expectations. My people knew that I would be coming but not when. If I was not pleased with what I saw, I would let them know, and they knew that and did not want me to "gig" them. Gravitt would take care of housekeeping, such as soldier appearance, building and ground maintenance, and troop training, and I would zero in on operational matters. I felt it imperative that I show the flag often in view of the wide dispersion of operations. My job description read:

> Adjutant General: Responsible for the personnel and administrative support systems for the 5th Infantry Division (Mech) and Fort Polk. Exercises direct supervision over enlisted management, officer and enlisted records, personnel

actions, central processing facility, casualty operations center, postal, publications, forms/records management, reproduction services, retirement services, congressional inquiries and the Standard Installation/Division Personnel System (SIDPERS). Supervises operation of the 5th Adjutant General Company, 5th Infantry Division (Mech) Band, and the 5th Replacement Detachment. Total workforce supervised is 443: 25 officers, 6 warrant officers, 348 enlisted and 64 civilians.

Quite a gaggle of geese!
Most of what these folks did involved other people. Job dedication and knowledge were paramount. I tried to lead by example, understanding that they were human and mistakes would occur, and they did. I just hoped that the mistakes did not result in my standing before the commanding general. I wanted the adjutant general operation to be totally responsive and professional, earning the respect of all. This was best for those served and those providing the service.

The offices and work areas of most of my troops and me were located in the old hospital complex. The complex consisted of a long hallway that was perhaps seventy-five yards long, with offices on the left and several long wings on the right with open office space. The main entrance was located in the center of the complex. The building was a typical, wooden, WWII hospital that had been reconfigured to serve as office space.

The command suite consisted of a private office for my civilian deputy, a retired warrant officer, and my military deputy. My secretary occupied a large open room guarding the entrance to my office. Sergeant Major Gravitt had a private office, and my congressional liaison staff of two people and a secretary had an office in the command suite. My office had been the hospital commanders' office. The office had a private latrine, which was nice to have after morning PT, and a closet to store my field gear. The room was large and comfortable, with a conference table and chairs, leather chairs, coffee table, and sofa. The entire command suite had hardwood floors. This boy from Barnhart thought he was in high cotton.

I had a jeep and driver. Often, Sergeant Major Gravitt would have the driver running an errand in the building, and rather than wait on the driver, I would drive myself to division headquarters or elsewhere.

Sergeant Major Bill Gravitt was as good as they came. He was "old Army" from the brown-shoe days. He had fought in Korea and Vietnam as an infantryman. He was tough as nails and rode herd on my NCOs, and I had a lot of them. Sometimes, I thought he was a little hard, but he made sure that they represented the NCO corps in a professional manner. Every Friday at precisely 1330, he held an NCO call under several scraggly trees near my office. I usually listened to what he was saying, and if he were particularly tough on them, he would poke his head in my back door and say, "Sir, you might want to say a few words to the NCOs. I have been a little hard on them, and they might appreciate you to talking to them." I would do as Gravitt asked, but I would think, Sergeant Major, *You stirred them up, you settle them down.* However, I continued to play the good guy with Gravitt, the bad guy. The good guy's role was not necessarily the one with which I was comfortable, but there was no way Bill Gravitt could be the good guy.

Bill Gravitt was very protective of the AG image and me.

Each time I drove the jeep to wherever I wanted to go, he had a talk with me. The talk went something like this: "Damn it, sir. You shouldn't be driving. You do not see other colonels driving. You have a driver. You have as many, if not more, people soldiering for you than most of the battalion commanders. I just don't think it is right for you to be driving yourself."

Bill Gravitt was never shy about letting me or anyone else know what he was thinking.

I just liked driving that jeep, but I would retort and say, "Sergeant Major, I am a busy man, and I don't have time to wait on a private."

I am sure that galled Gravitt.

He who has learned to obey will know how to command.
—Solon

My second day at Polk, I took PT with the 5th Adjutant General (AG) Company. Later, Gravitt and I would alternate, taking PT with the 5th Replacement Detachment and the 5th AG Company. The 5th

AG Company, which was battalion-sized, had both females and males assigned just as the 2nd Infantry Division did.

Gravitt met me, and we observed the company forming for calisthenics. We took a position behind the formation and participated in the exercises. The entire company had been formed by platoons based on their work areas, with their officer and NCO supervisor serving as platoon leader and platoon sergeant. The company began the run as one entity at a brisk pace. Soon, soldiers began to drop out of the formation, and after about one and a quarter miles, a third of the company was strung out along the route. The company was no longer a cohesive military unit.

"Sergeant major, what is the division standard for morning runs?"

"Minimum standard is two miles, sir. Eight-minute miles."

"How far do you think we have run?"

"Not two miles yet, sir."

"How far is it to the company assembly area?"

"About a mile, sir."

"Tell me about the company commander."

"He's green, sir, and hardheaded. Likes to do things his way. Not open to suggestions from the NCOs or the other officers. You need to have a long talk with him."

"Roger. How's the first sergeant?"

"Top-notch, but the company commander won't listen to him."

"What is the company commander doing with this long run at this pace? Trying to impress me?"

"Yes, sir."

"Well, he has."

We returned to the assembly area, and waited for the remainder of the company and the company commander. I told Gravitt to get a couple of NCOs and police up the stragglers, have the first sergeant take charge of the company, reform them, and dismiss them as a unit while I had a talk with the company commander.

The company commander and I retired to his office in the orderly room. I told him how I wanted PT conducted. I figured I needed to get his attention early on.

There would be a platoon of recently arrived soldiers, an overweight platoon, and the remainder of the company. The platoons would be commanded by senior NCOs and would take calisthenics with the company, but they would do their morning run separately and on a different route from the rest of the company. The goal was for all soldiers to finish with their platoon or the company; therefore, the pace would be set to ensure they did. I would rotate between the platoons and the company on an unannounced schedule to observe and make corrections. Individuals from the "newbie" platoon and overweight platoon would be integrated into the company run when they progressed to that point.

I explained to the commander that PT was not just to keep a soldier physically fit but also to develop esprit de corps and unit cohesion. Soldiers needed to feel like part of a unit. And if they could not keep up and had to drop out of the formation, they were not being trained, and they certainly did not feel like part of the unit. All soldiers had to be brought to the minimum standard of two miles in sixteen minutes with a goal of three miles in twenty-four minutes. Soldiers who could do more and wanted to do more were to be encouraged to run on their own after the company was dismissed.

Further, the AG company would form at 0545 each morning rather than 0600. This would allow the company to complete calisthenics and begin the run at the time other units were forming. The company would look sharp. The AG guidon bearer would have the guidon flying high. A strong-voiced NCO would lead "Jodie calls," and the company would proceed by the other units forming up. I assured the company commander this would develop esprit de corps, and it did. The soldiers loved it, and their voices were strong as the company passed by other units. I got a few calls from battalion commanders to cease and desist, as I was disturbing their morning formations. I would let the soldiers know this, and that morning, we would run around the complaining unit's billets and assembly area. The soldiers really loved doing that.

I also wanted a weekly status report on the progress of the individuals in the overweight program. The Army required all soldiers who did not meet weight standards to enter the program. Those who were progressing had one year to meet the standards. I would periodically meet with the overweight soldiers for individual counseling.

The company commander had a difficult job, as only a few of the soldiers assigned to the company (twenty-eight that I recall) worked under his direct supervision. Thus, a turf battle could develop between him and the soldier's supervisors. They had competing interests and priorities. The supervisor needed the soldier to accomplish his AG tasks, and the commander needed the soldier to accomplish his soldier tasks. I did not want turf battles. Common sense was required on the part of each, and give and take was required. Soldiers did not need to be caught in the middle. The company commander, my officers, and my NCOs often had a difficult time coming to an accord, and Sergeant Major Gravitt and I ended up as the referees. To alleviate this problem, I directed that each Thursday be a training day and that AG soldiers would be under the control of the company commander, performing their soldier tasks at the company, such as attending mandatory classes as well as firing and cleaning weapons. All offices would be manned but only with a skeleton staff.

Sergeant Major Gravitt had purchased several acres between Fort Polk and DeRidder, which he planned to farm upon retirement. The acreage had a two-story farmhouse that he was remodeling, a barn, and various pens where he had his hogs. Chickens, guineas, dogs, and some peacocks completed his menagerie. There was open land for farming and a swamp at the back of the property. The swamp held alligators, snakes, and other assorted creatures.

Mrs. Gravitt, who was slender, attractive, and elegant, always dressed as if she were going to a tea (and she may have been), but she did not fit my image of a farmer's or a sergeant major's wife.

The first time Bill and I were in the field observing quarterly field exercises, he sidled up to me around 1700 and said, "Colonel, if you have no objection, I'm taking the jeep and going to garrison to check on things and get the message traffic. There may be something you need to see."

I had no objection, and Bill took off. He returned well after dark and reported there was nothing I needed to see. The next afternoon, he did the same thing, except an NCO came looking for him.

"Have you seen the sergeant major, sir?"

"He's gone to garrison to check on things," I said.

"Guess Mrs. Gravitt still won't feed the hogs."

When he returned that night, he did have several things I needed to see.

The third afternoon, he did the same thing, but this time, I challenged him.

"Mrs. Gravitt won't slop the hogs?" I said.

"Hell no, and she won't feed the chickens, either."

I left it at that. I could do without him for a few hours, and he did check on things, albeit at both the office and his farm.

Bill Gravitt retired shortly before I left the AG post.

The NCOs conducted the retirement ceremony. The ceremony included the troops and band passing in review as a final tribute to Gravitt. The NCOs put on a good show. They had flowers for Mrs. Gravitt and presented the sergeant major with several mementos of his time at Polk and in the army.

I escorted Mrs. Gravitt and Sergeant Major Gravitt to the parade field located between my office and the 5th Replacement Detachment. As a seventeen-year-old kid, Bill Gravitt had lied about his age and joined the Army. He retired with over thirty years of honorable, dedicated service. I reviewed Sergeant Major Gravitt's military career, said a few words of praise, and presented him with the Legion of Merit, which had been approved by a special awards board at DA.

The Legion of Merit is one of only three US decorations issued as a medal to be worn and displayed around the recipient's neck rather than hung from the chest, the standard practice for displaying most decorations. Notable recipients of the Legion of Merit are Admiral Hyman Rickover, father of the nuclear navy, and Audie Murphy.

Bill Gravitt joins George Wallace, Ed McGlynn, Sid Guidry, and Walt Dick, who all had a direct, profound, and positive effect on the military career of this boy from Barnhart. Any success I achieved can (in great part) be attributed to the support and mentoring of these fine senior NCOs.

A few situations occurred that I found funny then and still do.

One afternoon, my secretary came in and told me that one of the female soldiers needed to talk with me. I had an open-door policy, but I wanted Sergeant Major Gravitt to see the soldier first, as he could often help them without my involvement; however, Gravitt was not in his office. I knew the soldier. She was a good troop, and I told the secretary to show her in, but to stay in the office while I talked with her.

I told the young specialist to have a seat and inquired about what I could do for her.

"Sir, I have been letting the train run on me."
"You have been doing what?" I asked
"Letting the train run on me. You know, sir."
"No, I don't know."
I asked my secretary if she knew. She did not know.
I asked the soldier to explain.
"Sir, it is hard to explain," she said. "You know, letting the train run on me. The other females are talking about me. I am so embarrassed."
Bill Gravitt poked his head in the door as he saw I was talking to a soldier.
"Sergeant major, what in the hell is letting the train run on you."
"Sir, it is a gang-bang. Servicing three or four males while the others watch."
"I see," I said.
I was embarrassed for not knowing. The secretary was just embarrassed, and the soldier was embarrassed because the other females were talking about her.
We got her an appointment with a shrink, moved her out of the billet room she shared with three other females, and reassigned her to duty at Eagle Hall.
I do not know if that train kept running.
Another afternoon, Gravitt came in and said that he hated to bother me but that he had a situation he thought I should handle. A man, his wife, and their daughter, a private, wanted to see me. They would not talk to him because they wanted to talk to the big boss. I told him to show them into my office.
I figured the couple were farmers based on their dress. The father wore overalls, had on brogans, and held a "givme" cap in his hand. He was stout, perhaps six-foot-three, 210 hard pounds, with a ruddy complexion. He had a handshake like a vise. The mother was small, probably pretty at one time, with a sun-bleached face. The cotton dress she wore had seen many washes. They both talked in a soft, low voice.
The daughter was tall, had the body of an athlete, and was attractive. She said nothing. I thought her shy at the time. She was not.
The father told me they were poor people farming near Jasper, Texas, and had with them their most prized possession, their daughter. They wanted to see the man who would be responsible for her and ask that he watch over and take care of her. Her being in the Army

frightened them, but it was a chance for her to have a better life. The mother said that they were a Christian family and that the daughter had only been away from them when she had gone to basic training. They hoped their daughter could come home on weekends, as Polk was not far from Jasper.

I talked with them and explained where she would live and work, the normal duty day, and other things I thought might reassure them. I promised to look after her and thanked them for entrusting their daughter to my care.

They thanked me and left.

I had already decided where she would work. She was a 71L clerk-typist, and a slot existed for a typist in the officer records branch processing OERs. Her supervisor would be CW2 John Harrison.

John was outstanding in every respect. He was smart, energetic and career-motivated, and he had a good future ahead of him. I explained the situation to John, and he told me that he would keep an eye on her. And by golly, he did.

I would see the soldier periodically, inquire about her parents, and ask how she was doing. She was doing fine, and I knew it. She was an outstanding athlete as well as a leader, and she starred on the AG female softball, volleyball, and basketball teams, all of which won company-level championships. She was excellent in the field and the company, and she was an overall good soldier. Soon, she was a specialist four (E-4).

About eight months after she arrived, John came to see me and said, "Sir, I got married over the weekend."

"Great. Why wasn't I invited? Who's the lucky gal?"

"The Jasper girl."

"Do her parents know?"

"Yes, sir, her father gave me permission. They were at the wedding. We got married at the justice of the peace."

The company was in the field somewhere in the Kisatchie National Forest, with the troops preparing individual fighting positions, and others preparing positions for crew-served weapons (machine guns and mortars).

It was hot and getting hotter, so I told the soldiers they could remove their fatigue jackets and work in their T-shirts.

I was roving around and observing when I spied Kowalski. Kowalski was a case. She was loudmouthed, heavyset, all muscle, and she kept the others entertained with her constant chattering.

"Kowalski!'

"Yes, sir."

"Do you have a bra on?"

"No, sir," she said.

"Well, get one on."

She looked like she had two pigs wallowing around inside her T-shirt.

"It's too hot, sir. It irritates me."

"I'm going to irritate you if you don't put a bra on."

My rater for most of my Polk assignment was Lieutenant Colonel (P) Richard M. Scott, the division G-1. Dick was on the promotion list for colonel and primarily worked officer assignments, which were always a hodgepodge of problems because of the politics involved. He was an infantry officer, knew little about my business, and told me so.

"You run your shop. You can go direct to the chief of staff without coming through me. I don't need to hear from you unless you need my help."

I could work with that.

The chief of staff, my intermediate rater and real boss, was Colonel Cecil N. Neely. Colonel Neely would later be selected for promotion to brigadier general along with the 1st and 2nd Brigade commanders, and the commanders of the division artillery (DIVARTY) and the division support command (DISCOM). There were some exceptional colonels at Fort Polk.

Colonel Neely presented an imposing figure. He was tall, heavyset, looked like a professional football player, gruff in manner, short-tempered, profane, impatient, and could multitask with the best. On several occasions, I saw him put members of the division staff as well as his secretary near tears. I can only remember Colonel Neely "getting in my knickers" a couple of times, and that was over the division band.

I knew nothing about music. I am tone-deaf. Apparently, Neely was not. Monthly, a division retirement and awards ceremony, which was followed by a review, would be held on the parade field near headquarters. The band would provide the music for the occasion and would be one of the units marching in the review. I dreaded these ceremonies, as more than once, I got the hook and it all went the same way.

Neely would crook and waggle his finger at me. I would hurry over to where he was standing, and he would say, "Colonel, do you know your right foot from your left foot?"

I would respond, "Yes, sir."

And he would say, "Well, you're going to be leading that goddamn band if you don't get them shaped up."

Because I did not recognize the problem, I would let it go and say nothing to the bandleader, a CW4. I was sure he knew which member required additional practice. I had more than enough to say to the bandleader at other times that did not involve music.

In my initial interview with Colonel Neely, he told me that I had one of the most important and visible positions on the installation and that all at Fort Polk thought they knew how to sail my ship, including wives, officers, soldiers, and civilians. I had been selected because I had recent division experience, and that being in the 2nd Infantry Division was a plus as it was a tough place to soldier. He expected me to run a tight ship, but he would not tell me how to steer the ship, as I was the captain.

He said, "I expect good things from you, so don't let yourself down. If you have bad news, get to me quickly so I can get involved to help put out the fire."

What I heard him saying was he had enough on his plate without me coming up on his radar screen.

He went on to talk about me having the best of both worlds, as I had two budgets and two personnel authorizations, one as the division adjutant general and one as the installation adjutant general. He understood my situation very well. If I had division soldiers training in the field, I had civilians and a residual group of installation soldiers operating essential activities at garrison. Thus, there was no degradation of missions, which was not the case in the 2nd Division, where some routine missions suffered from lack of attention during field exercises.

Because I received dollars and people from both the division and installation, I generally received at least my fair share, allowing me to move monies and soldiers between division and installation accounts when necessary. All was transparent but never visualized or understood by any other entity at Polk, primarily because I was responsible for strength accounting for both the division and installation. What Neely did not know but I soon found out was that I was operating a subsidiary of the Government Printing Office (GPO), which resulted in another source of funding, ensuring that I received top-of-the-line reproduction equipment. My repro section did printing jobs for the federal government throughout Texas, Louisiana, and Arkansas.

He also told me that I could (and therefore I did) select soldiers from the replacement stream to perform key duties, particularly the band. If they were smart, could type, had an athletic background, or play a musical instrument, they were a potential candidate for assignment to the 5th AG Company or 5th Mech Band. The 5th AG Company rarely failed to win an installation championship in softball, basketball, or flag football.

I asked about my being a major having to work with lieutenant colonels and above for a time. Neely responded, "It could be a problem. We thought about that when we selected you. Apparently, it was not a problem in the 2nd Infantry Division, and I don't think it will be a problem now."

It was not, because I dealt directly with brigade commanders instead of their subordinate battalion commanders just as I had done in the 2nd Infantry Division. I suspect that Neely or General Palastra, the commanding general, had contacted someone from the 2nd ID for a recommendation before they had hired me.

Neely did tell me one thing that put me in a difficult situation more than once. He told me that the ADC-M, Brigadier General John Malcolm Kirk, had a habit of going directly to the staff for information and issuing orders to the staff.

He raised his voice and said, "You don't work for Kirk. You work for me. If he tells you to do something, you tell me. Any information you provide Kirk, you send through me. You do nothing for Kirk unless you clear it with me. Got it?"

"Yes, sir," I said.

It was obvious that a turf problem existed between the two.

Brigadier General John Malcolm Kirk was much like Brigadier General Hardass from my 2nd Infantry experience. Small, wiry, sharp-witted, extremely intelligent, and demanding, he loved soldiers and was probably the best trainer in the Army. Eventually, he was selected to head up the training directorate at DA, a major general's position. One difference from my 2nd Division time was that Kirk liked me.

His eventual downfall was his lack of tact. He simply did not care who he pissed off if he thought that they were in any way letting soldiers down. A poorly trained soldier was letting the soldiers down. I saw him take over squads and teach them how to accomplish a particular task, and I saw him get down on his belly in the dirt and give individual instruction to a soldier having trouble with his weapon.

Kirk emphasized training in individual infantry and armor skills and how to lead squads, platoons, and companies. A hallmark was his manual on aggressive tactics, which was tested during brigade rotations at the National Training Center at Fort Irwin, California. The 2nd Brigade of the 5th Mech defeated the opposing force (OPFOR) at the National Training Center on their home territory. It was the first time the OPFOR had been beaten during the initial phase of a training exercise. Kirk engineered that victory.

I had great respect for John Kirk as a soldier, leader, and person.

Annually, 5th Mech officers would evaluate training of reserve and national guard units at Camp Shelby, Mississippi. Kirk headed up this effort. Apparently, he was unhappy with the performance of the Mississippi National Guard and came down hard on their leaders, who cried to their senators, which resulted in General Palastra having to make a special trip to Mississippi to smooth over ruffled feathers. A similar incident happened when he was the training director at DA and on the promotion list to major general. This time, the recipients of his wrath were from the Massachusetts National Guard, and their senator was Teddy Kennedy. This unfortunate clash resulted in General Kirk retiring. The Army lost a great soldier.

Nothing I ever did pleased him, but I soon realized that was just his nature. If he called me to his office, I would be chided about being a staff puke with spit-shined boots, or if I had been in the field training, he would holler at me for tracking dirt on his clean carpet.

Colonel Neely's direction not to deal with Kirk put me in a difficult situation. Kirk would call me wanting information or asking me to take a specific action. I was in no position to tell a general no, and usually, his requests made sense. Initially, I sent responses to Kirk through Neely, but I would get a call from Kirk wanting to know when I would respond to his query. I realized Neely was not forwarding my information to Kirk. I decided to deal with Kirk directly. I am sure Neely knew. At first, I would tell Neely I was going to see Kirk or brief him after I had seen Kirk. This worked, but eventually, I was confident enough to say the hell with it and deal with them individually. However, I was still walking a fine line, and I knew it.

This I could do only because I had value to both!

Kirk used me, as did Neely.

Each wanted the mission accomplished.

My senior rater and the commanding general of the 5th Infantry Division (Mechanized) and Fort Polk was Major General Joseph T. Palastra, Jr. General Palastra could best be described as a hard-nosed soldier. A West Point graduate, the son of a career-navy enlisted man, he was religious but did not wear it on his sleeve. A nonsmoker, he rarely drank except for an occasional glass of wine. He had served three tours in Vietnam, during which he received the Silver Star and two Bronze Star medals with V-device.

He went on to serve as a lieutenant general commanding I Corps and Fort Lewis at Fort Lewis, Washington. Subsequently, as a four-star general, he became the commander of US Army Forces Command (FORSCOM) at Fort McPherson, Georgia, responsible for all combat units stationed within the continental United States (CONUS).

Anyone can become angry—that is easy. But to be angry with the right person, to the right degree, at the right time, for the right purpose and in the right way—that is not easy.
—Aristotle

General Palastra had a short temper, and I suffered his anger on several occasions.

The first occurred shortly after my arrival at Fort Polk. I was responsible for publishing the daily bulletin, which contained items of an official nature. The bulletin served as a daily communication from the commanding general to all personnel on the installation, including family members. Traditionally, the adjutant general signed the bulletin for the commanding general.

When summoned to his office, I reported to him. As he left me at attention, he berated me for disobeying one of his standing orders, specifically that no formations other than PT were to be held prior to 0800 each day, as the first hours of the duty day were to be spent by soldiers in physical training, personal hygiene, and breakfast.

My SIDPERS people had included an item that a class for all new unit adjutants would be held on a certain date beginning at 0730 hours. I was not aware of the general's policy, but my SIDPERS chief, a major, should have been. The major informed me that he had thought the policy came from my predecessor and had not been aware that it had come from the commanding general. Regardless, it was not an auspicious beginning with my senior rater.

Later, I received an envelope from General Palastra containing a daily bulletin. He had redlined a misspelled word on the bulletin with a cryptic note, "If you can't get this straight, I will find someone who can."

Now, I hated having to proofread and sign that bulletin. Invariably, the bulletin would not be ready for my signature until late in the duty day. The bulletin would contain poorly written items requiring rewriting and retyping. It resulted in an unnecessary burden on my secretary and the reproduction section, which had to stay after duty hours to reproduce and distribute the bulletin.

I had a female second lieutenant whose duties included a responsibility for the bulletin. This young officer had no ownership in the bulletin, as I was her proofreader. Therefore, I decided I would have her sign the bulletin "For the Commander" as an assistant adjutant general. Any problems with the bulletin would have a direct negative effect on her OER. I figured Palastra would tell me to sign the bulletin, but I never heard a peep. If there was a problem with the bulletin, I never heard about it. I suppose he as well as I allowed lieutenants to make mistakes.

One of the funny incidents with Palastra, although not at the time, involved his wife. I was summoned to his office, and Mrs. Palastra was there. General Palastra wanted to know why my bus had gone by a bus stop without picking up passengers. Apparently, Mrs. Palastra had observed a bus that had not stopped at a bus stop where soldiers were waiting. She followed the bus to the AG billets and demanded to know for whom the driver worked. The young soldier blustered, "Colonel Taylor."

Now there were several layers of leadership between this trooper and me, but I had made a big deal about the bus and the work that my soldiers had done in refurbishing the bus. Bill Gravitt and the NCOs picked a sharp, junior enlisted soldier weekly to drive the bus. It was a reward for the trooper, as he or she was free to do whatever they wanted when not driving.

I explained to General Palastra that my bus was not the post shuttle bus. It was used to transport my soldiers to and from work and meals. I went on to explain that billets for my soldiers, who worked in the old hospital complex, were two miles from their offices and a mile and a half from the DISCOM consolidated mess and that most of my junior enlisted members had no car. This resulted in many lost hours, as my soldiers had to depend on the post shuttle bus, which only ran every thirty minutes. I had found an old, worn-out, and rusting International bus in the installation motor pool. The installation transportation officer had signed the bus over to me. My mechanics and soldiers had refurbished the bus and were using the bus to get to and from work and meals.

The more I talked, the madder I became, especially because his wife had been the catalyst. I am sure General Palastra recognized my anger. He dismissed me, and as I shut the door behind me, he laid into Mrs. Palastra, telling her that he ran the installation, not her.

Early one morning, I received a call from General Palastra's aide-de-camp informing me that the general wanted to see me. I could tell by the aide's voice that it was not a social call. After I jumped in my jeep, I drove to headquarters. When I arrived outside the general's office, I found a closed door, and both the aide and secretary with their heads down.

I could hear both Colonel Neely and General Palastra in a heated discussion that went something like this:

"Sir, you can't relieve him. He is too good an officer."

"The last time I looked, I command this installation, and I can do anything I damn well please."

I could only presume they were talking about me. The voices quieted, and after what seemed like an eternity, Colonel Neely appeared.

"What are you doing here?"

"General Palastra wanted to see me."

"You have too much work to be up here 'chitchatting' with the general. Get back to work."

I had no clue about what I had done to piss off Palastra.

Another time when I was called by General Palastra's secretary to come see the general, I knew it would not be good. When I reported, I was left at attention, and he threw something, which hit me in the chest. I discovered that it was an ID Card. He hollered, "How the hell can a 'dirt bag' who has been kicked out of the Army and shoots out road lights on my installation still have an ID card in his possession."

"I have no idea, sir."

"Well, you damn well better find out."

After I retrieved the ID card, I headed for "Eagle Hall" and my out-processing section. Army regulations required unit commanders take possession of a soldier's ID once the commander initiated paperwork to have a soldier discharged for reasons of unsuitability. Commanders often failed to do so. Therefore, my folks had initiated procedures to do so, but often, the soldier would say he had lost his card. The soldier would be asked to sign a statement to that fact, and the statement would be turned over to the provost marshal for appropriate action, which had been done in this case. I reported this to General Palastra, and as I departed his office, he was telling his secretary to have the provost marshal come see him.

One task that caused me much misery was outside of my ability to correct. Army regulations required that any soldier being held past his expiration term of service (ETS) for medical treatment or any other reason had to be approved by the General Court-Martial Authority, which was General Palastra. Invariably, the hospital would notify my staff that a soldier required continued treatment the day of his ETS. My folks would prepare a staff paper outlining the situation and coordinate the paper with the staff judge advocate (SJA), and I would carry the paper to General Palastra. This would take some time, which resulted in the action getting to Palastra at the end of the duty day or even after duty hours, so I had to take the paper to his quarters. This incensed Palastra, and it particularly upset him if it happened on a

Wednesday, as he often played golf in the afternoon. I explained that I had no control over the hospital commander, as I was not in his rating chain. Palastra allowed that might be correct, but I was responsible for preparing all personnel actions requiring his signature, so it was my problem to work the issue out with the hospital commander. I begged and pleaded with the hospital commander, and usually, I would get a couple of days' notice. Occasionally, notification came the day of the soldier's ETS, and I would get another ass-chewing.

A matter I discussed with my officers and senior NCOs early on was the following: If a member of the command group showed up in their area, they were to let me know. The bandleader, a CW4, said that I would get many calls from him. I did not ask him to elaborate. Soon, I received a call that General Palastra would be visiting the band at 0900 that morning. It was now 0850, and the band practice/training area was across post. When I arrived at the band area, I spotted General Palastra's jeep and driver. When I entered a small auditorium, I witnessed a strange sight. General Palastra was sitting in a chair with his back to the band. His helmet was in his hands, and his eyes were closed. The band played for about ten minutes. General Palastra turned, shook hands with the bandmaster, thanked the band, and proceeded to leave. He gave me a "what you doing here" stare, got in his jeep, and left.

I asked the bandleader to explain what I had just seen.

"He comes up here periodically. We play him some tunes. I guess it relaxes him."

I told the bandleader not to call me.

Fort Polk was the first time I had supervised a band, and it would be the last, for which I am eternally grateful. They were prima donnas because of the attention they received, and they believed that they were different and unique and wanted be treated as such. They did not want to train with or run PT with the AG company. They wanted to do both separately. I knew that if I allowed them to do so, it simply would not happen. I had the responsibility of ensuring that they were physically fit and trained in their soldier skills, including weaponry. In fact, bands by Army doctrine at the time had the additional mission while in a combat zone of providing rear-area security. Therefore, the band received the same training as the rest of my soldiers.

Major Larry Hamilton, my deputy, kept up with the band, and he had a full-time job juggling their schedule. Every village, town, and city in a two-hundred-mile radius wanted the band to provide music for a variety of functions. Recruiting command wanted to use them in promotional activities. ROTC units wanted them to provide music at balls and proms, and the installation wanted them for various activities. They were required to be at all battalion or above-change-of-command ceremonies, and the requests for their participation was endless. The 5th Infantry Division (Mech) band enhanced the image of both the Army and Fort Polk, but sometimes they tried my patience.

One morning, I arrived at the office to find a call waiting for me from a professor of military science (PMS) at one of the Louisiana universities. The band had played at the university's military ball the previous night and was now on the road to another engagement. The PMS told me that when he was cleaning up after the ball, he had discovered that three of the fifty state flags used to decorate the ballroom were missing. He suspected that the band had taken them. I asked what states, and he told me.

I called CW4 Kelsey, my chief of enlisted records, and asked him to review the 201 files (individual personnel record) of members of the band to determine those who came from the states whose flags were missing. He did, and there was one band member from each of the three states. It did not take a rocket scientist to deduce who had taken the flags. The bandleader was called, the soldiers questioned, and the flags returned.

General Palastra and Penny pinning on my silver oak leaves upon my promotion to lieutenant colonel.
July 1, 1980

There were several things that General Palastra did in addition to commanding a damn fine Army combat division that stand out in my mind.

The 256th Infantry Brigade of the Louisiana National Guard, the division's "round out" brigade, came to Polk for their two-week annual training each summer. The PX parking lot would immediately fill up with assorted military vehicles, and the PX would be crowded with long lines. Penny would not go to the PX when the guard was on post. These people were at Polk to train, not shop, although it was recognized that they had ID cards that authorized them to shop in the PX when on active duty for training. Shopping at the PX was much like shopping at a Wal-Mart, except better, as there were no state or federal taxes. Big-ticket items like cameras, stereos, and TVs were bargains. General Palastra wanted to accommodate the guard, but the training mission came first. After all, they were to go to war with the division if necessary.

He directed that each Saturday afternoon and Sunday be guard time at the PX. Guardsman found at the PX during other times would be apprehended by the MPs, their vehicles booted, and their battalion commander called to retrieve them. This solved the overcrowding problem and improved guard accountability. I worked with the 256th during their training, and it would be three days after the training cycle started before they had any idea about who had shown up and who had not.

It was a kick for Penny to go by the PX and count the number of booted vehicles. After a couple of days, there were no military vehicles in the parking lot.

A delegation of city leaders from Leesville wanted to meet with General Palastra to complain about soldiers getting into fights in their bars, speeding, spitting on the street, public drunkenness, and the list went on and on. The more they complained, the tighter Palastra got. Finally, he had enough.

He explained that his mission was to train soldiers to kill and not be killed. To do that, he took them to the field, sometimes for several weeks, and the macho and testosterone built up. When they returned to garrison, the soldiers wanted to hit the bars and let off a little steam. Those soldiers that did get in trouble with civilian authorities would be appropriately disciplined by the military. However, if the problem was as dire as presented, he would declare Leesville off-limits to all soldiers except those married soldiers who lived within the city limits.

The backtracking and bootlicking began as they saw all those government dollars blowing away on the wind, a wind that they had created.

> *I have one criticism about the Negro troops who fought under my command during the Korean War. They didn't send me enough of them.*
>
> —Douglas MacArthur

Racism is ugly under any circumstance, but it is intolerable in your Army. Racism was prevalent in Louisiana during the 1980s, and I suspect it still is, as many Louisianans are still fighting the Civil War. It was usually subtle, but sometimes it was not.

The senior officers, colonel and above, had been invited to a function in Leesville. Conspicuously missing from the list of invitees was Colonel (P) Charles E. Honore, the commander of the 1st Brigade. Chuck Honoree, a black officer, would later be promoted to major general while he was serving as the deputy commanding general of the Fifth United States Army at Fort Sam Houston, Texas. General Palastra contacted the organization hosting the function and let them know that all his senior officers would be invited or none would attend the function. Colonel Honoree received an invitation.

There was much for white soldiers to do off-post, but little for blacks. White soldiers could hit the nightclubs, bars, and honkytonks or head to Shreveport, Lake Charles, or New Orleans, as many had cars. The blacks did not, and when they did go off-post, they found an intolerant and racist civilian populace in the surrounding area. Hence, black soldiers were limited to post activities, and those activities were limited. The bowling alley, theater, enlisted club, and craft shop were all excellent but did not fulfill all blacks soldiers' needs for excitement and fun.

The night belonged to black soldiers, and they frequented on-post facilities in mass. A few beers, wine, or malt liquor combined with boredom and a sense of isolation often resulted in trouble. The primary area of mischief became the dimly lit parking areas around enlisted billets. A group of blacks would congregate and intimidate the whites, particularly females. Sometimes there were fights and car windows smashed.

This situation was insufferable, and it took little time for General Palastra to act. He directed battalion commanders and their senior leaders, both black and white, to move into the barracks and set up roving patrols in the parking lots. All battalion commanders and most of their senior leaders were married, so it only took a short time for the foolishness to stop.

AWOLs were another area where General Palastra had no tolerance. He believed that if a soldier went AWOL, it was because the chain of command had let the soldier down. They did not know the soldier, and they were not aware of or were not helping the soldier with his or her particular problem. Battalion commanders shook in their boots when they had to explain why one of their soldiers had gone AWOL. I knew one battalion commander and his wife who would spend the night at the Leesville bus station when one of their soldiers had been reported AWOL, hoping to intercept the soldier before he left the area.

General Palastra felt that if you had a cold or flu, you should be home in bed, not at work spreading your germs to others. He also tried to end his duty day at precisely 1700. This was much different from any general that I had worked for before or since. Colonel Neely would leave around 1745. As he passed by my office on his way home, he would honk the horn on his old pickup, and I knew that I would not be needed the rest of the day.

It is funny what you remember from the past. Many senior commanders and staff, Colonel Joe Ecopi and me being the exceptions, drove pickups to work. Most pickups were old and secondhand—the more battered, the better. I suppose this was done to present the image of a rough, tough, and virile southern fighting man or whatever. Some were Yankees, so I am not sure what they were thinking. Perhaps they wanted to fit in with the rest.

Colonel Ecopi, the division artillery commander who was later promoted to brigadier general, and I drove Ford Pintos to work. Ecopi was hard on the division staff and his three subordinate battalion commanders but never me. I wonder if it was because we drove Pintos.

Another interesting phenomenon was that everyone except Palastra, Ecopi, and I chewed tobacco. The monthly command and staff conference was a hoot, as several coffee cans would be in continuous movement among the attendees to collect their spit. I wanted to puke when the mucky thing was handed to me to pass to another.

I also expected any day to see someone growing a full beard, Civil War-style, and the rest following suit.

Most, including me, carried a small bottle of Tabasco sauce on their person, and it would appear any time food was served. Tabasco is an amazing additive to Army chow.

A few months after my assignment to Polk, my old boss, Bill Gourley, had been promoted to brigadier general and had been assigned as the director of Enlisted Personnel Management, MILPERCEN. I knew that Gourley would not have learned yet to say no to other generals when they pressed him for soldiers. I persuaded General Palastra to send Gourley a back channel inviting him to Fort Polk. Gourley accepted, and it was his first visit to a field command. I was in charge of his visit, setting up briefings, lunch, dinner, and an opportunity to address enlisted soldiers. We pressed Gourley hard for more soldiers, particularly critical vacancies of senior NCOs, master gunners, and track mechanics. I knew that once Gourley had the spigot turned on at MILPERCEN, it would take several months to turn it off, and it did. In the meantime, I received calls from my friends at MILPERCEN, calls chiding me for taking advantage of Gourley's newness and proclivity for saying yes to anyone who outranked him.

I visited with Gourley in my office for a time, and he indicated that he wanted me to work for him after I completed my tour at Fort Polk. I hesitated to commit because I wanted to keep my options open. I saw General Gourley when TDY to MILPERCEN and visited with him at the Worldwide Military Personnel Conference held in Atlanta, Georgia, and many times when we were both assigned to MILPERCEN and later at the European Personnel Conference held in Garmisch-Partenkirchen, Germany. Over time, he realized I did not want to work for him, and our relationship became somewhat strained.

Captain Fred Barrell, my chief of enlisted management, and I were to make a presentation at the aforementioned conference in Atlanta, but

I was summoned to an audience with the DCSPER, DA, Lieutenant General Maxwell R. Thurman. Fred was left to make the presentation on his own.

General Thurman, known as "Mad Max" or "Maxatollah," a bachelor and a workaholic, rarely returned to his quarters at Fort Myer. Instead, he maintained several sets of uniforms in his office at the Pentagon. He would shave and shower in the Pentagon Officer Athletic Club (POAC). He was the author of the recruiting slogan "Be all you can be" when he was the commanding general of the USA Recruiting Command (USAREC).

He was brilliant, demanding, ruthless, and he did not suffer fools lightly. He was particularly hard on colonels and generals, and he had no compunction about berating them before their subordinates. It was not unusual for staff officers working directly with Thurman to develop a physical illness or pass out from sheer exhaustion in the halls of the Pentagon. Subordinates either hated or loved Max Thurman, but all admired his vision for the Army, his organizational skills, and his intelligence.

Thurman would be appointed a four-star general as the vice chief of staff of the Army (VCSA). He later commanded SOUTHCOM, which, on December 20, 1989, invaded Panama (Operation Just Cause) to capture Manuel Noriega. It was highly unusual for the VCSA to continue to serve after relinquishing the position, but Thurman was a master at manipulating the system and the administration of President George H. W. Bush in this case.

General Thurman was at the conference to meet with installation, division, and MACOM adjutant generals. His message was that reenlistments had been so high that the Army was in danger of breaking congressionally mandated strength levels. He directed that commands meet reenlistment quotas received from DA at the 100 percent level. There would be reenlistments neither greater nor lesser than the DA-imposed quota. The only acceptable performance was 100 percent, not 97 percent and certainly not 103 percent. We were to return to our commands, brief our commanding general, and then brief all subordinate commanders of the new requirement. He also told us that he was sending a back channel to our commanding general, one informing him of the DA mandate. If they had a question, they were to call him directly, and he would explain the requirement to them. I can assure you that no commander wanted to call Max Thurman.

This was a sea change. Commanders took great pride in reenlisting more soldiers than their fellow commanders, and competition between units and installations was keen. In fact, awards were given to commanders and their reenlistment staffs for reenlisting the highest percentage of soldiers.

I welcomed the change, as I had long felt that commanders reenlisted too many soldiers who were poor performers in the competition to reenlist as many soldiers as possible. These soldiers often reenlisted for another duty station. Thus, the poor performers were shuttled back and forth within the Army. Eventually, they were discharged for unsuitability, and it was my people who had to process the paperwork.

I returned to Polk and briefed General Palastra. He had all commanders assembled, and I briefed them. I had been taught when briefing to be brief, be brilliant, and be gone. This was not a problem in this case. There were no nuances, and no need for a lengthy explanation.

Penny and Ross drove to Fork Polk after Ross graduated. Penny had rented the house to a couple with two kids, or so we thought. Actually, the couple was divorcing, which resulted in the kids being unsupervised by a father, which is usually trouble.

Penny had shipped our household goods before Ross had graduated, and they had camped out for a few days. The household goods had arrived, and I had the mover unpack all the boxes, so items were scattered throughout the rented house when Penny arrived. I tried to put all in their places, but doing so after work, I made little headway.

Furious, worn out from the drive to Louisiana, she told me that she could not deal with the mess. She and Ross were going to Austin to visit her parents for a few days. Then she was going to take Ross to various Texas colleges and universities and shop him around for a basketball scholarship, which she did. Most schools were interested and offered various forms of aid, but a full ride would be dependent on how he did as a walk-on freshman. This kid from Virginia had not shown up on their radar screen when they had been recruiting.

Penny left Ross with Uncle Phil for the summer and returned to arrange the household in her usual efficient manner. She became active in the Polk Red Cross and Officers' Wives' Club, organizing her girls for various activities. I had some twenty-five to over thirty officers working for me at various times, and most were married. The AG ladies' group was the largest at Polk.

Her main interest became pursing her college degree. Northwestern Louisiana State University, which was located in Natchitoches, offered many courses at the Leesville/Polk Education Center. Later, she would drive to Natchitoches three nights a week for on-campus courses. Natchitoches was an attractive, historical town, and the university campus was quite pretty. We went to the campus for several events and visited the town a few times. The movie *Steel Magnolias* starring Julia Roberts, Sally Fields, Shirley MacLaine, and Dolly Parton and *Horse Soldiers* starring John Wayne and William Holden were both filmed in Natchitoches.

Penny graduated Northwestern at the end of the fall semester of 1982. She was so proud of that diploma, and so was I. Grandmother Farr came up for the graduation ceremony and spent a few days with us.

School and ultimate graduation were one of the few things Penny found to enjoy at Fort Polk. She loved Louisiana history and became interested in bird watching. There were many different types of birds to watch, but she never really cared about her Fort Polk activities. She was merely being the good Army wife, marking time until she could get back to Virginia.

Two traumatic incidents occurred while at Polk that soured her on the whole deal. First, Ross went off to college. She was no longer in control of an important part of her life. Her little boy was now a man showing independence, although reluctantly, and he was out of the house and her sight. The empty nest syndrome was alive and well in the Taylor household.

The experience of choosing a college had not been easy for either Penny or Ross. Penny had all kinds of ideas about where he should go, and Ross had none.

Finally, it was time to go with no decision made.

The decision was made by default.

I knew where Ross was going. Tarleton was the only institution of higher learning about which I had personal knowledge, and it held a special place in my heart and mind.

When I reached Tarleton State University, I drove to Wisdom Gym and the office of the basketball coach, Sherman Perry. After I left Penny and Ross in the car, I found Coach Perry and told him I was giving him an early Christmas present, but that it came with a string attached. Ross had only recently applied to Tarleton, and acceptance paperwork had not been received; however, I was sure Perry could take care of that small detail. Perry had reviewed Ross's high school film. He told me that he had no idea that he had had a chance to get Ross and he was delighted with his Christmas gift.

Penny and I left Ross and his possessions standing with Coach Perry on the steps of Wisdom Gym. When we departed, I could see students moving into Bender and Ferguson Hall. The trip home was quiet, except for some periodic weeping.

If there are no dogs in heaven then when I die, I want to go where they went.
—Will Rogers

The other traumatic incident involved the loss of her precious dog, Gigi. After about a year, we moved into government quarters on Fort Polk at 5511B Gardner Street. Our neighbors were interesting people. He was a lieutenant colonel serving as the deputy commander of the "Warrior Brigade," the headquarters for all units not assigned to the 5th Mech. He had a most unusual childhood. He and his wife were both Jewish, and when he had been a child, he had been hidden from the *Gestapo* in an attic for almost five years. A male Anne Frank, he was in demand as a speaker in the local communities.

Both he and his wife were unusual, as were their children. I would be out mowing my portion of the lawn on a Saturday morning, and he would call my deputy, Major Larry Hamilton, about some trivial matter; however, he would not say a word to me. She would discover Penny was hosting a luncheon or tea for her girls and ask if she could borrow Penny's flower arrangement, silver, and china. Penny never saw anyone at her home, so we presumed she used them to set her family table. Once, she found a cigarette that I had dropped in their carport and berated me about the possibility of her children's exposure to such filth. More than once, the children, a fat little boy and fat little girl, would get off the school bus and find their mother gone and the house locked. The woman rode the shuttle bus, as she did not know how to drive. Penny would see them shivering in the cold and have them come in for a snack, but never did the children nor the parents so much as say thanks. In addition, the woman either was scared of Gigi or did not like dogs, as she would eye Gigi warily any time we had her in the front yard.

Gigi was becoming blind and incontinent, and it was time to put her down; however, Penny was not ready. Penny would get up with me at 0515 every morning and put her out in our small, fenced-in backyard. One morning, she put Gigi out, and a few minutes later, she went to let her back in; however, she was gone. The backyard fence had enough space that Gigi could have slipped under the fence and went into the neighbor's yard or out the back and into the Kisatchie National Forest, which was immediately behind our duplex.

Penny and I looked all around the duplex. We even walked into the forest with no luck. Penny was now beside herself. I went to morning PT and asked Sergeant Major Gravitt if he could get a few volunteer soldiers to help me look around the housing area and in the forest. After I returned to the house, I continued to look. I remembered that it was a dog's instinct to crawl off and hide when it neared death. I figured that was what Gigi had done. Shortly, Sergeant Major Gravitt and fifteen or so soldiers arrived, and we thoroughly searched the area to no avail.

I went on to work. Around midmorning, the thought occurred that perhaps Gigi had crawled into the neighbor's backyard. The woman had seen her, gone outside to shoo her away, and hit Gigi with a broom or something, and in her weakened condition, Gigi had died. Being frightened, the woman had placed Gigi's body in a garbage sack and deposited her in the trash dumpster. I immediately went home and checked the dumpster. It was empty. The trash had been picked up that morning.

I never told Penny this. Perhaps I am wrong, but that woman could never look me in the eyes. She would quickly duck back in her house and avoid us if she realized we were outside.

A Boy from Barnhart

Dogs are not our whole life, but they make our lives whole.
—Roger Caras

Each day, I would trek fifty yards out into the forest for ten days or so, thinking I might smell a decomposing body, but I never did. Penny grieved over Gigi until we left Fort Polk. The day we left, she asked me once again to go into the forest, thinking I might find some bones. Penny wanted and needed closure. She blamed herself for not standing at the door and watching Gigi that cold, dreary February morning. Penny said that she did not ever want another dog.

The social life at Fort Polk was that of a typical Army post. A monthly "Hail and Farewell" was held on a Friday night for all officers and wives at the Officer's Club. The command group and principal staff would have a monthly cocktail party in the home of one of the officers. A three-day, semiannual goals conference held at an off-post site, such as Alexandria, Shreveport, or Lake Charles, for key officers and their wives included both work and nightly social activities.

Penny and I would host a periodic function like a cocktail party or barbeque and beer bust for my officers and their wives. I would hold weekly officer calls on Friday night at the Officer's Club for my officers, and the wives would usually join us for dinner. Most Wednesdays after my weekly staff meeting, officers would go to a local barbeque for lunch.

There would be installation-wide activities for the Fourth of July, Mardi Gras, the US Army's birthday, and an annual retiree open house for which I was responsible. The Officers' Wives' Club would host periodic functions, such as a casino night and dinner theatre.

Some other fun things we did included a weekend retreat for the AG and G1 officers and wives and attending the 1982 NCAA Final Four Basketball Tournament at the Superdome in New Orleans. This was a neat trip, because we stayed in the VIP suite at Jackson Barracks, the headquarters of the Louisiana National Guard, and saw some great basketball.

Lieutenant Jim O'Neil, an outstanding young officer, was the chief of my personnel actions branch in charge of some very visible and important functions, including the operation of the Fort Polk Casualty

Operations Center (COC). The COC was responsible for all casualty notifications within the state of Louisiana and ten counties in Texas. The DA COC, which was operated by the Army adjutant general, would notify the Polk COC of the death or serious injury of a soldier whose family resided within the Polk geographical area of responsibility. Polk then became responsible for notifying the deceased or injured soldier's family and designation of a casualty assistance officer (CAO) who would assist the family in settling the deceased's estate and obtaining any government benefits due the soldier. The Polk COC operated 24-7-365. It had assigned some very responsible NCOs. Notifications had to be timely, professional, and flawless. The battalion responsible for quarterly duty as the installation support battalion would provide the casualty notification officer (CNO), chaplain, and CAO. These officers trained by the Polk COC were also provided a detailed brochure spelling out their specific duties and covering most situations that might arise. The Polk COC also used officers from the Louisiana National Guard and US Army ROTC units when notifications some distance from Polk were necessary.

One day, I received a call from Major General Ansel M. Stroud, Jr., the Adjutant General for the State of Louisiana. General Stroud had been called by a friend that had a son assigned to one of the ranger battalions at Fort Lewis, Washington. The friend had heard that a plane carrying soldiers from the battalion had crashed in the California desert, and he was concerned that his son might have been on that plane. The son was the battalion commander's driver.

Each morning, the COC briefed me of casualties received during the night and the status of notifications. My folks had nothing on the crash. I told General Stroud that I would call the DA COC and find out what I could. General Stroud told me he had called but that DA would tell him nothing, as the information had to come through the Polk COC. He asked I call him if notice did come. He wanted to serve as the notification officer. When I called DA Casualty, I was told that a C-130 had crashed in California and that the battalion commander was reportedly on the plane. However, because most were burned beyond recognition, positive identification had not been made. I notified General Stroud and cautioned that he could release no information, especially that the battalion commander might have been on the plane. I called Stroud each morning to tell him I had received nothing from DA. Finally, notified that the soldier had been killed, I informed General Stroud. By this time, we had become good telephone friends, and he told me anytime I came to New Orleans, he wanted me to stay in his private suite at Jackson Barracks.

The rest of the story is that Lieutenant O'Neil's father was an advertising executive and that his firm had the University of Louisville account. Thus, his father had several tickets for the 1982 NCAA Final Four Tournament, which was to be played in New Orleans, four of which he would give to Jim. Jim knew that both Penny and I were basketball aficionados and offered me two tickets. Jim, his wife, Penny, and I drove to New Orleans for the games and stayed in General Stroud's suite at Jackson Barracks. Penny and I would stay at Jackson Barracks again when we were visiting New Orleans. Once was for Mardi Gras, as the 5th Mech Band marched in the annual parade.

Jackson Barracks suffered extensive damage during Hurricane Katrina, with most of it under twenty-two feet of water, and all buildings were destroyed or significantly damaged. Built in 1834 and a national historical site, $250 million in state and federal funds are being used to restore this venerated and old installation.

Another pleasure during this time was getting to visit with Mike and Ann Torrans, our friends from Turkey and Vietnam, and Dexter Hancock, our friend from Japan.

Mike, a DAC, worked in civilian personnel and held a reserve commission as a lieutenant colonel. He would later retired as colonel. Mike would do his annual reserve training with me. Mike and Ann lived in Leesville, where Ann taught school.

Dexter was completing an internship with the Bayne-Jones post hospital for his master's degree in hospital administration. Dexter, now a lieutenant colonel, had bought an airplane and was paying for it by giving flying lessons or ferrying folks to different places. He flew Penny one time for sightseeing and a meal. Dexter would come to the house and fix one of his gourmet meals, which we always enjoyed. Shelley, his wife, came to Polk once, and we all drove to New Orleans for a weekend and ate at Antoine's. Dexter retired as a colonel and is now enjoying the good life in Alabama. I do not remember where Shelley was during Dexter's time at Polk, but I think she was teaching at Penn

State, her alma mater. I lost a bet to the Hancocks when Alabama beat Texas in the national championship football game.

Penny and I went to see a few of Ross's basketball games, but not nearly as many as we would have liked. I remember his game against Baylor University during his sophomore year, when he ran circles around their guards.

In July 1981, General Palastra departed Fort Polk for his next assignment as chief of staff of the Eighth US Army/US Forces in Korea, located in Seoul, Korea. Colonel (P) Neely, now on the promotion list to brigadier general, had the division staff assembled at the main gate of Polk. We saluted in unison as General and Mrs. Palastra drove off. We then retired to the Officer's Club, where we entertained each other with Palastra stories. Neely kicked the occasion off by saying, "Palastra fired each of you once, except for Taylor. He fired Taylor four times." I believe most of us did not want to see General Palastra depart, as we had great respect for him—one hard-nosed soldier indeed.

He may have fired me four times, with Neely talking him out of it, but he took care of me on my OER. The last two remarks read, "General officer potential. Capitalize on it."

Major General Edward C. Peter succeeded General Palastra. General Peter's previous assignment had been as chief of the Office of Legislative Liaison (OCLL) in the Pentagon. He had fought in both the Korean and Vietnam War and had been awarded two Silver Stars. General Peter's last assignment would be as a lieutenant general serving as the commanding general of Fourth Army at Fort Sheridan, Illinois. He had a wealth of combat and command experience, but I never felt that he was comfortable as the commanding general of the 5th Infantry Division (Mechanized).

Shortly before Palastra departed, Neely called to inform me that the division protocol officer was leaving and that he wanted one of my female officers to replace her.

"Taylor, you know what I want."

"Yes, sir. Blonde, blue eyes, small waist, long legs, and big tits, right?"

"Yeah, and she'd better be pretty, too."

Now it just so happened that I had recently been assigned a second lieutenant by the name of Votsmier that fit the bill exactly, and I do not think that Neely knew about her.

I called Neely back and told him I was sending Lieutenant Votsmier up for an interview.

"She'd better be good."

"Yes, sir, she is."

Later, Neely called me. "Damn you, Taylor. I knew you had one. Lieutenant Votsmier will do just fine." Soon, Lieutenant Votsmier became known as Lieutenant "Titsmier," and that spoke volumes about how well she was endowed. The fatigue jacket is not flattering to the female figure.

The first day after General Peter assumed command, Neely had the principal staff officers, including Lieutenant Votsmier, lined up in a hallway at division headquarters to introduce each. When he reached Votsmier, Neely said, "And this, sir, is your protocol officer, Lieutenant 'Titsmier.'" The staff could barely keep from laughing as Neely never realized his faux pas, and I do not think Peter caught it, either. Votsmier made an outstanding protocol officer. She was professional in every aspect. I am sure she was aware we called her Lieutenant "Titsmier" behind her back, but she could soldier with the best.

My initial briefing to General Peter went quite well, but he quizzed me extensively about my congressional liaison activities as I knew he would in view of his prior assignment. I explained that most were health and welfare inquires received either in writing or by phone from OCLL. Inquires from a Louisiana congressional representative either Senator J. Bennett Johnston, Senator Russell B. Long or the local representative, Claude "Buddy" Leach would be brought to his attention. A response would be prepared for his signature, if appropriate. Any inquiry that might reflect unfavorably on Fort Polk would also be brought to his attention. My congressional liaison folks answered routine phone requests from OCLL, and I signed all written responses to inquires not involving Louisiana congressional representatives. I told him my folks briefed me daily on the status of all active congressional inquiries.

This seemed to satisfy him, and he admitted that we had a good reputation at OCLL for timely and professional responses. However, my congressional liaison folks soon began to spend more and more time in his office, briefing him on routine congressional matters. I began to think that his comfort zone remained at him being a staff officer dealing with congressional inquires rather than commanding. Eventually, I discussed the situation with Neely, and we decided to move my folks to the command group so that they did not have to keep running back and forth to see Peter.

Another area in which Peter showed interest was the annual retiree open house, for which I was responsible. This was an all-day affair. It was held on a Saturday and involved the entire installation. There would be static displays of tanks, howitzers, helicopters, and armored personnel carriers, with soldiers available to answer questions about the equipment. The medical folks would be there to give immunizations and eye tests and check blood pressure. The staff judge advocate would prepare wills and powers of attorney. Other activities, including the Officers' Wives' Club, NCO Wives' Club, Red Cross, PX, and VFW would all have information booths.

The day started with a welcome from the commanding general and chairman of the Fort Polk Retiree Council. Speakers from DA would brief on the status of the Army and recent and pending legislation of interest to retirees. I would introduce each to the audience. Attendance for the day's activities would be over 1,200 retirees. Attendees rode buses to dining facilities for some good army chow, which they enjoyed. All manner of problems could arise during this long day.

The Fort Polk Retiree Council assisted me in the planning for this effort. The council met quarterly or more often if necessary and consisted of nine retirees from the serviced area of Louisiana and the ten counties in Texas. A retired major general chaired the council.

Determined to have the best possible open house, I called the Army retirement services officer (RSO) at DA and asked who put on the best open house. The answer was Fort Carson, Colorado. A friend, Lieutenant Colonel Frank Foster, a classmate from the adjutant general career course, happened to be the adjutant general of the 4th Infantry Division (Mechanized) at Carson. I called Frank and asked if I could come and observe their open house. Frank agreed, and I went and stayed with Frank and his wife, Linda, and had a great time. Moreover, I borrowed several of Frank's best ideas while I was there. Frank introduced me to his division commander, Major General

Hudachek. He told me there was another officer I should meet. Frank considered the officer to be one of the best and brightest he had known and thought he would go to the top of the Army. He introduced me to Brigadier General Colin Powell, the assistant division commander. Obviously, Frank knew what he was talking about.

General Palastra did not get involved in the planning for the open house other than to tell commanders to give me whatever support I needed. General Peter wanted to get involved in the details, and he nearly drove me crazy, rehearsing the welcome speech that I had written for him. I listened to that speech several times as he rehearsed and asked me how it sounded.

"Fine, sir," I always said.

One morning, Neely called and told me that Claude Anthony "Buddy" Leach, Jr., a democrat, local Leesville boy, and member of the US House of Representatives, was on his way to my area to talk to my civilians. He wanted me to meet Leach and show him around. Leach, the incumbent, had Buddy Roemer running against him, and the race happened to be tight, with both throwing dirt on the other.

I met Congressman Leach at the front entrance of my complex, held out my hand, and tried to introduce myself. Two burly men on either side of Leach brushed me aside as Leach headed for my printing and reproduction section, where most of my civilians toiled and where the union representative for the American Federation of Government Employees (AFGE) worked. It was obvious Leach knew where he was going. When I tried to enter the room through double doors with Leach, the two thugs took me by the arm, and one said, "You do not want to go in there, colonel." One closed the doors, and both stood in front of the doors, precluding anyone from entering. Leach stayed in the room a short time and left as he came. This was my introduction to Louisiana politicians. Roemer defeated Leach, and I was to have a similar experience with Roemer. I do not have a favorable impression of either Louisiana politics or politicians. Louisiana has a long and rich history of political arrogance.

I discovered that the Adjutant General's Corps was to access additional second lieutenants from ROTC over and above worldwide authorizations. This was necessary because of projected shortages of

AG field-grade officers in the out-years. To fill the predicted shortages, it was necessary to start accessing lieutenants and grow them so they could eventually fill the projected vacant major and lieutenant colonel authorizations twelve to eighteen years down the road.

I saw an opportunity to obtain and train second lieutenants above my authorizations. When I called the AG officer assignment branch, I asked that they assign me eight of the brand new second lieutenants, which they did. My reputation at AG branch was that I turned out good lieutenants while I weeded out the poor ones.

My philosophy, which I reinforced with my captains and majors, was that it was best for the Army and the individual to return poorly performing lieutenants to civilian life rather than allow them to invest some ten or more years in the Army only to be kicked out. Army policy required an officer be discharged if he were twice passed over for selection to the next higher grade. It was my experience that too many lieutenants were promoted to captain, ones who could not perform as a captain, eventually not being selected for major twice.

The Army had a mechanism to weed out poorly performing second lieutenants that was rarely used. Second lieutenants were automatically promoted to first lieutenant after eighteen months of active service. However, an officer in the grade of lieutenant colonel or higher could delay the promotion for six months to give a poor performer the chance to improve. If the lieutenant had not progressed, his promotion could be denied, and he would be separated from the service.

After some seventeen years, I was confident that I could identify second lieutenants who had a future in the Army and those who did not. The only lieutenants who gave me pause were the lieutenants who graduated the Historical Black Colleges (HBC). Too many officers from these institutions were behind both their white and black counterparts from integrated universities. The primary deficiencies were in oral and written communication. Some could not write a complete sentence, much less a paragraph. I found, however, that with counseling, training, and mentorship, most of these officers could compete favorably with their peers over time. Some could not, as some white lieutenants could not, and it was these officers that I wanted to identify.

My strategy was that I would serve as the senior rater on all lieutenant OERs. I cautioned my captains and majors not to send me a bad OER on a lieutenant without counseling statements attached. It was neither professional nor fair to write a poor OER unless the officer had been counseled regarding their deficiencies throughout the rating period and given guidance as to what they could do to improve their performance. If I received a bad report without counseling statements, I would include this entry in their OER: "This officer does not take care of his subordinates."

I had one lieutenant from a HBC that caught my attention early on, as he spoke the hip-hop language of the ghetto. I simply could not understand what he was trying to say. He wrote the same way. I directed his rating officer, a black captain who was also from a HBC, and his indorsing officer, a black major, to counsel this officer often and ensure they documented the counseling, giving the officer a copy of the counseling statement and having him sign and date the statement. I further directed that when the officer briefed me, either informally or formally, both would rehearse him. I wanted to ensure that this lieutenant had every opportunity to succeed, as I did with all officers, but I suspected it was futile in his case.

The major came to me and asked that he be allowed to serve as the senior rater of the lieutenant rather than me. The major believed that the officer had potential and that his mentorship as a black officer would succeed where mine as a white officer might not. I knew it was wrong, a mistake, but I acquiesced.

The lieutenant's rater was one of those officers promoted to captain who was not capable of functioning at the level expected of a captain. He had gone to law school at an HBC, but upon graduation, he had been unable to pass his state bar exam. Therefore, he had been commissioned in the Adjutant General's Corps rather than the Staff Judge Advocate Corps.

He apparently wanted to continue pursuing a law career. I received a call from the DISCOM commander, who wanted to know if I knew that my captain spent more time in his headquarters than mine. Colonel Taylor reported that anytime a black soldier was to receive nonjudicial punishment, my captain was there as the spokesperson for the soldier. I did not know this, but I soon got the captain straight, explaining that his duty position was in the AG, not the DISCOM, and he was not a lawyer, so he should stop trying to act like one. I presented him with a counseling statement.

This same captain allowed the lieutenant to take a job as a disc jockey at the Officer's Club. Only a lieutenant colonel or higher could approve outside employment. I found out when a shoving match ensued between the lieutenant and another officer over only black music being played at the Officer's Club. This resulted in an MP blotter entry. The chief of staff and the commanding general also reviewed the blotter, so I soon got a call to explain. I made another counseling statement for the captain, and there were several more over time. The rating I gave the captain was such that he realized that he had no future in the Army.

The division was in the field, conducting a brigade-level training exercise, and I was at the tactical operations center (TOC) for morning briefings. I was handed a note to report to the division inspector general (IG). What the hell? I had no idea why the IG wanted to see me. It must have been important to pull me out of the field.

The division IG, Lieutenant Colonel (P) Guy A. LaBoa, was a friend. Guy had been the division G3 (Operations) and was now the IG. Guy would go on to command the 4th Infantry Division (Mech) at Fort Carson and later the First US Army at Fort Gillem, Georgia, retiring as a lieutenant general. He was not friendly that day, just professional.

He told me that one of my lieutenants, the one previously mentioned, had written a letter to the NAACP accusing me of racial discrimination. The NAACP forwarded the letter to the DOD IG and requested an investigation and response. The DOD forwarded the letter to the DA IG for investigation. Guy told me later the DA IG had intended to conduct the investigation, but he had talked DA into sending the action to him. Colonel LaBoa placed me under oath and told me that the session would be recorded. He then proceeded to question me. I discerned that the key point was the following allegation: "I had directed a 'black book' be kept on the lieutenant, and I intended to have him kicked out of the Army."

I explained all that had transpired with this lieutenant. I had never used the words "black book" in my conversations with the officer's rating chain, although I might have said, "Keep a book on him," when I was referring to the counseling statements. The lieutenant had not mentioned in his letter to the NAACP that his rater and senior rater were black.

I went on to tell LaBoa that when it came time to write a report on the lieutenant, the major asked me to look at a draft and advise him before the report was sent to MILPERCEN. The report was a "zinger," but it was poorly written. I asked the major to let me see the counseling statements written by him and the captain, but there were none. Any counseling—and I doubted that there had been much—had been done orally. Accordingly, I suggested that the report be rewritten and watered down because of a lack of counseling statements. I also told the major that I would senior-rate the lieutenant on all future reports.

Subsequent questioning of the captain and major by Colonel LaBoa confirmed all that I had done and said. The captain divulged that it was he who told the lieutenant that a "black book" was to be kept. Later, LaBoa called to tell me that his report had been sent to DA, DA had forwarded it to DOD, and the matter was closed. I am quite sure it was the captain who suggested the lieutenant write the NAACP.

There is twist to this tale that would have cooked my goose had it surfaced. I had a habit of calling my lieutenants by nicknames when I was being friendly with them much like President Bush did when he told the head of FEMA, "Good job, Brownie." Lieutenant Jim O'Neill became Jimbo. Tommy became Tombo, and so on. This lieutenant's first name was Samuel, and he was called Sam. When I was heading down the hall one day to one of my offices, my mind elsewhere, I saw Sam at the water cooler and said, "Morning, Sambo." I immediately knew I had committed an egregious and unpardonable blunder, but Sam mumbled, "Morning, sir." He either did not hear me or was too damn dumb to realize that I had committed a terrible racial slur. It was spontaneous and without malice but inexcusable. This slip of the tongue was a wake-up call, and I became conscious of how I addressed lieutenants the rest of my career. Sometime afterward, when I was visiting with Guy LaBoa, I told him, and he told me I was a very lucky fellow.

Later, when I was chief of the Adjutant General Officer Assignment Branch at MILPERCEN, I had my captain assignment officer review his captain files to identify those who had been consistently poor performers. I did the same with majors and lieutenant colonels. The purpose was to forward files of those officers who had not already been passed over to a "show cause" board. I loathed assigning officers to a command when I knew they were poor performers and would continue to be poor performers. They were a blemish on the reputation of the AG Corps. It was much like a banker purging his books of bad loans. One of the officers identified was now Captain Sam. His performance had not improved with time. The "show cause" board selected him for separation, and soon, he was a civilian.

There were three Taylors assigned to the division: Colonel (P) James Taylor, the assistant division commander for support (ADC-S), who eventually retired as a major general; Colonel Sam Taylor, the DISCOM commander; and me. Sam Taylor, no relation, was an outstanding officer, and I am confident, had he not been retired on a medical disability, would have been promoted to flag rank.

I would receive calls from battalion commanders, and the conversation would go as follows:

"Herb, I'm returning your call."

"Good to hear from you, but I did not call."

"Shit! I was hoping it was you," they would say.

"Understand."

"Talk to you later."

"Roger."

"Out."

Those lieutenant colonels knew, as did I, if colonels Jim or Sam called, it was not to make small talk.

I had bought Ross a Chevy Nova from one of my lieutenants the summer before Ross's sophomore year. The car was adequate to get Ross around Stephenville, Austin to visit his grandparents, and Polk to visit us. I remember paying a thousand dollars for the vehicle.

After we arrived in Austin for a visit with Grandmother and Granddad Farr, Penny handed me a bill from a local automotive shop that her dad had given her. He told Penny that he had Ross' car in good shape, but it still needed some work. The automotive shop apparently wanted to be paid before they did more work on the car. The bill was for over $850.00. The car was hardly worth that much, but Granddad Farr was on the hook for payment. I went to the mechanic and paid him. I was pissed, but I said nothing. I was anxious to see the vehicle and inspect all that had been done. Several days later when I arrived at Tarleton and Crockett Hall, the athletic dorm, made small talk, and asked about his car, Ross informed me the car would not start.

One of his roommates said, "It's not a problem. Ross never knows where his car is anyway."

I was intrigued.

We proceeded to the parking lot and found the Nova. We tried to jump start the car, but it would not turn over. We bought a battery. The car now started, and I noted that the car had new tires, spark plugs, wiring, and a muffler. I saw that the wiper blades needed replacing and that the state inspection was overdue. I asked when the oil had last been changed, but Ross did not know. It was not an item on the $850.00 invoice.

We went to Montana's for dinner, along with a couple of Ross's teammates. Montana's is the place to eat in Stephenville. Owned by a Tarleton graduate, the servers are cute (Tarleton girls), the food good, and the bartender makes a terrific martini. I was no longer out of sorts. I listened as the boys talked, and the yarn about Ross's not knowing the location of his car slipped out.

Apparently, a Stephenville restaurant would comp Ross for food based on how many points he had scored. Ross had driven to the restaurant one night after a game. He ate, left, and absentmindedly walked back to Crockett Hall. A few days later, he looked for his car in the parking lot and did not find it. He was not worried and told his friends it would show up, and it did. Several weeks later, he walked out of the restaurant and spied his car.

"Surprise, surprise, there is my car!"

Around the end of April 1982, I moved up to be the deputy chief of staff working for Colonel (P) Richard H. Sharp, who had replaced Colonel Neely as chief of staff.

Lieutenant Colonel Ed Donnan replaced me as the adjutant general. Ed and I had served together in Japan and had been classmates at the adjutant general career course. Major Doug Williams, the chief of my Personnel Services Division, and an outstanding officer, had orders to Fort Jackson, South Carolina. I requested AG Branch assign Major Malcolm Weaver, who had supported me so competently in Korea, to replace Doug, and they did. The AG shop was in good shape with super leaders. I had received a max OER from General Peter, and I looked forward to serving in the command group for at least a year.

Colonel Sharp and I got along well. Later, Colonel Sharp, who was promoted to brigadier general and assigned as the ADC (M) with the 24th Infantry Division at Fort Stewart, Georgia, dropped dead of a heart attack during his morning PT run. The Army lost a fine soldier.

General Peter did not particularly like field duty, so Colonel Sharp spent much of his time in the field, representing the commanding general. During his absence, I would serve as the acting chief of staff. Again, my time as SGS in Japan served me well.

Early one morning, the installation provost marshal, a colonel, called to tell me that a weapon was missing from one of the battalions in the field. He recommended that the post be closed and all vehicles entering and exiting be searched. This was the first time a weapon had gone missing during General Peter's watch. Colonel Sharp, the division staff, and brigade commanders were at Fort Hood participating in a FORSCOM command post exercise.

General Palastra's policy was that if a weapon could not be accounted for, the unit would remain in the field, as peer pressure would come to bear and the responsible soldier would usually disclose the weapon's location. He would also close the installation, requiring all vehicles to enter and exit through the main gate. Closing the installation served two purposes: Vehicles could be searched for the weapon, and it provided a legal basis to search for illegal drugs and to confiscate government property. The amount of government property entering and exiting the post daily in soldiers' and DACs' cars, generally tools, was beyond belief.

I knew that if I called General Peter and woke him, he would have many questions and would agonize over the decision to close the post. Further, if the weapon was exiting the post, the window of opportunity to intercept the weapon would be greatly reduced. I told the provost marshal to close the post and the TOC to inform the battalion commander to remain in the field. When I told General Peter about the lost weapon upon his arrival, he remarked, "You and I make a good team. I like the way you operate."

The traditional tour for assignment as a division adjutant general was two years versus three years for a normal tour. This allowed more lieutenant colonels to serve in the position, establishing a larger pool of AG officers competitive for promotion to colonel and selection for senior service college.

AG Branch called to tell me that orders would be forthcoming, orders assigning me to the Office of the Adjutant General, (OTAG), DA. I knew this would please Penny, but it did not please me. I felt my assignment as deputy chief of staff would be as career-enhancing as any position in the OTAG, if not more so, and I really enjoyed wearing fatigues and being with soldiers.

Colonel Sharp directed I prepare a back channel to the commander of MILPERCEN for General Peter, requesting I remain assigned to Polk. I did this. Shortly, a reply was received, one stating that I was needed for a highly visible and critical position with the OTAG and that Fort Polk had sufficient officer strength to replace me. Colonel Sharp asked General Peter to call the commander of MILPERCEN and press the issue, but Peter declined.

I had no desire to be assigned to Washington, D.C. If I had to return to the D.C. area, I preferred to be assigned to MILPERCEN. My preference was an assignment to Germany. Penny, of course, preferred Washington, so she was ecstatic.

I was awarded my fifth Meritorious Service Medal when I departed Polk.

19

A Unique Assignment

We visited our parents and Ross in Austin, Big Spring, and Stephenville before we headed to Virginia. Ross's athletic achievements had been considerable, and his grades were excellent. He started for Tarleton as a freshman. He was named all-conference both his freshman and sophomore years, and he was on the academic honor roll all four semesters. We were proud of our son but sad as we left him. I do not remember seeing Ross play a game his junior or senior year. We kept up with his achievements through the student newspaper, *The J-TAC,* and clippings from various newspapers sent by family and friends.

Penny and I arrived at 9140 Conversation Way to find our tenant had not taken care of the home as we had hoped. Several doors, including the refrigerator door, had been sprung or otherwise damaged. The carpets had been soiled. The home was filthy, and the wallpaper in the master bedroom had a thin, orange film on it from marijuana smoke. Penny was particularly distressed by the dirty bathrooms.

All the problems could be corrected with money and hard work; however, before we started, we took photos of all the problems, which would come in handy. The woman had been required to put up a five-hundred-dollar security deposit, which I refused to return. The five hundred dollars in no way covered the purchase of new carpet, doors, and a refrigerator. She worked for a lawyer as a paralegal, so we soon received a letter from the attorney demanding the return of the five hundred dollars. It gave me great pleasure to respond to the attorney, with copies of the photos attached, and tell him we would not return the deposit. We never heard from him or her again.

The neighbors were pleased to see us return. Apparently, her teenage children, a boy and a girl, had had several well-attended, loud, wild parties, which had resulted in sleepless nights along with beer bottles and trash on their lawns. I am now pontificating, but I believe few women can raise children by themselves, especially boys. A boy can only learn to be a man from a man. There are exceptions but few, very few. The number of "deadbeat dads" in today's society appalls me. I suspect the courts, which have to deal with them and later their progeny, see it the same way.

It was now time to go to work. My new boss, Colonel James N. Lanier, had graduated from Wake Forest University, where he had played football. Jim was movie-star handsome, and he had the look and demeanor of a future general officer. He proved to be a grand boss.

The DA Adjutant General (TAG), Major General Robert M. Joyce, had pulled together various morale, welfare, and recreation (MWR) elements, attempting to have them established as a separate command with him as both the commander and the TAG. It was also the opinion of many that Joyce envisioned this new command to be a three-star position.

Joyce was a visionary. He recognize the need for Army-wide MWR activities, such as golf courses, officer clubs, hotels, movie theaters, bowling alleys, craft shops, child-care centers, and a myriad of other activities, to operate using a business model. He planned to keep the fees as low as possible but make money to use for recapitalization. His was an idea whose time had come, as the Army could no longer subsidize MWR activities without detriment to the larger mission. Joyce would see his dream reach fruition in November 1984 with establishment of the US Army Community and Family Support Center, a two-star command. This command would provide oversight and policy support that included contracting, human resources, and financial management services for all Army installations, including over thirty-eight thousand NAF employees.

In the meantime, I was to be a small part of the larger effort to establish the new command. Colonel Lanier offered me the choice of being chief of US Army Community Services (ACS) or the US Army Child-Care and Youth Activities Program. Neither position thrilled me. I asked Lanier where the greater need existed, and he said chief of the child services/youth activities division, as ACS was up and running while the child services and youth activities division struggled. He went on to say that no youth activities staff had been hired, so I would be starting that program from scratch. Then he dropped the bomb.

All military services had been admonished by way of a government accounting office (GAO) report for operating child-care facilities that did not meet minimum standards. The GAO directed the services to either bring their centers up to standards or close them. The Army was cited as having the worst facilities, with 95 percent of the facilities having at least one instance of "imminent danger," which, if not corrected, could result in the death of a child.

The GAO report required the services to report to congress actions taken to meet minimum standards, but typically, they did not provide the monies necessary to meet the standards. This was particularly onerous as most Army child-care facilities were housed in WWII wood.

My questions to Lanier: "Where did the GAO get this information? What were the minimum standards, and on what basis did they cite the Army as having 95 percent of their facilities with an imminent danger situation?"

His response was, "Welcome to Washington."

I learned that the GAO report had been initiated by Congresswoman Patricia Schroeder. Schroeder was an ultraliberal from Colorado, co-founder of the Congressional Caucus for Women's Issues, and as Democratic Whip, a powerful presence in Washington. She not only had women's issues in mind, but child care in particular.

What I never ascertained was if Schroeder schemed to put pressure on the services to improve child-care facilities or if this was done through the impetus of the National Association for the Education of Young Children (NAEYC). NAEYC is the largest membership organization of early childhood professionals and others dedicated to improving the quality of services for children and their families. It is a very vocal lobbying organization, and military child-care center directors and policy makers at the departmental level were members. Some, including my senior child-care program manager, M. A. Lucas, held leadership positions in the organization. I am confident that representatives from NAEYC, the military service program managers, including my own M.A. Lucas, convened with Congresswoman

Schroeder and helped the GAO and Schroeder's staff draft the directive to the military departments.

I do know that there were no minimum standards at the Department of Defense (DOD) or service level and that the 95 percent figure was bogus, extrapolated from a couple of installation surveys, but probably not too far off the mark. I am confident that these women conspired with Congresswoman Schroeder to target the services and particularly the Army, because it was the largest program, and because the services would not give their programs the attention the women felt the programs deserved without congressional intervention. It did receive the desired interest. The Army child-care program had the direct, personal interest of the US Under Secretary of the Army, VCSA, DCSPER, and MACOM commanders.

I did not like the job. I wanted to work with soldiers and do good things for them. I had no interest in how many slats there should be in an infant's bed or how far apart the slats should be so their little heads do not slip through or get caught and strangle them. I resolved that I would do the best job possible, regardless of my personal feelings. Eventually, I came to recognize that taking care of soldiers' children and their families was taking care of them. I believe my initial hesitancy stemmed primarily from not knowing a thing about an area in which I needed to become an expert quickly.

> My job description as chief of the child services/youth activities division read:

Responsible for developing plans and policies for the operation of the Army's Child Development Services and Youth Activities Programs to include providing staff management and technical supervision for the programs at HQDA level. Develops facility design guidance and standards for construction of new facilities, and conducts liaison with external DOD and Army agencies concerning child care and youth activities. Monitors MACOM/installation compliance with minimum program and facility standards. Serves as Chairman of the DOD Morale, Welfare and Recreation Coordinating Committee, Child Care Subcommittee.

M. A. Lucas, my program manager for child-care services, was a pistol. Smart, energetic, and totally dedicated to her program, she and her small staff achieved unbelievable results. Married to a US Navy officer, she was honored as a distinguished alumna by Pennsylvania State University for her work in the child-care field. The Army owes a debt of gratitude to Mary Alice Lucas for the excellent state of child-care programs and facilities that exist today.

She drafted, coordinated, and received approval to publish an Army regulation governing child-care activities at the installation level and, in coordination with the Corps of Engineers, developed minimum standards for fire, health, and safety within child-care facilities. This was a complex task, as there were no OSHA standards for child-care facilities and only thirty-eight states had standards ranging from a bare minimum to the idealistic. My part in all this was to ride herd on M. A. so standards were realistic and not cost prohibitive. Lucas like most bureaucrats had a propensity to gold-plate her programs.

We were successful in getting our request for new facility construction in the Army budget and submitted to congress, where Congressman Schroeder was an ally in obtaining approval of various projects. A female and a high-ranking President Ronald Reagan political appointee from California serving in the Office of the Secretary of the Army (SECARMY) was particularly helpful in running interference within the Army staff when the issue became motor pools versus child-care centers. This woman was extremely smart but rough around the edges, actually coarse, not ladylike, and very overweight. I remember the first time I briefed her. As I was leaving her office, she told me, "If you need my help, let me know. I have the biggest pair of balls you have ever seen." And she did.

One morning, we were in a Pentagon conference room briefing a group of senior officers with this woman and Lucas, the only females in the room. It came time for Lucas to brief, and as usual, she was focused, animated, and persuasive. She had lost a button on her skirt earlier that morning and had used a straight pin to hold the skirt together. The pin did not hold. Lucas walked right out of the skirt and was standing there in her slip. She was so focused that she did not realize the skirt lay at her feet. I was aghast, as was everyone else. The woman rose and got Lucas back in her skirt, closing it with a safety pin, while Lucas continued to brief.

Today (October 2010), M. A. Lucas is the director of Child, Youth, and School Services at the US Army Family, Morale, Welfare, and Recreation Command. She is the voice and conscience of the Army in those important areas.

Sue Bradshaw became my program manager for youth activities. Sue had been a special services representative during the Vietnam War, overseeing a vast network of recreational activities for soldiers in isolated combat areas. She was friends with many general officers. One four-star would come by the office periodically to visit her and often took her to lunch. Sue was well known on the DA staff and respected, which was good because she was revitalizing a program that had no DA oversight up to that time. The youth activities program did not receive the same attention as child care, but Sue was able to push through several of her programs, including an Army-wide youth soccer program with installations competing against each other for the Army championship.

One area that did receive interest from the DA staff was the Boy Scouts of America (BSA) Jamboree held annually at Camp A. P. Hill, Virginia. Sue was responsible for coordinating and providing liaison between the BSA, the Army staff, and Fort A. P. Hill. This undertaking consumed much of Sue's time and energy.

Sue and her husband, an attorney, lived in a restored historical townhouse in Old Town, Alexandria, Virginia not far from her work. One morning, Sue and I had arrived at the office early, just about the time a snow emergency was declared and government workers were directed not to report to work. I told Sue to go home, as nothing would be accomplished that day. Sue had ridden the Metro that morning, and the Metro was no longer running, so she had no way to get home. She and I got in my car and headed for her abode no more than a mile away. The trip took two hours. My trip home took almost six hours. This was just one of several reasons that I did not enjoy living in Northern Virginia as much as Penny did.

I served as chairman of the child-care subcommittee of the DOD MWR Coordinating Committee, which was chaired by a US Air Force three-star. My subcommittee consisted of the child-care chiefs from the US Army, Navy, Air Force, and Marines, all of whom were women. We would meet periodically, and quarterly, I would meet with other subcommittee chairs and report to the coordinating committee, which consisted of general officers from each service. The US Air Force three-star would throw a DOD proposal out for consideration, and invariably, the response from the services would be in character. The Army general would say, "Good idea. We can support it." The US Air Force general would say, "Good idea, but we have a better one." The US Navy admiral would say, "We don't care what you come up with. We will do it our own way," and the US Marine general would say, "The idea sucks, and we ain't going to do it." This is an exaggeration but not by much. Little was done, and rarely could consensus be reached. Basically, the services "flipped off" the DOD.

During this time, an acquaintance of mine approached me about serving as the Army representative to the US Armed Forces Sports Working Group, a subcommittee of the USA Olympic Committee. He was the incumbent, and his term would soon expire. He had attended most of Ross's high school basketball games and knew I was interested in sports. I was intrigued, but the child-care/youth activities job was out of the Army mainstream, and so was this opportunity. I told him my reason for not wanting to do so. I wonder how that would have turned out if I had thrown my hat in the ring.

One morning, I was walking the bowels of the Pentagon on my way to coordinate a paper with the Corps of Engineers when I spied my old friend from Fort Polk, Brigadier General John Malcolm Kirk. General Kirk was in deep conservation with two full colonels. He saw me and exclaimed to the two colonels, "Now there is a soldier. He hasn't spent his career riding a desk. He knows what a soldier looks and smells like."

I was somewhat embarrassed, and I am sure the colonels were. Kirk asked me to come to his office. We entered, and I have never seen such a sight. He had camouflage netting strung from floor to ceiling. His desk was behind a sandbag bunker. There was a sandbag machine gun positioned in one corner, a mortar positioned in another with various soldier items scattered about. He had been taken out of the field, but he had taken some of the field with him. General Kirk was particularly vocal that day about officers homesteading at the Pentagon.

"Taylor, they come here, learn how to work the budget cycle, write a couple of articles for publication in service journals, become pseudo-subject-matter experts, and forget what it is to be a soldier. Hell, they are no different than a bunch of tenured professors."

I got the distinct impression that he was unhappy as the director of training and particularly dissatisfied with the politics of serving on the DA staff as a general officer. He had not yet been promoted to major general and would not be. Shortly, he locked horns with that paragon of virtue, Senator Teddy Kennedy, over the training of the Massachusetts National Guard, and was eased into retirement. The Army lost a superb soldier.

I was floating along and thinking that all was going well and that my supervisors thought I was doing a bang-up job. Colonel Lanier had told me so, as had General Joyce. I had an uneasy feeling about my senior rater, Colonel Roland W. Eisenbarth, primarily because I never saw him. General Joyce would call and want to be briefed immediately, so there would be no chance to pre-brief Eisenbarth. I did try to back-brief him, but he was often tied up, so I would send him a memo of my discussions with General Joyce. After a time, Lanier told me not to bother, as General Joyce had told him that Eisenbarth just got in the way and "mucked" things up. I was not comfortable with that arrangement and suggested General Joyce senior rate me rather than Eisenbarth. Lanier said he would approach General Joyce at the appropriate time.

There were rumors that Mrs. Eisenbarth had announced at a cocktail party that Colonel Eisenbarth had bought his general officer uniform and accessories in anticipation of his selection for brigadier general. Colonel Eisenbarth had been the executive officer for the VCSA prior to assuming his duties in the OTAG, and he was considered a lock for promotion. The brigadier general board did not select him, and upon announcement of the board results, he had apparently gone into seclusion for over a week without General Joyce's authorization. Basically, he was AWOL. An officer in a position to know told me this a year or so later.

I was presented my OER by Lanier and quickly perused his comments, which were great. He wrote, "LTC Taylor definitely possesses general officer potential." Most all possess potential for a higher grade, so I would have been more pleased had he made a direct statement that I should be promoted to general officer. However, I was collecting the words "general officer potential" in my OERs, so I was not unhappy.

I was shocked at what I saw in Eisenbarth's portion of the OER. The words were fine. Jim Lanier had probably written them for Eisenbarth, as that was tradition when you wanted to make sure one of your officers was taken care of, positively or negatively. However, the kick in the gut was that Eisenbarth had marked me in the third block for potential. A rating that low was a killer if I had any thought of being a general officer. Frankly, this boy from Barnhart was devastated and went into a deep funk where drinking too much was not enough.

Later, I discovered Eisenbarth had marked two officers in the first block, five in the second block, and three others beside me in the third block. The three lieutenant colonels marked in the third block, along with me, had all been senior rated by Eisenbarth after Eisenbarth had been passed over for brigadier general. Colonel Lanier told me he had twice gone to Eisenbarth and asked him to change his rating, as there was no way I should have been rated so low. Eisenbarth had refused. He had gone to Joyce and asked him to senior rate me. Joyce said he would not do that but that he would senior rate me on my next OER.

I blame Joyce for poor leadership, because knowing Eisenbarth's mental state, he should not have been allowed to rate anyone. Lanier suggested I go to Eisenbarth and ask him to change his rating, and if he refused, go to Joyce. I told Jim I had too much pride to beg anyone for anything.

There was one who thought himself above me, and he was above me until he had that thought.
—Elbert Hubbard

Pride is one of my character defects. One dictionary definition of pride is an excessively high opinion of oneself. I do not think that is a good trait. Who was I to think I had any potential for promotion to general officer? Perhaps, just perhaps, Eisenbarth's evaluation reflected a true validation of my potential. I needed to accept that it was what it was and get on with serving my country the best I knew how.

In late May 1983, I went to see Jim Lanier and asked him to give me another job. I had done about as much as I could with youth activities and child care, and the programs needed to be viewed through a new pair of glasses. He agreed and said he and Joyce had already decided to move me to the operations directorate to help get the new command off and running. He went on to say that decision had been taken out of their hands that very day, as Joyce had been informed I had been selected for attendance at the Army War College starting August 8, 1983.

That was indeed good news. The Army War College is the Army's senior military educational institution and is one of the most competitive selection panels the Army conducts each year. Selection is made from a pool of lieutenant colonels who have at least twelve months in grade and colonels who have less than twenty years of active commissioned service. Many are considered, but few are selected.

General Palastra, my old boss from Fort Polk, had been promoted to lieutenant general and sat as the president of the selection board. Several officers who had served under him at Fort Polk were selected. I would be joining a long line of notable alumni of the Army War College. Generals John J. Pershing, Dwight D. Eisenhower, George S. Patton, Omar Bradley, Mark W. Clark, William Westmoreland, Creighton Abrams, Alexander Haig, H. Norman Schwarzkopf, Tommy Franks, and Admiral Bull Halsey were some of the well-known people who had graduated from this prestigious institution. This boy from Barnhart was going to have the opportunity to play in the big boy's sandbox.

During my farewell call with Jim Lanier, he told me he had become disenchanted with the Army and was thinking about retiring. I thought he was nuts, as he was sure to be selected for brigadier general. Jim did retire shortly thereafter and went to work for USPA&IRA, selling financial products to military personnel. Jim started out as an agent/broker with an office in Fairfax, Virginia. I began investing in mutual funds and bought an insurance policy through Jim in 1985.

The company, which is now known as First Command Financial Planning, Inc., has its corporate headquarters in Fort Worth, Texas. First Command purports that out of all members of the military, their clients include 40 percent of the flag officers, 33 percent of commissioned officers, and 16 percent of the noncommissioned officers. Jim's success in the financial field and rise through the First Command corporate structure can only be described as meteoric. He became the president and chief operating officer in 1992, and he was elected chairman of the board in 2007.

Penny was thrilled that I had been selected to attend the Army War College, as she would not have to move. I could attend the college as a "roadrunner" (one who leaves his wife at his current duty station and goes home on the weekends). The college was two and a half hours away from our home by car.

20

Army / Civilian Master's Degree

The Army War College is located at Carlisle, Pennsylvania, on the five-hundred-acre campus of Carlisle Barracks. Carlisle Barracks is the Army's second oldest military installation founded in 1757 by the British Army. The barracks served as an arsenal during the War for Independence. The main magazine, which was erected in 1777, still stands, and today, it is a museum. George Washington stayed and worshiped here while he was assembling troops during the Whiskey Rebellion.

The Carlisle Indian Industrial School was located on the barracks from 1879 until 1918. Men, such as Jim Thorpe (named the greatest athlete of the half-century) and Glenn "Pop" Warner (the coach), became legends while at Carlisle Barracks. Many of the buildings used by the Indian school still stand. The athletic dorm is now a guesthouse for visiting VIPs. The gymnasium, although refurbished, still looks much as it did during Thorpe's time, and the athletic field and track remain essentially the same.

The Carlisle area is a history buff's delight, because it figured prominently in the War for Independence and the Civil War. The Gettysburg battlefield is nearby as is the Amish country and Harrisburg, the state capital. Penny would visit me once or twice a month for official functions or sightseeing. She loved to shop for antiques and stay in historic inns and bed and breakfasts. I recall we purchased an antique desk, hall tree, and several chairs during these sorties.

Our photo for the Army War College Student Directory.

I was slow in notifying the college that I would need a BOQ room, so I ended up in a vacant World War II building with another student named Colonel Roger Hakola and a recently arrived member of the faculty. There were some thirty-five "roadrunners" attending the college. Most had left their wives at their previous duty stations because their wives worked. All were drawing a housing allowance or had been furnished government quarters at their previous duty station; therefore, they were not eligible for billets at Carlisle Barracks. The installation provided two excess WWII barracks to accommodate these students. Over the years, students had refurbished and turned the buildings into accommodating facilities.

This was not the case with our building. It had apparently been used as offices in the past. There were separate rooms within the building and a community bathroom at the end of the building. The latrine had several commodes and showerheads. We each took a room as a bedroom and another as an office. We were able to scrounge beds, desks, refrigerator, microwave, and TV from family housing. I did purchase and install a small window air conditioner to get me through the summer because the building, though heated, was not air-conditioned. The living conditions were austere but not uncomfortable.

The three of us ate out most of the time. There were several pubs, cafes, and restaurants within Carlisle and some good inns in nearby Boiling Springs and Mt. Holly Springs. We took turns deciding where we would eat. I do not think we missed a single eating establishment within the area.

The War College student body consisted of approximately three hundred students. There were around 190 Army officers, forty from the other services, thirty senior civilian employees of the federal government (CIA, FBI, NSA, DIA, and State Department), and forty officers from other countries. My seminar group consisted of eleven army officers, a US Marine Corps officer, a US Air Force officer, a State Department civilian, and a brigadier general from Austria.

Most officers were either colonels or lieutenant colonels on the colonel promotion list. There was a smattering of officers like me who had not yet been selected for promotion and a few foreign officers who were brigadier generals.

My seminar group was unique in two ways. First, the US Marine Corps officer, Lieutenant Colonel Wesley K. Fox, had been awarded the Medal of Honor for bravery during the Vietnam War, and the US Air Force officer, Colonel Robert B. Hinckley, had been a prisoner of war for almost five years. Web surfers can find much information about Wes Fox and some about Roger on the Internet. I enjoyed listening to both recall personal accounts of their ordeals.

Second, my former boss from ODCSPER days in the Pentagon, Colonel R. J. Wooten, was the seminar group leader and my faculty advisor.

Not to Promote War, but to Promote Peace.
—Army War College motto

In practical terms, the college provides a professional military education in national security affairs with emphasis on the development and employment of military forces in land warfare. The course is a rigorous examination of the military profession with a balanced curriculum of lectures, seminar studies, military planning exercises, operational war games, and individual research.

The college is a means of intellectual recapitalization for the Army. Its mission, which is increasingly urgent as military history disappears from the curricula on American campuses, could be indelicately expressed in the words of the Spartan king quoted by Thucydides, "The Nation that makes a great distinction between its scholars and its warriors will have its thinking done by cowards and its fighting done by fools."

The Commission on Higher Education of the Middle States Association of Colleges and Schools accredits the college.

I do not remember any of my class being selected for a fourth star. There were a few three-stars and several major generals and brigadier generals chosen. One that received notoriety is Major General William F. Garrison, then colonel, and the youngest Army officer to be promoted to colonel, brigadier general, and major general.

Bill Garrison was the commanding officer of Operation Gothic Serpent, the unsuccessful action to capture key leaders loyal to warlord General Mohamed Aidid in Mogadishu, Somalia. Garrison took responsibility for the debacle, in which eighteen American soldiers died. In my opinion, the blame lay at the feet of Secretary of Defense Les Aspin, who denied Garrison's request to use tanks during the operation, as it might have received too much interest from the press. The resulting failure of the mission did just that and effectively ended Bill's chance for selection to lieutenant general and higher.

Had the mission been a success, it probably would never have made the news. As a failure, it did. The bravery of the soldiers of Operation Gothic Serpent was of the highest order, with two soldiers posthumously receiving the Medal of Honor for valor on that bloody urban battlefield.

Sam Shepard portrayed General Garrison in the film *Black Hawk Down*, which chronicles the events of the Battle of Mogadishu. Bill served as an assistant professor of military science at Tarleton State University from January 1974 to June 1976 when he was a major. He is retired to Hico, Texas.

During his welcome address to the student body, the commandant of the War College, Major General Thomas F. Healy, made the statement, "You can walk on the grass while here." This meant that a bunch of "Mickey Mouse" rules would not encumber us. He stressed the year afforded an opportunity to become reacquainted with our families, to wind down, and to enjoy ourselves. The only grades would be pass or fail, and what we got out of the college would be in direct proportion to our effort. There would be no honor graduate or distinguished graduates.

We believed none of this, and for the first two months, we were all looking over our shoulders knowing there was an unknown system the college was using to evaluate us. The atmosphere remained tense as would be expected when you have a group of highly competitive individuals, each trying to gain an advantage over the others.

Eventually, we realized General Healy spoke the truth. The school was organized like a civilian university. Most classes were over by mid-afternoon, which left time to do research in the library, prepare a briefing/speech, complete readings for the next day's class, or participate in athletic activities. There was a core curriculum and many elective courses to choose from. We were typically done with classes by noon on Friday, and there were no weekend classes. The only time we wore uniforms were Friday mornings when we had lectures by high-ranking military or civilian leaders. The atmosphere was laid-back and nonthreatening.

Many classes were taught by visiting university professors. This often made for animated discussion.

General Healy strongly suggested that the sixty students who did not already have a master's degree take advantage of the Cooperative Degree Program with Shippensburg State University leading to the award of a master's degree in public administration. I did this.

The degree program required thirty semester hours, an internship, and a thesis. Shippensburg granted nine hours for War College attendance. The remaining twenty-one hours were taken at classes held at Carlisle Barracks, Harrisburg, or the main campus, each a short drive. The classes were held at night. There were several weekends that I stayed at Carlisle Barracks to study for a test, write, practice a presentation, and/or work on my research papers. I spent many an afternoon and evening at the War College or Shippensburg library.

The War College required students to complete a research-based essay for publication in a military journal or suitable for submission to the Army or DOD staff for consideration. The title of my effort was the following: "The Military Retirement System: Is Change Needed?" I used the War College manuscript as the basis for my Shippensburg thesis, changing the format from military to civilian. I receive a passing grade from the War College and an A from Shippensburg. In fact, I made A's for all my graduate courses.

I thoroughly enjoyed my internship spent with the tax collector for the borough of Carlisle and Cumberland County. The tax collector and his employees operated a manual system that had not evolved from the original system established during the 1700s. There were no computers in sight, and all had an aversion to trying anything new. Another student who was a computer whiz and I eventually convinced the reluctant tax collector of the benefits of automation. Once given the green light, we surveyed his office, determined all documents coming or going within the office, and identified those that could be consolidated or revised. We worked with a company in Harrisburg to develop software to create, collect, store, manipulate, and relay office information to accomplish the manual tasks and made recommendations regarding desktop computers. I stopped by to see the tax collector as I left Carlisle, and the computers and software were soon to arrive and employee training to begin. I wonder how it all turned out, as his employees seemed unwilling and perhaps incapable of learning "them newfangled gadgets."

Fifty-nine of the sixty students who arrived without a graduate degree had one by the time they departed.

Some reminisces from my time at the War College include the following in no particular order:

Lieutenant General Richard G. Trefry, the longtime Army inspector general, stating to the assembled students, "A woman's ass and a whiskey glass will get you in trouble every time."

The two-week operational war game, in which we planned and executed the invasion of Iran. This, of course, was during the Cold War, and the exercise was to counter a Soviet thrust to take over the

Strait of Hormuz. Our mission was to deny the Soviets control of oceangoing traffic to and from the oil-rich gulf states. I bet the Pentagon is fine-tuning contingency plans for Iran as I write.

The sobering briefing from the intelligence community on the Single Integrated Operational Plan (SIOP). The SIOP is a blueprint that specifies how American nuclear weapons would be used in the event of nuclear war. The SIOP integrates the nuclear triad of bombers, land-based intercontinental ballistic missiles (ICBM), and submarine-launched ballistic missiles (SLBM). The SIOP is a highly classified and sensitive document to which few are privy. We were not shown the actual SIOP. Instead, we were briefed on the intelligence community's consensus of the Soviet Union's SIOP. It was unnerving to see American missile, communication, and electrical sites, cities, and military installations disappear as SLBM, then ICBM, and finally Soviet strategic bombers rained death and destruction. All were visually depicted on a large, lighted map of the United States.

An Israeli student, a brigadier general and hero from the Arab-Israeli War of 1973, spent more time traveling the United States speaking to and soliciting money from Jewish organizations and audiences than attending classes.

The National Security Seminar was held from June 4 to June 8, 1984. Prominent members of academia, business, government, and the media attended presentations by high-level government officials while they interacted with students. The purpose was to invite folks who did not have a longtime association with the military and allow them to get to know us. It was a "grassroots" campaign to engender good will among the bourgeois. Each student sponsored a guest and escorted them as we went about our daily routine. General Healy hosted the obligatory welcome cocktail party and a farewell barbeque. Penny attended the barbeque. My guest was Aubrey L. Dunn, a New Mexico state senator from 1964 to 1980, and a candidate for the 1982 Democratic nomination for governor. He was a partner in a real estate and investment company, and owned a farm where he raised apples and livestock. He was an interesting fellow, and apples were his passion. He gave Penny several pieces of costume jewelry with an apple motif. He and I cut classes one afternoon and toured the Gettysburg battlefield. He told me that was the highlight of his visit.

The trips to US Naval Base Norfolk, Langley Air Force Base, and Quantico Marine Base were most informative. The US Navy, Air Force, and Marines put on impressive "dog and pony shows." I was awed by the F-15 Eagle fighter demonstration. On a tour to Washington, D.C., I had the opportunity to receive briefings at the Organization of American States (OAS) and the World Bank. All were beneficial to my understating of how the world turns.

I located and viewed the names of well-known graduates contained on the large bronze plaques, which lined the outside walls of Root Hall. There was a plaque for each class beginning with the first class, the class of 1904. The name and rank of each member of the class are stamped alphabetically in raised letters on the large bronze tablets. I visited the War College in 2004 and again in 2008, and this boy from Barnhart took pride in seeing his name alongside so many fine soldiers.

I often left the barracks at noon Friday, arriving home around 1445, and had the yard mowed by the time Penny got off work. We then had most weekends free to sightsee, see a play at the Kennedy Center, attend a movie, or just "jell." I would leave around 0430 on Monday morning and arrive at the barracks in time to shower and dress before classes started at 0800.

I began negotiations with the Adjutant General Officer Assignment Branch in early January. I realized that if I were selected for colonel, I would probably never get to Germany, so this was my last chance. The AG Branch chief was adamant that I was coming back to Washington, D.C. He and I sparred for a couple of months. He finally told me that the commanding general of MILPERCEN had approved me to replace him. That was dirty pool on his part; however, it was a super job, and I felt honored to be chosen. Penny was again delighted that her life would not be interrupted.

Ross graduated from Tarleton State in May 1984 with a degree in biology. He worked that summer for Tarleton until he started a two-year program at the University of Texas Medical Branch (UTMB) in Galveston to pursue a degree and license as a physical therapist. His exploits on the basketball court had continued with his being named the TIAA (Texas Intercollegiate Athletic Association) MVP during both his junior and senior year. He led Tarleton to their first conference championship as a four-year institution and set the all-time Tarleton scoring record in basketball. Wow, I was proud.

He had an entry in the 1985 edition of *Who's Who among Students in American Colleges and Universities* based on both his athletic and academic achievements.

The War College held graduation ceremonies on June 11, 1984. General John W. Vessey, Jr., chairman of the Joint Chiefs of Staff, gave the address and the First US Army Band provided the music. It was the first graduation ceremony where Penny and I did not have to hurry to get to our next duty station. I remember we took a leisurely stroll around the main campus before we departed for Springfield, Virginia, and home.

I did not attend graduation at Shippensburg University. I had them mail me my diploma.

21

MILPERCEN Redux

The daily drive to and from the Hoffman buildings in Alexandria, Virginia, where MILPERCEN and other government agencies were located, began once again. I hated the trip, which took at least forty-five minutes each way, and that was on a good day. Traffic in and around Washington, D.C., has to be some of the worst in the world. My route home along I-495 (the Beltway) to the I-95 (West Springfield) interchange was daily chaos and often gridlocked. I could take two alternate routes, if I knew there was a traffic jam at the interchange. However, each resulted in a drive of over an hour. A two hour drive plus ten to twelve hours in the office made for a long day.

> My job description read:
> Chief, Adjutant General Branch responsible for the worldwide assignment, career management, and professional development of over 4,000 Adjutant General's Corps officers (LTC, MAJ, CPT, and LT). Serves as assignment officer for 600 AG LTCs. Conducts field visits to counsel officers and commanders on assignment and professional development matters and keeps them abreast of the Officer Personnel Management System. Slates and assigns AG officers selected for LTC level command and Division/Installation AG positions. Monitors strength management by installation/command ensuring support of the Officer Distribution Plan (ODP). Maintains interface with the Commandant, AG School as the Adjutant General's Corps proponent for personnel and administrative matters.

I was blessed in that I had a great job and super people working for me. All officers assigned to MILPERCEN were handpicked and personally approved by the commanding general. The right credentials were important for credibility along with the gift of tact, diplomacy, and common sense when one was managing the careers of peers. The officer was his own best career manager, but the needs of the Army commonly took precedent over the desires of the officer. This resulted in the assignment officer often having to say no. I had disagreements with the AG branch over the years. But once told to "shut up, suit up, and ship out," I did. I would find that some officers did not and would continued to badger their assignment officer or more likely find a senior officer, colonel, or above to plead their case. This would call for my involvement in the conflict.

Some had the support of a general officer who would send a back channel to the commanding general of MILPERCEN, for which I would have to craft a response justifying my actions. I am quite sure that I made a few enemies, as did my assignment officers.

Captain Melanie Reeder and later Captain Rose Walker were responsible for assigning lieutenants. Both retired as full colonels. Melanie went into public affairs. She was attractive and articulate, and she represented the Army at various command levels when dealing with the public. Rose Walker ended her career, serving in a brigadier general position, as the commander of the Soldier Support Institute (SSI) at Fort Jackson, South Carolina.

Two cubicles over from the AG Branch was the Transportation Branch. Captain Ann Dunwoody was an assignment officer in the branch at the time. On November 14, 2008, Dunwoody became the first woman in US military history to achieve the rank of four-star general. My sentiment at the time was that all three of these female officers were destined to wear stars. I had no thought that one day Dunwoody would wear four of them. Timing, luck, and who you know are all as important as demonstrated performance for progression in the general officer ranks. I suspect Ann Dunwoody had them all.

Captain Sean Byrne and later Captain Todd Sain were responsible for the assignment of captains. Sean Byrne and Malcolm Weaver were the most outstanding of the many captains who worked for me. Sean had served as an enlisted soldier, finished his enlistment commitment, gone to college on the GI Bill, and had been commissioned as a second lieutenant.

The chief of the General Officer Management Office (GOMO) could select anyone he wanted to work for him. He looked to me to nominate officers for his consideration. I nominated Sean, and he was selected. Sean did an outstanding job in GOMO and was subsequently selected to be the military assistant/aide to the Vice President of the United States, George H. W. Bush. When Bush was elected president, he asked Sean to continue to serve as his military aide, but he was willing to release Sean back to the Army if that was Sean's desire. Sean asked me for advice about what he should do—along with others, I am sure. I told Sean he already had President Bush's signature on his OERs, and he needed to get back into the mainstream Army. I suppose you cannot say no to the president, because Sean continued to serve President Bush.

I was invited to attend Sean's promotion ceremony to major, which was presided over by Bush, and I had the opportunity to chitchat with Bush. What a nice man. Sean told me Barbara Bush never forgot a birthday, including his children's, and was a genuinely sweet and caring person. I have a photo of that occasion hanging on my office wall. The food after the promotion ceremony was lavish, as were the surroundings.

Sean went on to perform superbly in the 82nd Airborne Division, Korea, the Pentagon, and Iraq. Sean recently retired as a major general after he commanded the US Army Human Resources Command, the successor organization to MILPERCEN.

Major Chip Ecks was my assignment officer for majors, and had he stayed in the Army would have likely worn stars. Chip left AG Branch to attend the Armed Forces Staff College in Norfolk Virginia. Upon graduation, Chip could have chosen any assignment he wanted, but opted for location rather than job. Chip was assigned to the United States Air Force Academy in Colorado Springs, Colorado, as an Army representative. Chip retired as a lieutenant colonel to go into the corporate world, and continues to live in Colorado. Major Dick Ledman replaced Chip.

Major Steve Strippoli, later Colonel Strippoli, was the Professional Development Officer (PDO). Steve, in accord with assignment officers, slated officers for both military and civilian schools. Years before, the PDO had suggested I attend graduate schooling, and asked for a college transcript. He soon called to say, "There is no way in 'hell' I can get you into any graduate school with your grades."

Mrs. Ruth Williams and Mrs. April Wray were my administrative support people, and performed an invaluable service answering phones, which jingled constantly, along with maintaining records, and other office duties.

I was the assignment officer for lieutenant colonels, and there were six hundred of them, so in addition to my duties as branch chief, I had a full plate. I had a few interesting encounters during my tour that made the job stimulating.

Brigadier General Wilma Vaught, US Air Force, was the commander of the US Military Entrance Processing Command (MEPCOM) in North Chicago, Illinois. MEPCOM had the mission of ensuring that each new member of the US Armed Forces, including the US Army, Marines, Navy, Air Force, and Coast Guard, met the mental, moral, and medical standards required by the Department of Defense and the military services. Military Entrance Processing Stations (MEPS) located in cities throughout the United States accomplished this mission by testing, examining, and processing applicants for enlistment into the US Armed Forces. A major or lieutenant colonel commanded a MEPS depending on its size. Command of MEPCOM and the MEPS rotated between the services. I had responsibility of providing officers—captain through lieutenant colonel—to staff the various stations. I sent only the best majors and lieutenant colonels to command positions, so I had a good reputation with MEPCOM.

I received a call from General Vaught, and she told me the Army soldiers under her command were top-notch. Because the Army represented the largest service in her command, she asked that I send her a sharp lieutenant to be her aide-de-camp. I said that I would and asked if she preferred a female. She exclaimed, "Hell no! It is bad enough as it is with people thinking all female officers are lesbians. I do not need a female aide to fan that fire. I want a happily married male." I sent her a married male lieutenant, but I had no idea if he was happily married.

Captain Byrne was trying to reassign a captain assigned to the US Army Recruiting Command (USAREC), which was located at Fort Sheridan, Illinois. The captain had been assigned to USAREC since he had been a second lieutenant, and he was now a senior captain. USAREC was dragging their feet, saying that he was too valuable to their operation to be moved. The captain was a computer whiz. No officer is irreplaceable, and the officer needed to be moved for schooling and career progression. I told the USAREC chief of staff, a colonel, I was moving him and would send them a replacement.

Shortly, I received a call from Major General Alan K. Ono, the USAREC commanding general. Ono said, "Taylor, have you seen the movie or read the book *The Godfather*?"

"Yes, sir, I have."

"Do you remember the scene where the fellow woke up with a horse head in his bed?"

"Yes, sir."

Ono then hung up on me. Ono was an Adjutant General's Corps officer, and I did not need him as an enemy, so I told Sean to back off.

Later, the captain resigned his commission and went to work for USAREC as a civilian. I do not understand why Ono did not level with me. I would lock horns with Ono again after he had been promoted to lieutenant general and had been assigned as the DCSPER.

Brigadier General Charles A. Hines was assigned as the director of the Officer Personnel Management Directorate for MILPERCEN. He would be my senior rater. Hines was a black officer with a PhD and a protégé of General Max Thurman.

His first officer call, which took place shortly after his arrival, was to brief us on a paper, maybe his doctorial thesis, that he had written. In his opinion, it proved that black officers did not rate other black officers fairly. At the end of the presentation, he berated all assembled regarding the poor quality of MILPERCEN briefing charts. I found this strange, as his charts had been lettered by hand and were unprofessional. Most briefing charts used outside the organization, including mine, were prepared by the MILPERCEN graphics art section and were first-rate. In addition, most of the officers in attendance believed as I did, namely that black officers rated black officers fairly. White officers rated them unfairly by giving them inflated reports to avoid any hint of prejudice.

I had very little contact with Hines; however, officers did began to complain, and the word was to be wary when around him. My time in the box came on December 12 and 13, 1985, a sad time for the US Army.

Early on the morning of the 12th, a chartered DC-8 aircraft crashed on takeoff from Gander, Newfoundland. The plane carried 256 people, of whom 248 were soldiers in the 101st Airborne Division, 186 from the 3rd Battalion, 502nd Infantry alone. The soldiers were returning from a six-month deployment with the Multinational Force and Observers on the Sinai Peninsula in Egypt to their home base at Fort Campbell, Kentucky. Impact forces and a severe, fuel-fed fire destroyed the aircraft. All were killed and burned beyond recognition. This is still the greatest peacetime loss of military personnel in US history.

MILPERCEN was involved, as notification to families would be coordinated out of the casualty assistance office. It soon became a nightmare when it was discovered the unit had carried their personnel records with them as well as their health and dental records, which, of course, were destroyed. This was against Army regulations and division SOPs, as records were to remain at home station to preclude the very thing now unfolding. A positive identification of the deceased could not be made without the health and dental records, and notification to families could not be made without a positive identification.

General Thurman, VCSA, had directed General Hines set up a task force to recover any residual medical and dental records from installations where the presumed deceased soldiers had been previously assigned. Personnel records were available at MILPERCEN, so that did not present a problem.

Hines called a meeting of his three division chiefs: combat arms, combat support, and combat service support. I happened to be the senior officer in the combat service support division (CSSD) when the call came. Colonel Gerry Early, the division chief, and the other branch chiefs were out of the building or otherwise not available.

General Hines directed that a list of installations where a soldier had been previously assigned be prepared and their personnel records brought to his office. A representative from the enlisted personnel management directorate (EPMD) was also at the meeting. A list was received from Fort Campbell of all personnel who might have been on the plane.

I returned to CSSD and got the branches activated, and by the time I returned to Hines's office, records and lists were being delivered. Hines had prepared a message template for his secretary to type to the various installations once Hines had personally gone through each soldier's records to verify that the information was correct. In many instances, it was not—when you want something bad, you generally get it bad. It was now around 1900 hours, and I realized that no one was hanging around to assist. I asked Hines's deputy, a full colonel, if I could help. He told me Hines had told him this was too important to trust others to do and he would do it himself. The deputy said he was going home and I could stay if I wanted.

I went to General Hines and asked if I could be of assistance. He said no, but I knew he was thinking of some way he could use me. I asked if I could help do what he was doing, and he indicated that I could. I checked the records. He checked the records I had checked, and after a while, he stopped checking the records. He then began to proof and sign the messages that his secretary had typed while I continued to check records.

It was near midnight, and I calculated it would be a few more hours before we would finish. I suggested there was no reason for us both to lose sleep, that he should go home, and that I would wrap up. He said he was sending the messages "Personal For" from him to the installation commanding general and only he could sign the messages. I quickly drafted a memorandum to the communications center, giving me one-time signature authority to sign for him. Hines appeared to be weary and pleased to go home. The result of my effort to help Hines was that he took good care of me on my OER.

Gerry Early, my rater, was being reassigned to command the Eighth Personnel Command in Korea and had written OERs on his branch chiefs. As was custom, he had prepared draft comments for Hines along with a recommend senior rater block check for each officer. Both Early's comments and his proposed comments for General Hines were superlative. However, he recommended that Hines check me and one other officer in the second block and the three other branch chiefs in the first block. Again, a second block rating was the kiss of death.

Hines did not agree with Early's recommendations. He senior rated me in the top block and moved another officer to the second block. Luck, timing, and who you know can make a world of difference. The reason I know this is I was acting division chief while Early was on PCS leave, and Hines's secretary unintentionally gave me Early's memorandum to Hines.

General Hines retired as a major general and served for several years as president of Prairie View A&M University.

God could not be everywhere, and therefore, he made mothers.
—Unknown

Mother died on December 30, 2009, and I am writing this having just returned from her funeral. It is so hard to lose your mother. We buried her on January 2, 2010. The new decade begins with sadness, but also relief, because I know she is in a far better place than I could hope.

Mother was my first love, the one person who loved me unconditionally more than any other. I always knew that regardless of my failures or my accomplishments, she loved me just as I was (and am). My heartbreak was her heartbreak, and my joy was her joy. She was the one who would say she no longer liked pie when there were the four of us at the table and only three pieces of pie. Mother lived through her children. I am so unworthy of the endless love she gave me.

Mother's Obituary Photo

Elanor Alyene Shaw Taylor, 90, went home to be with the Lord on Wednesday, Dec. 30, 2009. Alyene was born Nov. 30, 1919, near Locker in San Saba County, Texas, the daughter of Walter Green (Pappy) Shaw and Martha Samatha (Mama Shaw) Blasingame Shaw. She is listed as El Nora on her birth certificate but a cousin added the name Allene. When she started school her sister Gladys, who was her teacher, changed the spelling to Alyene. Her friends called her Alyene and her husband called her "squirrel," a name given to her by her brother J. R. Shaw who thought she looked like a little squirrel when she was born.

She attended Locker school, then attended Richland Springs High School where she graduated in 1938. She married Norvel (Shorty) Ross Taylor in Kerrville, Texas, on Sept. 30, 1939. He was a rancher, and they first lived near Maryneal, Texas. They moved to Suggs Switch between Mertzon and Barnhart, Texas, where they lived until 1956 when they moved to the Woods Place between Barnhart and Big Lake, Texas. In 1962, they moved to Crane, Texas, where N. R. went into the grocery business. In 1964, they moved to Big Spring, Texas, where they purchased a grocery store. They moved to Slaton, Texas, in 1993 to be near their daughter. After 68 years of marriage, her beloved N. R. passed away on Aug. 4, 2007.

Alyene was the youngest of five children. She was preceded in death by sisters Thelma Gladys, Bessie May, Billie Iva; and brother J.R. Shaw. Alyene was a loving wife and mother. She was raised by Christian parents and knew the Lord from an early age. She led her husband to the Lord by her godly example and together they created a Christian home where their children and grandchildren could see Christ in action. She was a Sunday school teacher for many years. Her witness will be missed by those who knew and loved her. She was a member of Bible Baptist Church in Slaton.

She is survived by son Herbie Ross Taylor and wife Janice of Salado, Texas; daughter Norvel Nantippe Cox and husband Jackie, of Ransom Canyon, Texas; grandsons Herbie Ross Taylor Jr. and wife Kristi of Frisco, Texas, and Michael Wayne Martin and wife Melanie of Austin, Texas; great-grandsons Micah Jeb and Jared Ross Taylor of Frisco and Ryan Austin, Reed Nicholas and Riley Jackson Martin of Austin. Service will be held at 1 p.m. Saturday, Jan. 2, 2010, at Bible Baptist Church in Slaton with the Rev. Chris Downer officiating. Interment will follow in Resthaven Memorial Park in Lubbock.

I visited Mother shortly before Thanksgiving and silently prayed to God that he take her home. That is a terrible thing to do, to admit. She was so unhappy, so miserable, and she so wanted to get out of the nursing home. Her physical and mental health had slowly spiraled downward once she lost her beloved Shorty. Dementia had set in, and I was not sure how cognizant she was of her surroundings. She recognized Janice and me, but meaningful conversation with her during our last visit was negligible. She would look at me with pleading eyes and repeatedly mumble in a barely discernible voice something I could not understand. I finally realized she was asking me to take her home. I told her I could not do that, and in a clear and strong voice, she said, "You could if you wanted to."

She, of course, was right. I could, but I could not. We Americans may be the only people I know who do not care for our elderly in our homes. Instead, we resign them to a nursing home and to the care of strangers who may or may not care for them. Her last words trouble me, and I have conflicting emotions. If Mother had been a dog, we would have put her down long ago.

Mother died alone in her sleep early on the morning of December 30, 2009.

I miss her.

I would periodically receive invitations from division, installation, or corps AGs to visit, brief, and conduct one-on-one professional development interviews with their officers. I usually took Sean Byrne with me. I would interview majors and lieutenant colonels while he interviewed captains and lieutenants. These forays outside Washington, D.C., were a welcome respite, as it was revitalizing to be with soldiers doing soldier things.

There would usually be a welcome cocktail reception at the officer's club. I would brief all officers in a theater or conference room the following morning, and then Sean and I would begin the individual interviews. The visit would end with a dinner attended by senior officers at either the officer's club or the adjutant general's quarters.

I had received an invitation from the AG of III Corps and Fort Hood to visit and brief. I was not looking forward to the visit. First, there were many AG officers at Fort Hood, and interviews became tedious and perfunctory when you tried to accommodate large numbers. Second, one of the officers to be interviewed was Major Margaret "Peggy" Bahnsen. Major Bahnsen was married to Brigadier General John "Doc" Bahnsen, Jr., the III Corps and Fort Hood Chief of Staff.

Doc Bahnsen was a war hero with a Distinguished Service Cross, our nation's second highest award for valor, five Silver Stars, four Legions of Merit, three Distinguished Flying Crosses, four Bronze Stars with V-device, two Purple Hearts, and a variety of lesser awards. Doc Bahnsen intensely disliked Adjutant General's Corps officers, particularly those assigned to the Washington area. I never knew why Bahnsen had an aversion to AG officers, as he was married to one, but he did. Some AG officer had done him wrong somewhere.

The previous year, Bahnsen had served as the president of the major selection board and had refused to select for promotion any AG officer who was not serving in a combat unit. This was devastating for the morale as well as the health of the AG Corps. AG Branch simply was unable to rotate all captains into a combat unit, as there were other high-priority positions that had to be filled. Phil Remling, my predecessor, flew to Fort Hood and confronted Bahnsen, but Bahnsen refused to budge.

I was going to Fort Hood to tell Peggy Bahnsen that I was reassigning her to Washington for career progression. I knew I would hear from her husband, and I did.

The last night, the III Corps AG invited Sean and me to his quarters for cocktails and dinner. In attendance were Doc and Peggy Bahnsen, Major General James L. Dozier, the DCG, III Corps and Fort Hood and his wife, the two division AG's and their wives, and the host and hostess.

I was waiting for Doc to attack, and he did. He called me over and told me his wife did not need an assignment to Washington, that was so much "horse hockey," and he would not stand for it. I knew Doc had spent a tour in Washington and reminded him of that fact and suggested that the assignment was probably beneficial to his career. That comment greatly irritated him. Thankfully, we were called to the dinner table. The dinner went reasonably well, with only a few barbed comments from Bahnsen.

After dinner, he went after me again. I now realized this was moving to an "I do not like you, and I am going to whip your ass" situation, and I began trying to extricate myself. Peggy also realized the situation was reaching critical mass and literally took Doc by the ear. She told him, "We are going home," and they did.

When I returned to Washington, I issued orders assigning Peggy to Washington and called Peggy to let her know. She told me I had not heard the last of it. Soon, Gerry Early told me Bahnsen had called the MILPERCEN commanding general. The commanding general wanted to know if there was not some way we could accommodate General Bahnsen without hurting Major Bahnsen's career. I told Early that the staff college list would soon be released, and my source had informed me that Peggy had been selected, so it was a moot issue.

I heard no more from General Bahnsen. I recall that Peggy attended the US Armed Forces Staff College, now the Joint Services Staff College, at Norfolk, Virginia, and that Doc retired in that area. I am not sure how it all turned out. I just do not remember. I do know this: I was not attempting to bait, pick a fight, or get back at General Bahnsen. Peggy had a good career ahead of her, and she needed time on the DA staff to prepare her for increased responsibility. It was my job to see that she got that opportunity.

General Dozier had an interesting story. In December 1981, then Brigadier General Dozier was kidnapped by the leftist Italian "Red Brigade" terrorist group. General Dozier was the Deputy Chief of Staff for Logistics and Administration, Allied Land Forces Southern Europe in Verona, Italy, at the time of his kidnapping.

Four men posing as plumbers took him from his apartment in Verona. His wife was not kidnapped but was left bound and chained in their apartment.

According to Steven Emerson's book *Secret Warriors,* the Italian government did not want to mount the rescue operation initially and would not permit the United States to rescue General Dozier, either. Mr. Emerson reports that President Reagan contacted H. Ross Perot and asked him to rescue General Dozier using his private force. Mr. Perot accepted the mission, and while in the air between Texas and Italy, the Italian government heard about the private rescue mission and was convinced that in order to save face, they should launch their own rescue.

One of the fun things Penny and I did was attend the European Military Personnel Conference held in Garmisch-Partenkirchen, Germany. My former boss, Brigadier General Bill Gourley, had invited me to speak at the conference.

The Garmisch-Partenkirchen area is delightful, situated in a long valley with the Zugspitze, the tallest mountain in Germany, on its southern end. The town is a resort area in Bavaria, southern Germany, not far from the border with Austria. Located there is a civilian-run American Armed Forces Recreation Center (Edelweiss Lodge and Resort) that serves US and NATO military and their families.

We flew to Germany from the Washington/Baltimore International Airport via New York and Frankfurt to Munich, where we rented a car and drove the short distance to Garmisch-Partenkirchen.

After the conference, Penny and I spent a few days in the area. We rode the tram to the top of the Zugspitze. We walked from the base of the Zugspitze back to town through the farms and fields located in the valley. Along the way, we stopped at a Gasthaus for a late lunch of schnitzel, beer, and schnapps.

We drove to Innsbruck, Austria, for a day and leisurely motored through parts of Bavaria and the Black Forest. We stayed at a Gasthaus and eventually arrived in Stuttgart. There, I addressed and interviewed AG officers. Finally, we arrived at Patrick Henry Village, the American enclave near Heidelberg. I had an office call with my boss from Fort Polk days, Brigadier General Cecil Neely, now the chief of staff of V Corps, which was located in Heidelberg. Neely had not changed. When I walked into his outer office, he was shouting at his secretary to get some son of a bitch on the phone.

I spent a day with Lieutenant Colonel Earl Halbrook, who commanded a personnel and administration battalion, briefing and interviewing his officers.

Penny and Earl's wife drove to Rothenberg, a medieval town, to shop. Their car broke while there, and they returned to Heidelberg in the car on top of a wrecker. They thought that was great fun and laughed about the strange looks they received while they were zipping down the autobahn aboard the wrecker.

We had a wonderful evening in Heidelberg with Earl and his wife and Colonel Mary Willis, the commandant of the AG school at Fort Harrison, who had also come to Germany to speak at the personnel conference. The friendship I formed with Earl Halbrook would continue for the remainder of my military career.

Along with the European Personnel Conference, I attended the annual Worldwide Military Personnel Conference, which was held at various locations within the United States. There, I would brief people on the status and future of the AG Corps. The year the conference was held in Washington, we had officers waiting in line to be interviewed. We had asked that officers call for an appointment prior to the conference.

Some did, but most did not, so we continued the interviews long into the night.

This was the time that Lieutenant Colonel Patricia Hickerson who commanded the 38th Personnel and Administration Battalion, located in Germany, accused me of lying to her. I had not, but Pat was adamant that I had made a promise to her that I had not kept. Pat was on the fast track for future promotions, and I did not want her for an enemy. I do not know why Pat had a bee in her bonnet, but all was soon forgiven. Pat would retire as a major general. She and Earl Halbrook would later figure prominently in the most difficult career decision I made while I was serving my country.

Colonel Mary Willis and I had a good relationship. I often visited with her by phone and always had an office call with her when I was visiting Fort Benjamin Harrison to address AG basic and advance courses. As commandant of the Adjutant General School, Mary served as the proponent for all issues involving AG officers and enlisted soldiers. Mary would retire as a brigadier general.

Colonel Mary Willis and Lieutenant Colonel Herb Taylor.

The TAG, Major General Bob Joyce, was the titular head of the AG Corps, but he had abrogated that responsibly in his drive to establish a community and family support command. Mary Willis should have picked up that responsibility by default, but she had been hesitant to do so. Gerry Early and I were the only ones giving any thought or taking any action regarding the future of the AG Corps.

I convinced Early that the top officer to replace Mary Willis was Lieutenant Colonel (P) Frank Foster, my AG advance course classmate and fellow division AG. I considered Frank to be one of the best and brightest in the AG Corps, and certainly the most innovative. Frank and his lovely wife, Linda, did not want to go to Fort Harrison, and both expressed their dissatisfaction on several occasions. I told Frank the Corps needed him, so he went. Frank is considered the founding father of the AG Corps "regiment," and in 1987, he activated the Adjutant General's Corps Regimental Association, of which I am a founding member. Frank is the only colonel inducted into the AG Corps Hall of Fame.

Frank opted to retire when he completed the required three years in grade as a colonel. I am confident that had he not retired, he would have worn stars. Frank and Linda established Medals of America (http://www.usmedals.com), which is located in Fountain Inn, South Carolina. Today, it is probably the largest mail-order business in the United States specializing in military medals, ribbons, and related paraphernalia.

The two years that I spent managing the careers of AG officers were two of the most rewarding years of my life, but also two of the most frustrating years. The job was rewarding in that I was helping develop the future leaders of the Army while maintaining the force. The frustration came from four sources.

The first was the "careerist" who always put themselves ahead of the needs of the Army. These people demanded an inordinate amount of both phone and face time.

The second were those officers who thought they wanted a career in the Army but were actually only looking for a paycheck. It took time to identify and selectively remove them from the Army's rolls.

The third were married Army couples, and there were many. I would have married couples show up for an interview who wanted to be interviewed together. It was my preference that they be interviewed separately because one would invariably have a better performance record than the other. I am confident that telling an officer in front of their spouse that their record reflected that they were a poor performer and not likely to be selected for promotion to the next higher grade had a negative effect on their relationship. This was especially true when the other spouse had an outstanding performance record. It was not an issue when they were both poor performers, although I would have two people who left the interview room mad at the Army and me. The issue when they both had outstanding performance records became one of assignment and precedent. Specifically, was it imperative they be assigned together, and if so, which career had precedent, the male's or the female's? Every installation and command had jobs that were considered career enhancing, but these positions were limited, which made it hard to ensure that both had an opportunity to prove themselves in difficult and demanding positions. The bottom line was that married Army couples required intense management to ensure that both the needs of the Army and that of the officers were met. The needs of the Army always came first, which often left one or both spouses frustrated and unhappy.

The final issue involved females in general. There were many outstanding female officers in the AG Corps who were groomed along with outstanding males for positions of higher responsibility. This was done primarily by assignment to high-priority and visible assignments and schooling. AG selection rates for promotion to each grade mirrored the Army average in all grades except major. The reason why this happened at the grade of major was simple, but it was not politically correct for me to espouse. I took heat on this issue from various sources, primarily senior AG officers, captains not selected for promotion, the MILPERCEN leadership, and the AG school as proponent for the AG Corps. All thought the assignment process was to blame.

The reality was that there were only so many career-enhancing jobs available, and those were shared between outstanding male and female officers. Female captains began to leave the Army when they were senior captains because they either had married or had started a family and an a Army career no longer fit into their plans. This resulted in a number of male captains not being selected because they had not had the tough assignments qualifying them for major. Females had filled those assignments, and they were no longer in the Army.

My take on the issue of women in the Army is that a male-only force would best serve the military and consequently our nation. However, the reality is that our all-volunteer force cannot be manned without females. The solution, of course, is a return to the draft where all males, regardless of socioeconomic background, have an equal opportunity to serve their country. This will not happen in my lifetime!

My assessment is tempered by the fact that females have had remarkable success during both peace and war. I just do not think females should be put in harm's way.

I had now been selected for promotion to full colonel, so I was no longer my own assignment officer. My records had been moved to colonels division. It was also time for me to move, as the AG Branch chief job was a two-year assignment. It was one of those high-visibility positions that competitive AG lieutenant colonels needed to be cycled through for promotion to colonel.

The G1 of I Corps and Fort Lewis, Fort Lewis, Washington, and I had visited in late 1985, and he told me Lieutenant General Palastra, my old boss at Fort Polk, wanted me to be his adjutant general. I called GOMO to get an idea of how long General Palastra would be at Fort Lewis and was told Palastra would most likely get his fourth star and be moving. I still thought about going. I had always wanted to see that part of our great nation. Penny balked, so I turned the offer down.

Colonel Phil Remling, who I had replaced in MILPERCEN, was being reassigned from his position in the US Army Intelligence and Security Command (INSCOM) to command the garrison at Fort Hamilton, New York. I was nominated to and approved by the INSCOM commanding general to replace Phil. Penny was pleased, as INSCOM headquarters was located in Arlington, Virginia. Upon my departure from MILPERCEN, my quarterly article in the July-September 1986 issue of the *Soldier Support Journal* ended as follows: "I leave you with these thoughts. Take care of yourself, your family, and your fellow soldiers. If you do, you, your family, your Corps, and your Army will prosper."

I was awarded my sixth Meritorious Service Medal.

22

Silent Warriors

I would find my assignment to the US Army Intelligence and Security Command (INSCOM) to be the most enjoyable and satisfying of my Army career. This was due largely to the outstanding people I worked for and those who worked for me. Equally important, INSCOM had a real-world mission to collect intelligence against organizations and states that had the intent of doing harm to the United States and its people. While the majority of the Army was training, INSCOM soldiers and civilians were performing their wartime mission without fanfare. They were indeed silent warriors.

INSCOM conducted intelligence, security, and information activities at the tactical, operational, and strategic level in all intelligence disciplines for ground commanders and national decision makers. The principal intelligence disciplines included the following:

- Human Intelligence (HUMINT)
- Signals Intelligence (SIGINT)
- Imagery Intelligence (IMINT)
- Measurement and Signature Intelligence (MASINT)
- Technical Intelligence (TECHINT)
- Open Source Intelligence (OSINT)
- Counterintelligence (CI)
- Communications Security (COMSEC)
- Information Systems Security (INFOSEC)
- Operations Security (OPSEC)

Only wise ruler and brilliant leaders who are able to conduct intelligence with superiority and cleverness, are certain to achieve great results.
—Sun Tzu

The structure of INSCOM resembled an inverted iceberg. The majority of people and organizations comprised the large portion of the iceberg. The "black" or covert operations comprised the small portion of the iceberg. In this case, the "open" or large portion was above water, and the tip of the inverted iceberg, namely the "black" operations, was below the water. They were unseen but there nevertheless. I cannot write about the "black" world for security reasons; however, I can say it existed, and you and I are safer as a result.

The command was a forty-minute drive from home. It was located at historic Arlington Hall Station in Arlington, Virginia. Arlington Hall Station was a hundred-acre installation that had been a private girl's school from 1927 until the Army commandeered the facility under the War Powers Act in 1942. It was to be used by the newly established Army Signals Intelligence Service, the precursor to the National Security Agency (NSA).

Arlington Hall

The headquarters, shown above, is where cryptanalysis of the Army Signals Intelligence Service broke the Japanese diplomatic code nicknamed *Purple*. Later, they were able to decipher Soviet encryption in a super secret project code named *Venova*. *Venova*, in addition to exploiting Soviet diplomatic communications, exposed Julius and Ethel Rosenberg's involvement in a Soviet spy ring.

The building, which was old but superbly maintained, had elegance and style. My office was on an upper floor at the end of a long, wide hall that extended the entire length of the building. A staircase provided access to the hall near the center of the building. There were no elevators. Offices for my staff were located on each side of the hall. My suite consisted of a reception area where my secretary, Liz Branch, toiled. There were separate offices for my military deputy, Lieutenant Colonel Danny Braudrick, and my sergeant major, Walt Dick. My office consisted of a desk, conference table, and easy chairs. A door led to a large balcony where I could have sunbathed had I been so inclined.

Entrance to Arlington Hall Station was through a security gate manned by military police (MP). The headquarters building was entered through a military police checkpoint where all briefcases or packages were opened and screened by the MPs. This was also done when one was exiting the building. There was a roving patrol of MPs inside the headquarters building during both day and night. Visitors or people without security badges had to be escorted within the building.

The entire building was a sensitive compartmented information facility or SCIF (pronounced skiff). A SCIF is an enclosed secure area that is used to process Sensitive Compartmented Information (SCI) level classified information. Access to a SCIF is limited, and all of the activity and conversation inside is presumed restricted from public disclosure. The building was technologically advanced, with computers at all workstations. I could send e-mails via encrypted satellite links up to Top Secret. I could not send e-mails containing SCI.

The ability to use e-mail to correspond with subordinate INSCOM commands was the best thing since sliced bread, as these commands were located across the globe. I no longer had to wait until the wee hours of the morning to get an overseas call through the Pentagon switchboard as I had to do in Korea. Communication was instantaneous. I did utilize secure landlines dedicated for INSCOM use (no waiting) when the subject matter did not lend itself to written communication.

INSCOM operated the worldwide classified cable communications system used for back channel traffic between general officers and other senior government officials. I was cleared to use this system, but I rarely did.

I was "read-on" to several high-level compartment classified projects. I was only given access to that portion of the project that I needed to know to do my job. I usually had no idea what the overall project entailed, although I was sometimes able to deduce this information. I had a Top Secret clearance and was cleared for special intelligence information (SI).

The history of the headquarters building suggested that the building was haunted. This tale went back to the early days when the government first requisitioned the building, and was a carryover from when the building served as a girls' school. The basis of the legend was that a student in the girls' school had become pregnant, and because of social mores at the time, she had hanged herself in her dormitory room. The room had never been occupied after her death. I heard this account from various people early in my assignment to INSCOM and thought nothing more about it. One day on my way to another office on an upper floor, the room was shown to me, and it was indeed empty and appeared much as it might have in the 1920s. This piqued my interest.

I like soldiers and the MPs knew that they could come by my office during their rounds and Liz Branch would give them a cup of coffee, and if I was not busy, I would engage them in conversation for a few minutes. I began to quiz the MPs, and they all purported to have seen the ghost, specifically a female, or felt her presence. Some told me they had been physically touched by the ghost. On widely separate occasions, two swore they had been picked up by the ghost and deposited headfirst in large, circular trash bins (MP blotter entry). This all happened at night.

I do not believe in ghosts or haunted buildings, although I do believe in angels. There were occasions when I worked past midnight and there were often strange noises outside my office. I never ventured alone along the long hallway and down the stairs without calling the main MP desk and asking for an escort. The MPs never sent one. There were always two.

My job description read:

Deputy Chief of Staff, Personnel for a 16,000 person major Army command (MACOM) located in and outside the continental United States (CONUS) with a worldwide Intelligence, Security and Electronic Warfare mission. Exercises staff supervision over personnel programs to include military and civilian personnel management; recruiting and retention; human affairs; personnel services; safety; awards and decorations; alcohol and drug abuse; morale, welfare, and recreation; non-appropriated fund and EO and EEO programs. Represents the commander at DA/DOD/NSA levels on personnel related issues. Responsible for development and integration of DCSPER portion of short, mid and long-range plans and contingency plans, and Military Intelligence (MI) personnel proponency.

Lieutenant Colonel Danny Braudrick, my military deputy, arrived at INSCOM shortly after me from the Naval Postgraduate School at Monterey, California, where he had completed a master's degree. Danny was first-rate in every respect, and we made a good team. Danny was a MI officer, so he spoke and understood the military intelligence vernacular and kept me straight in that regard. Danny and his wife, Mary, were good friends with both Penny and me.

Al Ressler, my civilian deputy and a GM-15, had forgotten more about civilian personnel management than I would ever know. Al was relatively young to be a GM-15. He was smart, energetic, and ambitious. He would depart INSCOM shortly before me and rise through the civilian ranks of the intelligence community. The management of civilians in the intelligence field was vastly different from normal civilian personnel management because of the classified nature of their duties. Al was the driving force in developing and implementing the excepted civilian intelligence personnel management system (CIPMS) for DA. I was blessed to have Al by my side.

Sergeant Major Walt Dick was an outstanding NCO, well known and respected within the intelligence and personnel community. He had spent many years with military intelligence organizations and spoke their language. I rarely travelled to subordinate INSCOM commands without Walt Dick.

I had an exceptional front-office team, and my civilian and military division chiefs, GS-13/14s and majors, were equally adept. The captains, NCOs, and midlevel civilians were also good. My job was to ensure that they had the resources to do their jobs, get out of their way, and let them do it.

The general officers I worked for at INSCOM were individually and collectively the best of my career. Each let me do my job. My relationship with all was one of mutual respect. Perhaps part of our close professional relationship was that we had shared similar experiences and were relatively close in age. The fact that during most of the time I was assigned to INSCOM I wore the eagles of a full colonel was more likely the real reason. I was almost a peer but not quite.

My senior rater was Major General Harry E. (Ed) Soyster. General Soyster was a West Point graduate with movie-star handsomeness and a field artilleryman by trade. He had never served with or had an assignment in military intelligence. He was a protégée of General Max Thurman, the VCSA, who was also a field artilleryman. In fact, when Thurman hosted a function at his quarters, Mrs. Soyster assisted as his hostess. Thurman was also godfather to the Soyster children. I suppose that the Soysters were the family Max Thurman never had.

Thurman had sent Soyster to INSCOM to clean the place up after some unwanted press from the days of Major General Albert Stubblebine and his interest in parapsychology and support of the CIA's Stargate Project. Stubblebine retired, and General Soyster had a reputation for being anti-anything paranormal. Even so, there were still those who would tell of Stubblebine's demonstrations during which he could bend spoons and forks using only his mind, and there were still a few of the bent spoons and forks around the headquarters. There was also some tightening up that needed to be done with alleged misuse of "black" funds. Soyster did all this quietly and quickly.

During my initial office call with General Soyster, he told me I ran the INSCOM personnel system and that he would keep the brigadier generals from interfering in my business. He indicated that there had been times when the brigadier generals had tried to influence the assignment of officers to and within INSCOM. He raised his voice and exclaimed, "I am the only one who makes colonel assignments. You make all the rest. If, in my absence, you need an assignment for a colonel, contact me. Do not let the brigadiers get involved. Do you understand?" It was the first and last time General Soyster raised his voice even slightly with me. He did on occasion with others.

It was obvious that the assignment of colonels was a sensitive issue with General Soyster. He had two brigadiers: One served as his chief of staff, the other served as the deputy commanding general. Apparently, one had approved an assignment in General Soyster's absence, which had caused a problem.

There came a time when one of the brigadiers did try to get involved in the assignment of a colonel while General Soyster was temporarily out of contact on an overseas mission. I had to tell the brigadier to back off, which he did.

The other thing that General Soyster told me that was refreshing and much different than any general I had worked for before or since was that he would not try to help the MILPERCEN commanding general do his job. He would not send back channels to MILPERCEN requesting favors or special treatment. It was for me to work things out in INSCOM's best interest with MILPERCEN, but let the system work.

General Soyster was promoted to lieutenant general shortly before I left INSCOM, and he was then assigned as the director of the Defense Intelligence Agency (DIA). He was, of all the generals I worked for, the one I would most want to work for again.

I participated as a member of the INSCOM staff in General Soyster's departure ceremony and his promotion to lieutenant general. The event occurred right before Christmas, and there had been a heavy snowfall. The ceremony was moved inside a large wooden gym-like structure at Fort Myer where all official military and civilian ceremonies involving high-ranking officials were held during inclement weather. The Army band provided the music. It was a privilege to march to the music and pass in review with INSCOM soldiers in honor of General Soyster.

My first rater was Brigadier General Ira C. (Chuck) Owens, the INSCOM chief of staff. Chuck Owens had a master's degree from Shippensburg State just like I did. General Owens would later serve as the deputy commanding general of INSCOM and eventually be promoted to lieutenant general and assigned as the Army G2. General Owens was well versed in tactical, operational, and strategic intelligence. He was all soldier, having served as the G2 of the 82nd Airborne Division and J2 of the Joint Special Operations Command (JSOC), both at Fort Bragg. I never once saw General Owens visibly upset. He was a pleasure to work for and was supportive of all I tried to accomplish. Along with General Soyster, he is one of the three I would most want to work for again.

Brigadier General Floyd L. Runyon, another Shippensburg graduate, replaced Chuck Owens as chief of staff and became my rater. Runyon was a cryptologist and most of his experience had been in strategic intelligence serving with and commanding military intelligence units that worked closely with the National Security Agency (NSA) at Fort Meade, Maryland. Runyon was the strong, silent, and cerebral type, indicative of the personality normally associated with success as a cryptologist. He also was a pleasure to work for, as he left me alone to do my job.

Brigadier General Michael M. Schneider, a Texas A&M graduate, replaced General Runyon and was my last rater in INSCOM. Mike Schneider had begun his career as an infantry officer and then transferred to the Military Intelligence Corps, where he had served in both tactical and strategic units. He was another boss with whom I enjoyed working.

Again, it was my lot to be assigned to INSCOM as a promotable lieutenant colonel. My promotable status did not seem to cause a problem, and the generals certainly had no problem with it. Eventually, my day came on March 1, 1987. Brigadier General Chuck Owens, in the absence of General Soyster, and Penny pinned on my eagles.

Promotion to Colonel.

The morning of my promotion ceremony, Penny presented me with a set of sterling silver eagles to be used in the ceremony. Along with the gift was a card that read:

Herb,

After chasing these "birds" all these years I hope they make you very happy. I am very proud of you—maybe I haven't said that often enough through the years. Wear these with pride and may they give you a great sense of accomplishment and also some peace.

All my love,

Pen

We had flown Ross in for the ceremony from Dallas, where he was now working as a licensed physical therapist, having graduated from UTMB. It was a good time for the Taylor family. I had told Penny that it was her day, too, and that Ross and I would do anything she wanted to do. She wanted to go to the Smithsonian Museum of American Art, a place she had been many times but never tired of visiting, so that was what we did. Penny wandered, looked, and studied the paintings while

Ross and I found a seat in one of their cafes and talked. Eventually, we ended up at the Museum of American History, where we had dinner in the Smithsonian's members-only dining room. The Smithsonian no longer offers a private dining room for members, which is a shame, as it was an excellent place to wind down after a day at the Washington mall.

Never trade luck for skill.
—Army aphorism

The US Army puts such a high premium on command that few commissioned officers who have not previously commanded at company, battalion, and brigade levels ever wear stars. However, most professional staff officers who have a superlative performance record may possibly cap careers with eagles on their shoulders, but only if they are lucky. I suppose this boy from Barnhart was lucky. I know this boy from Barnhart was lucky.

One of the benefits of being assigned to INSCOM was the opportunity to travel. General Soyster encouraged me to visit each major subordinate command annually to show the INSCOM flag and to serve as his eyes and ears. I would divide my trips into a European visit and Far East visit. I would travel to Europe so that my visit would coincide with Oktoberfest in Munich, Germany, and to the Far East during the spring when that part of the world is most pleasant. Each trip would take three to four weeks.

The principal INSCOM unit in Germany was the 66th Military Intelligence Brigade, which was located in Augsburg with other smaller INSCOM units scattered throughout Germany, including the Russian Language Institute in Garmisch-Partenkirchen. The institute had an unusual mission in that it trained FAOs (foreign area officers) for the Army. FAOs, once trained, served as defense attachés, security assistance officers, staff advisors on military affairs and operations, and liaison officers to foreign militaries throughout Europe. They were essentially intelligence collectors. Interestingly, the institute used former Russian soldiers and defectors as instructors. I had the opportunity to visit and share meals with these fellows and found them fascinating. My visits were prior to the time of the Berlin wall coming down, but already the

Iron Curtain was leaking like a sieve. INSCOM units were having a field day, interviewing and extracting intelligence from defectors.

Sergeant Major Walt Dick and the chief of my officer branch would accompany me on these trips. We would fly to Frankfurt, West Germany, and then on to Berlin and backtrack to visit INSCOM units in West Germany. I would then travel alone to visit Diogenes Station at Sinop, Turkey.

The visit to our field station in West Berlin was most enlightening. Field Station Berlin was collecting signals of intelligence from Soviet units located in East Germany, primarily the Russian Eighth Guards Army and the East German National People's Army. The field station in conjunction with the Berlin Brigade arranged for me to travel into East Berlin. A Berlin Brigade representative accompanied me, and we passed through the infamous Checkpoint Charlie into East Berlin. We took a short drive along a major thoroughfare, parked, and walked to a large department store that was several stories high. My instructions were that I was not to stare at East German civilians or salute Russian or East German officers. Frankly, they paid us little mind, but it was obvious that we were being watched. I was amazed at the drabness of their buildings and the starkness of their streets and surroundings. The department store was filled with items of every sort from clothes to kitchen utensils to knickknacks, all cheaply made.

Field Station Berlin had elaborate security arrangements to conceal the true nature of their mission. Even so, the unit adjutant told me that each Christmas, the senior Soviet commander in East Germany would send a message wishing the members of Field Station Berlin a merry Christmas, listing each member of the unit by name. Apparently, the Soviets had a good collection capability as well. I was told it was relatively easy to intercept Soviet message traffic, as they used a lot of Morse code and often communicated in the clear over landlines. The field station was located on the highest point in West Berlin. It sat at the top of a mound that appeared to be a large hill covered with trees. Actually, the hill consisted of rubble removed from the city after WWII.

We would return to Augsburg for a few days and then head to Munich for Oktoberfest. While at Augsburg, I visited with Lieutenant Colonel Claudia Kennedy who commanded the 3rd Operations Battalion, one of the 66th MI Brigade's subordinate battalions. Claudia

Kennedy was the first Army female promoted to lieutenant general. She retired after she had served as the Army's chief of intelligence (G2).

Oktoberfest was great fun. I did not like beer but drank my share and then some. I did like the German food served at the fair, such as *Haxn* (knuckle of pork), *Wurstl* (sausages), and *Steckerlfisch* (grilled fish on a stick). Sergeant Major Dick would over indulge and suffer mightily the next day. I remember having a queasy feeling a couple of times as well.

While in Munich, we made a side trip to Dachau, the first Nazi concentration camp opened in Germany and the second camp to be liberated by British and American forces. Over two hundred thousand prisoners from thirty countries were housed in Dachau, of whom two thirds were political prisoners and one third Jews. Over thirty-five thousand prisoners are believed to have died there, primarily from disease and malnutrition. Holocaust scholars draw a distinction between concentration camps and extermination camps, which were camps established for the sole purpose of carrying out the extermination of the Jews. Dachau was primarily a concentration camp but came to symbolize Nazi cruelty, as it was one of the first places where the previously unknown Nazi practices were exposed to the world. I cannot comprehend man's inhumanity to man and how this could have happened. A real danger of history repeating itself exists today from radical elements within the Muslim world.

Sergeant Major Dick was a devout Catholic, and every Sunday, he attended mass. I attended a mass with him in Heidelberg, Germany, at a beautiful cathedral several centuries old. The mass was conducted in Latin with a sprinkling of German. Sergeant Major Dick told me to do what he did, but he appeared slow in responding to the ritual. I think the language barrier confused him, or perhaps it was all the beer he had drank the night before. I can still see in my mind's eye that ancient church. It was stunning and reeked of history.

We usually stayed in Garmisch for a few days, primarily to recoup. Each unit we visited wanted to wine and dine us, which meant a lot of late nights. After a while, the body begged for rest. Once, we were in a Garmisch hotel bar, and all the patrons were singing what I was told were verses from the German national anthem that had been banned after WWII. Later, people began to arrive at the hotel dressed in their WWII uniforms, and what splendid uniforms they were. Apparently, it was a reunion of one of the WWII German Army combat divisions. Music began to drift out from the hotel's main ballroom. I loved the old German marching songs they were singing, all very patriotic and nationalistic.

Eventually, we would end up back in Frankfurt. Sergeant Major Dick and whoever else was travelling with me would return to Washington, D.C., and I would fly to Istanbul and stay at a military-leased hotel near the airport. This was a much nicer hotel than the one Penny, Ross, and I had stayed in so many years ago. The rooms and food were better, and the tanning factory was no longer there.

The commander of Field Station Sinop would send one of his two twin-engine militarized commercial aircraft to pick me up and fly me to Sinop. On the way up, I was talking with the pilot, and he wanted to show off his recently installed autopilot. He asked, "Where you from, colonel?"

I answered, "D.C."

He entered some numbers in a console that set between him and the co-pilot. The plane began a gradual turn, and simultaneously, a printout emerged from the console. The printout contained information about flying times, distances, fuel stops, and other information for a flight to D.C. He said, "I will have to make a few landings and takeoffs, but the autopilot will do the rest." He then turned the plane back toward Sinop. I was impressed.

The landing at Field Station Sinop airstrip was worth the price of admission. The airstrip began near the edge of the Black Sea and ended near the base of a large cliff. The pilot had to fly out over the Black Sea, turn, line the aircraft up with the runway, fly yards above the water, land, and then make a hard braking stop. The pilot told me that there was little room for error. It must have been even more exciting in a US Air Force C-130 that brought supplies and mail in twice a week.

Field Station Sinop was a brigade-sized unit located on a peninsula atop a high cliff overlooking the Black Sea. The commander was Colonel William P. Walters, a classmate from CGSC whom I knew well. The command was known in military circles as Diogenes Station after the Greek philosopher, Diogenes, who had been born in Sinop.

In addition to US Army personnel, there were US Navy personnel collecting information on Soviet submarines and warships in the Black

Sea. The Black Sea gave the Soviets access to the Atlantic Ocean via the Mediterranean and Aegean Sea and various straits. There was also a small US Air Force element, a Turkish contingent, and NSA representation. The unit was self-contained with supply by C-130 aircraft. It was a thirteen-month, unaccompanied hardship tour made even more difficult because of repeated assignments to Sinop. Soldiers would do their tour at Sinop, rotate back to the States for assignment, generally with the NSA, and twenty-four months later, were again sent to Turkey. This was necessary because all spoke Russian and each became subject experts on that part of the world.

Alcohol and depression problems, primarily rooted in boredom, were areas that Bill Walters and his medical people had to monitor constantly. Sitting at a console and listening to Russian communications for eight hours with little to occupy their off-duty time was not conducive to the soldier's mental health. Bill Walters did the best that he could within his limited resources to provide soldiers with off-duty opportunities. There was an all-ranks' club that served alcohol for a limited period each evening, a library, a craft shop, a gym, a chapel, a very small PX, and other activities. But that piece of the world became very small during a thirteen-month tour. The isolation and working conditions sometimes resulted in sexual harassment, unwanted advances, and fraternization problems.

Once when I was there, the female soldiers were making dresses for a fashion show, and other soldiers were practicing for a Christmas pageant. There was also a radio station manned by volunteer soldiers that broadcasted a few hours each day. There were no cell phones, televisions, e-mails, or other amenities that the soldiers of today enjoy. The US Air Force flew in mail twice a week, but that was erratic during the winter because of weather.

The town of Sinop was small, home to around twenty-five thousand, and it was isolated, which meant it had few recreational activities or even sightseeing opportunities for the soldiers. I had dinner with the mayor of Sinop once at a nice restaurant by Turkish standards. The mayor was young, energetic, and supportive of the field station. He and Bill Walters enjoyed an amiable relationship. I remember that General Soyster brought the mayor to Washington for a visit at INSCOM's expense.

Bill did offer trips to the US Air Force base at Incirlik, Turkey, on the Mediterranean with nice beaches, and soldiers would ride a ferry for a three-day trip to Istanbul. Some soldiers even braved a ride in a decrepit bus to Istanbul. Field Station Sinop, more than any other INSCOM command, required a strong, mature leader of high moral standards. The commander was out there by himself with no one to turn to when problems arose. Bill Walters was that person.

I remember two incidents most about SINOP. One afternoon, Bill and I were in the operations center, and a soldier motioned to Bill to put on headphones. Soon, they were laughing uncontrollably. They were monitoring communications between the commander of the Soviet space station Mir and the ground. Apparently, a cosmonaut on a resupply ship had erroneously connected the fresh water supply to the same apparatus used to remove waste from the Mir. The commander of space station Mir was screaming, "I want him flogged. I want him flogged."

Upon arrival at Diogenes Station, I immediately noticed that all sidewalks and walkways had handrails. I did not ask why, but I was curious. The next morning, I found out why. The fog coming in off the Black Sea was so thick that you could not see your hand in front of your face. Bill told me that more than one soldier had tried to move from one point to another without using the sidewalks and handrails and became totally lost and had to wait until the fog cleared. He also told me the fog would clear by 1000 hours but the handrails would still be needed because of the wind, and he was right. The wind came in, and the fog went out; however, the wind increased in velocity until you could not stand unless you were holding on to the rails.

This boy from Barnhart did not envy the soldiers of Diogenes Station.

My trips to the Far East involved visiting Field Station Hawaii (tough duty), the 500th Military Intelligence Group at Camp Zama, Japan, my old stomping grounds, and the 501st Military Intelligence Brigade in Korea.

I would visit Field Station Hawaii on my way to Japan. When I returned to the States from Korea, I would spend a couple of days lying on the beach in Honolulu to give my body, especially my liver, a rest. Field Station Hawaii was located in a large underground bunker constructed during WWII. My visits to the commands in Hawaii and Japan were relatively uneventful, as the units were usually at 100 percent strength. Every soldier wanted an assignment to Hawaii, and many volunteered for Japan, so there were mostly happy campers in these commands.

The visit to Camp Zama gave me a chance to revisit all the places I had been before. I especially enjoyed the opportunity to return to traditional Japanese bathhouses and to visit Quarters 8 at Camp Zama, where Penny, Ross, and I had had such good times so many years before. I have found over the years that most places I return to after having been away for a time have changed, sometimes significantly. I really do not like change, so I am often disappointed. This was not true of Camp Zama. Most of the installation appeared as it had been when I had lived there. Quarters 8 had changed relatively little. The yard and front of the house were the same. The lady of the house was kind enough to show me the interior of the home after I told her who I was and that I had once lived there. The kitchen and the bathroom had been remodeled, and the kitchen expanded. A small, enclosed screen porch had been built onto the back of the house, but the rest was exactly as I remembered it.

It was a gorgeous spring day, so I told my driver that he was no longer needed, as I would walk back to the VIP billets. I needed the exercise and fresh air, and I wanted to recall the people and places that I had known while I had been at Camp Zama. I remember that I became very melancholy as I walked down that curvy road lined with pine and cherry trees in bloom. The feeling remained as I was coming off the hill, passing by Clayton Kano's parents' home and the two-story concrete building, where we had stayed for a month when we had first arrived in Japan. It was more than just feeling sad. It was a premonition that my life was not going to turn out as I had planned. I felt a heavy weight on my shoulders and a tiredness that I could not explain. It soon went away after a shower in the VIP quarters and a couple of scotches at the Zama Officer's Club, which had not changed. The feeling would come periodically over the years. Thankfully, it did not last long, but it was always lurking in the back of my mind.

My first trip to the 501st MI Brigade was as a promotable colonel. I had been told by people at headquarters INSCOM that the commander,

Colonel Earl Riddle, could be difficult to work with. I had Sergeant Major Dick and a captain with me. We had a long sedan ride through terrible traffic from Camp Zama to Narita International Airport, which was some distance outside Tokyo, to catch our short, two-hour flight to Seoul. We were to leave at 1800 hours and arrive in Seoul around 2000 hours. The departing flight was late by several hours, so by the time we got to our billets in Yongsan, Korea, it was around 0100 hours. My escort officer told me he would pick me up for breakfast at 0530 and that Colonel Riddle had scheduled briefings for me starting at 0630. I was fighting jet lag, so that was a short night.

Have you ever met someone you immediately disliked? Well, I walked into that conference room and shook hands with Earl Riddle, and he immediately did not like me. I could feel it, and I think it was obvious to others. Earl became my nemesis. Apparently, he considered me a greater threat to the 501st than Kim Il-sung and the North Korean Army. He would write sarcastic notes belittling me about how much better the Eighth Army was supported with people than the 501st, and he accused me of filling other INSCOM units at a higher fill rate than the 501st. This was not true. I made sure the 501st and Field Station Sinop were maintained at 100 percent strength because of their mission.

We were having the semiannual INSCOM Command and Staff Conference and had gathered at the headquarters for briefings from various intelligence agencies within the Washington metropolitan area. We then boarded a bus for a three-day stay in Charlottesville, Virginia, where we had a unit with a classified intelligence mission. We were to receive more briefings, but the main purpose was to give General Soyster the opportunity to present his commanders with their annual OER and for all to socialize and "kick back." The seating arrangement on the bus was such that Earl stared daggers at me all the way down and all the way back. I had tried to shake hands with him at the headquarters, but he had brushed me off. Earl Riddle remains a riddle to me even today.

One of the funny situations that arose from the Riddle affair was a trick my deputy, Danny Braudrick, in collusion with Colonel "Holly" Hollingsworth played on me prior to the Charlottesville trip. "Holly" was a Texas A&M graduate and a "good ol' boy" and the INSCOM deputy chief of staff. Danny and Holly created an official-looking document that they had gotten General Owens to sign. The document stated that because of budgetary reasons and in an attempt to develop interpersonal relationships between commanders and staff, each staff member would share a hotel room with a commander. I had been paired with Earl Riddle. Danny brought the document into my office and handed it to me and said, "You are not going to like this." I read the document, went ballistic, and headed to General Owens office. I was ready to fall on my sword, knowing that General Owens was screwing with me, but not in the way I had thought. I handed the memo to Holly and told him I needed to see General Owens. Holly told me the general was busy, that General Owens had personally paired me with Riddle, and that I would be making a mistake to discuss it with him. About that time, Danny showed up with a shit-eating grin on his face, and I knew I had been had. Danny was always screwing with me. I guess because I was easy to fool and upset.

On the return from Charlottesville, we stopped at Vint Hill Farms Station for a change of command and retirement ceremony in honor of Colonel Lee J. Holland. Colonel Holland was the military attaché in Iran and was taken hostage along with fifty-three other Americans on November 4, 1979. They were to remain hostage for 444 days after a group of Islamist students and militants took over the American embassy in support of the Iranian Revolution. They would be released minutes after Ronald Reagan was sworn in as president. This incident precipitated the conflict between the United States and Iran, which continues today.

Vint Hill Farm Station was a seven-hundred-acre Army facility with a classified intelligence mission, and it was located forty miles southwest of Washington, D.C. The installation was in a rural area surrounded by horse farms. The dominant feature of the post was a vast array of antennas inside security fences. The base had supported the Army and the National Security Agency for many years, beginning in 1942, in the signals intelligence-gathering mission. I found the bucolic setting to be a place of serenity, and it was vastly different from the hectic life inside the beltway. It must have been a great place to be assigned, as it was located near many Civil War battlefields and the sights of Washington, D.C., without the disadvantage of having to live inside or near the beltway.

When I returned one year from a Far East tour, I left balmy Honolulu to fly into a snowstorm at Dulles International. The pilot announced that we were the last plane to land because they were closing both Dulles and Washington National. Penny was to meet me, but she realized the storm was a bad one and it was unlikely that she could make it to Dulles. I called her, and she suggested I stay at a hotel near the airport. I figured that they would all be filled, and I really wanted to sleep in my own bed and next to her for a change.

I caught a cab, but the driver told me he did not think we could make it to Springfield, and he did not want to take me. The cab ride was around fifty dollars, and I told the cabby I would give him a fifty-dollar tip if he got me home, so away we went. We motored along the Dulles Toll Road and the beltway slowly but steadily. Once we left the beltway, the snow began to pile up, and driving became difficult. The cab company was radioing for all their cabs to return to their base in D.C. and to call in their status. The driver ignored the calls, but eventually, he told me we were not going to make it to my house and he needed to return to base. I upped the tip another fifty, and we slowly moved forward. My house sat on a hill, and the grade was quite steep. The cab became hopelessly stuck in the snow a little over a quarter mile from home. I knew I could make it home, but what about the cabdriver? He told me he had seen a shopping mall a mile or so back and that was where he would stay until the storm cleared.

I gave the driver all the cash I had on me, which was around $150.00, grabbed my luggage and briefcase, and headed up the hill. The snow was up to my waist in places. It had drifted up to my knees everywhere. Eventually, I had to leave my bag and later my briefcase lying in the snow. I was covered in sweat and totally exhausted when I rang the doorbell for Penny to let me in the house. It was another day before the snow stopped and several days before I could recover my belongings. Thankfully, I was not carrying classified material.

This boy from Barnhart does not miss the snow and cold of Northern Virginia. I can tolerate heat, but cold gets in your bones and stays there.

I have just returned from the funeral of my friend and high school classmate, Karman Weatherby, dead from a heart attack at the age of sixty-nine. He died on March 11, 2010, and never knew what hit him.

Karman was an athlete, and excelled in football, basketball and track. He was an Eagle Scout, Vietnam veteran, recipient of the Purple Heart, a lover of music, particularly rock and roll, and a music trivia buff. He had a sarcastic wit, loved jokes, and enjoyed life as much as anyone I have ever known. He was a surgeon. Many people in the San Angelo and West Texas area owe their lives to Karman's skill.

Most important, Karman was a Christian who led a spiritual life representative of his beliefs. He had participated in the "Walk to Emmaus" and enjoyed his Emmaus fellowship. The First Methodist Church of San Angelo overflowed with people standing in the aisle at his service. Many people mourned for Karman and his family.

Karman married his high school sweetheart, Carolyn Becknell, in Ciudad Acuna, Mexico, on January 16, 1959. Penny and I were to accompany Karman and Carolyn, but because we were cutting high school classes, we decided Penny should not go. I went, and while there, I bought a bottle of apricot brandy, which I proceeded to drink. I spilled the brandy on the seat cover of Karman's car, a new Chevrolet, which made Karman unhappy. I have known Carolyn since I was a boy at Barnhart, as her father worked on the Bar S and I played basketball against Big Lake and Karman while at Barnhart. It had been a long and lasting friendship.

The Weatherby and Becknell union was a fruitful one. They had four children: Tim, Jay, Amy, and Kristin. His ten grandchildren knew Karman as Daddy Doc as did his e-mail friends. The grief and sadness the Weatherby family is feeling is understandable, as they now realize that Daddy Doc lives only in their memory. I grieve with them, and my heart is heavy. Karman was many things, not the least of which he was a good husband, father, grandfather, and friend. Karman was a beautiful person, but most of all, he had a beautiful spirit, a beautiful soul.

Rest in peace, my friend. Yours was a life well lived.

One of my strategies while at INSCOM was to invite general officers from the Total Army Personnel Command (TAPA), the new designation for MILPERCEN, to visit INSCOM for briefings and to meet my people. This served two purposes: One, I knew that the generals, once they understood the INSCOM mission, would return to TAPA with our personnel requirements visible on their radar screens, ensuring that their people met and possibly exceeded our needs. Two, their visits gave my people face time with the generals, which might prove beneficial to them in future. I also had a TAPA general as the keynote speaker for the INSCOM Worldwide Personnel Conference, which I held annually for adjutants, S1s, and deputy commanders.

A flag officer I did not invite to INSCOM was Vice-Admiral William Studeman, the director of the National Security Agency (NSA). He wanted to see me. The director of NSA, also known as the DIRNSA (pronounced "durnsa"), is a heavyweight in the intelligence community. He is recommended by the secretary of defense, nominated by the president, and confirmed by a majority vote of the US Senate.

Admiral Studeman's office had called General Soyster's office and said the admiral wanted to visit INSCOM for personnel discussions with me and that he did not want any INSCOM briefings or office calls with INSCOM generals. General Soyster had misgiving about the visit because protocol dictated that Studeman should have an office call with him and he felt, rightly so, that if Admiral Studeman had an issue with INSCOM, it should be discussed with him and not one of his underlings. Therefore, General Soyster had the message relayed back to NSA that he welcomed a visit and office call with Studeman followed by discussions with me, which was what happened.

The issue that Admiral Studeman had with INSCOM stemmed from a less than congenial relationship between his personnel chief, a US Air Force colonel, and me. INSCOM was responsible for providing personnel support to NSA. In fact, NSA reimbursed the Army for my salary and some of my people for this mission. This effort was accomplished by me requisitioning soldiers from TAPA for assignment to the 704th Military Intelligence Brigade, a subordinate INSCOM unit, to work in the huge copper-shielded NSA building at Fort Meade, Maryland. The disconnect occurred when I received a call from TAPA that the US Air Force colonel and his deputy, a female Army lieutenant colonel, were visiting TAPA with a by-name list of soldiers they wanted assigned to the 704th for subsequent detail to work in the NSA. TAPA wanted to know if they were to deal with me or with the NSA, and if it was me, they wanted me to ensure that NSA stop pestering their assignment managers. I had asked the NSA colonel on several occasions to stay away from TAPA. He would for a while, and then I would find out he was back at TAPA with by-name requests. I met with the colonel at NSA and told him to cease and desist or I would have to get my general and his admiral involved, and neither he nor I wanted that to occur. I was wrong, because he now had them involved. Thankfully, I had briefed General Soyster on the problem, so he was aware of why Studeman wanted to see me.

Admiral Studeman met with General Soyster for a brief time, and I escorted the admiral to the INSCOM command conference room, trailed by the US Air Force colonel and his deputy and Colonel (P) Schneider, the INSCOM chief of staff. The conference room consisted of a large screen at the front, with two smaller intelligence-dedicated screens on either side, ten to twelve rows of elevated theater seats along the back and sides, and a massive table in the middle of the room where the principals sat. I was prepared to give the admiral an overview of the assignment process, but instead of taking a seat at the conference table, he climbed several rows to sit at the back of the room while I stood. Colonel Schneider took a side seat on the first row at the back of the room, and the colonel and lieutenant colonel sat on seats arrayed around the sides.

The admiral began to pepper me with questions about how the Army selected, trained, and assigned soldiers, both officer and enlisted, with emphasis on military intelligence skills. It was apparent he was testing me to determine if I knew the personnel business. Eventually, he and I moved to a philosophical discussion about women in the military. Two questions I remember him asking were the following: "Females make up what percent of Army military intelligence skills? What percent do you think they will be in five years?" I rattled off the total percentage and the percentage for each discipline. I had recently sat in on a breakdown of all intelligence specialties at TAPA, so I was able to give him concise projections for five years and a guess for ten and fifteen years. The US Air Force colonel tried once to interject himself in our discussion. The admiral cut him short, and he got the message that his input was neither solicited nor wanted. Colonel (P) Schneider said nothing.

Admiral Studeman thanked me for my time. I escorted him to his sedan, and I was followed by the US Air Force colonel and the Army lieutenant colonel. Then they departed.

Colonel Schneider called me to his office and said, "A very impressive performance, colonel." I never had trouble with NSA after the admiral's visit. In fact, I soon received a memo from NSA inviting me to a series of executive briefings and a tour. This allowed me to get into the bowels of the NSA building and view their array of supercomputers.

Sergeant majors conduct the reenlistment program within the Army. The program at DA is managed by a sergeant major, and each major command and installation has a sergeant major that runs his or her programs. I had a sergeant major that ran the INSCOM program. He had a budget of two hundred thousand dollars. My reenlistment sergeant major, not to be confused with Sergeant Major Dick, told me he had received a call from the DA reenlistment sergeant major that informed him General Ono, now a lieutenant general and the DA DCSPER, wanted to see me about a reenlistment problem in one of our subordinate battalions located in Germany. This particular battalion had soldiers in a low-density discipline that was difficult to recruit without a large enlistment bonus. It was even more difficult to reenlist soldiers, as they could take their Army training, experience, and security clearance and quickly obtain high-paying civilian jobs with DIA, CIA, or defense contractors.

My reenlistment NCO and I traveled to the Pentagon, where we met with General Ono and several of his straphangers. It was the first time I had been in the DCSPER's office since I had been assigned to ODCSPER some six years before. Little had changed, and I suspect did not change until September 11, 2001, when the then DCSPER, Lieutenant General Tim Maude, and several of his people were killed in the terrorist attack on the Pentagon.

General Ono wanted to chide me about the poor reenlistment rate for the aforementioned discipline. He told me he was doing his part in providing DA monies to fund enlistment and reenlistment bonuses, but we were not doing our part because soldiers in that discipline were getting out of the Army. I suggested he provide even more money to allow us to compete with the other users of that discipline. He went ballistic and threatened to cut off funds entirely. You do not disagree with a three-star in front of his subordinates. I let him huff and puff, and finally, he talked himself into increasing the reenlistment bonus. I, of course, had to pledge that INSCOM would work harder to reenlist soldiers. After the meeting was over, General Ono asked me to remain, and we had a pleasant chat.

Outside agencies robbing INSCOM was a recurring problem. Civilians, particularly low-level clerical personnel, were the primary problem. It was nearly impossible to hire a low-level secretary or clerical person with the requisite security clearance. INSCOM had to hire a person and then try to get the person cleared. Because all of them had to have a Top Secret clearance, it could take up to nine months for a clearance to be processed. In the meantime, these people could not get into Arlington Hall. Consequently, I had anywhere from fifteen to thirty folks, normally women, waiting clearance. I would loan them out to other agencies that did not have a need for them to be cleared just to keep them busy. Finally, an employee would be cleared. Shortly, they would be offered a high-paying job by another agency, usually a defense contractor. I am told it took an average of twenty-five thousand dollars to complete a Top Secret clearance, so INSCOM employees represented a lucrative market for the "beltway bandits." I am not sure Al Ressler was able to completely solve this dilemma, although I remember he got the lawyers to agree to new hires signing an employment contract that enabled us to keep them for at least one year after their security clearance was finalized.

It was around this time that INSCOM hosted the Worldwide Reenlistment Conference at a hotel near the airport in San Antonio, Texas. We received logistical support from our SIGINT battalion located on "Security Hill" at Kelly Air Force Base. There were no officers present at the conference except for Colonel Phil Remling, my predecessor, and me. I was there to welcome conference attendees and to introduce the keynote speaker, Colonel Remling. I flew to San Antonio the night before, and Phil and I had dinner at a Mexican restaurant.

The next day after my welcome to the reenlistment NCOs, our SIGINT battalion picked me up and took me to "Security Hill" for briefings. It was here I learned that the battalion was the first to learn of the Chernobyl disaster at the Chernobyl nuclear power plant in the Soviet Ukraine. Their personnel were monitoring Soviet communications and happened to stumble on the disaster, as it was occurring, which enabled them to notify national command authorities even before the Soviet high command knew of the incident.

I cannot recall the trips that Penny and I took during my assignment to INSCOM except for a few. A vacation in the US Virgin Islands stands out. We were to leave early one morning from Baltimore/Washington International Airport. A snowstorm was due to arrive the evening prior, so we drove to Baltimore and spent the night near the airport. It was quite a shock to leave the frigid cold and blowing snow of Baltimore and arrive in the stifling heat of Saint Thomas. It did not take us long to acclimate. Penny was soon sunbathing, and I was snorkeling. Penny would not even try to snorkel, saying, "I will breathe in water and drown."

A small and rocky prominence jutted out into the bay, dividing the beach at our resort from another beach. I decided I would climb the mound and see what was on the other side. I discovered it was a topless beach. The scenery would change each time a cruise ship anchored in the harbor at Charlotte Amalie, necessitating me to climb the hill. Eventually, Penny got curious, followed, and told me, "I now know why you were climbing that hill. I thought you were getting some exercise." I tried to talk her into to walking the beach with me, but she would have none of that.

We took the short ferry ride to Saint John Island and toured the island. I found the snorkeling to be much better than Saint Thomas. I saw some beautiful fish while in the water at Saint John. Saint John is an exclusive travel and honeymoon destination with several resorts and one of the top ten beaches in the world. It is also the most expensive of the US Virgin Islands, attracting a high level of affluent tourists. The island's affluence has earned it the distinction of being the "Beverly Hills of the Caribbean." That explains why we stayed on the island of Saint Thomas. The prices, while not cheap, were much cheaper than on Saint John.

We had a lazy, restful time sunbathing, reading, snorkeling, and touring the islands by jeep. We took most of our meals at our resort as we were on a package deal, but we did eat several meals in Charlotte Amalie while we were shopping at the duty-free shops. I vividly remember that the sex was great. I suppose it had something to do with the heat of the tropics. It was hard to return to the cold and hustle and bustle of our everyday lives.

In October 1988, Colonel Frank Foster, commandant of the Adjutant General School, invited me to be the graduation speaker for one of the AG basic courses. I flew to Indianapolis, and a waiting staff car took me to the VIP quarters at Fort Harrison. I had dinner that evening with Frank and Linda in their wonderful two-story, brick quarters with hardwood floors and twelve-foot ceilings, a place built in the 1920s. Fort Benjamin Harrison was closed as part of the 1996 Base Realignment and Closure Commission (BRAC) recommendations. The site has since been redeveloped and includes residential neighborhoods and a golf course, and it is the location of Fort Harrison State Park.

The next morning, prior to addressing the class, I noticed that there were several senior members of the AG Corps in the audience, which I thought unusual for a basic course graduation. I was not that great of a speaker for them to take time out of their schedules to hear my remarks. I gave my fifteen-minute talk to the graduating class. Immediately thereafter, Frank rose from his chair and addressed the assembled audience and announced that I was being awarded the Order of Horatio Gates Bronze Medal for exemplary meritorious service to the US Army Adjutant General's Corps. Major General Gates was the first adjutant general of the Army. During the Revolutionary War, a gold medal was presented to General Gates by congress to commemorate his victories over the British in the battles of Bennington, Fort Stanwix, and Saratoga. These three key battles prevented the British from occupying the strategic Hudson Valley and isolating New England from the other colonies. The original die used to make General Gates' gold medal is used to make the Order of Horatio Gates medals.

This award was much unexpected. Today, the medal is encased in a frame along with the presentation certificate, and it hangs in my office with other medals received over the course of my Army career.

The Army Security Agency (ASA) was integrated into INSCOM in 1977. Prior to that time, ASA had operated as a separate command providing cryptology support for the Army. ASA was small and close-knit, and even by 1987, many Army cryptologists could barely accept the fact they no longer operated independently. The soldiers of

ASA had established a fund to which each member contributed monthly to guarantee a college education for the children of any ASA soldier who died while on active duty. The legality of the fund was questionable, but over the years, it had grown to a significant amount. The monies had transferred to INSCOM and had been deposited with a large D.C. bank that managed the money. Once a quarter, a representative from the bank would brief General Soyster and his advisory board, of which I was a member, regarding the status of the fund. The fund increased each quarter, and had grown to over nine hundred thousand dollars. The advisory board decided to make the money available as a grant, a gift, to any child of an INSCOM soldier, active or retired, to use for college, provided they met certain standards. Even then, the fund continued to grow.

General Soyster was looking to terminate the fund, but he was reluctant to do so because of pressure from former ASA members. Their position was that they had raised the money and it should be used for the purpose originally intended. Finally, upon the advice and urging of the DA IG, the money, which was now over one million dollars, was turned over to Army Emergency Relief (AER).

AER is a private nonprofit organization incorporated in 1942 by the secretary of war and the Army chief of staff. AER funds are made available to commanders to provide emergency financial assistance to soldiers—active and retired—and their dependents when there is a valid need. AER funds made available to commanders are not limited and are constrained only by the requirement of valid need. Although sponsored by Department of the Army, AER receives no funding from the government.

I used the fund over the years to help needy soldiers, and I continue to contribute to AER during their annual fund drive.

During the entire duration of my assignment, plans were being made to transfer INSCOM to a new headquarters building being constructed at Fort Belvoir, Virginia, near Mount Vernon, the plantation home of George Washington. Arlington Hall, although certified as a SCIF, was not adequate for the purpose for which it was intended. Further, it lay on direct line of sight with the Soviet embassy in northwest Washington, D.C., an embassy that was known to have technical capability to monitor American communications in the Washington area. The new INSCOM building was to have a portion underground. Additionally, Arlington Hall was coveted by the Department of State for their Foreign Service Institute and National Foreign Affairs Training Center, so a move by INSCOM was a win-win situation for both.

General Soyster had chosen the garrison commander of Arlington Hall Station to plan for the move relieving the INSCOM staff of this onerous task. This individual had been selected for promotion to colonel and subsequent reassignment to Korea. General Soyster called me to his office and told me that he had never tried to influence the personnel system with regard to an individual's assignment but that he needed the garrison commander to remain until after the move to Fort Belvoir. He asked how he should go about making that happen. I suggested a phone call to the commander of TAPA, as I was aware of General Soyster's aversion to back channels, but he said he wanted to use that as a last resort. He directed I prepare a back channel, which I did.

Several days later, he called me to his office and handed me a response from the director of Officer Personnel Management at TAPA, a brigadier general, that provided the typical TAPA response, "I regret that I am unable to accommodated your request as the officer is required for a high-priority assignment. It is his time to move, and if your request is approved, some other officer will have to move early."

General Soyster was livid. "I have never asked TAPA for help, and the commander TAPA did not even respond to my request. He had one of his horse holders turn me down." I asked General Soyster to give me a chance to work the problem before he took further action.

I drove to TAPA to see my old friend Colonel Ez Cummings, the TAPA chief of staff, and laid the situation out for him. He told me that the TAPA commanding general had been TDY, that he had not seen General Soyster's request, and that the director of Officer Personnel Management had responded in his absence. He said, "Let's go talk to the boss." I lay the circumstances out to the TAPA commanding general, emphasizing that General Soyster had never asked TAPA for anything. The general told me he would look into General Soyster's request and let General Soyster know his decision soon.

I returned to INSCOM and headed to General Soyster's office. He saw me and waved me in and said, "You do good work, colonel.

I just got a call from the commanding general of TAPA explaining he had been out of the net, apologized for not answering my request, and told me it was approved." General Soyster's faith in the personnel system was renewed. I would bet he never sent another back channel to TAPA.

General Soyster called me to his office and told me he had been selected by the secretary of the Army to be the president of the next brigadier-general selection board. Him telling me this was unusual because board membership was kept secret to preclude board members from being inundated with back channels from general officers and others supporting their "boy." General Soyster told me he would like me to give him the names of five AG colonels that should be promoted to brigadier general and two that should not. I told him I probably knew twenty AG colonels that were qualified to be and would make super brigadier generals. He said, "No, I only want five, and rank order them." He also told me the two who should not be promoted were to be officers who were competitive, but who did not take care of their people.

I went back to my office and spent some time deciding who would be number one and who would be number five. The two who should not have been general officers was easy. I, of course, did not include my name on either list.

I was leaving the headquarters some three weeks later when General Soyster got out of his sedan. He had just completed his duty on the selection board and wanted to talk. He told me that an AG colonel had been the board's lone female selection for promotion to brigadier general. He went on to tell me that he had twice gone to the secretary of the Army to tell him that there was no female better qualified than a male to be a brigadier general. He told me that after the second time, the secretary of the army told him, "You either pick a female, or I will disband the board and appoint a new one." General Soyster said he and the board members were not willing to fall on their swords over the issue.

I have often wondered how I would have fared if the board had not had to select a female. This female was the only AG colonel selected for promotion.

I was in my office when Lieutenant Colonel (P) Patrick Hughes came in to see me. Pat had been slated to replace Earl Ritter as the commander of the 501st Military Intelligence Brigade. Pat was a classmate from CGSC, a friend, and an all-around good fellow. We visited for a while, and Pat asked, "You reckon someone around here would pin on my eagles?" Pat was on leave before he departed for Korea, and his promotion date had arrived. I arranged for one of the generals to conduct the ceremony. Pat was a welcome relief from Earl. I never heard a peep from Pat about poor support. He once told me, "I'm satisfied with getting my fair share."

Pat went on to great success in successive assignments, and he was ultimately selected for lieutenant general and appointed as the director of the Defense Intelligence Agency (DIA).

One thing that always fascinated me was the way I would be taken to visit one of our "black" units. A nondescript vehicle with Maryland, D.C., or Virginia license plates rather than government plates would be used to transport me. The driver would take me on a circuitous route that added thirty to forty-five minutes to the normal trip. All to ensure we were not being followed. I loved the "spook" business.

Around January 1989, I began to think about my next assignment. Penny, of course, wanted me to stay in the area, but I had decided it was time to return to Texas and position myself for retirement. I understood her preference for the stimulating cultural, economic, and social climate of Washington, D.C., to the less urbane charms of living on or near Fort Hood and Killeen, Texas, but it was time to go home. Penny's argument was I was more likely to find a job in D.C. than Texas and she had a nice salary. We could "sock away" a lot of money before we decided if, when, and where we wanted to live in Texas.

I told Penny I would see what colonel's division had to offer in the D.C. area. When I called Lieutenant Colonel (P) Earl Halbrook, now my assignment manager, I told Earl I really wanted to go to Texas, but would not be adverse to another assignment in the Washington area. Earl told me he really wanted my job and he would see what he could do. There are often strange twists in the Army. Once, I had been Earl's assignment manager, and now he was mine.

The primary reason for wanting to return to Texas was that I knew my career was nearing an end. The OER that I had received from Colonel Eisenbarth and a decision that I had made to not compete for a highly visible and prestigious position ensured I would finish my career as a colonel.

I may have been able to overcome the Eisenbarth OER had I commanded as a lieutenant colonel or colonel. I had missed my chance to command as a lieutenant colonel, even though I had been selected as an alternate on the command list. I was chagrined to find on arriving at AG Branch that my number had come up while at the War College. The officer who had served temporarily as the AG Branch chief had apparently decided that I did not need to command because I would be a War College graduate and soon selected for colonel. Therefore, he had gone to the next lieutenant colonel on the command list when my number came up. This ensured that I would not command as a colonel. The Army was not going to select me for colonel-level command without commanding as a lieutenant colonel.

The other factor weighing on my decision was that I had burned one bridge too many. I had received a call for Colonel Patricia P. Hickerson, who at the time was the administrative assistant to the chairman of the Joint Chiefs of Staff, General Colin Powell. Pat told me she had been selected for colonel-level command and would be departing in June 1989, and General Powell wanted her position to be filled by an Army officer. She was in the process of notifying TAPA to provide nominations for the position and asked if I wanted to compete for the position. If so, she would ask TAPA to include me as one of the nominees. Pat intimated that General Powell would select whomever she recommended. Pat also hinted that working for General Powell was a sure ticket for promotion. I think Pat probably called other AG colonels she considered competitive for flag rank.

I asked Pat to give me a day to think it over. Two reasons influenced my decision to tell Pat that I was not interested: One, the OER from Eisenbarth would probably result in Pat not recommending me, as my file would not be competitive with the other nominees, but that was not the real reason. I simply no longer had the fire in my belly to work the protracted hours that would be necessary toiling for General Powell. Pat told me that the position was seven days a week with a minimum of fourteen-hour days and that I could forget about a family life. I had grown accustomed to having weekends and holidays off, not to mention my nightly cocktails. It was a difficult decision to make, and I vacillated; however, I eventually realized I was not willing to pay the price necessary to be successful in the position.

Even today, I wonder if Pat had already decided that it was me she wanted to replace her and that it would have been a done deal had I said yes. I shall never know.

Pat Hickerson retired as a major general.

Earl Halbrook soon called to tell me that there was a colonel's position at Fort Hood, which had become vacant. The position was the deputy chief of staff for personnel, administration, and logistics (DCSPAL) with the Test and Experimentation Command (TEXCOM). He also told me he was getting pressure from TEXCOM to fill the position. Additionally, he had been selected for colonel-level command and would have to find another officer to replace me at INSCOM. I told Earl I really wanted the TEXCOM assignment and to stall them because I could not be released from INSCOM until the summer. I expected that because Earl was not going to be my replacement, he might decide he could not stall TEXCOM and go ahead and fill the position, but he did not.

Penny and I listed our home for sale with Bill Bisson, who had been the realtor who had sold us the home. Bill worked his magic and within a month, we had signed a contract with a lieutenant colonel returning from Germany for an assignment in the Pentagon. We had made an additional monthly payment each of the years we had been in the house, building up equity. Penny and I walked away from 9140 Conservation Way with a nice return on investment from the home.

In reviewing the OERs written by my raters and General Soyster, my senior rater, I found the following comments: "Strong flag-rank potential," "Select for general officer," "A future flag officer," and "Herb Taylor is the best AG officer I've seen, at any level, in the entire Army." In his final report on my performance, General Soyster wrote, "A must selection for general officer. I have never known a better G-1 or DCSPER." General Soyster wrote this after he had served as president of the brigadier general selection board, so he must have considered me competitive for promotion. In his senior rater comments, Major General

Stanley H. Hyman, General Soyster's successor, wrote, "Promote this fine commander-oriented personnel expert to brigadier general now. The army needs him." General Soyster and General Hyman both gave me top block reports.

I was awarded the Legion of Merit upon my departure from INSCOM and inducted as an honorary member of the Military Intelligence Corps. There was a ceremony, but I do not remember the details. The folks at Woodburn Mental Health Center gave Penny a fine farewell party, and many people spoke of how much Penny meant to them and the organization. Penny shed a few tears as she thanked the assembled crowd. She hated to leave her job and co-workers. A video was made of the proceedings, and I use to play the tape just to remember the sound of her voice; however, I have not done so in several years. I think Ross now has the video.

This boy from Barnhart was going home, home to Texas.

23

Last Hurrah

The military is a horse of a different color. While soldiers come from the greater American culture with all its subcultures, the Army has a culture all its own and a language all its own, and it is organized unlike the rest of American society. I had been a part of this culture for twenty-five years in a variety of assignments, and I thought I had seen and done most of what there was to do and see.

TEXCOM was different from any Army unit with which I had ever been associated. The testing community spoke a unique language, a technical language, that I never fully learned and certainly did not comprehend. Fortunately, my organization supported the operational testers in traditional ways, so I did not have to become an expert in the testing field. However, I often sat in conferences and briefings and wondered what the hell they were talking about.

The other difference I found in TEXCOM was that, with few exceptions, the officers assigned to the command were serving in the grade in which they would either be discharged or retired. This was true from captain through major general. I cannot recall a single officer being promoted while he or she was assigned to TEXCOM. I remember two officers who worked for me who were promoted after they left TEXCOM. Many of the officers at the grade of captain and major had been passed over for promotion and were waiting for the next shoe to drop—not being selected a second time. Consequently, they would be discharged, or if they had twenty years of service (and few did), they would be retired. The lieutenant colonels and colonels were waiting to reach their mandatory retirement point, which was twenty-eight years of active, commissioned service for lieutenant colonels and thirty years for colonels. The commanding general of TEXCOM, a major general, of which there were two during my time, I do not believe harbored visions that they would be selected for lieutenant general. The TEXCOM assignment was out of the Army mainstream, and was a final assignment for most officers.

It could be said that most TEXCOM officers had reached their highest level of competence. This is not to say that the officers assigned to TEXCOM were not good officers, because most were. It was simply a fact that few would ever be promoted.

The lieutenant colonels and colonels were particularly good. I do not remember even one who had retired in place. This was not true for the captains and majors, as some were giving only what was required and a few were giving less. For the most part, the civilians were outstanding. Many had engineering, physics, or operational research and systems (ORSA) degrees. They were intelligent and highly motivated as an opportunity for promotion and advancement existed within the civilian workforce.

One anomaly between the military and the civilian pay structure that I never understood was the difference in responsibility versus salary. This anomaly was especially apparent between the salaries of members of the senior executive service (SES) and general officers. Flag officers, brigadier general through general, have their pay capped. It is not unusual to have a civilian reporting to a general and drawing a higher monthly salary than the general. This was the case in TEXCOM. The technical director, a SES position occupied by Marion R. Bryson, reported directly to the commanding general of TEXCOM. But Bryson drew a monthly salary greater than the commanding general by several thousand dollars a year. There is something wrong with this scenario in my mind. I suppose it all results from the fear of a man on a white horse by our nation's founders, but more likely this is because of the prohibition of the active duty military to lobby congress, though civilians are not similarly constrained. Their union, the American Federation of Government Employees (AFGE), does this for them. This anomaly is present in lesser grades as well. Al Ressler, a GM-15, reported to me at INSCOM but had a higher annual salary than I did.

I have no quarrel with the prohibition against the unionization of the military. In fact, I wholeheartedly agree with the prohibition.

However, it does show that the squeaky wheel gets the grease. I would argue that a large percentage of the members of the AFGE vote the Democratic ticket, whereas the military does not vote as a bloc.

We were offered quarters on Fort Hood in the colonel's area. The quarters were slightly more than 1,800 square feet, had a carport rather than a garage, and simply would not accommodate our furniture. We were able to rent a single-story home at 516 White Oak in Harker Heights, which was adjacent to Killeen, for only a hundred dollars more that my housing allowance. A lieutenant colonel who had been transferred to be the professor of military science at Sam Houston State University in Huntsville, Texas, owned the home. The home was older, probably built in the early 70s, but it was spacious and reasonably clean and had a nice backyard. We would find the home to be very comfortable.

Penny began to look for a job—any job—as soon as we arrived. There were few jobs available, and those that were available paid little, as there were many wives of soldiers also looking for a job. I remember her being furious after interviewing for a secretarial position at a local business. The owner had told her, "Honey, I don't pay much because you girls are a dime a dozen." "Honey" and "girl" were two words that incensed Penny. Eventually, Penny was hired as a secretary with the Killeen Independent School District (KISD) in their special education department. Over time, Penny became the coordinator for the Deaf Education Program. KISD had responsibility for all deaf education within the area, servicing children in school districts from Lampasas to Temple. Penny was happy in this job, as she felt needed. She enjoyed working with the deaf children and helping their parents. And she learned to "sign."

KISD had a contract with Scott and White Medical Center, which was located in Temple, to provide medical insurance for their employees. Penny was authorized to use the military medical facilities at Fort Hood at no cost; however, appointments were difficult to get, and waiting times were excessively long for dependents. We decided it would be best if she took the Scott and White medical insurance, even though it was not cheap. This decision would prove to be paradoxically both wise and unwise.

My job description read:

Deputy Chief of Staff for Personnel, Administration, Security, and Logistics for a 2200+ person command geographically dispersed at six separate CONUS installations with an Army-wide test and experimentation mission. Exercises staff supervision over multifunctional programs, to include military and civilian personnel management, administration, logistics, safety and security. Responsible for the day-to-day activities of the contracting officer's representative for a multimillion-dollar test support contract. Supervises 61 military/civilian personnel and an annual operating budget of $1.1 million in support of base operations.

I was the GI, G2, and G4 for TEXCOM, and I had oversight over the test support contract. I would find my TEXCOM assignment to be enjoyable because I worked for good people and had good people working for me as I had had in INSCOM. The primary irritant was that the command was in a constant state of flux, some driven internally but most externally from higher headquarters. This caused my personnel and logistic folks to be constantly reacting to situations over which they had little control. This proved frustrating to all concerned. My leadership style was to be proactive rather than reactive, but it was difficult to do in the fluid environment in which I found myself.

The TEXCOM headquarters building was less than a year old. It was a three-story, brick building, and my organization occupied nearly half of the first floor. The headquarters was a secure building with access by key card. My office suite consisted of a private office for me, one for my deputy, and a reception area occupied by my secretary, Oteeka Davis. My deputy initially was Lieutenant Colonel Bill Fesler and then later Lieutenant Colonel Chuck Grossman. Bill was an Army aviator, and Chuck was a military policeman. Both had an alternate specialty of logistician. I had little experience in logistics, so Bill and Chuck had to keep me straight in that regard, which they did. They were both outstanding officers and good citizens and became good friends.

The first day I walked into my office and met Oteeka, I was not sure that our relationship would be cordial, much less develop into one of friendship. She was certainly pleasant that morning, but behind her desk on a wall, a list of tasks that secretaries did not have to do was tacked up. I remember two: "I do not have to put up with your idiosyncrasies. Those are your problems," and, "I do not have to make and serve coffee. You are capable of doing that yourself." I looked at the sign and then Oteeka and remarked, "I do not drink coffee," which I did not, and over the years, I had taken a lot of guff from others for that.

"You are a soldier and don't drink coffee?"

I had to be on my best behavior with Oteeka for a time, but she eventually warmed up to me and me to her. She did serve coffee to my visitors, but I do not think she liked it unless she knew and liked the visitor.

Oteeka's dad had been a soldier and had been killed in Vietnam when she had turned twelve. She had been notified of his death while at the Girl Scout camp located on West Fort Hood. She was married to Russell, who owned a car repair and body shop in Killeen. They had one child, a son named Jason. He was a good high school football player and very smart. He graduated from Texas A&M and went to medical school. Today, Jason is an Army doctor at Fort Lewis, Washington, specializing in cardiology, specifically implants, pacemakers, defibrillators, and angiograms.

Oteeka and Russell both loved boats, big boats. I remember that they had one that they bought on the Hudson River near West Point, New York. They brought the boat to Texas by way of the Intracoastal Waterway. They had the boat at a marina on Lake Travis near Austin. They once had Penny, me, Bill, and Theresa Fesler for a day of swimming, cruising, and riding Sea-Doos.

Penny and I were particularly close to Oteeka and Bill Fesler and his wife, Theresa. Bill, Theresa, and Oteeka would be of great aid and support to Penny and me during a difficult time. Bill retired and immediately went to work as a GS-12 in one of the test directorates. Today, he is the civilian deputy for logistics and does the same job as he had done when he worked for me. Oteeka was promoted several times to work in civilian personnel and is now retired.

Both Oteeka and Bill were runners and spent their lunch hour running the hills of West Fort Hood. Shortly after my arrival, Bill said he and Oteeka would take me for an easy jog. Oteeka turned toward home after a mile or so, easily getting in her two miles for the day. Bill kept going, and I followed. Shortly, I breathlessly asked Bill, "How far do you intend to go?"

Bill replied, "I usually do six miles, but we will take it slow today and do a little less."

I turned and headed back to the gym, but where was the gym? Bill continued on for a while but realized I was probably lost and returned to guide me home. Oteeka, Bill, and I continued to run during our lunch hour, but each would go his or her own way and at his or her own pace after we had jogged together for a short distance.

Bill was a helicopter pilot flying the Huey. He told me he loved to get his seat as far forward as possible so he could see better—that is, until he got to Vietnam and bullets began to pop through the thin skin of the Huey. He then hunkered down in his seat and made himself as small as possible. Bill said he went through four Hueys on one mission.

Lieutenant Colonel Betty P. J. Osweiler was the boss of the personnel and administration division responsible for both civilian and military personnel management. Major Don McNally headed up the military personnel branch, and Nora Roberts was the guru for the civilian personnel operations office (CPOO). A couple of captains, several NCOs, and civilians also worked under Betty's supervision. Additionally, Betty was responsible for overseeing the operation of the technical support library. Faye Wilbur was the librarian.

Nora Roberts spent a lot of time with the command group. This was not unusual because Army officers generally did not have a good understanding of the civilian personnel system and needed a lot of hand-holding. Nora came to us from the civilian personnel office at Fort Hood, and this relationship proved beneficial during our numerous reorganizations. Nora has since passed away. Major McNally retired as a major and went to work for the Texas Employment Commission.

Betty was married to Major John Osweiler, who was working for the III Corps and Fort Hood AG at the time. I had known both Betty and John when I was chief of the AG Branch at MILPERCEN, and I was their assignment officer. John worked with me in the combat service support division, and Betty was the AG at Fort Belvoir, Virginia. John and Betty both retired as full colonels and now live in Pennsylvania. Betty would succeed me upon my retirement as the chief of the personnel, administration, and logistics directorate (PALD), the new name for my organization. We continue to keep in touch by Christmas card.

My logistics branch was headed up first by Major Rich Powell and later by Major Art Faison. Their primary job was to interface with the test support contractor. The branch was also responsible for the movement of material and equipment upon the closing of five test directorates at other installations and their relocation to West Fort Hood. The safety officer, a captain, also resided in the logistics branch along with a couple of other captains. Rich Powell was promoted to lieutenant colonel after he departed TEXCOM.

The maintenance, engineering, and supply (MES) division was headed up by Jim "J. C." Callaway. The division, which was composed entirely of civilians, performed everything from carpentry to mowing lawns to setting up audiovisual equipment to moving furniture to issuing pens, pencils, and paper. The MES provided anything that the officers, NCOs, or civilians needed in the way of support.

I had a couple of retired sergeants major who ran my security office, processing security clearances and issuing building passes.

My rating officer the entire time I was at TEXCOM was the chief of staff, Colonel Kenneth E. Kimes. Kenny Kimes was a super boss. He was tough but fair, and he had the perfect temperament for the job. He was always calm, cool, and collected, at least outwardly. I rarely saw Kenny lose his temper or raise his voice, but he did have a wicked stare that alerted you that you were getting dangerously close to a line you did not want to cross. Kenny was an aviator by trade and possessed that competitive attitude that I found most military aviators to have. He had commanded an aviation brigade in Germany prior to his assignment to TEXCOM.

Kenny was a good friend as well as a boss, and we had some good times together. If Kenny was on leave, TDY, or otherwise absent from the headquarters, he would have me occupy his office as the acting chief of staff. Kenny was working hard to quit smoking (which he eventually did), and he kept candy in his desk to use as a substitute. I would eat the candy in his absence, and if I did not finish eating it all by the time he returned, I would take it to my office to eat. This irritated Kenny to no end. He took to hiding his candy, but I would usually find it. In fact, the week before I retired, I sat in for Kenny while he was TDY and ate his candy.

My first senior rater was Major General Robert L. Drudik, the TEXCOM commanding general. Drudik had been awarded the Silver Star, Distinguished Flying Cross, and three Bronze Star Medals with V-device for valor, and the Purple Heart while he had served two tours in Vietnam. He had been seriously wounded, and he had a very visible scar across the right side of his face. Because of this experience, Drudik was instrumental in influencing the design of the new C-17 aircraft, which allowed the aircraft to be converted into a flying hospital. Drudik always took the opportunity to shower the military medical community, even in private conservation, with accolades for saving his life.

General Drudik had what I thought was a peculiar hobby for a general. He had a passion for roses. He grew roses of every kind. A large portion of the backyard of his quarters on Fort Hood had been dug up and planted with roses. They were carefully tended, and when in bloom, they presented a beautiful sight. I discovered that he carefully picked and personally delivered them to patients at the Fort Hood hospital.

TEXCOM's motto was "Truth in Testing," coined by General Drudik and emblazoned on the TEXCOM unit crest and shoulder patch. Drudik felt that sometimes he had been unduly pressured by project managers and industry representatives to move a test along or to go easy on his report about particular systems. He would have none of that. Drudik always referred back to his *Bugle Notes* from his West Point years, turning the page to the passage that read, "Make us choose the harder right instead of the easier wrong, and never to be content with a half truth when the whole can be won."

During Drudik's tenure, TEXCOM had been instrumental in the beginning of the Army automation efforts and testing the early maneuver system, M1 main battle tank, the new manning systems field evaluation, the single channel and airborne radio system (SINGCGARS), and the Bradley fighting vehicle. One of the old-timers told me that one of the less visible TEXCOM tests was testing the underwear for female basic trainees. That must have been a very interesting test, especially for the data collectors.

I do not remember how long I worked for General Drudik before he retired, but I vividly remember his retirement ceremony. It was a hot, miserable summer day, and the TEXCOM troops were assembled in parade formation on the III Corps parade field. General Drudik and the reviewing party were late in arriving. The troops, including me, were drenched in sweat, and my helmet was killing me, which resulted in a first-class headache. Several people presented gifts to General Drudik and flowers to Mrs. Drudik, and then a lieutenant general spoke prior to General Drudik receiving his retirement award and making his farewell remarks. The lieutenant general was verbose, and his remarks were overly long. I hoped that General Drudik would be merciful and mindful of the troop's welfare and keep his remarks short. He did not and droned on for way too long, eventually breaking down and weeping. Finally, we were given the command to "Pass in Review," but by that time, several soldiers had passed out and were being treated for heat exhaustion.

This was to be my last time to march in a formal military formation. I remember most of the ceremonies that I participated in during my Army career. I do not recall any of the speeches. I do remember the pride that I felt as we passed by the reviewing stand and followed the color guard who was bearing the Army flag and our nation's colors as we listened to the heavy beat of the drum from the band. It was no different in this instance.

Major General William C. Page, Jr., succeeded General Drudik as the commander of TEXCOM. General Page was a career-long aviator. He served two tours in Vietnam and commanded an aviation company during his second tour. He was awarded the Distinguished Flying Cross and Air medals, but I do not know if they were for heroism or achievement. He was an exceptional administrator. General Page would leave TEXCOM to become the deputy commanding general of III Corps and Fort Hood for a little over a year prior to his retirement.

General Page used me in some unusual ways. He would send me to represent TEXCOM at the III Corps commanding general's weekly command and staff meeting. Often, these briefings were held on a Wednesday morning at the same time General Page held his weekly staff meeting. I was known by some of my peers as the "ghost" for sending my deputy to represent me at these meetings—I also did this for other meetings called by General Page that I had no desire to attend—and for my behind-the-scenes manipulation of TEXCOM activities. This reputation was deserved, as I was a close confidant of Kenny Kimes and General Page, to a somewhat lesser degree. My counsel was often sought by both.

There was one director of a test directorate, who was a colonel and a peer and who constantly complained to General Page that he was not getting his fair share of resources. General Page had gotten a "belly full" of this "crybaby" but wanted to give him a chance to redeem himself before zapping him on an OER. He called me to his office and told me that he wanted me to tell the director that he (General Page) had had enough and to cease and desist. I thought this inappropriate as I was not in this officer's rating chain and had no leverage over him. I suggested that perhaps Kenny Kimes in his role as chief of staff should meet with the officer. General Page responded, "No, I don't want the chief of staff to get crossways with the directors." I did as Page asked, and the colonel was contrite for a time.

TEXCOM had a subordinate command co-located at Fort Ord and Fort Hunter Liggett, California, the TEXCOM Experimentation Command (TEC). TEC was led by Dr. Marion R. Bryson, the civilian equivalent of a brigadier general, and had the only test organization of its kind that included an organic armor-mechanized infantry task force dedicated to the test and experimentation mission. TEC headquarters was at Fort Ord, and testing was done at Hunter Liggett. TEC also had a "skunk works" at Hunter Liggett, and it was doing many innovative and "off the wall" projects, primarily with laser technology.

Fort Hunter Liggett, named for Lieutenant General Hunter Liggett of WWI fame, is a beautiful place located on the southern end of the Salinas Valley with mountains separating the installation from the Pacific Ocean. The post consisted of some 165,000 acres purchased by the government in 1940 mostly from William Randolph Hearst. (Hearst Castle is down the coast.) The land had been part of the Hearst Ranch and contained two significant buildings, the Hacienda and the Mission San Antonio de Padua. The Hacienda, which was built in 1930, had been the Hearst ranch house with an attached bunkhouse for the cowboys, and it was being used as an officer's club and VIP billets by TEC. The mission was founded in 1771 and was the site of the first

Christian marriage in Northern California. The mission continues to operate under the Franciscan order with one old padre. Several movies have been filmed on Fort Hunter Liggett. There are many Spanish missions located on or near the California coast. The missions are some twenty-one miles apart, the distance a military column could easily travel by horseback in a day.

I made several trips to Hunter Liggett, flying in to Monterey or Fort Ord by either commercial or military aircraft. The trips were made primarily to witness live-fire combined arms tests and to observe the testing of laser technology. Hunter Liggett lay in the flight path of major airlines flying between Los Angeles and San Francisco, requiring close coordination with the FAA, as the laser beams could blind pilots if they inadvertently escaped out of the test area.

I was the driving force in obtaining DA approval to replace TEC's M-60 tanks with the M1A1 Abrams main battle tank incorporating steel-encased, depleted uranium armor. This required close coordination between TEC, the receiving unit, and the US Marine Corps, the losing unit. The US Marines were willing to relinquish their tanks as they were receiving an upgraded version of the M1A1.

On one of my visits, Colonel Kimes and a couple of others had flown to Fort Ord by an Army C-12, King Air, a twin-prop civilian aircraft converted for military use to witness a live-fire test of combined arms tactics at Hunter Liggett. Other staff members had come on another C-12. I was standing on a knoll overlooking a valley, watching through binoculars the mock battle unfolding in the distance. It was incredibly noisy, as Apache helicopters and US Air Force A-10 "Warthogs" entered and exited the maneuver area. I kept feeling a tap on my shoulder and finally realized it was Kenny Kimes. Kenny told me we were leaving and going back to Fort Hood. He told me that he had just notified one of our GM-15s that his sister and two of her small children had perished in a house fire, and we were flying him back to Sweetwater, Texas, where his sister's family lived. The C-12 was waiting on a dirt strip at Hunter Liggett near the maneuver area. It was a long trip back to Sweetwater. What do you say to comfort a man who has suffered such a loss? We refueled at Kirkland Air Force Base in New Mexico and landed at Avenger Field, the civilian airport in Sweetwater, where the fellow's family was waiting. The crew chief opened the exit and the GM-15 walked off the plane. We taxied out for takeoff. The pilot had not shut down his engines. The rest of the flight to Fort Hood was quiet, as Kenny and I were lost in our thoughts of what we could do to help the man through this tragedy.

While many of Texas's municipal airports were postwar gifts to the host communities, the case was reversed in Sweetwater, where the existing municipal airport became a training facility in May of 1942. The lasting legacy of the field was formed when the base became the training facility for the Women's US Air Force Service Pilots (WASPs). Licensed, female, civilian pilots were recruited and trained to fly military aircraft, ferrying them from factory to shipping point and flying damaged planes back for repair on occasion. This enabled more male pilots to be sent into combat.

Jacqueline Cochran, one of the most famous women pilots of the twentieth century, persistently lobbied US Army Air Force General Henry "Hap" Arnold to establish a flight-training program for women during World War II. Hard-pressed for pilots by midsummer of 1942, General Arnold approved Cochran putting her pilot plan into action. A WASP flight school opened at Houston's Municipal Airport in late 1942, outgrew its facilities, and was relocated to Avenger Field in Sweetwater. The school operated from February 20, 1943, to December 7, 1944, during which time it became the first and only all-women military flying school in the world. The program successfully trained women to fly every kind of aircraft, including bombers and fighters. Of the twenty-five thousand women who applied for WASP flight training, only 1,830 were accepted into the program. Of this number, 1,074 went on to gain their silver wings and fly over sixty million miles on operational duty. Thirty-eight of them lost their lives serving their country. Considered civilian employees during the war, WASP pilots finally gained military benefits after special legislation passed in 1977. I am a lifetime member of the National WASP WWII Museum, which is located at Avenger Field.

Many of TEXCOM's tests were conducted using the multiple integrated laser engagement system (MILES), the test support contractor providing the instrumentation, wiring, and data collection. MILES is a training system that provides a realistic battlefield environment for soldiers involved in training exercises. MILES provides tactical engagement simulation for direct-fire, force-on-force training using eye-safe laser "bullets." Each individual and vehicle in the training exercise has a detection system to sense hits and perform casualty assessment. Laser transmitters are attached to each individual and vehicle weapon system and accurately replicate actual ranges and lethality of the specific weapon systems. MILES training has been proven to dramatically increase the combat readiness and fighting effectiveness of our military forces.

Joe Owens, a retired Army major general, was the manager of the test support contract. The contractor operated under a cost-plus-incentive fee (CPIF) contract worth approximately fourteen million dollars annually. The contractor billed TEXCOM for the actual cost to perform a TEXCOM-directed mission, and profit came from how well the mission was performed and included any cost savings. I was responsible for grading the performance of the contractor, and my appraisal accounted for approximately 55 percent of the total evaluation. Quarterly, I would meet with the commanding general to render my report on the contractor's performance, generally rating them at the 95 percent level, which resulted in the contractor receiving a bonus in the two-hundred-and-fifty-thousand-dollar range. Joe Owens was an outstanding manager and had an excellent workforce consisting primarily of retired military personnel.

My logistics branch was responsible for bird-dogging the contractor and reporting how well the contractor was performing. Consequently, I might not see Joe Owens more than once or twice a month, but the week prior to the quarterly evaluation, Joe would drop by every day just to chat.

One of the missions I tasked the contractor to perform was maintenance of all TEXCOM vehicles. TEXCOM was authorized few vehicles, but over time, the command had acquired a fleet of over three hundred M880s, a commercial utility cargo vehicle (CUCV, pronounced "cuck-vee"). The CUCV was a military-modified, commercial, off-the-shelf Dodge pickup designed to replace the ubiquitous Jeep of WWII and Vietnam fame. The Dodge did not work out, so the Army began procuring Chevrolet pickups and Blazers, which also could not stand up to military needs. Consequently, the Army was replacing the commercial pickups with the high-mobility multipurpose wheeled vehicle (HMMWV, pronounced "hum-vee").

The Army was selling the M880s primarily to foreign armies but also to fire departments and police.

I saw an opportunity to scratch an itch by obtaining some of these vehicles. Units that supported TEXCOM tests had to use their own vehicles for data collection and other purposes. Units complained about the wear and tear on their vehicles and the cost of shipping the vehicles if they came from an installation other than Fort Hood. I was able to convince the Fort Hood property disposal officer to allow me to cull the vehicles and transfer ownership of the best conditioned to TEXCOM. HQDA discovered what I was doing and sent a message to TEXCOM to cease obtaining the vehicles and to turn in what we had on hand. I convinced General Page that the "turn in" of the vehicles was a massive effort throughout the Army and that HQDA would eventually lose oversight of the effort and that he should ignore the DA directive. He did this, but I knew he was uncomfortable doing so.

Mr. Walter W. Hollis, the Deputy Undersecretary of the Army (Operations Research), Office of the Secretary of the Army, was visiting TEXCOM, and over lunch at the West Fort Hood Officer's Club, General Page decided to tell Mr. Hollis about our M880 program. I was called to join them and give details about what we were doing. I explained to Mr. Hollis that we had both Dodge and Chevrolet pickups and Blazers and that I initially had the vehicles serviced and repaired at the local Dodge and Chevrolet dealerships in Copperas Cove but had found that too expensive. Consequently, I had tasked the test support contractor with the mission of maintaining the vehicles under the parameters that any vehicle costing over five hundred dollars in any fiscal year would be cannibalized and used for spare parts. Mr. Hollis was a friend of the test community and asked if he needed to weigh in on the issue at DA. This, of course, was what General Page wanted. I told Mr. Hollis that if he got involved, it would only pique DA interest and likely cause them to send a direct order to General Page to turn in the vehicles. I further told him if DA did issue a direct order, we would ask for his assistance, but it was my view that no order would be forthcoming. Neither General Page nor TEXCOM ever heard from DA. TEXCOM, now OTC (Operational Test Command), continue to use the pickups and Blazers. Recently, Bill Fesler e-mailed me that the test support contract was now some 290 million and that OTC had over four hundred vehicles.

One of the many facilities and buildings that I was responsible for included the large tunnel complex that had been used for the storage of nuclear weapons and several of the concrete bunkers that had been used for storage of conventional ammunition and bombs. These facilities were used by Killeen Air Force Base and were one of the early US national stockpile sites for storing nuclear weapons. This classified site, also known as "Baker," secretly held both US Army and USAF special weapons. The tunnel complex was vast with many large rooms, cranes, and two locomotive engines that supplied electricity. The concrete bunkers were covered with dirt for camouflage on which trees now grew and maintained a constant temperature of sixty-seven degrees. I used them for storage, machinery, and carpenter shops. Concrete machine gun positions and huge steel doors had guarded the tunnel and were still in existence at its two entrances.

On June 15, 1963, Killeen Base was turned over to the Army. In October 1969, Killeen Base was designated as West Fort Hood, and the airfield's name was designated as Robert Gray Army Airfield. The base was named after a Killeen native and John Tarleton Agriculture College (JTAC) student who was a pilot of a B-25 bomber on the famous Doolittle Raid on Tokyo in 1942. Gray was killed flying a combat mission in Burma. With the change in operations at West Fort Hood, the nuclear weapons were removed. They had been secretly kept there since 1947.

I stored computer files and tapes in a climate-controlled vault in the tunnel complex, but I was unable to use the rest of the tunnel because ceiling and walls were beginning to drip water and the asbestos in the facility was a danger to occupants. I needed more space as we began to close the test directorates at Fort Sill, Benning, and Rucker, and I needed to move their people and equipment to Fort Hood. I had local engineers survey the tunnels with a view to removing the asbestos and refurbishing the facility for offices. The projected cost was in the millions of dollars and simply not cost effective.

I kept a golf cart in the facility primarily to show both curious, active-duty and retired generals and dignitaries through the facility. We received requests to tour the tunnel from people who had been associated with the building of the facility and its use as a nuclear storage area, and we were pleased to accommodate them.

The need for space consumed a significant amount of my effort during the last two years of my time in the Army. I was able to obtain congressional approval, thanks to Congressman Chet Edwards intervening on TEXCOM's behalf, to gain out-of-cycle funds to build a motor pool and maintenance shops for our unauthorized vehicles, an arms room, and offices. I also designed—yes, personally designed—a three-story office building to be co-located with the TEXCOM headquarters that was built after my retirement from the Army.

I hate war as only a soldier who has lived it can, only as one who has seen its brutality, its futility, its stupidity.
—Dwight D. Eisenhower

The command sergeant major for TEXCOM was a fellow by the name of John Rottman. John stood six-foot-seven and weighed about 240 pounds. He was all muscle, gruff, and no-nonsense. Lieutenant Colonel Betty Osweiler had much the same personality as Rottman. We used to joke behind their backs that if they mated, you would end up with a Rottweiler.

We had all gone to a conference at our higher headquarters in Rosslyn, Virginia, to determine the leadership structure for the command. The decision to be made was the following: Should the headquarters remain in the Washington area, or should the headquarters be relocated to Fort Hood? We had recently been assigned to the new headquarters, and the writing on the wall was that the TEXCOM commander's position would be downgraded to a brigadier general position regardless of the location of the headquarters. I had no dog in the fight because I felt that it would work either way and I knew that I would be retiring before an actual move would be made. Rottman did, though, because if the headquarters remained in Washington, he would most likely be required to move to Washington. Rottman felt strongly that the major general should be at Fort Hood, where the soldiers were, and he had no desire to serve with a general in D.C.

The last night of the conference, with no decision being made, there was a formal party with an open bar, "motivational speaker," and sit-down dinner. The get-together was to allow participants to "wind down" as tempers had flared on several occasions. Rottman approached and asked what I thought about the conference. Rottman and I had been allies for a couple of years, standing firm against some of the policies the generals and others wanted to implement. I told him it was a waste of the taxpayer's dollar. He agreed, and over drinks, I asked if he had ever been to downtown D.C. and seen the Vietnam Memorial. He said he had not. He also said he would like to see the capital and the mall but had no desire to see the memorial. I said I had lived in the town off and on for ten years and was a good tour guide, so off we went with our two seats at the dinner vacant.

We caught the Metro and arrived at the mall, which was near the Smithsonian, between the Capital and the Washington Monument. In the distance was the Lincoln Memorial, and I directed him that way, knowing the Vietnam Memorial was only a short distance from the Lincoln. That is somewhat of a trek, as those of you who have been there know, but an enjoyable walk on a cool autumn evening.

When we arrived at the Lincoln Memorial, we took a good look, and as we descended the stairs, I told him, "John, the Vietnam Memorial is just over there, and that is where we are going." Once we entered that hallowed area and I explained how and where to find the names of those on the wall that we personally knew who had fallen, I had the privilege of watching this hard, tough man sob until there were no longer tears but just the need to talk to someone and explain who they were and what had happened. It was not my first time there, and most of my tears had already been shed; however, I had to bite my lip to console this hunk of a man who had lost most of his squad of eight men as a squad leader in 1967.

I will not forget that night!

Another memorable recollection from this time was that I bought Penny a dog for an early Christmas present. Bill Fesler had a female Schnauzer with puppies, and I bought her last two, one of which was the runt of the litter. My plan was to determine the one we liked best and give the other to Bill Farr's daughters, Sarah and Megan, for their Christmas present. I named one Missy and the other Anna Bell. Why I picked Anna Bell as a name I do not recall.

Penny had said that after Gigi died, she never wanted another dog, but I knew she would fall in love with one of the puppies after they had been around for a while. Missy, the runt, proved to be the most playful and inquisitive of the two, so she was the one we decided to keep. The first night we had Missy, after Anna Bell had gone with the Farr girls, she began to whimper. We had been keeping the dogs in our bedroom at night, which was a mistake. I told Penny to do something about that dog, as I could not sleep. I felt Penny reach off the bed, pick Missy up, and deposit her between us. Missy immediately stopped crying, and she slept between us from then on. Missy was a great comfort to Penny and later to me as events began to unfold.

Two incidents occurred during my assignment to TEXCOM that turned my orderly life topsy-turvy, irrevocably changing it forever. The first was Penny's diagnosis of ovarian cancer.

Penny had complained for some time that she felt bloated, had a queasy stomach, and was tired all the time. She had been to the Scott and White (S&W) Clinic in Killeen on two separate occasions, and she had been told to use Tums or drink Pepto-Bismol as she might be developing an ulcer. During the Christmas holidays in late December 1990—I believe it was a Wednesday—she said she could not fit into her blue jeans and showed me her stomach, which was definitely swollen. I begged her to go to the emergency room, but she already had an appointment scheduled for Friday morning at the main S&W Clinic in Temple and wanted to wait for that appointment.

She was feeling a lot of discomfort by the time we got to S&W on Friday morning, as her abdomen had continued to swell, and she was frightened. She was taken into an examining room, and within fifteen minutes, a nurse came and escorted me to the room. There I found Dr. Dudley P. Baker, the head of the department of obstetrics and gynecology, and Penny. Dr. Baker told us it was his diagnosis that she had ovarian cancer. He also stated he must operate immediately to remove the cancer and would schedule the operation for the following Monday. He then took us to another room where he took a long needle and removed over eight pounds of the vilest looking fluid from Penny's stomach. Dr. Baker told Penny that the removal of the fluid should allow her to rest easily over the weekend.

Neither she nor I rested at all that weekend. I can only imagine what Penny was thinking. I know we were both in shock. I could not process what Dr. Baker had told us. The word "cancer" being applied to Penny was unthinkable. She was the healthiest person I knew. How could this be happening? We had no idea about the extent of her cancer, and we could find little information about ovarian cancer. What we did find was not good, especially if the cancer was stage III or IV. I thought that the ovarian cancer diagnosis might be wrong. Penny had had a hysterectomy in 1973 when we were in Japan, but the ovaries had not been removed because of her young age. Prior to the hysterectomy, she had taken birth control pills for a number of years, which available literature indicated might help prevent ovarian cancer. I prayed for the doctors not to find cancer.

Dr. Baker said the operation would take five to seven hours. I think he called it debulking surgery necessary prior to initiating chemotherapy. It took eleven. He came to the surgery waiting room and took the family into a separate room. He told us it was stage IV ovarian cancer. The cancer cells had spread outside the abdomen and metastasized on the liver and bladder. He described the cancer within the abdomen and on the liver and bladder as minuscule growths that resembled popcorn. The reason the operation took so long was due to him surgically removing each of those minute growths. He said he thought he had found and removed it all, but I suspect all doctors say this. He said that once Penny recovered from the operation, he would began an intense regimen of chemotherapy and bathe the peritoneal area with a powerful concoction of drugs. He offered no prognosis when asked but was upbeat and gave us hope. I think we all felt Penny would beat this terrible disease. I knew, as did Penny, from reading literature about the disease that less than 20 percent of patients with stage IV ovarian cancer survived longer than five years.

Penny did not deny the diagnosis that she had stage IV ovarian cancer, but she defied the verdict that she had been given a death sentence. She was not going to crawl in a hole and pull the dirt in after her. She was not going to sit quietly by and accept the verdict without a fight. She was going to use every fiber of her being to beat "the Big C."

She and Dr. Baker immediately established a rapport that was more than the usual doctor-patient relationship. They genuinely liked each other, maybe even loved each other, and it was evident. Penny trusted Dr. Baker explicitly, and there was no doubt in my mind that he believed he could cure Penny. We expect a lot from our doctors. We ask them to be nothing less than perfect and to give us miracles as well as medicine. We want more than medical care. We want kindness, humor, honesty, consideration, even love. We want them to be superhuman, godlike, but with a human touch. We want our doctors not only to care *for* us but also to care *about* us. Most of all, we want them to give us hope. All this and more, Penny got from her relationship with Dr. Baker.

Her oncologist was Dr. Jacob Benjamin Green III, a taciturn fellow that Karman Weatherby told us was one of the best. I remember the chemotherapy starting some three weeks after the initial operation. Initially, she received intraperitoneal (IP) chemotherapy with the drugs given through a thin tube inserted into her abdomen. Then she received chemotherapy intravenously through a semi-permanent catheter that I had to clean and dress periodically. The treatments took around three hours each session. The oncology treatment room was a cold, sterile place, and it was always filled with very sick patients. It was depressing. Penny took her treatments sitting in a chair and generally read or dozed. She told me you could do a lot of thinking while sitting in a chair and taking chemo. It took Penny a day or two to recuperate from a treatment before she could go back to work. I know she was weak and sick; however, work got her out of her head, and it was something she wanted to do. She did not lose her hair for which she was grateful, although it thinned somewhat. Her initial operation and round of chemotherapy would not be her last.

Penny and me at the TEXCOM Christmas Party, 1990.
She was so sick, but we had no idea at the time.

In the spring of 1994, we had a mini-reunion for RCHS in Salado. George and Verlis Tucker, Marion and Judy Daily, and James and Kay Easter Johnson rented a house near the Mill Creek golf course. The guys played golf while the girls visited and shopped. One evening, we all went to the German restaurant in Walburg. Bill and Mary Williams drove up from San Marcus, where he was ranching at the time, and we had an enjoyable time visiting and listening to a band in the *biergarten*. In May 2010, we had our fiftieth high school reunion at Marion and Judy's home on Lake Granbury. Kay and I were visiting, and she told me that as she and Penny hugged good-bye in 1994, Penny told her that this would be the last time that Kay would see her. She told Kay that her family could not accept that she was going to die. Penny never told me she felt that way, although she did gently and obliquely try to prepare me for that event. I simply refused to think about it or accept that there was the possibility she would die from the disease. I realized now that my view probably hurt her and caused her unnecessary grief. Life can either be accepted or changed. If it is not accepted, it must be changed. If it cannot be changed, then it must be accepted. Acceptance that all is right in God's world is sometimes hard to do.

One way that Penny forced me to deal with the eventuality of her death was to buy a prepaid funeral policy with the Cook-Walden Funeral Home in Austin for burial next to her parents at the Cooke-Walden Cemetery in Pflugerville. I balked at doing this, but one day, the salesperson arrived at the house and I had no choice but to listen to the presentation. One of the benefits of military retirement is that you and your spouse may be buried in any national cemetery. I had in my mind that we would be buried in Arlington National Cemetery, but Penny did not want to be buried at Arlington. When I asked why, she said, "No one will come to visit us there." We eventually bought a policy for both of us that included the lots, type of coffin, and many other matters that you do not think about until you are faced with the responsibility of planning a funeral. I though it all somewhat morbid at the time, but I later realized how wise Penny was in insisting we buy the policies. It relieved me of worry in an already difficult time.

Shortly before Penny was diagnosed with cancer, we signed a contract to purchase a home in the Mill Creek subdivision of Salado, Texas. The subdivision was built around the Mill Creek golf course, an eighteen-hole facility later expanded to twenty-seven holes, that had Salado creek running through the property. We contracted for the home through Jim Thorn with Mill Creek Reality. The builder was Larry Lilly, the brother of Bob Lilly of Dallas Cowboy fame. Larry was in the process of building the house. I offered to buy the home at the price Larry was asking, provided we could make some cosmetic changes to the home, change the landscaping, add a deck and fence built to our specifications, and install a yard sprinkler system. Larry agreed. I suppose the house was overpriced, or Larry was looking to get his start in Mill Creek and use our house as a representation for his work, which he later did. Larry and his family lived in the home and paid us rent for a few months until Penny recovered from her surgery. We were able to purchase the house in cash using the profit from the sale of our home in Virginia.

When he learned of Penny's illness, Larry offered to let us out of the contract, but we had decided that Fortress Hood would be our last Army assignment. We had been looking for a place to settle almost from the time we had arrived at Hood. Some weekends when we did not have a military function, we went scouting for a place to retire. Our treks took us to Austin, Kerrville, Fredericksburg, Granbury, Stephenville, Wimberley, and San Antonio. General Joe Owens suggested we visit Salado, where he resided. Joe had also been talking to me about going to work for him. Salado was thirty-five miles from Fort Hood, so it would be convenient to use the commissary and PX, but it was far enough away that we would not have the undesirable elements of pawnshops, cheap hotels, and used car lots associated with a military town. I had recently taken up the game of golf, so the Mill Creek golf course appealed to me. We were already familiar with the Stagecoach Inn and restaurant from our time at Hood during the early sixties. Once we visited Salado, we fell in love with the quaint village.

Salado was founded at the Old Military Road crossing of Salado Creek on October 8, 1859, coincident with the founding of Salado College. It developed as both an industrial and agricultural center with a gristmill within the town limits and seven other mills within nine miles on Salado Creek. The first Grange in Texas was organized here in 1873, and Salado ranked second in size and importance in Bell County until the early 1880s. Salado College attracted residents of education and refinement and gave prestige to the village. The Chisholm Trail came right up main street, and the stage lines that served Central Texas included Salado among their stops. After the railroads were built to the north and east of Salado, the newly created towns drew most of the trade, and Salado steadily declined. Population dwindled to around two hundred people in 1950. Since that time, Salado has grown slowly and is recognized as a very pleasant place to live and work. Eighteen of the old buildings are listed on the National Register of Historic Places, and Salado has twenty-three Texas historical markers.

The revitalization of Salado began in the 1950s as the fame of the dining room of the Stagecoach Inn spread. It continued with the founding of the Central Texas Area Museum in 1959, the construction of the first new residential area, Mill Creek, in the early '60s, and most importantly, its location on Interstate Highway 35. The many shops catering to visitors have led to the popularity of Salado. Today, Salado has approximately 130 businesses of many kinds, adding to the charm of this small village. Salado incorporated in 2003 and now faces the ills of the typical small town, including taxes, poor roads, and local politics. Salado schools are excellent, but taxes are high. Salado yet does not have a traffic light. I suspect I will look for another place to live when that abomination occurs.

We moved from Harker Heights to 701 Blaylock Circle in March or April 1991. The address was later administratively changed to 800 Blaylock Circle. Penny was unable to help with the move because of her illness, but Oteeka, Bill and Theresa Fesler, their son, Randy, and a friend of Randy's came to our rescue. I rented a U-Haul truck. Oteeka and Theresa packed, and Bill and the boys loaded and unloaded. It took at least four trips to get all our furniture moved, but they did it in one long day. Grandmother Farr was at the house in Salado and made the decision as to where each piece of furniture was to be placed. Her instinct in this regard was much better than mine, and Penny was pleased with her arrangement of the furniture. However, I do not think Penny got much enjoyment from her new home. She was just too ill to care. Penny and I drove to work each morning from Salado, me to West Fort Hood and Penny to Killeen, a thirty-eight minute drive for each of us.

In early January 1992, we got some good news. Ross was to be inducted into the Tarleton State University Athletic Hall of Fame.

There was a ceremony at Tarleton in early spring, and Ross asked me to be his presenter. I sat on the dais with Dr. Dennis McCabe, the new president of TSU, and we became acquainted with each other. I would have many meetings with Dr. McCabe in later years as a member of the Tarleton State Alumni Association (TAA) board of directors, including a term as president of the organization. Ross was presented a plaque that outlined his exploits at TSU. A similar plaque hangs on the wall in the Tarleton Athletic Hall of Fame area in Wisdom Gymnasium on the TSU campus.

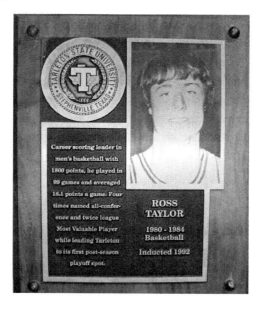

Ross's plaque in the Tarleton State University Athletic Hall of Fame.

The second life-changing occurrence was my retirement from the Army. The end of the Cold War symbolized by the tearing down of the Berlin Wall in 1989 ushered in the clamor for a "peace dividend" as it always does after a war. There was no longer any "big, bad Russian bear" to fight, or so it was thought, and congress and the George H. W. Bush administration began developing plans to significantly and systematically drawdown our nation's military. In fact, the "peace dividend" was a political slogan popularized by Bush purporting to describe the economic benefit of a decrease in defense spending. It was used primarily in discussions relating to the guns versus butter theory. The first Gulf War, better known as Operation Desert Storm, came along, and the plans were temporarily put on hold; however, immediately following the war, the plans were implemented.

Title 10, Section 638 of the US Code authorizes the armed services to convene boards for the selective early retirement of active-duty regular officers in the grade of lieutenant colonel, colonel, brigadier general, and major general. This section overrides other sections of the code, which states, in my case, that officers in the grade of colonel will be mandatorily retired upon completion of thirty years active-commissioned service provided they have not been selected for promotion to brigadier general. I, therefore, expected to serve until July 30, 1994.

The first selective early retirement board (SERB) was for lieutenant colonels, and the number selected was significant. I immediately called one of my contacts at DA and asked if there was to be a SERB for colonels. He answered in the affirmative. He told me that if I thought the percent of lieutenant colonels selected for early retirement was high, the percent for colonels would be even higher. He went on to tell me that all colonels who had served at least four years as a colonel and whose name was not on a list of officers recommended for promotion would be selected for early retirement. Those in command, selected for command, or within one year of their normal mandatory retirement date would not be selected. The handwriting was on the wall. I needed to prepare for retirement.

I talked with General Owens and told him that I thought I would be a civilian soon and that I indeed wanted to work for him. I also told him that my reading of Army regulations indicated I should get a legal ruling to make sure there was no conflict of interest issue resulting from my oversight over his contract. Joe thought that if I did not raise the issue, it would never become an issue. Regardless, I wanted to get a decision from the lawyers to protect both the contractor and myself. I sent a letter to the judge advocate general (JAG) at Fort Hood asking for an opinion about if there would be any prohibition of my going to work for a contractor whose work I had supervised. The Fort Hood staff judge advocate (SJA) forwarded my letter to the DA SJA for a decision. The DA SJA responded with a bunch of legalese and legal precedents opining that I should not work for the contractor until one year after my retirement.

Shortly after I moved to Salado, I met and became friends with Gary Souter, the director of human resources at S&W. Penny and I had been invited to join a social group that met for monthly cocktails at a member's home, and then we went to dinner at the Mill Creek Country Club. Gary and his wife, Deborah, were members of that group. Gary was a "good ol' boy" from Louisiana. He had served as an officer in Vietnam, and we hit it off immediately. He also wanted me to come to work for him, but he first needed to get the position authorized. The position would be titled "training manger," and the salary would very nicely supplement my retirement income. I, of course, told Gary I wanted the job and could be available to go to work immediately. Therefore, I had some assurance that my life after the Army would open up to a new adventure. I had not known what I wanted to be when I grew up and still did not, but the position at S&W appeared to be one that would be both enjoyable and rewarding.

> *Any man or woman asked in this century what they did to make life worthwhile in their lifetime can respond with pride and satisfaction, "I served a career in the United States Military."*
> —Ronald Reagan

Around mid-March 1992, I was called by General Page's secretary to standby, as General Page needed to talk with me. I knew the drill. HQ DA required a general officer to personally present the letter notifying an officer of their selection for early retirement. The board results were kept secret until all officers had been notified. I, of course, knew, and General Page knew I knew; however, we both had to play the game. I had been in General Page's office the day before and commented, "This would be a good time to retire."

General Page told Kenny Kimes after I left, "He knows. This is supposed to be close-hold, but he always knows before anyone else," and he was right. I did.

General Page presented me the letter signed by the DA DCSPER, and I chuckled. Page looked at me with a strained look on his face, and I told him, "This is the same letter I wrote for the DA DCSPER when I was chief of the Army Retirement Branch in 1976 for the Vietnam drawdown. You would think they would have changed the letter by now." The letter began:

> As I know you are aware, Congress has mandated a smaller Army to meet the changing threat we face and will face in the foreseeable future. Unfortunately, this reduction requires the early retirement of some of our most experienced and professional officers. We have made these most painful decisions very carefully to ensure officers affected are treated fairly and with the dignity they deserve as a result of their contributions to the Army. It is my difficult duty to confirm your selection for mandatory early retirement. Your retirement date will be 31 August 1992, unless you voluntarily select an earlier date.

I fully understood the need for the reduction of senior officers as the Army transitioned to a smaller Army. There needed to be room at the top for younger guys to be promoted, or the Army would stagnate. Nevertheless, the Army was putting many experienced and productive soldiers on the street who were in their early fifties. I had had only one permanent job in my life, and I felt that I had been fired. This was tempered somewhat by the fact that 60 percent of the colonels serving on active duty on January 1, 1992, were gone by December 31, 1992. I had lots of company.

Last Official Photo.

My work in TEXCOM had become routine, and I had accomplished all that I had set out to do. My lieutenant colonels had all missions under control, so I began to kick back and take care of personal business in preparation for retirement. I found that I had a lot of time on my hands, so I read. The TEXCOM technical library belonged to me, and in addition to storing all test reports and related documents, some of which were Top Secret, it was a full-service library that included periodicals and the most recent best sellers. I would go to the library, select a book, and leave without signing for the book. This drove the librarian, Faye Wilbur, bonkers, and she would bring a sign-out card to my office for me to sign. It became a game for me to slip into the library when Faye and her assistants were not looking and take a book. I was always careful to return the book to its proper shelf space, but some books remained in my office for a lengthy period. Faye, when she was inventorying, would find books missing and come to my office looking for them. She usually found one, two, or more lying around.

I knew an OER would be written upon my retirement and that an entry was required as to the date of my last PT test and if I had passed or failed. It had been over six months since I had taken the test, and during that period, I had not trained for the test. However, I damn sure wanted that date to be current and reflect that I had passed. My ego was involved here. I called CSM Rottman and told him I wanted him to administer the test. John said he would, but in retrospect, it was stupid to ask him, as I had seen him grade PT tests before and he was a stickler for doing pushups and setups correctly. It was no different in my case, and he did not count a few; however, I had no problem meeting minimum standards. The two-mile, timed run was next. I remember the minimum standard for a colonel of my age was two miles in sixteen minutes and nine seconds.

Well, I wanted to beat the minimum standard by a couple of minutes. I took off, and after a while, John was pulling up beside me in his pickup and saying, "Slow down, sir. You have plenty of time." Then he was saying, "Sir, the pace is too fast. You will burn out." Then he was hollering, "Stop, sir. This is ridiculous. You are going to kill yourself." Then he was gone.

Finally, I hit the finish line and collapsed. I rested for a while and breathlessly asked, "How did I do?"

"You passed," he said, "But you scared the shit out of me. Slobber was coming out your mouth, snot from your nose, and your breathing was like a train engine. I expected you to collapse at any moment, and I would have to give you mouth-to-mouth, and I sure as hell did not want to do that."

I had not wanted a retirement ceremony and preferred to quietly slip out the door. My folks had hosted a potluck retirement luncheon for me, which was held in our main warehouse, where I was roasted and presented with gag gifts. I had also made farewell calls with key TEXCOM personnel and friends, and I saw no need for a ceremony. Kenny Kimes thought otherwise and said, "You have many friends and admirers, and they want to see you appropriately rewarded. You need to do this for them."

The ceremony was held on the Friday morning before I retired on the following Monday. General Page had moved over to the Fort Hood command group by then and was TDY. I asked Kenny to conduct the ceremony. The TEXCOM command conference room was standing room only, and Grandmother and Granddad Farr had come from Austin. Penny and Grandmother Farr were presented with flower bouquets. Kenny had Penny and me come to the front of the room and face the audience, and he made some nice remarks about both of us. Penny was presented with a certificate signed by the Army chief of staff, one thanking her for her selfless service, and a TEXCOM certificate of appreciation, and then she was asked if she wanted to make comments. She thanked several people in the crowd who had come to the hospital and who had helped her through a difficult time. I remember she singled out Kenny, Art Woods, Betty Osweiler, Chuck Grossman, Bill Fesler, Oteeka, Waylon Smith, and others. Tears came to her eyes, and her voice cracked; however, she did a fine job.

I was presented with a retirement certificate signed by the Army chief of staff and one from the secretary of the army. I noticed Colonel Earl Halbrook, who had come from III Corps, in the audience, and I was glad to see my friend. Kenny then began to talk about a special award I was to receive and proceeded to give the history of the Horatio Gates Gold Congressional Medal. I was then presented the Order of Horatio Gates Gold Medal to go along with my bronze medal. I am sure that Earl and Lieutenant Colonel Osweiler were instrumental in obtaining approval from the Adjutant General's Corps Regimental Association awards board for me to receive the award. I was then presented my second award of the Legion of Merit, my retirement award. I made a few remarks, thanked all for coming, stated how much I enjoyed working with them, and I ended by saying, "Life is much like a book. I am soon to write the next chapter." Colonel Kimes then invited the crowd to come and shake hands with Penny, her mother, her father, and me. That was the only time that any emotion welled up. I would see a face, shake a hand or hug a person, and remember a time and place when we had shared a life experience.

Me, Penny, Grandmother Farr, and Granddad Farr at my Retirement Ceremony.
(August 28, 1992)

We then went to another area where coffee, tea, sodas, and finger foods were served. It was a time to visit, reminiscent, and say good-bye. I have not seen most of those folks since. The ceremony was videotaped, but I have not looked at the video in years.

The morning of August 31, 1992, I reported to the III Corps and Fort Hood out-processing facility at 0600 hours, along with fifteen or more colonels. There we were to receive final pay, sign documents to be sent to the Veterans Administration (VA) for a determination regarding any service-connected physical disability that we might have, and be given our DD Form 214, certificate of release, or discharge from active duty.

The young specialist four handed me the 214 and said, "Be sure to hang on to this, sir. It is all that you have to prove you were in the Army." I looked at the document and read that I had served twenty-eight years, one month, and eleven days on active duty. Counting the four years at Tarleton State, where I wore a uniform, I had been in Army greens for my entire adult life.

I walked out of the building at 0645 and heard the "Jody Calls" as units went about their morning PT. It was a beautiful, clear morning, and I thought what a great day to be a soldier. Then it hit me like a punch to the stomach: My soldiering was done. This poem, written by Colonel Eldon W. Carey, a former Salado resident, expresses how I felt at that moment:

Old Soldier's Lament

Whom shall I serve when my service is done
When I no longer march to the beat of the drum
When the call of the bugle has faded and died
And old comrades at arms have long since left my side

Where shall I go when the going is o'er
When no mission awaits me on some distant shore
When calls, oh so urgent, have ceased to resound
From the hills and the fields of that still testing ground

How will it be with no banner to wave
With no cause to espouse that can warrant the grave
With no troops to lead, no vision to see
Who will I be when I'm no longer me

Colonel Eldon W. Carey
United States Army (Retired)
November 26, 1972

I stopped by a Wal-Mart on my way back to Salado and purchased a large footlocker. I placed one set of Greens, BDUs, Dress Blues, boots, hats, belts, various accruements, some medals, dog tags, and my personal 201 file in the locker and manhandled it to the attic.

I was no longer a soldier, no longer Colonel Taylor. I was no longer me!

Yet, I remained a boy from Barnhart!

PART IV

Later Years

24

Trying Times

> *These are the times that try men's souls.*
> —Thomas Paine

Thomas Paine wrote these words when he was advocating colonial America's independence from Great Britain. People like nations go through the crucible of fire at various times. These were to be the times that tried my soul. Penny had a life-threatening illness. I had no job, and our psychological health was at an extremely low ebb. I needed to be strong for Penny to encourage her and to give her hope. I would like to think I did this, but I am not certain. I had been in control for most of my life, but from September 1992 through December 1992, I was not! I was in limbo, and I was mentally and emotionally impotent. My single accomplishment during this time was to study for and pass the exam for a real estate license, which I never used.

In early January 1993, I received a call from Gary Souter, and he said, "Colonel, I need you to come in for an interview. I have a job for you." (Gary always called me colonel.)

"Is it the training manager job?"

"No, I have fired the manager and assistant manager of the child-care center, and I need you to run that place until I can hire someone for the job. I will move you to the training manager job when I find the right person to replace you."

Gary wanted me to interview with the chief of his recruitment staff and one of her minions as a matter of courtesy. The interview was strained. I found out later that both were friends of the child-care center manager and assistant manager, and both were incensed that Gary was hiring me without advertising for the job. Gary said he had to get the approval of his boss, Mr. Robert Mason, the CEO of Scott and White Hospital. He told me Mr. Mason would be an easy interview but not to be alarmed if he dozed off, as he suffered from an unknown malady and his medicine caused him to nod off. I had been in Mr. Mason's office for a short period when he asked if I golfed. I responded that I did. He stated he was having a hard time with his driver and asked if I had ever used an iron to tee off. I responded that I had but usually only on par threes. Then he went to sleep. Gary and I sat there for a very long three minutes. He woke, and very alertly, he said, "I have reviewed your resume and think you will do a fine job," and that ended the interview.

On the way back to Gary's office, I asked when I was to start work, and he responded, "This evening."

Gary had invited all parents with children in the center and other interested parties to meet the new manager. The meeting was well attended by a mix of people who were mad at Gary for firing the previous managers and a few who were glad to see them go. Gary introduced me, and I gave a brief overview of my time as the Army child-care guru and promised that the welfare of their children would be my primary concern. I then asked for questions. The first question was asked in a hostile tone: "What do the children call you? Colonel? Mr. Taylor? Boss? What?"

I answered, "Certainly not colonel. I think Mr. Herb will do just fine." That seemed to satisfy the crowd, and the remainder of the session was what parents wanted stopped or started. I listen and told them I would consider their concerns and make appropriate changes wherever possible.

I reported to work at 0515 the next morning. I opened the door at 0600, and the first child, an infant, was brought in. I would see the father in his pickup each morning as I arrived for work, and he would be standing at the door with the baby when I opened. I closed the center at 1800 each evening, but it was usually 1900 or later before the last child left, as nurses and doctors often had emergencies with which they had to attend. I fed the children two full meals a day, breakfast and lunch, plus a snack in the morning and afternoon. The cook arrived at 0600 along with two caregivers, one to take care of the infants and the other to handle the rest until the full work staff was on duty by 0730.

The cook was excellent with a good work ethic, but the majority of the caregivers were not. They often called in sick after they were due to report for work, leaving me shorthanded until I could call in one of my temporary workers. This exacerbated my staffing problem, as the center was several caregivers short when I took over, and I was soon to fire others. My combination secretary, receptionist, and bookkeeper arrived at precisely 0800 and departed at precisely 1600, and she didn't take a lunch break. She was an excellent worker, but her hours left me with a myriad of problems to deal with—0600 to 0800 and 1600 to 1900. I often had to act as a caregiver for those children who arrived early or left late. I had that infant more than once by myself until the cook could relieve me.

I can only describe the Scott and White Child-Care Center as a facility waiting for a calamity to happen. The center was understaffed. There were few people who wanted to work as temporary workers. The pay scale was ridiculously low. Hardly any people wanted to work at that pay, and those who did were generally people you did not want taking care of your children. The facility was first-rate, all clean and child-friendly, but in that center, children were warehoused and their basic needs were met, nothing more. The center was being touted as a learning center where all aspects of a child's development—physical, emotional, and mental—would be enhanced, but that simply did not happen.

My first act was to learn the qualifications of my staff and determine manning shortfalls. Most had a personnel file with their application for employment and little else. I found that not even one had undergone a background check as required by Texas law, that none had received a physical to determine if they had a communicable disease, and that there was only one who had been certified in CPR or first aid. The center had not yet been accredited by the state and was soon to be visited. Gary was able to get the state to cancel their visit until the new management had a chance to get on board. I am confident that had the accreditation people from the state of Texas visited on my first day, the center would have been closed, and parents told to come get their children. It was that bad.

The center was not profitable and would never be profitable. In fact, Scott and White subsidized it at a hundred thousand dollars a year simply because the fees charged were ridiculously low. The child-care center was one of the benefits of employment at Scott and White. New employees soon found this benefit was one they would have to wait and wait a long time to use. Center capacity was two hundred children, and the center was always at capacity. The waiting list, especially for infants, was extremely long, and turnover was minimal. In addition, I had an after-school program where we picked up some fifteen kids from first through sixth grade, kids who were in addition to the two hundred spaces, and accommodated them in a large multipurpose room.

The fees at the center had been set nonsensically low to benefit the doctors and nurses. I soon realized the political climate was such that an increase in fees was not going to happen, even though I was receiving some pressure from Mr. Mason to bring the center from the red into the black. I attempted to charge time-and-a-half bills for those children not picked up by closing time, but the clamor was such that I had to back off.

I told Gary from the very beginning that the center was an albatross, and he should get rid of it by giving it to the nursing department, as they already had the Child Life Program, which was run by Jan Upchurch and did for sick children what the child-care center was meant to do only much more. Gary was not willing to do this, as the child-care center was a pet project of Mr. Mason, and Gary was determined to make it work. I told Gary that I needed some professional help and asked if he would contact the head of the nursing department and see if she would allow Jan Upchurch to assist in getting the center up and running with SOPs and training. Gary agreed, as did the head nurse. Jan Upchurch was an immense help, and after a time, we had most of the problems solved except for staffing. Some caregivers (babysitters) I fired. Some did not like my rules and style of management and quit, and some I ran off. Consequently, I was always shorthanded with considerable turnover. I was lucky there was no significant incident during my tenure.

Jan Upchurch's ears perked up when I suggested the nursing department take over the child-care center, and eventually, that was what happened. Even so, Mr. Mason asked me on two occasions to remain as manager with a generous pay raise. I told him the only way I would stay was if Scott and White were willing to hire a professional who had a degree in early childhood education as my assistant manager.

He said he would think it over; however, nothing came of my proposal, and for that, I am grateful.

Eventually, the nursing department realized the center was a millstone and convinced Scott and White management to close it. Today, the building houses the S&W mental health offices. I consider that fitting, as the place almost drove me crazy.

Gary brought me up to be the personnel department training manger once the nurses took over the child-care center. My boss was Herb Rosencrans, a retired US Air Force lieutenant colonel and Gary's deputy. Both Gary and Herb were as good as any boss I had ever had in the Army. The only specific I was given about my new job was that I would be responsible for employee orientation, which was an all-day affair held on Monday of each week. In essence, Gary and Herb told me I was to develop my own job description, but they envisioned that I would teach classes primarily to supervisors on what I thought they needed to know to manage people in the S&W culture. S&W had a training department that consisted of several people that Gary had tried to get to teach human resource subjects, but they had refused, preferring to teach employees how to answer the phone, how to dress, and other such subjects. Both Gary and Herb mentioned that S&W sometime had difficulty with the Texas Employment Commission over unemployment benefits for employees who had been fired for cause. The commission was reluctant to deny benefits when there had been no warnings or counseling statements written when the employee was a poor performer or had committed violations of S&W policies.

The new employee orientation consumed one day out of the week, so I immediately set out to develop a supervisor's course for all supervisors regardless of position. My goal was to have all supervisors attend the course with emphasis on getting new supervisors through the course. Eventually, I developed a class that would be presented over a two-day period, one that included those subjects that all supervisors needed to know. Covered were such subjects as the hiring and firing process, how to conduct an interview, what you could and could not ask, the need to document performance and counsel problem employees, how to develop a job description and obtain approval for a new position, a review of the S&W employee handbook, which some supervisors had never read, and many other topics now lost to memory. One of the early attendees was Brad Cryer, who was in the supervisory chain for outlying S&W clinics. Brad wrote in his critique of the course that it was the best course he had ever attended and wanted me to take the course to the outlying clinics, particularly the one at College Station. The fact that Brad liked the course and talked about it in staff meetings resulted in supervisors volunteering to attend the course. I limited the course to twenty students each session and had a waiting list. In addition, I briefed the senior-level staff on the implementation of the new congressionally mandated Family and Medical Leave Act and other legislation that Gary felt senior-level management needed to be aware. Apparently, Gary and Herb were satisfied with my efforts as I received one of the highest year-end bonuses of any employee in the personnel department.

Penny's cancer was in remission for some thirteen months, and then it was back. There was a blood test to detect a marker for ovarian cancer (CA-125) that Penny would be tested for every three weeks. The marker, while not accurate for detecting the early stages of cancer, was used to monitor her late-stage cancer. It was the best diagnostic tool the doctors had at the time, and I think it still is.

Penny told me the cancer was back several weeks before it appeared on the results of a CA-125 test. I said, "You can't know that." And she responded, "I know my body." This resulted in another major operation and a ten-day hospital stay. Penny was very prim and proper, and I laughed when she told me, "I can't go home until I pass gas." I recall she recuperated from the surgery for some three weeks, and then she was itching to go back to work, which she did. She continued to work even while she was undergoing a second round of chemo. This time, she experienced nausea, a low blood count, and some hair and weight loss. She would rest a day, sometimes two, after a chemo session, and then she went back to work. I marveled at her stamina and willpower, but Penny was prone to do what Penny wanted to do. Large or small, setbacks were only obstacles to be overcome. The operations and chemo were beginning to wear her down, and it was showing. My hours at S&W were such that I was able to spend time with Penny in the hospital, at home, and in the chemo room. Gary and Herb were extraordinarily accommodating and supportive.

After the second operation, I wanted Penny to go to M. D. Anderson in Houston for a second opinion, as did her family. Her brother, Phil, was the most vocal of all the family in this regard. Penny was unwavering that she was pleased with her course of treatment and with Dr. Baker in particular. I brought the subject up with Dr. Baker during one of Penny's periodic checkups. Dr. Baker agreed that we were entitled to a second opinion but was adamant that M. D. Anderson used the same treatment method, as did S&W, and the same chemotherapy drugs. He further stated Penny would be just a number at M. D. Anderson and that she would not receive the same care and attention that she was receiving at S&W, as the doctors at M. D. Anderson would not know her. I still wanted her to go but realized that was not to be. It was her body, her life, and her decision.

My work situation changed dramatically when Gary got crossways with Mr. Mason over a personnel issue. I never knew if he was fired or if he quit, but he ended up suing S&W. His replacement was a fellow in his late thirties who came from a personnel job at a clinic in Florida. In my initial office call with the new fellow, I noticed that he winced when I told him I was retired military, and he remarked, "That is good to know." Both Herb Rosencrans and I thought that he was woefully lacking in experience and supervisory skills and way over his head as manager of a large personnel department. I imagine the new person was aware of our view and felt threatened by our age and experience, particularly our military experience. Shortly after his arrival, he sat in on the new employee orientation and did not like much of what I was doing, which resulted in the orientation being significantly changed. He then attended my course for supervisors. At the first break, he pulled me aside and said, "If you have to teach supervisors how to be supervisors, they should not be supervisors. They should be fired." He then departed. I knew then my days were numbered.

All was not gloom and doom, as there were many happy occasions after my retirement and Penny's diagnosis, not the least of which was Ross's marriage. Ross married Kristi Ann Tidwell from Peoria, Texas, at their home in Frisco, Texas, on August 21, 1993. Kristi was Ross's longtime sweetheart from college days. Kristi graduated Hillsboro High School and Tarleton State, and she had a master's degree from

East Texas State University, now Texas A&M University-Commerce. They were married in front of their fireplace just as Penny and I had been married at the Rocker b. Ross bought the home a couple of years after he entered the workforce, which was a very wise move. Frisco, a suburb of Dallas, is one of the fastest growing and most affluent cities in the United States. Ross was working in downtown Dallas at the time, so he had a rather long commute. The decision to buy the home is paying off now, as the home is almost paid for and his commute to a Plano hospital is less than fifteen minutes.

Grandmother and Granddad Farr and other members of the Farr family attended the wedding. It was a happy event for all. Ross was thirty-two, and it was time he married. Penny and I were pleased to have Kristi as a daughter.

Penny, Kristi, Ross, and me.
Ross' marriage—August 21, 1993.

Nine months after her operation, Penny's cancer was back. This was around October 1994. Again, Dr. Baker operated, and the operation took over ten hours. This time, he removed a portion of her colon, and she was fitted with a colostomy that she absolutely hated. The second week of recuperating in the hospital, she developed an infection. I think the doctors thought they were going to lose her, but they never said. The nurses did, and they said it was bad. I could tell from their actions that they were afraid Penny might not make it. Finally, the doctors were able to get the infection under control. I was scared. I can only imagine Penny's thoughts.

Penny bonded with one of the S&W chaplains named Judy Hoeschler, whom she loved. Judy was a Catholic chaplain. She was a great comfort to Penny and helped her immensely, both spiritually and emotionally.

This time, Penny did not return to work for several weeks.

A week or two after Penny was home from the hospital—it was a Friday afternoon after lunch—I was called into the new fellow's office. He did not ask me to sit, but he simply said, "I don't need you."

I was caught off guard and said, "Sir?"

He repeated, "I don't need you. I am giving you two weeks' severance pay. Clean out your office and turn in your keys."

I asked, "Is this personal?" even though I knew the answer would be no.

I turn to leave, and he said, "I guess I trust you. You can clean out your office over the weekend and turn your keys in on Monday."

I responded, "I will be gone shortly," and I was. I had very few personal effects in my office, as I had felt from the time I had come up from the child-care center that my time in S&W might be short. It was about this time that Gary got crossways with Mr. Mason. I figured my employment was contingent on Gary's employment.

I arrived home around 1500, and Penny was on the phone talking with her brother, Phil. She asked, "What are you doing home so early?"

I said, "I got fired." This hurt Penny because she knew I was hurt. Actually, only my pride was hurt. I had already considered quitting after the first of the year so that I could be available to attend to Penny's needs. Still, the fact that I had only two jobs my entire adult life and had been let go from both galled me somewhat. In addition, I thought it tacky that I was fired when the new person knew Penny's situation.

In retrospect, the new chap did not need me. I had already heard that all S&W training personnel, some four or five people exclusive of nurses, would be moved to the personnel department and that I was to be placed with that group. This I did not like and drove my thinking to quit after the first of the year. Further, the training folks could now be directed to assume my duties if desired.

Herb called me at home and told me that two other people along with me had been fired: One was a clerk who had recently gotten out of the Army, and the other was a problem child. Herb then told me he had been called in and had been demoted and relieved of his supervisory responsibility. I think the new fellow had a resentment of military people for whatever reason. Herb was later able to get the chap to keep the status quo until after the end of the year to allow Herb to get enough time to be vested. The new person agreed, and Herb retired.

Penny went back to work over my objections. She was ever so fastidious, and she agonized over the colostomy, afraid she might have to clean it at work and she and the bathroom would smell. This happened on occasion, but she had spray to cover any odor. She would clean the colostomy at night and again before work, but she would not let me assist her in any way. How she was able to do that I do not know, as later I also had the experience of wearing a colostomy for some eighteen months and I definitely needed help. I started taking Penny to work and picking her up after work, and she would be exhausted.

The oncologist had planned to start chemo using the new experimental drug Taxol after the surgery, but her blood count and physical condition was too low. They began to give her a succession of shots to improve her condition. The shots cost $250.00 each. Her drug allowance through KISD with the Scott and White health plan was $2,700.00 a year, which was reached quickly. Dr. Baker was able to get S&W to cover the cost. I once added up the cost of Penny's treatment and hospital bills, and it was over $750,000.00.

Around February 1995, her blood count was such that the oncologist began to treat her with Taxol, and the cancer remained in remission. The Taxol was given in a start-and-stop manner because after each treatment, her white blood count would become extremely low and the oncologist had to wait until her count reached an acceptable level. There were other side effects, such as nausea, anemia, and more hair loss. Penny was deathly ill, but she continued to go to work after each treatment.

In the meantime, I applied for several jobs, primarily in the Georgetown, Round Rock, and Austin areas. I did this because Penny wanted me to stay busy and not sit around the house with nothing to occupy my time. She knew me well. The job search was hopeless. In fact, only one company even bothered to acknowledge my application. I did receive an interview with KISD for one of their recruiter positions, but they filled the position in-house.

It was sometime around March 1995 when I finally realized and accepted that Penny was not going to survive the cancer. You cling to any hope though. It is like a drowning man grasping for a small piece of wood, hoping it will keep him afloat. We were on our way to S&W for blood work and had just passed the Fort Hood/Killeen interchange on I-35 when I said, "Penny, if you are not to survive this illness, please do not die without me being there." (No one can know how hard it is for me to type this sentence.) She did not answer, but she nodded her head and smiled.

Penny had a checkup in early May, and on the way to Scott and White, she told me the cancer was back. She immediately told Dr. Baker when he entered the examining room that the cancer was back. He told her, "No, Penny, it is not back. The CA-125 is normal." He finished the exam and told her all looked normal.

Penny again told him, "The cancer is back. I know my body." He told her to return the next week, and they would check her blood again.

We went in the day before for blood work. The next day as we were waiting for the exam, Sergeant Major John Rottman came over, and we had a quick visit. John's wife was a nurse in the gynecology department, and John was visiting with her. I thought John nervous, but I did not know why. We entered the examining room, and Dr. Charles Capon was there, no Dr. Baker. Dr. Capon was read onto Penny's illness and had examined her on occasion. He simply told Penny that the CA-125 marker showed the cancer was back. He told Penny it was now a quality of life issue. They could operate again and try some older drugs that they had not used but had no success with fighting ovarian cancer. He went on to say, "This might buy you some time, but you are not going to get well." Then he said, "We have done all that we can do."

I asked, "How much time does she have? Is it months, weeks, days?" There was no response. I asked again, "How much time does she have?"

Dr. Capon said, "It is not months."

The whole scene was surreal. I was hearing this but not understanding, and then I very clearly understood what we were being told. It was like a bad dream where you want to scream but cannot, and then you wake up. Penny told me, "I am going to see Judy," and she left.

I followed, but John was waiting at the door. He held me and said, "I'm sorry." I ran to catch Penny, but she was already on the elevator and gone. I remember the day as a Friday, May 12, 1995.

I sat outside Judy Hoeschler's office for over two hours as she and Penny talked behind a closed door. I was deep in my own thoughts and mad. I was mad as hell at God for this happening. How could he let this happen to Penny, to me? It is always about me, me, and me. Self-centeredness is one of my character defects. Penny emerged, and she was calm and composed. She told me Judy wanted to talk with me, that Judy could help me. My frame of mind was such that I did not want to listen to the pitch of a snake-oil salesman telling me that Jesus loved me and Penny was going to a better place than I could ever imagine. I would need to hear those words later but not then, not at that moment.

On the way back to Salado, Penny verbalized her disappointment over Dr. Baker not being there, and she wondered why he had asked someone else tell her she was going to die. She was deeply hurt by Dr. Baker's absence. I did not have the heart to tell her that in my opinion, he had played God, and when he had realized he could not cure her, he could not bring himself to be the one to tell her he had failed. She told me she would rest the weekend and go to work the following Monday. She had to have everything organized and written down for the person who would replace her. I thought that was a good sign, and perhaps it would be months. Sunday night, she told me, "I can't do it any longer. I have done all I can do. I can't go to work tomorrow." I knew then it would not be months, not weeks, but days.

I called the hospice people to come Monday, May 15th, and they were most helpful in their assistance to both Penny and me. They ordered a hospital bed for Penny and pain pills and instructed me to place them under Penny's tongue any time she had pain. They told me the pills acted instantly and would free her from even the most severe pain. I never had to use them, as I do not think Penny experienced pain during her remaining days, a blessing for which I am grateful. She wanted to move to the guest bedroom so she could see outside and people coming to visit. I had wanted to limit visitors, as I was afraid they would wear her out; however, she wanted visitors, and many came. Her friends from KISD, TEXCOM, and the village of Salado all came, some more than once. I also recall that Janet Parry Harkleroad, and Marion and Judy Daily came to visit with Penny.

I asked her mother to come and help, but I could tell after a few days the emotional strain of a mother watching her daughter slowly slip away was too much for her, so I suggested she go home. Her mother told me later that Penny told her, "I have had a good life." This was much comfort to me, and I hope it was to her mother.

I called Tippe and asked her to come. I also asked the hospice nurses if I should have Ross come, and they said yes. I picked Tippe up at the Austin airport on Monday, the 22nd of May. Ross had arrived on Saturday, so he was with his mother. Tippe did not believe me when I told her Penny was in her final days, but she did when she got to the house. One of us was always in the room with Penny. I slept alongside her bed on a futon at night. Tippe slept in the master bedroom, and Ross in a guestroom.

Penny wanted "The Lord's Prayer" and "Amazing Grace" sung at her funeral. She asked Jean Teal, a neighbor and member of the Salado Methodist Church choir, to sing "The Lord's Prayer" and the choir director to sing "Amazing Grace." Jean said she would, but the week Penny died, Jean told Penny she could not do it, as she would not be able to get through the song without crying. Jean told Penny she would sing it for her now if Penny wanted, and Penny did. Jean had a beautiful voice, and I can still hear the sound of that wonderful prayer coming from Penny's bedroom. I am certain that meant a lot to Penny.

Our Father, who art in heaven, hallowed be thy name. Thy Kingdom come, thy will be done, on earth as it is in heaven.
—Anglican Book of Common Prayer

A couple of days before she died, she wanted a bath. She was dead weight by then, and it took both Ross and me to get her in and out of the bath. Penny, bless her heart, was a fanatic about cleanness until the very end. It was the same day I heard her talking to Jesus: "Just leave the door open a little, so I can get in."

I asked Grandmother and Granddad Farr to come for supper the evening of May 27th. The hospice nurses told me death was near as she was hovering over the threshold between life and eternity. They said they could not be sure, it could be a day or two, but her skin had lost its pinkness and had become jaundice yellow, her breathing was becoming increasingly labored, and she had a sinking and darkening around her eyes. I know it was unimaginably difficult for the Farrs to look down at their daughter for the last time. Penny was able to mouth "I love you" as they left her room.

We were getting ready for bed, and Tippe came into Penny's room and said, "I'll sleep in here with her. You need to get some rest and sleep on a good bed." I started for the master bedroom when Tippe said, "She wants you to sleep by her. When I told you to sleep on a good bed, she shook her head to say no." I should have known but did not. I checked on her around midnight. I woke at 0300 and heard no breathing. I touched her skin, and it was already cold.

She had the most beautiful expression frozen on her face. It was one of wonder and amazement. It was as if she were seeing and experiencing something marvelous. There is no doubt in my mind that she was catching her first glimpse of God.

Grief and a host of heartbreaking emotions flooded my soul. I could barely catch my breath. I sobbed for a short time. Oh, the finality of it all. A wife, a mother, a daughter, a sister was gone. I realized I needed to compose myself and tell Ross and Tippe and call the Farrs, Bud, Bill, Phil, the hospice nurse, and the funeral home.

The hospice nurses arrived almost immediately. The first thing they did was ask for the pain pills, which they counted and then flushed down the drain. The funeral home people arrived within the hour. Tippe had me go outside on the deck when they removed Penny's body. I watched the hearse drive down the hill, and I think it was at that moment that my mind became numb to all that had happened and would happen. I was now operating on adrenalin, and my emotions, my feelings were deadened. It was if I had been anaesthetized.

The date was May 28, 1995, a Sunday.

Tippe's husband, Jackie, arrived that afternoon. The next morning, he was to drive me to Cook-Walden Funeral Home to make final arrangements. Shortly before we left, I received a call from Dr. Baker. He told me he had just heard about Penny and that he had planned to come see her that very day. I told him that Penny had been devastated that he had not been the one to tell her nothing more could be done, and that both he and she had lost a valuable opportunity for closure. Dr. Baker said nothing. He gave no explanation, and the conversation ended.

The one thing Penny and I had not discussed was what she was to wear. The funeral home had a variety of clothing for purchase. I decided on a simple dressing gown. The rest had already been decided. I gave the funeral home Penny's obituary that I wanted published in the Austin, Salado, and San Angelo newspapers. Her obituary follows:

Penelope "Penny" Ann Farr Taylor died peacefully at her home in Salado, May 28, 1995 after a long and courageous battle with cancer. Penny was with those who loved her at the time of her death.

She was born August 13, 1942 in Kansas City, Missouri, the eldest child of Louis L. Farr III and Lou Dickey Baucus Farr. Penny grew up with her brothers on the Rocker b Ranch in Irion and Reagan Counties, and attended elementary school in Barnhart.

She was a 1960 graduate of Reagan County High School, Big Lake, and graduated with honors from Northwestern State University, Natchitoches, Louisiana.

She married Colonel (Ret.) Herbie Ross Taylor, Sr. at the Rocker b Ranch on January 7, 1961. She lived in Izmir, Turkey; Camp Zama, Japan; Indianapolis, Indiana; Fort Leavenworth, Kansas; Springfield, Virginia; Fort Polk, Louisiana; and Fort Hood, Texas.

During her travels, she was an active member of The American Red Cross and the Officers' Wives' Club, serving as an officer of these organizations on several occasions. She also was employed by Woodburn Mental Health Center in Alexandria, Virginia for several years and most recently with Deaf Education, Killeen Independent School District.

Funeral services were held at the Salado United Methodist Church, May 30. Interment followed at Cook-Walden/Capital Parks, Austin, Texas.

Penny is survived by her husband Herbie Ross Taylor, Sr. of Salado; son, Ross Taylor, Jr. and his wife Kristi of Frisco; parents Mr. and Mrs. Louis L. Farr, III of Austin; brothers Dr. Louis L. (Bud) Farr, IV of Lubbock; William (Bill) Baucus Farr of Austin; Phil Sawyer Farr of Saginaw, and their wives and families.

The evening of May 29th, Jackie drove me to the funeral home to view Penny's body. I looked at her in the coffin and thought, You don't have to hurt anymore. Penny's tiny, little, worn-out body was there, but not Penny.

There was a heavy rain the early morning of the 30th, and Salado Creek was flooded, causing the single-lane bridge crossing the creek to be closed. This required people to take the back way to our house, which was difficult to find. Family and friends were arriving, and several called for directions, which required me to go get them because there was no direct or easy route to the house. The ladies of Salado Methodist Church brought food. The church service was to start at 1400, but before I arrived at the church, I received a call from the funeral home informing me that I-35 had been flooded between Austin and Salado and they were waiting for the water to recede. Thus, Penny's body did not arrive until near 1500. Most people milled around and visited outside the church while others went inside.

Salado United Methodist Church

Penny's funeral was more than "standing room only." The chapel of the old historic church was full, and some people had to view the service over closed circuit TV in the church's activity center. The KISD deaf education folks brought a few of Penny's children, and a deaf education teacher signed the service for the kids. Judy Hoeschler conducted the service, and she did a fine job. Bud gave the eulogy, speaking for the family. Her pallbearers were her nephews, Mike Martin, Jeff Farr, Lee Farr, and Zack Farr, and friends Bill Fesler and Don Lowe.

The church choir director sang "Amazing Grace" and "The Lord's Prayer." The service was short, simple, and upbeat. Bud got a few chuckles as he talked of growing up with Penny. The only time I almost lost it was when Penny's mother squeezed my hand. I knew what she was going through. I think Penny would have enjoyed the service. This girl from Barnhart was truly in a better place than I could ever imagine.

After the ritual, I was not able to visit with all those I would have liked. I much appreciated seeing Janet Parry Harkleroad and her mother at the service. There were also Shelley Hancock, S&W nurses, friends, and co-workers from TEXCOM and S&W. Also, Dr. Romaine, the head of the school of veterinary medicine at Texas A&M, was there for the Farrs. There were so many people who cared about Penny, the Farrs, and me.

Ross, Kristi, and I rode together to the burial ground. There were a few people other than family at the site, but not many. The time at the cemetery was no more than twenty minutes. Then Pen's family along with a few friends gathered at the Farr's. I made an appearance, but I really wanted to be by myself. I had a lot of pent-up emotion that needed releasing. Jackie drove Tippe, Mother, Daddy, and me back to Salado. They let me off at the house, where I had a good cry. The next morning, I met them for breakfast at the Stagecoach Inn, and they departed for Lubbock. I was now truly alone.

Later, Penny's marker was placed at her grave.

Penny's Marker, Cook-Walden Cemetery, Pflugerville, Texas.

One day, I will rest beside her, and a similar plain plaque will mark my time on this earth. I hope that our grandchildren and their offspring will visit and think ours were two lives well lived.

Dear Ancestor

Your tombstone stands among the rest
neglected and alone.
The name and date have worn off the
weathered marble stone.
It reaches out to all who care.
it's now too late to mourn,
you did not know that I'd exist,
you died . . . and I was born.
Yet each of us are cells of you
in flesh, in blood, in bone.
Our hearts contract and beat a pulse
entirely not our own.
Dear ancestor, the place you filled
some hundred years ago
spreads out among the ones you left
who would have loved you so.
I wonder how you lived and loved.
I wonder if you knew
that someday I would find this place
and come and visit you.

—Unknown

I believe they will come and visit, and they will know how Penny and I lived and loved because of this book.

25

Floating

The dictionary defines floating as "not secured in place; unattached; inclined to move or be moved about." That describes my emotions after Penny's death. Penny was both my compass and my anchor. I had lost my mooring and was adrift and floating. She gave purpose and direction to my life. I have wondered over the years what I would have been had Penny not been by my side. The thought frightens me. She was with me through grade school and high school, got me through college, and was the settling influence in my life thereafter. She was my girlfriend, sweetheart, lover, wife, and best friend. Then she was gone, and I was alone and floating. It was as if I were walking in a dream.

I think as I write this (May 26, 2011) had Penny not died, we would have been married fifty years on January 7, 2011. As it was, we were married for thirty-four years, four months, and twenty-one days.

Grief is an evil, insidious emotion. The worst part of grief is that you cannot control it. The very worst part is that you think it is over, and it starts all over again. I would be driving, eating, reading, working in the yard, preparing for bed or sleep; and, then I would be overcome with sadness, and the tears would flow. I hated this but found no way to get relief except for one activity, and that was golf. I realized that when I was on the golf course with other people and that little, white, round ball, I thought of nothing except the next shot. It was me against the ball, and for a time, it would bring relief.

I had taken up the game a couple of years prior to retirement at the persistence of my deputy, Lieutenant Colonel Bill Fesler. I played

Saturday mornings with a group of TEXCOM golfers on the Fort Hood course. I was terrible, and no one wanted me on their team. Thus, I usually ended up on Bill's team. Bill had infinite patience, and the other members of the group tolerated my consistently errant shots. Sometimes General Page played in our foursome. He hated anyone to stand behind him when he was on the tee box, which invariably Bill Fesler would do, and invariably, General Page would ask him to move. Page had a temper, so Bill's action would trigger that temper, and Page would shank or hook his tee shot. Bill and Page would have a side bet as to who would have the best round, and once Bill had made General Page mad, his game would suffer to the point that Bill could win the match. One day, General Page called me aside and said, "Colonel, Fesler works for you, and I want you to tell him to stop standing behind me on the tee box."

I responded, "Sir, if a general cannot get him to stop, why do you think me, a mere colonel, would be able to do so?"

Upon Penny's death, I joined the Mill Creek Men's Golf Association and began to play every single day. I believe a person cannot become a decent golfer unless they play often. I usually played with a group of perhaps twenty to twenty-five golfers who teed off every morning at 0900. The group would finish around 1330, and I would eat at the club and arrive home around 1430. I would then have the rest of the day and night to dwell in my misery. However, for a time, I did not think about anything except that little round, white ball. Thinking and being in my head without distraction was not a good place for me to be.

Eventually, I achieved a decent handicap, and in 1997, I decided to play in the Mill Creek Club Championship in the senior flight for fifty-five and over. I won senior low net and received a trophy. I never played in another club championship but continued playing with my morning group.

I was on the golf course the morning of September 11, 2001, playing with my neighbors, Ron Anderson and Dean Ekhoff, when Glen Barton, the course marshal, told us that he had heard that an airplane had hit one of the Twin Towers of the World Trade Center in New York City. I thought, What a disaster, and wondered how an airliner could get that far off course. I thought that it might have been a small plane. Glen was soon back with news about the second plane hitting the other tower, and I knew then that it was no accident. We headed for the clubhouse and watched it all unfold on TV. We all wondered who could have done such a thing and why.

It is now known that it was Osama bin Laden and his al Qaeda terrorist organization. The sad part is that President Bill Clinton and his administration knew about bin Laden and al Qaeda and the organization's capabilities. For whatever reason, he failed to take the actions that could have prevented the disaster. Regardless, the War on Terror that had its beginning on that infamous day continues. The US Army and Marine Corps have now been at war for over ten years, and the price in blood and treasure has been unbelievably high. The Army is broken and cannot continue at the same operational tempo. Long and repeated deployments have not only broken the morale of the individual soldier but their families as well. Suicide and divorce are the highest the Army has ever experienced. I wonder if Penny would have tolerated my going back for a third tour in Vietnam. Many soldiers have deployed five or more times.

I like to talk with soldiers and keep abreast of what is happening in the Army. Time has passed me by as weapons, communication systems, and even the uniforms have changed. The Army of today is not the Army of 1992. Digitization, networking, space-based technologies, precision-guided munitions, and unmanned aerial vehicles either were in their formative stages or did not exist at all when I retired. Even the organizations have changed, with emphasis on brigade combat teams rather than combat divisions. What has not changed is the need for the American soldier.

Again, I envision the inevitable downsizing of the Army because of national debt, reduced budgets, and drawdown of soldiers in Iraq and Afghanistan. I also am beginning to hear the familiar refrain that airpower and sea power are sufficient to protect the nation's interest. History tells me otherwise. There will always be a need for "boots on the ground." To gut the Army, in my opinion, would be a mistake, and the nation does so at its peril. The American people, including me, have found many reasons to complain about national policy with regard to Iraq and Afghanistan, but none of us can complain about the quality of our soldiers.

Shortly before Penny's death, probably February or March 1995, I received a call from Janis Petronis, the director of alumni relations at Tarleton State University. Janis asked if I would meet with her, a professor at Mary Hardin Baylor University in Belton, and the chief of staff at King's Daughters' Hospital in Temple. Both were Tarleton graduates. She wanted to discuss actions the university could take to increase alumni participation in university activities. We met in the boardroom of King's Daughters' Hospital and had a beneficial dialogue. I thought nothing more about the meeting until the week before Penny's death when I was surprised by a call from Matt Brockman, the president of the Tarleton State University Alumni Association (TAA). Matt told me that I had been recommended to serve as a member of the alumni association board of directors, and he asked if I would be willing to serve. I said that I would.

The first meeting was held in Granbury, Texas, shortly after Penny's death. This began a period during which I was actively involved in alumni association affairs, both on and off the Tarleton campus for six consecutive years. My time on the board was a godsend, because it gave me another distraction to get me out of my head. It was also to be fortuitous in another way, although I did not know it at the time. A member of the board was a pretty lady named Janice Irene Taylor Sullivan, who was to serve with me the entire time I was on the TAA board.

Janice was a divorcee and lived in Abilene, Texas. She was a broker selling financial products primarily to college and university professors. Her clients were employed at colleges and universities that stretched from Western Texas College in Snyder to Angelo State University in San Angelo. She also had an extensive client base at Tarleton. I was to discover that her ex-husband, Cavin Sullivan, had been one of my platoon sergeants when I had commanded Company D during my senior year at Tarleton. Janice finished her degree and graduated Tarleton in 1973 when Cavin was on a short tour in Korea. Cavin retired as a lieutenant colonel, and they divorced soon thereafter. Although we were on active duty at the same time, Cavin and I never served together.

My entire time on the TAA board was marked by a series of proactive initiatives taken by the board to improve its standing and visibility with its membership and the university. Luine Hancock succeeded Matt

Brockman as president for a one-year term (1996–7). Janice was then president (1997–8). I followed Janice (1998–9) and had the privilege of serving as president during Tarleton's centennial celebration in 1999. Tom Kemp followed me as president (1999–2000).

Significant accomplishments during Luine's term include the signing of a memorandum of agreement between the TAA and Tarleton that codified the relationship between the two. This took several meetings with Dr. McCabe, the president of Tarleton, and the TAA board, because there were several areas of contention regarding responsibilities that took time to resolve. Initially, there was an adversarial relationship between Dr. McCabe and the TAA, but over time, both became equal and cooperative partners in supporting Tarleton. The memorandum of agreement was the key to solidifying this mutually beneficial relationship. Equally important was Luine's efforts in negotiating a contract with First USA for a TAA-sponsored credit card and an initial payment of two hundred and fifty thousand dollars with three hundred thousand guaranteed over five years. These monies put the TAA on firm financial footing and enabled the TAA to support Tarleton in areas other than scholarships. The TAA awarded twelve scholarships in 1997 to deserving students whose parents or grandparents were Tarleton graduates and members of the TAA. Luine was recognized as a distinguished alumnus of Tarleton in 2011.

Janice's tenure was marked by the hiring of a part-time TAA employee to enable the organization to rely less on university support. This was the first time that the TAA had administrative support that reported directly to the organization. The Clyde H. Wells/TAA Golf Classic netted forty thousand dollars, and ten thousand donated by the Baylor Health-Care System was used to establish a scholarship fund to benefit nursing students at Tarleton. Fourteen scholarships were awarded, and the prototype of the TAA website was developed. Additionally, the TAA had engraved pens made from the first pecan tree cut to clear space for the new science building. The TAA board had actively supported legislation in Austin, which resulted in the fifteen-million-dollar construction project being approved.

Achievements during my tenure were centered around activities in support of Tarleton's hundredth birthday. The TAA commissioned Covelle Jones, a Tarleton graduate, distinguished alumnus, and a renowned sculptor, to design a centennial medallion to honor Tarleton's first one hundred years. All proceeds were to be used for scholarships. The Annual Distinguished Alumni Dinner, which is sponsored by the TAA and presided over by the TAA president, is held during homecoming. The purpose is to recognize that year's distinguished alumnus, distinguished young alumnus, distinguished faculty, and distinguished staff. I had the privilege of presiding when Joe Long, that year's distinguished alumnus, and his wife, Teresa, presented Tarleton with a gift of one million dollars for scholarships. In addition, Mr. Long committed to the TAA to provide a dollar for every two dollars contributed from other sources to support an O.A. Grant Excellence in Teaching Award to honor outstanding members of the Tarleton faculty. The inaugural presentation of the TAA/O.A. Grant Excellence in Teaching Award was presented to five Tarleton professors during the annual academic forum. The TAA hosted a free barbecue during Tarleton's centennial week, feeding over 2,400 Tarleton students, faculty, staff, alumni, and friends. The TAA awarded sixteen scholarships, and the golf tournament netted twenty-two thousand dollars. The net worth of the TAA at the end of the fiscal year was $455,000.00.

Tom's term was marked by moving management of TAA investments to a professional organization, namely Merrill Lynch, developing and refining a new TAA website and moving it to an off-campus host, and concluding a partnership arrangement with Hastings Bookstore, which ensured a 35 percent margin on all TAA merchandise sold. Tom was also influential in amending the TAA bylaws to change the terms of board members and officers to an annual rather than fiscal-year basis. His most noteworthy accomplishment (and the most meaningful of my time on the board) was his leadership in completing funding, design, and groundbreaking for the Tarleton Military Memorial, which is located in Heritage Park on the Tarleton campus.

The Tarleton Military Memorial began as an idea by Colonel Willie Tate of the US Army (retired). Colonel Tate served during WWII, Korea, and Vietnam. He attended Tarleton during its junior college days from 1933 to 1935. He was a star on the basketball team that went undefeated during his time at Tarleton. Will played for the legendary basketball coach, W. J. Wisdom, whose teams won eighty-six consecutive games. Wisdom's teams were so successful at defeating larger four-year colleges that the Southwest Conference schools would not play Tarleton. Will went on to play and graduate from the University of Texas, where he also starred on their basketball team. Will told me that in one game with Texas A&M, there were nine former Tarleton players on the court, four from Texas and five from A&M. Will attended Harvard Business School while in the Army, and upon retirement, he served as a vice president of Galveston College. Eventually, he found his way back to Stephenville and Tarleton. Will Tate is a great supporter and benefactor of Tarleton and one of the finest men I have ever known.

Cadet Raymond Jones, Colonel Will Tate, and Colonel Taylor.

Will brought his idea for a military memorial to the TAA board of directors, and in 1996, he was appointed chairman of the Military Wall of Honor Committee. The committee included Tom Kemp; Major General (Ret) Chris Adams, a former TAA president, and a distinguished alumnus; and Dennis Hancock, an architect, Tarleton alumnus, and Luine's husband; and me. We obtained the approval and support of Dr. McCabe to locate the memorial on the Tarleton campus and began to consider design and sources for funding.

Several designs were considered but rejected because of cost. Eventually, the memorial took shape in the form of a twenty-ton marble cube. The front of the cube is shown below. The reverse of the cube contains the names of all Tarleton faculty, staff, and students who were prisoners of war. The left side contains the names of general officers who attended Tarleton and those awarded the Silver Star or a higher award. The right side contains the names of Tarleton faculty, staff, and students who have been killed in action (KIA). There were over 210 KIAs in WWII alone.

Military Memorial-Tarleton State University

Leading to the memorial are three flagpoles. The first is for the Tarleton flag, the second for the flag of the state of Texas, and the last pole for our nation's colors. I donated the funds to cover the cost of the Tarleton flagpole. At the base of the flagpole is this plaque.

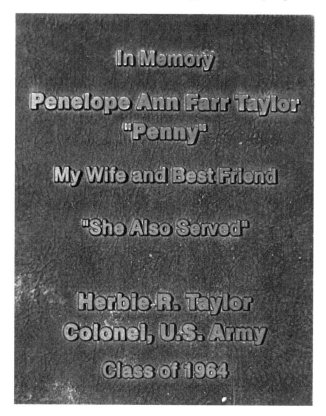

Penny's Plaque at Tarleton's Military Memorial.

There are fathers who do not love their children; there is no grandfather who does not adore his grandson.
—Victor Hugo

There were two occasions that especially brought me great joy. The first was the birth of my grandson, Micah Jeb Taylor. Micah was born August 14, 1995, the day after what would have been Penny's fifty-third birthday. The second was the birth of Jared Ross Taylor on October 1, 1997. Both were born at Presbyterian Hospital in Plano, and I was there for their births. They are big guys now, but what a wonder it was to see them right after they came into this world. It is a memory that I will carry with me to the grave. My only regret is that Penny was not there to share my joy.

Micah is learning to drive now, and we have had fun on the back roads of the farmland near Salado. Soon, it will be Jared's turn. Both boys play in the band, and skateboarding is Micah's passion. I suspect that will change to cars and girls soon enough. It appears that Jared will be the athlete of the family. It will be enjoyable to watch the boys grow up and become men.

This boy from Barnhart is so proud of his grandsons.

26

A New Beginning

Marriage is the triumph of imagination over intelligence. A second marriage is the triumph of hope over experience.
—Unknown

I married Janice Irene Taylor Sullivan, a woman from Breckenridge, Texas, on April 29, 2003, at the courthouse in Belton, Texas. Judge Ted Duffield officiated, and Ron and Phyllis Anderson, our good friends and neighbors, witnessed the ceremony. The clerk asked when we applied for the marriage license, "Are you related?"

Janice quipped, "We may be, but we don't plan to have any children." We all had a good laugh.

Janice has three children. They are Melissa Irene (forty-three), Brent (forty-one), and Shaun (thirty-two). Melissa has one child, Anastacia "Staci" "Tinkerbell" Irene Autrey, and Brent has five children. They are Cassie, Leigh Ann, Brianna, Caleigh, and Gavin. Melissa is married to Ronnie Ives, and they live in Arlington, Texas. Neither Brent nor Shaun is married. Janice and I began our courtship when Staci "Tinkerbell" was around ten, so I have had the privilege and pleasure of watching her grow into a woman of twenty-one. Staci, the daughter I never had, has brought a new dimension and much joy to my life.

Herbie and Janice.

Our marriage has been full and rewarding. It has also been filled with the usual trials and tribulations that you'd expect to find when two people marry in late middle age. I lost both my parents, and Janice's mother suffers from Alzheimer's and colon cancer, her stepfather from dementia and heart problems. Thus, Janice, as the oldest of her siblings, has had to take on the task of being responsible for her parents. Janice is a caring and nurturing person, and she was a great comfort to me and my parents in their last days. Tippe was the one responsible for my parents, as she moved them close to her and had to deal with their daily problems. She and her husband, Jackie, were devoted to my parents, and I will be eternally grateful for all they did.

Janice has had to nurse me through three major operations. One that involved a twenty-nine-day hospital stay at Baylor Medical Center in Dallas, and two major surgeries at S&W. She also had to assist me with the colostomy that I had for eighteen months before it was finally reversed. She is a Stephen Minster in the Salado United Methodist Church and an active member of a twelve-step program for people with an addiction to alcohol. Much of her time has been and is being spent helping others.

We have had some enjoyable times together. I taught Janice to play golf (sort of), and in addition to playing at Mill Creek, we played at Tapatio Springs in Boerne, Texas, Dyess Air Force Base in Abilene, the Texas Tech course in Lubbock, and others during our travels.

Travel has been our greatest enjoyment. We have taken a train trip in vintage turn-of-the-century Pullman cars with a private dining car visiting the national parks in the western United States. We have taken three-week road trips to both the East and West Coast. We have been to Canada and stayed in Vancouver twice and Victoria once. We have ridden a train from Skagway, Alaska, to the Yukon Territory in Canada and from Anchorage to Denali National Park. We have taken a private plane and flown over and around Mount McKinley, the highest mountain in North America, and taken helicopter rides to Mount St. Helens and the Mendenhall glacier. We have cruised the coast of Alaska from Whittier to Vancouver British Columbia and from Galveston to Cozumel, Mexico. We have stayed at Marriot Resorts in Colorado (Vail), Missouri (Branson), Texas (San Antonio), and Tennessee. Janice took Staci to Europe for Staci's high school graduation, and she, Staci, and friends visited Disney World in Orlando, Florida.

During Spring break of 2009, Ross, Kristi, Micah, Jared, Janice, and I flew to Washington, D.C., to see the sights and take a tour of the capital. We then drove to Carlisle Barracks to visit the Army War College and stayed in guest quarters on the post. Along the way, we toured the Gettysburg Battlefield. The boys enjoyed seeing my name on the plaque outside Root Hall at the War College. We then drove to Baltimore and stayed at a Marriott Hotel on the waterfront. It was a good lesson for the boys in the history of this great nation and an enjoyable time for all.

Janice and I are booked for a seven-day cruise from New York to Halifax, Nova Scotia, to view the Autumn leaves (October 2011). Our next planned trip is to cruise the Mediterranean and spend time in Turkey, Egypt, and Israel followed by a cruise to New Zealand and Australia.

This boy from Barnhart has been blessed by marriage to two fine, beautiful, and loyal West Texas women. I have had a good life. What a journey. And to think there are still more chapters to be written as I trudge the road of destiny.

Living Life

Life is not a race—but indeed a journey. Be honest. Work hard. Be choosy. Say "thank you", "I love you", and "great job" to someone each day. Go to church, take time for prayer. The Lord giveth and the Lord taketh. Let your handshake mean more than pen and paper. Love your life and what you've been given, it is not accidental—search for your purpose and do it as best you can. Dreaming does mater. It allows you to become that which you aspire to be. Laugh often. Appreciate the little things in life and enjoy them. Some of the best things really are free. Do not worry, less wrinkles are more becoming. Forgive, it frees the soul. Take time for yourself—plan for longevity. Recognize the special people you've been blessed to know. Live for today, enjoy the moment.

-Bonnie L. Mohr

I

For My Descendants

If we take habitual drunkards as a class, their heads and their hearts will bear an advantageous comparison with those of any other class. There seems ever to have been a proneness in the brilliant and warm-blooded to fall in to this vice.
—Abraham Lincoln

I am an alcoholic! This admission is made without regret for my past or a desire to shut the door on it. It is what it is.

I hope that an examination of alcoholism and my drinking career may be of benefit to you, Micah Jeb, and to you, Jared Ross, and to those who are prone to be in or already in the clutches of this cunning, baffling, powerful, and very patient disease.

Alcoholism is a pejorative word. One, when thinking of the alcoholic, conjures up images of the homeless, the wino, the bowery bum, the criminal, the weak-willed, and the morally decadent. There are those who fall into these categories, but most do not. I have found that there is no typical alcoholic, although our actions and ultimate end are much the same.

I have attended twelve-step meetings with successful executives, physicians, attorneys, judges, and one well-known actress. Most, though, are like me: average Americans. All sections of the country and most occupations are represented, as well as political, economic, social, and religious backgrounds.

I fall into the category of the high-bottom or functioning drunk, one who has not yet lost his health, his wealth, his family, his friends, or his freedom, and the emphasis is on the "yet." I have never been arrested for DUI or public intoxication, seen the inside of a jail, owed money, or lost a home, job, or family. My health, while fair, can only be peripherally attributed to drinking. Regardless, I am a drunk just as surely as he or she who has lost all.

I have self-referred myself to alcohol treatment programs and hospital detoxification, and I have fought the demon, the elephant in the room, for years.

I am powerless over alcohol, and my life is unmanageable when I drink.

There is but one solution, and that is abstinence. I must put the "plug in the jug" and simply not take that first drink.

One drink is too many, and a thousand not enough.

I have spent much of my adult life obsessing about my next drink and the relief that it would bring.

Spirituous liquors shorten more lives than famine, pestilence and the sword!
—Noah Webster

Alcoholism has been recognized for many years by professional medical organizations as a primary, chronic, progressive disease that, if not controlled, ends in death. This acknowledgment of the disease concept has begun the breakdown of some of the stigma associated with alcoholism, mainly that it is not a result of immorality, lack of willpower, or insufficient discipline.

Even so, alcoholics, because of the perceived social stigma, embarrassment, and denial, tend to keep their drinking a secret. It is no different in my case.

I never understood the disease concept of alcoholism and why I could not drink like other people until it was explained to me in a rehab center and later emphasized in a twelve-step program.

I have an allergy to alcohol much as you might have an allergy to eating strawberries or peanuts, except that you would stop eating peanuts or strawberries after your first negative encounter. I do not stop drinking, although my experience is also negative. I do not break out in a rash. Instead, I break out in a drunk.

This phenomenon is expressed by the development of a craving for more alcohol once the first drink is taken, and the more one drinks, the greater the craving.

The alcoholic does not metabolize alcohol like normal people do. When a normal drinker consumes alcohol, it passes from the stomach and intestines into the blood. Alcohol is then metabolized by enzymes, which are bodily chemicals that break down other chemicals. In the liver, an enzyme mediates the conversion of alcohol to acetaldehyde. Acetaldehyde is converted to acetate by other enzymes and is eventually metabolized into carbon dioxide and water.

The acetate stage is where the problem occurs for the alcoholic. We have an enzyme that is of insufficient quantity and quality to process the acetone efficiently. The acetone, for reasons unknown, creates a craving in the alcoholic. The more alcohol ingested, the greater the amount of acetone. And the greater the acetone, the greater the craving. Thus, the alcoholic drinks until he "blacks out." Blacking out is much different than "passing out." During a "blackout," the alcoholic functions much as a sober person, but when he stops drinking, he has no recollection of what he has or has not done. Once the drinking stops, the obsession to drink begins, and the cycle starts all over, resulting in the alcoholic finding that he is unable to stop drinking without help.

Willpower and knowledge of the disease are of no help to the alcoholic.

Is alcoholism inherited? Alcoholism tends to run in families, and genetic factors partially explain this pattern. Currently, researchers are on the way to finding the genes that influence vulnerability to alcoholism. A person's environment, such as the influence of friends, stress levels, and the ease of obtaining alcohol, also may influence drinking and the development of alcoholism. Still, other factors, such as social support, may help to protect even high-risk people from alcohol problems.

Risk, however, is not destiny. A child of an alcoholic parent will not automatically develop alcoholism. A person with no family history of alcoholism can become alcohol-dependent.

I believe that I was born with a genetic predisposition to alcoholism. Although there is no alcoholism in my immediate family, I see other more distant relatives who show signs of the malady. I think my maternal grandmother had an alcoholic personality, and had she had money and access to alcohol, she may have been in danger. Further, it appears that some members of her family were itinerant preachers, outlaws, or alcoholics, and some were all three. My great-grandmother on my maternal grandfather's side was a Native American, and there was Native American blood on my maternal grandmother's side of the family as well. The problem Native Americans have with alcohol is well known.

Alcoholism is much like the disease of diabetes in that it cannot be cured but it can be controlled. Hence, there is the term "recovering alcoholic." Twelve-step programs sermonize that alcoholism has only three outcomes if the twelve steps are not practiced daily: death, imprisonment, or confinement to a mental institution.

> *We don't think ourselves into a new way of living; we live our way into a new way of thinking.*
> —Richard Rohr

The addictive personality remains after drinking stops unless the alcoholic undergoes a rigorous practice of the twelve steps, thus changing their actions and changing their thinking. An alcoholic cannot think their way into changing their actions. Instead, they must take action, the twelve steps, to change the way they think.

Alcoholism is a disease of the brain as much or more than a disease of the body.

Dr. Charles B., my first sponsor and accountability partner, would say, "If nothing changes, then nothing changes." He would go on to say, "If you do not change your actions, then there will be no change in your life. You may be sober or at least dry, but you will still be the same miserable bastard bringing chaos into your life and the lives of those around you, especially those who love you. And eventually you will drink again."

There simply is no progress without change.

There are only two things an alcoholic doesn't like: the way things are and change.

Why do I drink? The short answer is that that is what alcoholics do. I think the following, which was written as an exercise while I was attending an outpatient treatment program, may shed light on the reasons:

> I once believed you were my friend.
> I thought you made me happy when I was sad, gave me courage when I was afraid, comfort and companionship when I was alone, stroked my ego when I felt inferior, and how I needed that. You kept the demons at bay and allowed me to think when it was painful to think. You kept me from being afraid.
> But what a cunning, baffling, powerful, and insidious bastard you are. You were taking control of my life, my very soul, drink by drink, and leading me to an early grave. You made me insane. You helped me to believe that all was well in my world for a long time, but even in my craziness, I knew better, and through the grace of God, I have been able to remove you from my life.
> Who are you? You are alcohol, and you are no friend of mine.

More specifically, I have some very destructive personality traits. I am egotistical with an inferiority complex, and that is a bad combination. I am selfish and self-seeking, prideful in the extreme, inconsiderate, dishonest in matters involving my drinking, and impatient. Moreover, I am fearful, afraid that I will lose something I have or not get something I want.

I have been diagnosed as having OCD (obsessive compulsive disorder) and SAD (social anxiety disorder), both of which contribute to my alcoholism.

Consequently, I am uncomfortable in my own skin and find it difficult to accept life on life's terms. Daily living is my problem, not the drinking. The drinking is but a symptom of the problem.

Having a wealth of knowledge about the disease—I could probably teach in an alcohol rehab facility—and being aware of my shortcomings, why do I take that first drink? I am strangely insane in this regard.

I did not become a full-blown alcoholic overnight. My first drink and first drunk occurred when I was thirteen or fourteen and involved beer. I did not like the taste; however, I liked how it made me feel, and I wanted more. For the first time in my life, I felt like I belonged, and my feelings of inferiority disappeared. I drank only on weekends while in high school. Even then, I drank alcoholically. I did not drink beer like most of my friends. I drank liquor, any liquor, and my tolerance for liquor was prodigious. The amount of alcohol I ingested was more than the other guys; however, I did not get falling-down drunk as they did, and I did not get sick like they did.

In college, I drank very little because of a lack of money. When I did, I drank to get drunk. My drinking career took off in the Army. Booze was cheap, and the culture emphasized drinking. Many thought you were less than manly if you were not a two-fisted drinker, and I could drink with the best of them. It was all right to have a beer or martini at lunch and a few drinks at the Officer's Club after work, provided you did not show up on the MP blotter the next day or otherwise embarrass yourself or your boss.

I progressed to a daily drinker, a maintenance drinker. I would usually have a couple of drinks before supper and maybe a drink afterward. Over time, the number of drinks increased, and the drink glasses got larger.

Field duty and temporary assignments interfered with my drinking, but I was able to "white knuckle" my way through until they ended.

I became a man of principle. I did not drink on duty. I did not drink before 1700 hours. I did not drive when I drank, and I never drank more than two drinks if I was to be around my boss. He might have thought I had an alcohol problem or, heaven forbid, was an alcoholic.

Well before I retired from the Army, I realized I had a drinking problem and began to moderate. This was especially true during Penny's illness. I suppose this was because of my love for her and my sense of responsibility to attend to her needs, or perhaps I just felt needed. However, my experience was that when I tried to moderate, I realized my drinking was out of control.

When Penny died, I had no reason to get up in the morning other than to golf. My drinking then became decidedly alcoholic, as I began to isolate from family and friends and to binge drink. I would go to the liquor store and buy a half-gallon case of scotch and several cartons of cigarettes. I would rotate between liquor stores to make my purchases because I was embarrassed and did not want them to think I was an alcoholic.

I would return home, close the blinds, turn off the phone, turn on the computer, and drink continuously, stopping only for a few hours of sleep, until the six 1.75 liter bottles were empty. During this time, usually ten days or so, I neither bathed nor shaved.

Once the liquor was gone, I would bathe, shave, "dry out," and attend to whatever needed done in the way of bills, meetings, family, and other responsibilities. I began to have tremors in my hands that greatly affected my golf game, although I continued to play. I had a housekeeper who came weekly and a lawn care company that maintained the yard. I had nothing except playing golf and working with the Tarleton Alumni Association to occupy my time. I lived inside my head, and that is a bad place for drunks to be, especially me.

I was running against the wind, out of touch with my life, my family, and my friends.

This situation continued periodically for almost eight years until I married Janice, and she and I became active in a twelve-step program.

> *It is a painful thing to look at your own trouble and know that you yourself and no one else has made it.*
> —Sophocles

By going back into my drinking history, I believe that I could show that years before I realized I was out of control, my drinking even then was no mere habit, that it was indeed the beginning of a fatal progression. Nevertheless, the difficulty is that I had not suffered enough to have the desire to stop drinking while there was yet time.

I was never of a violent nature, but when I was in a dark mood that had been exacerbated by alcohol, there were times when I verbally maltreated Penny, Ross, and Janice. Years of living with an alcoholic is almost sure to make any wife or child neurotic. The entire family is ill to some extent. There were endless others who suffered from my temper, my tongue, and my anger.

The most painful thing about returning from an alcoholic spree is seeing the look of disappointment and hurt that these forays invariably put in the eyes of your loved ones. *The important thing I lost was my own self-respect.* Ultimately, I do not have a problem with drinking. I have a problem with living. The drinking is only the symptom of the problem.

In the words of Andy Dufresne, protagonist of the *Shawshank Redemption*, "Get busy living or get busy dying."

For a long time, this boy from Barnhart was busy dying.

My sponsor suggested I write a letter to my parents, one making amends for the hurts I had caused them. I think the letter succinctly sums up much of the preceding. I read the letter to Daddy at his grave and to Mother while she was asleep, as I did not want to upset her. She was unable to discuss my drinking without crying. The letter reads:

Dearest Mother and Daddy,

I am writing to apologize for the hurts and sadness that I caused you.

Most were caused either by my drinking or by my character defects or both.

I am an alcoholic.

I have many character defects. I am selfish, self-centered, egotistical, prideful, and dishonest; I am spiritually bankrupt.

You did not cause my alcoholism, you cannot control it, and you cannot cure it.

Neither can I cure it by willpower nor self-knowledge.

God can and will if he is sought.

I have sought God through both prayer and deed.

Today, I belong to a fellowship whose only requirement for membership is a desire to stop drinking. If I am to remain sober and lead a useful and productive life as intended by my creator, I must follow certain spiritual principles. One of these is to clean up the wreckage of my past and make amends to those I have harmed.

You, more than others, I harmed by word and deed. I realize I caused you great mental and emotional anguish by my actions. I was often selfish, inconsiderate, dishonest, self-seeking, and impatient in our relationship.

I did not live the Christian life you wished and prayed for me.

I cannot undo the past, but I do not have to repeat the past. I have asked God to remove every single defect of character, which stands in the way of my usefulness to him and my fellow man. I pray that he will give me the strength not to drink and to do his bidding and that, over time, all will see a change in me.

I have returned to the Church, as I feel called to do so.

There is a void, an emptiness in my heart, and the Church helps fill that void by bringing me closer to God.

Herbie

Some tell me that I have changed or at least mellowed. I work daily on being a better person. I think I have achieved some success, but much work remains. Thankfully, it is a program of progress rather than perfection.

There is no short-term solution to a long-term problem.

I will never be cured of alcoholism. What I really have is a daily reprieve contingent on the maintenance of my spiritual condition. Some days are better than others. I am willing to turn aspects of my will and my life over to the care of God as I understand him, but I often take it back. God does not move fast enough or does not do what I would like him to do.

I continue to try.

I have written this so that you, my descendants, understand you may have a genetic predisposition to alcoholism. I would tell you not to take the first drink, but that is unrealistic, as the nature of an adolescent is to experiment.

I do tell you that repeated experimentation could become a habit that could rapidly develop into an addiction.

I realize you think that would never happen to you.

I, too, thought the same thing.

II

Further Reading

Bahnsen, John C. "Doc," Jr. *American Warrior: A Combat Memoir of Vietnam.* New York: Kensington Publishing Corporation, 2007.

Bean, George E. *Aegean Turkey.* London: Ernest Benn Limited, 1966.

Berryman, Frank R., and Russie T. *From the Distant Past to the Present: A Genealogy of the Taylor and Berryman Families.* Utica, Kentucky: McDowell Publications, 1978.

Bowden, Mark. *Black Hawk Down: A Story of Modern War.* New York: Penguin Books, 1999.

Cather, Willa. *Sapphira and the Slave Girl.* New York: Alfred A. Knopf, Inc., 1940.

Choate, Wade. *Swappin' Cattle.* San Angelo, Texas: NewsFoto Publishing Company, fourth printing, 1990.

Cox, Jim. "Ranch on the Concho, Rocker b Reflects West Texas History." *Texas Parks and Wildlife* (1989).

Crawford, Leta. *A History of Irion County, Texas.* Waco, Texas: Texian, 1966.

A History of Irion County, Texas. San Angelo, Texas: Anchor, 1978.

Fall, Bernard B. *Street Without Joy.* New York: Schocken Books, 1961.

Fehrenbach, T. R. *Lone Star: A History of Texas and the Texans.* New York: Collier Books, 1980.

Ferber, Edna. *Giant.* New York: Doubleday, 1952.

Flippin, Ray. "Old-Fashion Cowboy." San Angelo, Texas: *San Angelo Standard Times.*
April 24, 2005.

Foreman, Mary Anne. "Leadership and Excellence, 1917–1998: A Look at Our Rich Military Heritage." *Alumni J-TAC* (1998): 8–10.

Fox, Wesley L. *Marine rifleman: forty-three years in the corps.* Dulles, Virginia: Brassey's, Incorporated, 2002.

Franks, Don R. *Concho Valley Archeology Society News* (Spring 1994).

Glasser, Ronald J. *365 Days.* New York: Braziller, 1971.

Greene, A. C. *A Personal Country.* Denton, Texas: University of North Texas Press, 1969.

Greene, A. C. *900 Miles of the Butterfield Trail.* Denton, Texas: University of North Texas Press, 1994.

Gusewelle, C. W. "Remarkable Military Maneuver at Ft. Leavenworth." *The Kansas City Star* (May 11, 1975).

Guthrie, Christopher E. *John Tarleton and His Legacy: The History of Tarleton State University.* Acton, MA: Tapestry Press Limited, 1999.

Hall, Sarah Harkey, *Surviving on the Texas Frontier: Personal Recollections of Surviving Life in Nineteenth-Century Texas.* Austin, Texas: Eakin Press, 1996.

Hamrick, Alma Ward, *The Call of the San Saba, A History of San Saba County.* Austin and New York: San Felipe Press, Jenkins Publishing Company, 1969.

Harkey, Dee. *Mean as Hell.* New Mexico: University of New Mexico Printing Plant, 1948.

Hilburn, Sam E. *A Place of Miracles: The Legacy of the Rocker b.* Dallas, Texas: Dockery House Publishing, 1999.

Irion County Museum and Historical Society. *A History of Irion County Texas.* San Angelo, Texas: Anchor Publishing Company, 1978.

Kelley, R. M., Colonel, Major Thomas Pirtle, and Captain Thomas Speed. *The Union Regiments of Kentucky.* Louisville, Kentucky: Union Soldiers and Sailors Monument Association, 1897.

Kelton, Elmer. *The Time It Never Rained.* Fort Worth, Texas: Texas Christian University Press, 1984.

Kelton, Elmer. *Sandhills Boy: The Winding Trail of a Texas Writer.* New York: Tom Doherty Associates, LLC, 2007.

Kennedy, Claudia J. *Generally Speaking.* New York: Warner Books, Inc., 2001.

Kerns, Wilmer L. *Frederick County, Virginia: Settlement and Some First Families of Back Creek Valley, 1730–1830.* Baltimore, Maryland: Gateway Press, 1995.

King, C. Richard. *Golden Days of the Purple and White. The John Tarleton College Story.* Austin, Texas: Eakin Press, 1998.

King, Larry L. *The Whorehouse Papers.* New York: Viking Press, 1982.

Knapp, Caroline. *Drinking: A Love Story.* New York: Dial Press, 1996.

Kurtz, Ernest. *Not-God.* San Francisco: Harper & Row Publishers, Inc., 1979.

Lackey, Jerry. "HOMESTEAD: Blackstone-Elkins Ranch." *Standard-Times* (April 6, 2008).

"HOMESTEAD: Owenses carry on ranching tradition." *Standard-Times* (August 8, 2009).

"HOMESTEAD: Train ride planted seeds for Blackstone success." *Standard-Times* (November 27, 2010).

"HOMESTEAD: Settlers were made of tough stuff." *Standard-Times* (October 14, 2007).

"Louis Lee Farr III, New TS&GRA President." *Sheep and Goat Raiser: The Ranch Magazine*, Volume 50, No. 11 (August 1970): 8–9.

Lutz, Joseph Brown. *Genealogical Findings for the Following Families: Taylor of Virginia, et al.* Cheyenne, Wyoming: 1939.

McMurty, Larry. *The Last Picture Show: A Novel.* New York: Dial Press, 1966.

Meyer, Milton. *Japan: A Concise History.* Boston: Allyn and Bacon, 1966.

Michener, James A. *Texas.* New York: Random House, 1985.

Moore, Harold G., and Joseph L. Galloway. *We Were Soldier's Once . . . and Young.* New York: Random House Publishing, 1992.

Myrer, Anton. *Once an Eagle.* New York: Holt, Rienhart and Winston, 1968.

O'Bryan, Suzanne. *Sauntering: One Woman's Life in the Country.* Georgetown, Texas: Chengalera Press, 1998.

Randall, H. Pettus. *Who's Who Among Students in America Universities & Colleges, 1985.* Tuscaloosa, Alabama: Randall Publishing Company, 1985.

Reeves, Frank. "Major Cow Factory." *The Cattleman* (August 1960): 34–6, 61–2, 64.

Reynolds, Russel B. *The Officer's Guide.* Harrisburg, Pennsylvania: The Stackpole Company, 1967.

San Saba County History, 1856–1983. San Saba, Texas: San Saba Historical Commission, 1987.

Schreiber, Colleen. "Owens Family Has Been Running University Lease for 120 Years." *Livestock Weekly* (February 7, 2008): 10–14.

Shaara, Michael. *The Killer Angels.* New York: Random House, 1974.

Sheehan, Neil. *A Bright and Shining Lie: John Paul Vann and America in Vietnam.* New York: Random House, 1988.

Summers, Harry, Jr. *On Strategy: A Critical Analysis of the Vietnam War.* New York: Dell, 1984.

Taylor, Harrison D. *History of the Taylor Family.* Hartford, Kentucky: 1875; reprinted as chapter 21 of *Ohio County, Kentucky in the Olden Days,* ed. Mary Taylor Logan (Louisville, 1926), pp. 101–11.

Taylor, Nathaniel L. *An American Taylor Family: Descendants of Richard Taylor (d. 1679) of North Farnham Parish in the Northern Neck of Virginia.* East Providence, Rhode Island: Draft work, December 19, 2009. Retrieved April 20, 2010 from http://www.nltaylor.net/pdfs/Taylorgen.pdf.

Taylor, Nathaniel L. "The False and Possibly True English Origin of Richard Taylor of Old Rappahannock County, Virginia." *The American Genealogist,* Volume 83, No. 3 and 4 (October 2009 and February 2010).

The Texas Trademark: "Flair for the Flamboyant." *Life,* Volume 61, No. 2 (July 8, 1966).

Tracey L. Compton. "BARNHART, TX," *Handbook of Texas Online,* http://www.tshaonline.org/handbook/online/articles/hnb09 (accessed November 06, 2010).

Tzu, Sun. *The Art of War,* translated by Samuel B. Griffith. New York: Oxford University Press, 1963.

Von Clausewitz, Carl. *On War,* edited and translated by Michael Howard and Peter Paret. Princeton, New Jersey: Princeton University Press, 1976.

Welch, June Rayfield. "Bill Blakley Looked Like a Texas Senator." *The Texas Senator* (1978): 64–5, 144–7

Werst, J. L., Jr., ed. *The Reagan County Story*. Big Lake, Texas: Reagan County Historical Survey Committee, 1974.

Wickham, Kenneth. *An Adjutant General Remembers: A Military Memoir*. Fort Harrison, Indiana: The Adjutant General's Corps Regimental Association, 1991.

III

Service Resume of Herbie R. Taylor

ACTIVE COMMISSIONED SERVICE:
28 years, 1 month, 11 days

RETIREMENT DATE:
31 August 1992

MILITARY SCHOOLS ATTENDED:
The Adjutant General School Basic Course
Manpower Control Course
The Adjutant General School Advance Course
National Security Management Course
Army Command and General Staff College
Personnel Management for Executives
National Security Agency Executive Management
Army War College

SECURITY CLEARANCE:
Top Secret
SI/TK
SCI

EDUCATIONAL DEGREES:
Tarleton State College (BS)—General Business
Shippensburg University of Pennsylvania (MS)—Public Administration

SOURCE OF COMMISSION:
Reserve Officer Training Corps

SERVICE NUMBER:
OF109654

PROMOTIONS

	Temporary	Permanent
2LT	20 Jul 64	20 Jul 64
1LT	20 Jan 66	20 Jul 67
CPT	1 Feb 67	20 Jul 71
MAJ	1 Jul 74	20 Jul 78
LTC		1 Jul 80
COL		1 Mar 87

US DECORATIONS AND BADGES:
Legion of Merit (with Oak Leaf Cluster)
Bronze Star Medal (with Oak Leaf Cluster)
Meritorious Service Medal (with five Oak Leaf Clusters)
Army Commendation Medal (with Oak Leaf Cluster)
Army General Staff Identification Badge

US SERVICE MEDALS:
National Defense Service Medal (with Bronze Service Star)
Vietnam Service Medal (with four Bronze Service Stars)
Vietnam Campaign Medal

US RIBBONS:
Oversea Service Ribbon (with numeral three)
Army Service Ribbon

US UNIT AWARD:
Meritorious Unit Commendation

FOREIGN AWARD:
Republic of Vietnam Cross of Gallantry with Palm

HONORARY AWARDS:
Order of Horatio Gates Bronze and Gold Medal

MAJOR DUTY ASSIGNMENTS:

Jul 64	Sep 64	Student, Adjutant General Officer Basic Course, United States Army Adjutant General School, Fort Benjamin Harrison, Indiana
Sep 64	Apr 66	Assistant Personnel Officer, later Assistant Chief, Personnel Management Branch; later Chief, Personnel Management Branch; and later Chief, Personnel Records Branch with additional duty as Trainee Classification and Assignment Officer, 1st Armored Division, Fort Hood Texas
Apr 66	Jun 68	COSMIC and ATOMAL Control Officer and Chief, Military Records Section, Allied Land Forces Southeastern Europe, Izmir, Turkey
Jun 68	Jul 69	Chief, Administrative Services Division, XXIV Corps, Phu Bai, Republic of Vietnam
Jul 69	Apr 70	Student, Adjutant General Advance Course, United States Army Adjutant General School, Fort Benjamin Harrison, Indiana
Apr 70	May 74	Adjutant, United States Army Personnel Center, Far East; and later Secretary of the General Staff, United States Army Japan/IX Corps, Camp Zama, Japan

Jun 74	Jun 75	Student, United States Army Command and General Staff College, Fort Leavenworth, Kansas
Jun 75	Mar 78	Chief, Service Retirement Section, United States Army Military Personnel Center, Alexandria, Virginia
Mar 78	Mar 79	Chief, Personnel Services Division, 2nd Infantry Division (Mechanized), Camp Casey, Korea
Mar 79	Apr 80	Chief, Personnel and Administration Team, Security Manager and Assistant Executive Officer; later Personnel Staff Officer, Office of the Deputy Chief of Staff for Personnel, The Pentagon, Washington, D.C.
Apr 80	Apr 82	Adjutant General and later Deputy Chief of Staff, 5th Infantry Division (Mechanized) and Fort Polk, Fort Polk, Louisiana
Apr 82	Jul 83	Chief, Child Services/Youth Activities Division, Office of the Adjutant General, Alexandria, Virginia
Jul 83	Jun 84	Student, United States Army War College, Carlisle Barracks, Carlisle, Pennsylvania
Jun 84	Jun 86	Chief, Adjutant General Branch, Officer Personnel Management Directorate, United States Army Military Personnel Center, Alexandria, Virginia
Jun 86	Jun 89	Deputy Chief of Staff for Personnel, United States Army Intelligence and Security Command, Arlington Hall Station, Arlington, Virginia

Jun 89	Aug 92	Director, Personnel, Administration, Logistics and Security, United States Army Test and Experimentation Command, Fort Hood, Texas

IV

Taylor, of Virginia: Documented Male Lines

Richard
b. unknown
m. Sarah
d. 1679 (VA)
|
Simon
b. 1667–70
m. Elizabeth Lewis
d. 1729 (VA)
|
John
b. 1704
m. Hannah Harrison
d. 1741 (VA)
|
Harrison
(Honest Old Taylor at the Mill)
b. 1735
m. Jane Curlet
d. 1811 (KY)
|
Septimus
b. 1773
m. Mary McMahon
d. 1814 (KY)

Richard McMahon
(Major Dick)
b. 1798
m1. Delilah Frances Grigsby Wise
m2. Sarah Rock
d. 1880 (KY)
|

Woodford Mitchell
(Woop)
b. 1841
m. Sarah Peter Rust
d. 1926 (TX)
|

Emmett Overton
b. 1882
m1. Mamie Beatrice Wood
m2. Willie Rhee Wood Graham
d. 1963 (TX)
|

Norvel Ross
(Shorty)
b. 1910
m. Elanor Alyene Shaw (Squirrel)
d. 2007 (TX)
|

Herbie Ross
(Pops)
b. 1942
m1. Penelope Ann Farr (Penny)
m2. Janice Irene Taylor Sullivan (Jan)
|

Herbie Ross, Jr.
(Ross)
b. 1961
m. Kristi Ann Tidwell
|

Micah Jeb   **Jared Ross**
b. 1995   b.1997

Note: There is significant but not definitive evidence that Richard is the son of Simon Taylor and Constance Berrington, who were married at Stanford-on-Soar, Nottinghamshire, England on June 14, 1641. A record of baptism for Richard has not been found to verify this premise.

V

My Descendants

Micah Jeb, Ross, and Jared Ross at Pop's home in Salado, Texas.
(2000)

Micah Jeb, Ross, and Jared Ross at Grandmother Taylor's Funeral.
(2010)

VI

Glossary

ACP	Advanced Command Post
ACP	Automatic Colt Pistol
ACS	Army Community Services
AD	Armored Division
ADC	Assistant Division Commander
ADC (M)	Assistant Division Commander (Maneuver)
ADC (S)	Assistant Division Commander for Support
AER	Army Emergency Relief
AFB	Air Force Base
AFGE	American Federation Government Employ
AFRS	Armed Forces Radio Service
AFSOUTH	Allied Forces Southern Europe
AG	Adjutant General
AGC	Adjutant General's Corps
AGOBC	Adjutant General Officer Basic Course
AGSIB	Army General Staff Identification Badge
AIT	Advanced Individual Training
ALFSEE	Allied Land Forces Southeastern Europe
APL	American Presidential Lines
APO	Army Post Office
AO	Area of Operations
ARC LIGHT	B-52 Strike
ARCOM	Army Commendation Medal
ASA	Army Security Agency
ATF	Allied Tactical Air Force
ATOMAL	NATO Term for Nuclear Information
AUS	Army of the United States
AWOL	Absent Without Leave
BCT	Basic Combat Training

BDU	Battle Dress Uniform, fatigues
BG	Brigadier General, flag officer, 0-9
BN	Battalion
BOQ	Bachelor Officer Quarters
BSA	Boy Scouts of America
BSM	Bronze Star Medal
CAO	Casualty Assistance Officer
CEO	Chief Executive Officer
CG	Commanding General
CID	Criminal Investigation Division
CLASS I	Supply item: Food, health, and comfort
CLASS II	Supply item: Clothing, tentage, and tools
CLASS III	Supply item: Petroleum, oil, and lubricant
CLASS IV	Supply item: Construction materials
CLASS V	Supply item: Ammo, all types
CLASS VI	Supply item: Beverage alcohol
CNO	Casualty Notification Officer
COC	Casualty Operation Center
COLA	Cost-of-Living Adjustment
COL	Colonel, field-grade officer, 0–6
CONUS	Continental United States
COSMIC	NATO Top Secret
CPT	Captain, company-grade officer, 0–3
CPIF	Cost-Plus-Incentive Fee contract
CSM	Command Sergeant Major, enlisted, E–9
CSSD	Combat Service Support Division
CUCV	Commercial Utility Cargo Vehicle
DA	Department of the Army
DAC	Department of the Army Civilian
DAV	Disabled American Veterans
DCG	Deputy Commanding General
DCS	Deputy Chief of Staff
DCSPAL	Personnel, Administration and Logistics
DEROS	Date Due to Return from Overseas
DIA	Defense Intelligence Agency
DINFOS	Defense Information Service
DIRNSA	Director, National Security Agency
DISCOM	Division Support Command

DIVARTY	Division Artillery
DMPM	Directorate Military Personnel Management
DMZ	Demilitarized Zone
DOD	Department of Defense
DODS	Department of Defense School System
EPMD	Enlisted Personnel Management Dir
ETS	Expiration Term of Service
FAA	Federal Aviation Administration
FIGMO	F* * * It Got My Orders
FOD	Field Officer of the Day
FORSCOM	Forces Command
FUBAR	F* * * Up Beyond All Recognition
G1	Personnel
G2	Intelligence
G3	Operations
G4	Logistics
GAO	Government Accounting Office
GM	General Management (Civil Service)
GOMO	General Officer Management Office
GPO	Government Printing Office
GS	General Schedule (civil service)
GSA	General Services Administration
HBC	Historical Black College
HMMWV	High Mobility Multipurpose Wheeled Vehicle
HQDA	Headquarters, Department of the Army
ID	Infantry Division
IG	Inspector General
INSCOM	Intelligence and Security Command
IP	Intraperitoneal
JAG	Judge Advocate Genera
JFK	Kennedy Airport
JGSDF	Japanese Ground Self-Defense Forces
JSOC	Joint Special Operation Command
JTAC	John Tarleton Agriculture College
JUSMMAT	Joint United States Military Aid to Turkey
KATUSA	Korean Augmentation to the U S Army
KIA	Killed in Action
KISD	Killen Independent School District

LAX	Los Angeles Airport
LOD	Line of Departure
LOM	Legion of Merit
2LT	Lieutenant, company-grade officer, 0–1
LTC	Lieutenant Colonel, field-grade officer, 0–5
LTG	Lieutenant General, flag officer, 0–11
MAC	Military Airlift Command
MACOM	Major Command
MACV	Military Advisory Command Vietnam
MARS	Military Affiliate Radio System
MAJ	Major, field grade officer, 0–4
MEPCOM	Military Entrance Processing Command
MEPS	Military Entrance Processing Station
MG	Major General, flag officer, 0–10
MI	Military Intelligence
MILES	Multiple Integrated Laser Engage System
MILPERCEN	Military Personnel Center
MILPERCEN-K	Military Personnel Center-Korea
MOS	Military Occupational Specialty
MP	Military Police
MPC	Military Payment Certificates
MSG	Master Sergeant, enlisted, E–8
MSM	Meritorious Service Medal
MSR	Main Supply Route
MWR	Morale, Welfare and Recreation
NAF	Non-appropriated Funds
NATO	North Atlantic Treaty Organization
NAEYC	National Assoc Education Young Children
NCO	Noncommissioned Officer
NCOIC	Noncommissioned Officer in Charge
NOK	Next of Kin
NSA	National Security Agency
NVA	North Vietnamese Army
OAS	Organization of American States
OCD	Obsessive Compulsive Disorder
OCLL	Office Chief of Legislative Liaison
OCSA	Office of the Chief of Staff, Army
OCONUS	Outside Continental United States

ODO	Officer Development Officer
ODP	Officer Distribution Plan
OER	Officer Evaluation Report
OHSA	Occupational Safety and Health Admin
OJT	On-the-Job Training
OPFOR	Opposing Force
OPLAN	Operations Plan
OPORDER	Operations Order
ORB	Officer Record Brief
ORSA	Operations Research Systems Analysis
OTAG	Office of the Adjutant General
OTC	Operational Test Command
PBO	Property Book Officer
PCS	Permanent Change of Station
PCV	Provisional Corps Vietnam
PERINREPS	Periodic Intelligence Reports
PDO[1]	Professional Development Officer
PDO[2]	Property Disposal Office
PFC	Private, enlisted, E–3
PMS	Professor of Military Science
POAC	Pentagon Officer Athletic Club
POV	Privately Owned Vehicle
PUF	Permanent University Fund
PT	Physical Training
PVT	Private, enlisted, E1–E2
PX	Post Exchange
RA	Regular Army
RCHS	Reagan County High School
ROTC	Reserve Officer Training Corps
ROK	Republic of Korea
RRFS	Radio Research Field Station
R&R	Rest and Recuperation
RSO	Retirement Services Officer
RVN	Republic of Vietnam
SACEUR	Supreme Allied Commander Europe
SAD	Social Anxiety Disorder
SECARMY	Secretary of the Army
SCI	Sensitive Compartmented Information

SCIF	Sensitive Compartment Info Facility
SEATAC	Seattle-Tacoma Airport
SERB	Selective Early Retirement Board
SES	Senior Executive Service
SFC	Sergeant First Class, enlisted, E–7
SGM	Sergeant Major, enlisted, E–9
SGS	Secretary of the General Staff
SHAPE	Supreme HQ Allied Powers Europe
SI	Special Intelligence
S1	Personnel, brigade level and below
SIDPERS	Standard Installation/Division Personnel System
SINCGARS	Single Channel Ground and Airborne Radio
SJA	Staff Judge Advocate
SNAFU	Situation Normal All Fucked Up
SOP	Standard Operating Procedure
SOUTHCOM	Southern Command
SOFA	Status of Forces Agreement
SSG	Staff Sergeant, enlisted, E–6
SSI	Soldier Support Institute
S&W	Scott and White Hospital
TA-50	Individual Combat Gear
TAA	Tarleton Alumni Association
TAG	The Adjutant General
TAPA	Total Army Personnel Command
TDY	Temporary Duty
TDRL	Temporary Disability Retired List
TEC	TEXCOM Experimentation Command
TEXCOM	Test and Experimentation Command
TIAA	Texas Intercollegiate Athletic Association
TL	Turkish Lira
TOC	Tactical Operations Center
TSU	Tarleton State University
USAF	US Air Force
USAREC	US Army Recruiting Command
USAREUR	US Army Europe
USARJ	US Army Japan
USARV	US Army Vietnam
USC	US Code

USDA	US Department of Agriculture
USFK	US Forces Korea
USMA	US Military Academy
USR	Unit Status Report
UTMB	University of Texas Medical Branch
V	Valor
VA	Veterans Administration
VC	Viet Cong or Victor Charlie
VCSA	Vice Chief of Staff, Army
VFW	Veterans of Foreign Wars
VIP	Very Important Person
WAC	Women's Army Corps
WASP	Women's Air Force Service Pilots
XO	Executive Officer
201 File	Individual Personnel Record